COMMODITIES TRADING
Foundations, Analysis,
and Operations

COMMODITIES TRADING

Foundations, Analysis, and Operations

ANDREW D. SEIDEL

PHILIP M. GINSBERG

PRENTICE-HALL, INC., Englewood Cliffs, New Jersey, 07632

Library of Congress Cataloging in Publication Data

SEIDEL, ANDREW D.
   Commodities trading.

  Includes bibliographies and index.
  1. Commodity exchanges. I. Ginsberg, Philip M.,
  date   II. Title.
HG6046.S44 1983   332.64'4   82-16164
ISBN 0-13-152678-2

Editorial/production supervision and interior design by Alice Erdman
Cover design by Edsal Enterprises
Manufacturing buyer: Ed O'Dougherty

Printed in the United States of America

10 9 8 7 6 5 4 3 2 1

ISBN 0-13-152678-2

Prentice-Hall International, Inc., *London*
Prentice-Hall of Australia Pty. Limited, *Sydney*
Editora Prentice-Hall do Brasil, Ltda., *Rio de Janeiro*
Prentice-Hall Canada Inc., *Toronto*
Prentice-Hall of India Private Limited, *New Delhi*
Prentice-Hall of Japan, Inc., *Tokyo*
Prentice-Hall of Southeast Asia Pte. Ltd., *Singapore*
Whitehall Books Limited, *Wellington, New Zealand*

to:

Ann, Nicole, and Pop

ADS

to the future:

Mia, Klindt, Laura, and Carrie

PMG

CONTENTS

PREFACE

‖‖‖

Over the past several years, interest in the commodities markets has grown dramatically. The reasons for this surge in interest are manifold. In part, base commodities are not as plentiful as they once may have seemed, and all business activities have become more sensitive to their availability. In addition, the commodities markets have not only presented an attractive investment alternative to the securities markets they have become an increasingly popular vehicle to hedge investments in other markets and capture arbitrage opportunities.

The commodities markets no longer just trade in goods intended for human consumption or manufacturing such as wheat, cattle, plywood, and copper. They now encompass financial commodities—mortages, commercial paper, foreign currencies, and government debt along with precious metals. Today the commodities markets have evolved into an effective mechanism to accommodate a wide range of business interests. They offer producers and processors an opportunity to shift their risks of loss owing to adverse price fluctuations; they offer security portfolio managers an opportunity to hedge their portfolio asset value against unseen economic circumstances, and they offer investors opportunities to capture returns and speculate on the future.

Despite the opportunities presented in the commodities markets, much of what passes for systematic analysis and management of commodity trading operations is based more on convention and intuition than on objective planning and empirically tested methodology. To be sure, few can afford to approach any investment opportunity ignorant of the underlying risks and institutional characteristics of the markets or naked to the use of the tools necessary to win. Yet in light of these requirements, it is remarkable how much of what passes for systematic commodity analysis clusters around two extreme performances: overtures of business and economic fundamentals on the one hand, and solo cords of mathematics and statistics on the other. The former all too often do not carry their analysis through to efficient and adaptable implementation, while the latter often sacrifice business context and practicality in their pursuit of rigorous decision rules. To a large extent this state of affairs is understandable. The application of economic analysis, statistical and mathematical methodologies, to commodity business problems is in its earliest stages, and its success is not yet common.

Unravelling the complexities of commodity trading is what this book is all about. It summarizes the various types of commodity markets and contracting and integrates this information with relevant aspects of economic analysis, statistics, and mathematics. Together, these foundations can provide a basis for systematic trading operations that can reduce risks and raise returns from levels otherwise achieved. Surely no single individual can be expected to master each of these disciplines or all of the ways they can be brought to bear upon all of the possible problems one can encounter in commodity business operations. Nevertheless, those responsible for the successful conduct of business must be well-enough versed in these areas to help translate real-life commodity market problems into tractable structures, to oversee the analysis, and to extract their business implications.

The book is directed toward several related audiences. On the one hand it is directed toward the MBA student, investor, research economist, commodity trader or broker, and financial manager. The intent is to help bridge the gap between the identification and specification of commodity trading problems and their analysis and control. On the other hand, the book is aimed at statisticians, mathematicians, and operations researchers to help them better understand the content and structure of problems arising in commodity trading that are ripe for their contribution.

Despite its quantitative bent, the mathematical level of the book has been kept as elementary as possible. A review of the statistical and mathematical foundations are covered in separate chapters. Although much of the technical material presented is not new, the book does bring together, in a unified framework, principles and applications of economics, statistics, and mathematics heretofore unavailable in a single text.

The book is organized as follows:

PART I focuses on the institutional aspects of the commodities markets: the contracts, exchanges and controls, and elements of finance with special emphasis on their application to commodity trading and investment. Included here are discussions of options, futures, and forward contracting. In addition, an overview of the role of the commodity markets, the participants, their objectives and interactions are presented together with a summary of major regulations and AICPA accounting recommendations.

PART II provides a summary of select aspects of operations research and time series analysis. Included here are elements of probability and statistics, decision theory, mathematical programming, and time series estimation and forecasting. Special emphasis is given to the application of these disciplines to commodity trading and provides a foundation for subsequent topics.

PART III addresses the technical analysis of commodity prices, with particular emphasis given to chart analysis and technical trading models. Among the topics included are stop-loss and non-parametric models, autoregressive moving-average models, and Kalman filter models. The section also includes several illustrative examples designed to highlight applications of these methodologies, their strengths and weaknesses.

PART IV explores the analysis of fundamentals in the commodity markets and its role in commodity trading activity. Here, elements of demand, production, and supply are summarized together with design features for fundamental models and guidelines for their development. In addition, operations oriented econometric models of several different commodities are presented. These applications include wheat, foreign exchange, gold, and money market instruments. Throughout these chapters, the models are used to illustrate the integration of fundamental economic information into commodity trading decisions. This is done from the vantage of different market participants with different trading objectives.

PART V ties together the topics covered in the previous chapters and turns to three aspects that encompass almost every activity of commodity trading. These aspects include the design and implementation of commodity trading strategies and tactics. Included here are elements of the probability of ruin, the planning horizon, and operational check lists. The chapter on portfolio selection and maintenance emphasizes the peculiarities of commodities and the implications of execution errors owing to illiquidity in the markets. The discussion of integrated, multi-commodity trading activity explores the financial constraints of the firm and the various trading desks and trading procedures to manage profits over different time bargains and across commodities. Here, inventory scheduling and the application of multi-commodity, multi-time period mathematical program procedures are applied to commodity trading.

While book length studies exist for many of the issues and methods the authors deem important, the intent of this book is to emphasize their integration. Accordingly it is necessary to be selective, drawing on those principles and methodologies that have stood the test of time or show promise of practical contribution. In this regard experience has been the leading edge of Ocams razor. As such the book attempts to portray, as candidly and rigorously as possible, the practical problems and issues that face anyone ambitious enough to "enter the ring".

ACKNOWLEDGMENT

||||||||||||||||||||||||||||||||||||||||||||||||||||||||||||||||||||||||||||||||||||||||||||||||||||||||||||||||||

The help and guidance of many people contributed to the preparation of this book.

In particular, we must express our gratitude to David C. Hildebrand, Prentice-Hall's editor of economics and finance, who encourged and enhanced our efforts and to Alice Erdman, Prentice-Hall's production editor, who tirelessly directed the manuscript through production.

We must also thank Neil Sheflin and Dennis Warner for their special contributions.

Finally, we are indebted to the following individuals for their valuable comments and suggestions: Martin Barrat, Jean Blin, Roger Gray, Roger LeRoy Miller, and Matthew Stirling.

Of course, the authors bear all responsibility for any theoretical and factual errors contained in the book. Similarly, the opinions, insights, and approaches to commodity trading are solely those of the authors.

Andrew D. Seidel
Philip M. Ginsberg

COMMODITIES TRADING
Foundations, Analysis, and Operations

I
COMMODITY TRADING:
Markets, Perspectives, and Problems

A commodity is anything useful or valuable—from soybeans to securities. It may be traded in different markets with distinct contractural arrangements and for a variety of business objectives. While each commodity has its own established conventions, the fundamentals of commodity trading, analysis, and operations cut across commodity classifications. Indeed, trading commodities requires the ability to compare risk and returns among them, their markets, and instruments. Part 1 is intended to help facilitate these comparisons.

Chapter 1 provides an overview of commodity contracting with some historical perspective. Chapter 2 summarizes and compares elements of cash, futures, and options contracting. Perspectives on asset and liability management are discussed in Chapter 3. Included here are notions of hedging, arbitrage, and speculation within and among commodities and markets. Elements of price formation are considered in Chapter 4. Here market linkages, processes, stability, and efficiency are given special attention. The pricing and application of contingent claims are the subject of Chapter 5. The types of options, their valuation and use, are among the topics covered. Elements of finance are presented in Chapters 6 and 7. Here measures of return and risk are discussed with special distinctions between financial and nonfinancial assets of reference. The regulation of commodities trading is discussed in Chapter 8. Among the topics covered are Internal Revenue Service and other government and private controls and guidelines. Accounting for futures contracting, spot, forward, and standby commitments, is the subject of Chapter 9. Included here are examples of accounting for financial assets of reference.

1

OVERVIEW OF COMMODITY CONTRACTING

||||||||||||||||||||||||||||||||||||||||||||||||||||||||||||||||||||||||||||||||||||||||||||||||||||||||||||||||||||

1 INTRODUCTION

If there is a persistent theme of economic performance, it perhaps can best be characterized in one word: uncertainty. As John Maynard Keynes noted in his epic book, *The General Theory of Employment, Interest and Money*, first published in 1936, "Investment based on genuine long-term expectation is so difficult today as to be scarcely practicable. . . . It needs more intelligence to defeat the forces of time and our ignorance of the future, than to beat the gun."[1]

Keynes' eloquent description of investment as the process of defeating the dark forces of time is as appropriate today as it was then. Economic forecasts notwithstanding, profitable investment is very elusive: The opportunities are scarce, fleeting, and subject to risk throughout their term to maturity.

To help capture these opportunities and to shift the risks, various forms of commodity contracting have evolved. Used properly they can help insulate the investor from unanticipated losses once an investment position has been taken. Moreover, they can offer a wider range of investment opportunities than otherwise would be available.

1. From *The General Theory of Employment, Interest and Money* by John Maynard Keynes. Reprinted by permission of Harcourt Brace Jovanovich, Inc.

But the commoditites markets are not a bromide for all business uncertainties: Not all commodities have established markets and not all commodities markets are the same. What are sound business objectives and opportunities in some commodities markets are inappropriate for others. As a first step toward the effective use of these markets, their general characteristics must be understood.

The purpose of this chapter is to provide an overview of commodity trading—its extent, origins, and select operational characteristics.

2 OVERVIEW OF THE COMMODITIES MARKETS

2.1 Extent of Trading and Types of Contracts

A *commodity* may be defined as anything useful or that can be turned to commercial or other advantage. Taken to its extreme, this definition includes several million commodities ranging from singing telegrams to titanium sponge. While each of these items have their own demand, supply, and methods of exchange, only a handful have achieved the status of worldwide trading activity. Although a small fraction in comparison to the total number of commodities, these base commodities nonetheless cover a wide and growing domain of items. This domain has four major categories: agriculture, precious metals, financial instruments, and manufacturing items.

There are three types of commodity contracts traded at present: cash, options, and futures. *Cash contracts* are traded by direct placement; that is, trade takes place off an organized exchange and is done directly between the buyer and seller. These contracts are for the exchange and ownership of the commodity. The delivery may be immediate or for some specified date in the future. The latter is referred to as a forward contract. Because cash contracts reflect ownership of the commodity they can be used as collateral. Any transference or liquidation of the contract must be done with the mutual agreement of both the buyer and seller.

Option contracts give the buyer the right but not the obligation to buy or sell an agreed amount of some item at an agreed price over some agreed time period. Commodity options are traded primarily by direct placement. Some countries allow commodity options to be traded on organized exchanges such as the London Options Market. Because an option does not impart ownership of the underlying asset the contract cannot be used as collateral.

A *futures contract* is a commitment to buy or sell commodities at a specified time and place in the future. The trade is made in an open outcry auction on an organized futures exchange and not by direct placement. The term "open outcry" is not limited to voice but includes hand signals, touch, and electronic messages that are presented openly to the trading members of the exchange. Futures contracts also do not impart ownership of the underlying physical commodity and cannot be used for collateral.

The exchange of base commodities and claims against them account for several trillions of dollars of trading worldwide. Not all of this trading activity represents an exchange of the physical items for final use. Indeed most of the trading is done for claims or potential claims against the physical items for some time in the future. This trading can greatly exceed the amount of the physical item. For example, in 1979 there was approximately $160 billion outstanding in 90-day U.S. treasury bills while the volume of 90-day treasury bill futures contracts traded on the Chicago Mercantile Exchange alone exceeded $1,900 billion. That the value of futures contracts can exceed the value of the underlying cash commodity at any time is no cause for alarm. In fact there may be cause for alarm if that were not the case. That futures claims exceed available supplies only reflects the myriad of positions that must be taken to cover the far more numerous different possible tomorrows. The intent and practice is not to take or make delivery on each and every futures claim. Rather it is to be in a position to take or make delivery on that claim that profitably meets the conditions of the one future that will emerge. The other positions are liquidated as the future unfolds and their relative or absolute unprofitability becomes self-evident. For example, speculators may take positions on the future price of gold that covers the known world supply. At the same time producers and manufacturers may take similar positions in gold to protect their forward production commitments. Moreover, arbitragers may take an equivalent number of similar positions in several of the gold markets —London, Chicago, and New York, for example—in their efforts to capture profitable intermarket price differentials. Furthermore, these positions may be taken in each of several different time horizons owing to the uncertain timing of influential events. Taken together these claims against the future can easily be a large multiple of the current available supply.

2.2 Historical Perspective

The history of commodity contracting is as old as the history of trade itself. Ancient documents originally believed to be the Code of Hammurabi reveal records of credit contracts based on the volume of grain and the weight of precious metals. From these and other records it is clear that early trading partners recognized the gains to be made from the absolute and comparative advantages of commodity production among regions. Economic mutual interests made it inevitable that markets and commercial interests would evolve to facilitate the capturing of these gains. Indeed the great trade networks of the Phoenician, Greek, Roman, and Byzantine empires included trade markets that specialized in the spot (immediate) and forward (future) delivery of specific commodities. That commodity markets and their forms of contracting first emphasized agricultural produce and precious metals and then raw materials closely follows the history of trade from agrarian societies through mercantilism, colonialism, and industrialization.[2]

Although contracting for forward delivery existed in pre-Christian empires these contracts were negotiated directly between the buyer and seller. These direct placement contracts were not standardized as to quality or size and were not transferable. Then as now, direct placement contracts were governed by the laws of contracts. Delivery was expected to be made and taken unless both parties agreed to the liquidation of their business commitment. It is in the degree of standardization, transferability, and liquidation of contracts that the direct placement markets now differ from the so-called futures markets.

One of the first recorded organized futures exchanges was the Osaka rice market in early eighteenth-century Japan. The rules of this market included standardization of contracts by weight and grade (quality), a specified and finite contract life, the settlement of trades through a clearing house, required lines of credit for traders with an exchange-approved clearing house, and the trading of both futures and cash physical commodities.[3]

Futures contracts in the West can be traced back to the medieval "lettre de faire." The American version of these contracts were "to arrive" agreements. Both had similarities to ancient forward contracting and with few exceptions were not easily transferable. The major alteration in "to arrive" contracts in the United States was their transferability. This emerged largely because of the standardization of terms and more precise contracting. By the late 1800s the transferable "to arrive" contracts had evolved into organized futures markets. Among the most notable survivors are the Chicago Board of Trade, the New York Mercantile Exchange, the New York Coffee Exchange, and the New York Cotton Exchange. Today organized futures markets exist around the world and include major exchanges in London, Hong Kong, New York, and Chicago.

From time to time throughout the history of trade, direct placement forward contracting and especially futures contracting have been attacked by leaders and governing bodies. Almost without exception, these attacks have come during some economic calamity. These events pressed the limits of the markets and the imperfections in them apparently exacerbated the economic problems. Forward and futures contracts, as well as options, often carried a premium to their cash commodity. This premium was assailed on ethical and religious grounds—especially when large numbers of potential market participants could not afford the premium or meet delivery.

2. Edward McNall Burns, *Western Civilizations Their History and Culture*, 5th ed., (New York: W. W. Norton & Co., Inc., 1958), pp. 60, 186.

3. Chicago Board of Trade, *Commodity Trading Manual* (Chicago: Chicago Board of Trade, 1982), p. 2.

Options and futures contracts also have been assailed as mere gambling because they do not have corresponding quantities of the commodities behind them as "collateral." Indeed, it has been argued that the potential financial chaos emanating from these contracts could destory the commodities themselves by undermining the financial integrity of producers. To be sure, imperfections in the options, futures, and forward markets have led to problems. The original absence of cash commodity trading on the Osaka rice futures exchange did contribute to erratic price fluctuations between the futures and cash markets for rice. Here the introduction of cash commodity trading on the Osaka exchange led to greater market coordination and in turn allowed arbitrage to eliminate uneconomic price differentials and reduce price instability. The Osaka story has been retold several times for various commodities in different parts of the world since localized meeting places for trade began.

At present governing bodies such as the United States Commodity Futures Trading Commission try to minimize the impact of periodic deficiencies between the rules of the market and the evolving needs of the market. But, despite periodic spasms, the basic economic origins of these markets ensure their existence in one form or another. These origins include uncertainty, the business nature of the production, storage, and consumption cycle, and the nature of price formation.

2.3 Uncertainty and the Transference of Risk

The demand for contracting among direct placement and organized exchange markets stems from the *uncertainty* created by fluctuating prices. Most commodities have regular fluctuations such as seasonal patterns associated with the production, consumption, and inventory cycle as, for example, with corn. However, superimposed upon regular fluctuations that the market can anticipate and adjust for are unanticipated events that can lead to unanticipated price fluctuations.

The fact that price changes are not anticipated creates uncertainty. This unpredictable variation in price may be viewed as a measure of *risk*. The inability to predict unanticipated price changes and the potential losses they imply creates a demand for contracts through which this risk can be transferred from those who want to avert it to those who are willing to assume it.

Business decision makers seeking to avoid risk, that is, *hedgers*, concentrate on risk transference. *Speculators* or investors concentrate on buying now (going long) for future resale, or selling forward (going short) in anticipation of some future purchase that promises a profit. Together hedgers and speculators make the market for risk transference.

Some academics [Black 1976] have questioned the need for commodity risk-shifting activities in the context of a corporation. It is argued that the very existence of a corporation and the trading of its equity upon organized securities exchanges is itself a sufficient form of risk spreading. This risk spreading among equity holders does not have to be further "leveraged" through participation in commodity markets.

While, theoretically, this may seem like a valid criticism, this view neglects the expectations and performance measurements upon which managers and financial directors are judged. Losses, shared by the diverse group of equity holders, are nonetheless, placed squarely upon the shoulders of the individual or division responsible for them. This failure of management, *management bankruptcy*, can be just as important to those who run corporate entities as *firm bankruptcy* is to the equity and bondholders of the corporation: While a corporation may end with its bankruptcy, the onus of management's failure is carried by the managers.

Be that as it may, one of the most important questions that the owners of a corporation must answer is what is the nature of the business? This, in turn, means deciding in advance what risk return profile the corporation wants to assume and whether to assume risk from unanticipated price or supply conditions or to shift it through further contracting. While no formal proof that futures contracting in particular helps diversify risk is attempted here, the weight of history seems overwhelming. It clearly suggests that the various types of commodity contracting can be useful business tools for controlling risk by those seeking to avoid it.

2.3.1 The Sixteenth-Century Vintner: a twentieth-century example[4]

To appreciate the role of commodity markets and their risk transference consider a sixteenth-century Italian vintner who produced and distributed wine. Domestic production required planting, maturation, harvesting, and processing before a drop could be sold. Because of the long period of time between planting and sales the vintner was subject to the risk that wine prices might change dramatically from the time the production expenses were incurred to the date of the sale. While these price changes could be favorable and widen profit margins they also could bring about substantial losses. One way to reduce these risks was for the vintner to engage in forward contracting to major consumers—for example, the local lord, other wine merchants, and taverns. These forward contracts also acted as collateral for loans from moneylenders and changers. Thus, with forward contracts the vintner could borrow against forward sales receipts to finance current production costs. At the end of the contract period, the vintner would repay the loan plus interest. Presumably the differential between the costs plus interest and total revenues left the vintner with a profit. In short, forward contracting helped the vintner produce his wine with reduced financial risks.

The forward markets could also help the vintner engage in foreign

4. Adopted from the New York Futures Exchange, *Financial Futures Course* (New York: New York Futures Exchange, 1981), pp IV-2 to IV-8, V-1 to V-5.

trade when he purchased wine across the border in France in order to supplement his own production. The vintner had Italian lire but had to purchase francs in order to buy the wine. Once a year after the spring festival he went to the center of town, exchanged his lire for francs, crossed the border, purchased the wine. brought it back, sold it to the local populace, and then recouped his lire, hopefully at a profit.

By dealing in this manner, the vintner undertook an exchange risk: From the time he sold his lire to purchase the francs, crossed the border, purchased his wine, came back, and sold it again for lire, the value of the lire in terms of the francs could have changed.

One way the vintner could eliminate that exchange risk was to go to money-changers and buy francs beforehand, knowing that he would need those francs after the spring harvest to purchase the wine. In this way the vintner could put a fixed rate of exchange on his conversion from lire to francs. He could take those francs and deposit them until he needed them. On the date of the fair, he could collect the proceeds of his deposit, cross the border, and perform the same business but without exchange risk.

If the vintner did not have lire on hand he could borrow lire, exchange the lire for francs, and put the francs on deposit until he needed them to purchase the wine. When the time came, he would purchase his wine, bring the wine back to Italy, and sell it, thereby generating lira income. That lira income would pay for the lire he originally borrowed, plus the interest on his loan, and presumably some profit differential.

2.3.2 The Sixteenth-Century Money-Changer: another twentieth-century example[5]

The example of the sixteenth-century vintner illustrates the need and role of hedging in the commodity market for foreign exchange. Here, the vintner was a hedger, that is, one seeking a means of protection against financial loss. The hedge vehicle in this case was the forward commitment to buy and sell lire at fixed rates. In this way the vintner could remove the risk of loss owing to an unanticipated rate of exchange between lire and francs. Here the vintner was transferring risk away from himself to someone else willing to accept it: the money-changer.

The money-changer may be viewed as either a speculator or arbitrager or both. As a speculator, the money-changer may have been willing to speculate that the rate of exchange between lire and francs would change in his favor and produce a financial gain. Alternatively, the money-changer could have been an *arbitrager*, that is, one who purchases or sells a commodity in one market and simultaneously sells or buys the same commodity in another market in order to capture a profit from a price discrepancy between the two markets. In the case of the sixteenth-century vintner, the vintner may be

---

5. Ibid

viewed as one market seeking to purchase lire at a certain price. At the same time another trader may have been trying to sell lire at another price. If the vintner is willing to pay a price that (unknown to him) is above the price the other trader will accept, the money-changer may profit by acting as a financial intermediary and buy from the other trader and sell to the vintner and keep the difference as an arbitrage profit. To be sure, the money-changer could act as both a speculator and arbitrager. Indeed, the money-changer could also act as a hedger in order to reduce the risk of loss from other commitments.

3 SUMMARY

Commodity trading has existed for thousands of years and plays an important role in the allocation of resources between markets and over time. The types of transactions illustrated by the example of the sixteenth-century vintner and money-changer are illustrative of the world commodity markets as we now know them, regardless of the specific commodity in question. Parallels to the above cases are easily found in other commodities, including agriculture, precious metals, and financial instruments such as U. S. treasury bills. Each of them is subject to uncertainty and risk of loss; only the specific details of the commodity and markets differ. These details, however, can be important. While principles of risk transference, speculation, and arbitrage may be the same regardless of the commodity or market, the differences in the types of commodity contracts can require significant changes in trading emphasis and operation. Here there is no substitute for understanding the specific types of commodity markets and the types of contracting that may be done. These topics are covered in the next chapter.

4 BIBLIOGRAPHY

BAKKEN, HENRY H., *Theory of Markets and Marketing*. Madison, Wis.: Mimir Publishers, 1953.

BLACK, F., *Journal of Financial Economics,* 3, No. 112 (January-March 1976), 167–79.

BURNS, EDWARD MCNALL, *Western Civilizations, Their History and Culture*, 5th ed., New York: W. W. Norton & Co., 1958.

Chicago Board of Trade, *Commodity Trading Manual*, Chicago: Board of Trade, 1982.

KEYNES, J. M., *The General Theory of Employment, Interest and Money*. New York: Harcourt, Brace and World, 1966.

New York Futures Exchange, Financial Futures Course, New York, New York Futures Exchange, 1981.

TEWELES, R. J., C. V. HARLOW, and H. L., STONE, *The Commodity Futures Game: Who Wins ? Who Loses ? Why ?* New York: McGraw-Hill, 1974.

2

ELEMENTS OF CASH, FUTURES, AND OPTIONS CONTRACTING

ıı

1 INTRODUCTION

Commodity contracting extends across both time and space (location) and can be performed with a variety of instruments. While there are many different types of contracts they all must specify price, quantity, grade, (quality) and delivery conditions. Nevertheless, comparisons among them are not a trivial exercise. These issues are addressed in Section 2 together with major differences in commodity markets. Section 3 explores elements of the direct placement cash markets, both spot and forward. Commodity options also are traded in direct placement and are discussed in Section 4. Here, the elements of both puts and calls as well as the returns to both writers and buyers of both kinds of options are introduced. Futures contracting on organized exchanges is discussed in Section 5. Section 6 explores the use of all markets as substitutes and complements for one another. A comparison of the commodities markets with the equities market is given in Section 7, while the direct placement and open outcry markets are compared in Section 8. Section 9 summarizes the characteristics of the various forms of commodity contracting.

No attempt is made in this chapter to spell out the fundamentals of supply and demand for any one commodity, or the strategic reasons for using a particular form or combination of commodity contracts. Rather, the intent of this chapter is to acquaint the reader with some essential institutional and practical elements of commodities contracting.

2   COMMONALITY AND VARIATION IN COMMODITY CONTRACTING

To the uninitiated the commodity markets appear arcane and Byzantine in their complexity; there are many different commodities, different grades of a commodity, different methods of exchange, and different types of contracts, all of which are couched in jargon that makes the simplest transaction a near mystery. Needless to say, the mystery is more apparent than real. All commodity trades have several characteristics in common and the difference in markets and contracts while sharp are far from unfathomable. The following paragraphs spell out these common characteristics and some of the variations in markets and contracting.

2.1   Common Characteristics of Commodity Contracts

All commodity contracts must specify price, contract horizon (or term of maturity), quantity, place of delivery, and grade (or quality). While each of these characteristics has a simple definition there are many variations in practice.

2.1.1   Price

The price of the commodity is specified in terms of the currency of exchange, for example, U.S. dollars or deutschemarks, and the quantity unit of measurement, for example, $17.00 per troy ounce. Depending on the contract the price may be specified absolutely or relative to some other specified price. An example of a relative price would be 20¢ per troy ounce over the price per troy ounce on some specified exchange on a specific date.

2.1.2   Contract Horizon

The contract horizon specifies the date or range of dates during which the commodity must be delivered and, in relation to the date the contract takes effect, also specifies the duration of the contract. For certain contracts the date for delivery is fixed and represents a specific day. For other contracts the delivery date may be at the buyer's or seller's discretion over some specified period, for example, the last ten business days in the month. In some contracts the delivery period can be as long as the life of the contract itself:

Here the buyer of the contract typically has an option to exercise the contract at any time up to the end of the contract period.

2.1.3 Quantity

The amount of the commodity to be delivered also must be specified. In the case of an exchange market, the quantity is always fixed. In the case of direct placement (between two parties off an organized exchange), the quantity may be variable but typically is fixed. In direct placement contracting the quantity may be variable in two distinct ways. First, the amount specified in the contract may be variable. For example, Bread Inc. may have a contract to buy at least 20,000 bushels of wheat but no more than 30,000 bushels under the terms of the contract. Second, the amount traded need not always be traded in multiples of some common trading quantity unlike the amounts traded on an organized exchange. Wheat is traded in multiples of 5,000 bushels on the Chicago Board of Trade, but Bread Inc. may enter into a contract with a private party for delivery of 23,000 bushels.

2.1.4 Place of Delivery

For contracts between two parties the point of delivery may be anywhere they agree. However, to meet an obligation on an organized exchange, the delivery points must be those approved by the exchange. An individual intending to take delivery on an organized exchange may have uncertainty as to where the delivery will take place as, for example, with contracts involving live hogs. For agricultural commodities the short i.e., the person making delivery, typically has discretion for the place of delivery. In currency futures the buyer has discretion as to delivery location. While premia or discounts are built into the various locations to help equilibrate them, the equilibration is rarely achieved.

2.1.5 Grade

Commodities are not always of the same quality or grade. Some gold bullion may be .995 pure and other bullion may be only .990 pure. In the case of the direct placement markets, the grade must be agreed upon by the trading parties and prices are adjusted to reflect the quality. On organized exchanges, the quality is fixed by a minimum standard such as .995 pure gold. Quality, of course, is not limited to precious metals or agricultural products but applies to financial items as well. Here the quality refers to a specific type of instrument, its term to maturity, and any rate of interest it may carry. For example, there are many kinds of US treasury bonds outstanding but the

Chicago Board of Trade will accept only noncallable bonds with at least 20 years to maturity as of the maturity of the futures contract.

2.1.6 Nomenclature

Trading in the futures markets is done for specific months as opposed to the cash markets where exact dates are used. The standard mnemonics for futures contract maturity months are

> F = January
>
> G = February
>
> H = March
>
> J = April
>
> K = May
>
> M = June
>
> N = July
>
> Q = August
>
> U = September
>
> V = October
>
> X = November
>
> Z = December

for contracts traded up to one year forward. For futures contracts traded more than one year forward the same mnemonic scheme is used with the addition of a color code, e.g. red for one to two years forward.

2.2 Variations in Markets

In general, there are two kinds of markets: the two-party direct place-ment market and the open outcry exchange market. The *direct placement* market refers to the direct communication and agreement between the buyer and seller whether or not a broker acts as a middle man. The open outcry exchange market refers to transactions made on an *organized exchange* where the ultimate buyer and seller do not communicate or enter into an agreement between each other. Instead their orders are traded between third parties with anonymity in an *open outcry* auction.

The direct placement market has two principal variations. One is referred to as the *cash market* since deliveries have to be made or taken on a specified date unless the two parties involved can agree on a liquidation before the delivery date. The other is the *contingent claim market*. For agriculture, manufacturing, and precious metals, contingent claims typically are referred to as options. In the financial markets contingent claims are often called standby commitments. Regardless of the specific commodity of reference, contingent claims, unlike a "cash" agreement, do not obligate the buyer of the claim to take or make delivery. Rather, these claims give their owner the right to take or make delivery according to some prescribed conditions.

For the most part, the open outcry exchange markets are the organized futures markets. A futures contract is a commitment to buy or sell a commodity at a specified time or place in the future. The price is established when the contract is made in open auction on a futures exchange.

In the organized futures markets, the buyer and seller make an agreement on and with the exchange. The exchange provides the machinery for the transactions—a location, record keeping, and financial settlements. This service is offered only to the members of the exchange.

Contracting in direct placement and exchange markets, whether simultaneously, in tandem, or independently is the nature of commodity trading. Each market has its advantages depending upon the business problem at hand.

3 DIRECT PLACEMENT: The Cash Markets

There are two different kinds of cash markets: the *spot* physicals market and the *forward* physicals market. In the spot physicals market, commodity transactions are made for current sale at current prices. Delivery is to occur within normal commercial periods, that is, the amount of time it would take to deliver the commodities from the warehouse to the point of location specified by the producer or purchaser, for example, two days.

The forward physical market, called the forward market, is a direct placement market where the purchase and sale of commodities is for future delivery. Prices are determined at the time of contract and may be stated as prices per unit or as a price differential per unit to some other market price, for example, 10¢ per bushel over the December CBT futures closing price on December 1, 1980.

The attributes of the cash markets are the following: A legal contract is made between two parties. Physical delivery is *expected* and *must* be performed. The grade or quality, quantity, location, and time of delivery are negotiated between the two parties and are specified in the contract. In this sense there is no standard cash contract. Moreover, cash market contracts are not generally regulated by government agencies. Most important is they are not cancellable unless mutually agreed upon. Payment is not standardized and depends upon the trade terms that exist between the parties.

For example, on July 1, an Iowa corn farmer cultivating 1000 acres in assessing prospects for his harvest has $1.50 per bushel invested in seed, fertilizer, fuel, and capital costs that include his diesel tractor, storage bins, and combine. Interest costs on land and capital are another $1.00 per bushel based upon an estimated yield of 100 bushels per acre. The local county elevator where he typically sells grain will buy grain now, July 1, for October 30 delivery at a price of $2.90 per bushel. Cash prices for spot delivery at the local elevator are now at $3.25 per bushel but are expected to decrease owing to a large expected harvest. If the farmer contracts with the county elevator on July 1 for October 30 delivery, he can lock in a price profit of 40¢ per bushel without worrying about spot prices deteriorating at harvest time owning to exceptional fall weather. Not knowing the exact yield per acre he will acheive, the farmer enters into a forward contract to deliver 70,000 bushels at $2.90 per bushel with a penalty for excess moisture. His own storage capacity will allow him to store the expected extra 30,000 bushels of corn. The farmer sells forward 70,000 bushels of corn in the forward market and ends up with a possibility to sell 30,000 bushels later in the spot market.

Since the final harvest quantities are not known with certainty at the time the forward contract was written, this "hedge" transaction does not eliminate all risk. Large losses could occur if severe damage from corn blight were to severely reduce the size of the crop. Forward contracting need not be less risky if *price certainty* is accompanied by *quantity uncertainty*. For example, the farmer may lock in a price only to experience a terrible harvest and be unable to deliver.

Nevertheless, a main business philosophy of farmers, manufacturers, and investment managers is based upon the avoidance of revenue loss that is beyond the purview of their planning horizon. The business plan is to eliminate unexpected fluctuations so that resources can be concentrated upon the business decision of planting, manufacturing, and investing. The purpose of contracting is to eliminate price and in some cases quantity fluctuations that are beyond the control of the individual players. The cash markets are one place where this contracting is done. They are, however, not the only one.

4 DIRECT PLACEMENT: The Options Market

Options contracts are agreements that give the purchaser of the option the right but not the obligation to exercise the contract. The option contract specifies the length of time over which the option may be exercised, the type and amount of the commodity to be bought or sold, the price at which the purchase or sale will take place (called the striking price), the price (value) of the option, and the delivery point(s).

Options that represent claims to buy are referred to as *call options*. In this case, the underlying asset upon which the option is written can be "called" from the owner of the asset or writer of the option. That is, exercising a call results in the purchase of the asset from the writer.

Options that represent claims to sell are said to be *put options*. Exercising a put results in the sale of the underlying asset to the writer. Option contracts between two individuals are direct placement contracts and are not regulated by the Commodities Futures Trading Commission, the Securities and Exchange Commission, or any other government organization. While the CFTC has some authority over commodity options on organized exchanges, it has no clear jurisdiction over all option contracting for the physical commodity.

As distinct from a cash contract, an option contract, before it is closed or exercised, only has a probability that actual physical delivery will take place: The delivery may or may not take place. The stochastic nature of these contracts makes their valuation difficult. Nevertheless, it is now recognized by both market participants and the academic profession that options contracts play a role in the efficient use of resources. Even without the formal trading of commodity options on U.S. exchanges the value of these contingent claims in the direct placement markets is useful in setting investment strategies and tactics. A discussion of the valuation of alternative types of options and their use in setting investment and hedging strategies and tactics is deferred to Chapter 5. Suffice it to say the contracts can be substitutes as well as complements to cash market direct placement and futures contracts.

4.1 Types of Options and Rationale

Of the many types of options that have evolved, all of them can be categorized as either puts or calls and either European or American. Other options contracts, such as strips, straps, or straddles are merely combinations of puts and calls. A put option gives the *buyer* of the option the privilege to sell a certain amount of a commodity at an agreed-upon price known as the *striking price* sometime within the life of the contract. A call option gives the buyer the right to buy. A *European option* allows the buyer to exercise only on the last day of the option life. An *American option* offers the buyer the right to exercise the option at any time during the life of the contract.

The *writer* of the option stands behind the terms of the contract and must buy the commodity from the buyer of a put if it is exercised and must sell the commodity to the buyer of a call if it is exercised. Options are often transferable, and a seller may not be the original writer. Option dealers may specialize in the purchase and resale, or, brokerage, of options where such organized trading is permitted as in securities.

Whether an option is a put or call, it offers the holder (buyer) an opportunity to reduce risk or sell a commodity at a price higher than the purchase price. The rationale behind a put option is the buyer's expectation that within a certain period of time the price of the commodity may fall to a level lower than the exercise price agreed to in the option. If this should occur, the buyer of the put would be able to exercise the option and sell to the writer at the agreed price and, if need be, buy it in the market at the lower price. Similarly, a call option is based on the buyer's expectation that the price of the commodity may rise in the near future. If a price increase should come to pass, the buyer of the call would have the opportunity to buy the commodity at the lower price from the writer.

4.2 Intrinsic Value and Premium

The price or value of an option is the sum of two elements; the intrinsic value and the premium. The *intrinsic value* of an option is the difference between the striking price and the market price of the underlying asset when the option is in the money, that is, when the option can be exercised at a profit. This value is zero when the option is out of the money because a rational investor would not exercise the option under these conditions. The option *premium* is the "markup" of the option value over the intrinsic value. The premium over the intrinsic value may be viewed as the price of an opportunity to capture a possible profit. As the option is further in the money the expected profit over the intrinsic value becomes smaller and, in turn, the premium becomes smaller. These terms and relationships are illustrated in Figure 2.1 and 2.2, respectively.

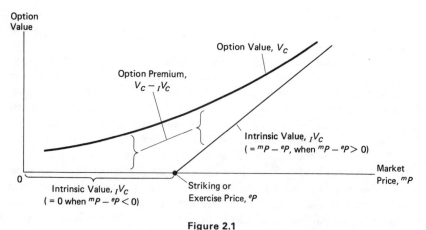

Figure 2.1

INTRINSIC VALUE, PREMIUM, AND VALUE OF A CALL OPTION

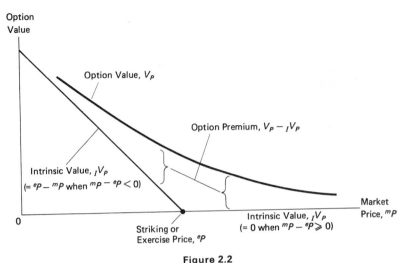

Figure 2.2

INTRINSIC VALUE, PREMIUM, AND VALUE OF A PUT OPTION

4.3 The Role of Options and the Redistribution of Risk

Regardless of the type of option, put or call, European or American, options perform several services to the economy. Among their most important contributions is the redistribution of risk from those seeking to avoid it (hedgers) to those willing to accept it (speculators).

The *redistribution of risk* is easily demonstrated by example. Consider a manufacturer of electronic components committed to future sales at set prices. If the prices of precious metals used in the manufacture of these products may rise in the near future, the producer faces the risk of profit erosion owing to increased production costs. In this case the manufacturer could reduce the risk of reduced profits by purchasing call options in precious metals. This would offer the manufacturer the opportunity to buy the metals at some acceptable price regardless of the price movements in the market. Here the price of the option may be viewed as an insurance (or assurance) premium for the reduction of risk. In this example, the manufacturer is a hedger. On the other side of this transaction is the writer of the option. The writer would be willing to sell the call option for either of two reasons. First, he may speculate that the market will not move far enough during the life of the option for the hedger to exercise the option. If this should occur the writer would capture some portion of the premium as a profit. Second, the writer may have other business commitments that require the offering of a call option to reduce risk of a possible loss.

Another common example can be found in the financial markets. A financial institution may buy a put option (standby commitment to sell) for a certain amount of government bonds at a certain price (based on a certain rate of interest) in order to hedge against the possibility of a rise in interest rates and a resulting capital loss if the bonds have to be liquidated during this time period. The party who writes the standby commitment may do so with the belief the premium will cover any likely fluctuation in interest rates during the life of the option or because of countervailing business that lock in the premium as a profit.

The risk profiles of hedgers and speculators and the redistribution of these risks between buyers and writers of options are illustrated in Figures 2.3 through 2.6. Figure 2.3 illustrates the risk of a long position with and

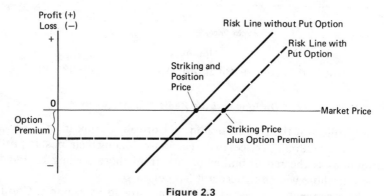

Figure 2.3

RISK OF A LONG POSITION WITH AND WITHOUT AN OPTION
(STRIKING = POSITION PRICE)

without a put option to limit those risks. Without the option the individual or firm with the *long position* will gain (or lose) $1 for every $1 the market price moves above (or below) the position price. With a put option that has a striking price equal to the long position price, the maximum the holder of the long position can lose is the price of the option. However, the holder of the long position with a put option will not be able to capture gains by exercising the option until the market price has moved above the position price plus the cost of the option.

Figure 2.4 shows the risk of a *short position* with and without a call option. Without the call option the holder of the short position will gain (lose) $1 for every $1 the market price moves below (above) the position price. With a call option the holder of the short position can limit losses to the price of the option. Here the holder of the short position with a call option would not be able to capture gains from exercising the call until the market price fell below the position price (same as the striking price) less the

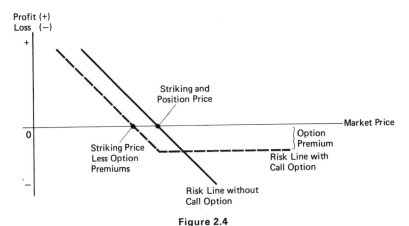

Figure 2.4

RISK OF A SHORT POSITION WITH AND WITHOUT AN OPTION
(STRIKING PRICE = POSITION PRICE)

cost of the option. In both cases, Figures 2.3 and 2.4, the position price and the striking price need not be the same. If the striking price is above (below) the long position price the put is said to be "in the money" ("out of the money") and typically carries a higher (lower) value to offset this differential. Similarly if the striking price on the call option is below (above) the short position price it is said to be "in the money" ("out of the money") and typically carries a higher (lower) value to offset this differential.

Figure 2.5 reveals the speculative risks between a call option buyer

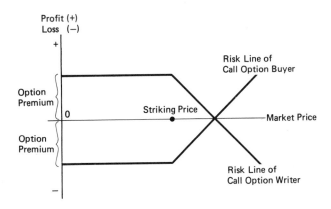

Figure 2.5

COMPARISON OF SPECULATIVE RISKS OF A CALL OPTION
BUYER AND WRITER

and writer, and Figure 2.6 illustrates the comparative risks of a put option buyer and seller. As can be seen the risks between buyer and writer are inverse images of one another: The speculative risk to the writer is just the opposite of the risk to the buyer.

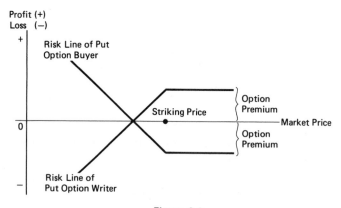

Figure 2.6

COMPARISON OF SPECULATIVE RISKS OF A PUT OPTION
BUYER AND WRITER

It must be noted that options trading is not the same as gambling. To be sure, the speculator may be likened to the gambler. However, the party on the other side of the table, the hedger, surely cannot be considered a gambler. Indeed the hedger's objective is to avoid risk, not to take it. Insofar as options enable hedgers and speculators to satisfy needs or desires that otherwise would be unfulfilled, both hedgers and speculators are better off. Gambling does not provide the same opportunities: One side's gain is the other side's loss.

4.4 The Contribution of Options to the Economy

Options offer at least two other benefits to the economy. First, they can lower price in a competitive market owing to the efficiencies gained from the redistribution of risk. Second, they can contribute to price stability by increasing supply when prices rise and increasing demand when prices fall.

One of the benefits of the redistribution of risk is the lessening of expensive inventories by a manufacturer, portfolio manager, or some other hedger. Insofar as options enable these hedgers to lower their business costs by replacing expensive ("physical") inventory investment with less expensive options, these cost savings can be passed on to the consumer. In general, the inefficient allocation of risk may be viewed as a market imperfection. Insofar as these market imperfections result in higher costs, a healthy options market can reduce these costs by reducing the degree of market imperfection. Whether these savings will be passed on to the consumer depends, of course, on the nature of the market. Generally speaking, in a competitive market these reductions in costs will be passed on. However they may not be passed on to consumers under conditions of imperfect competition. But this is not a problem of options. Rather, it is a more fundamental problem of the marketplace.

Options are often criticized as serving only the purposes of speculators and, in so doing, contributing to unstable prices. Speculators have often been accused of market manipulation resulting in price destabilization in their quest for profits. As reprehensible as this may be it is not a criticism of speculators or speculation per se. As soon as a speculator manipulates a market by capturing or "cornering" a large percent of that market either alone or in collusion with others that person or group no longer is taking a chance or speculating on the outcome of a business investment. Here, speculation in a business investment has been abandoned in favor of the speculation of the highway robber—the risk of getting caught. Speculation is no more at fault for criminal market manipulation than the accounting profession is for the fraudulent activities of one of its members or clients. Looking beyond the emotion of this accusation it becomes clear that options neither serve only the purposes of the speculator nor contribute to price instability. As we have seen, options offer a redistribution or risk from hedgers to speculators. While they may offer an uncertain opportunity for profit to the speculator, they also offer risk avoidance to the hedger. As far as price instability is concerned, speculators presumably operate with a profit motive. If they are to achieve this aim they must sell commodities when prices rise above their long position price or must buy when prices fall below their short position price. By increasing supply when prices are high and increasing demand when prices are low these actions only serve to put downward pressure on rising prices and upward pressure on falling prices. In so doing these actions serve to maintain price stability and thus to counteract price instability.

5 ORGANIZED EXCHANGE CONTRACTING:
The Futures Markets

In the United States, futures contracting, as distinct from forward contracting, is done on organized commodity exchanges. There exists only government-regulated trading for futures contracts. The regulating bodies are the Commodity Futures Trading Commission (CFTC) and the surveillance committees of the exchanges themselves. *Futures contracts* are commitments to buy or sell commodities at a specified time and place in the future. These contracts do not exist between two individuals. A futures contract exists only between the buyer or seller of a contract and the exchange itself or its representative, the clearing corporation. In order to buy or sell a futures contract "earnest money," that is, good faith money, in the form of *initial* and *maintenance margins* must be posted with a broker and ultimately the clearing corporation. When an order is generated through a broker or a member of the exchange, it is transmitted to the "ring" or "pit" of the exchange where the order is executed electronically or by outcry between floor traders. The only negotiation done in a ring is for price and number of contracts. All other contract conditions are standardized. Prices are "hit" by answering the cry of a floor trader or broker. Even though a price is hit and a purchase and sale recorded, no contract exists between the traders or brokers. The contract is made with the clearing corporation of each exchange. In essence, two separate contracts are created, one for the buy side and one for the sell side.

Futures contracts are settled or reconciled at the end of every day, unlike options or cash direct placement contracts. That is, gains and losses from buying or selling are assessed by the market price at the end of the day. This price is the *closing* or *settlement price* of the particular futures contract. This process of accounting is called "daily marking to the market." The daily gains are credited to the trader's account and the daily losses must be paid up immediately in the form of maintenance margin.

Because the futures contract is settled at the end of the day by posting gains and losses to each trader's account, the value of the futures contract is reduced to zero by the end of the day or the beginning of the next session of trading. Thus, no one pays a premium for acquiring a futures contract as would be the case of either a call or put option contract. While the futures contract can be said to have no value at the beginning of trading or at the time a futures contract is purchased, it is the accumulation of intraday gains and losses from price movements over time that classifies them as risky assets. Indeed holding futures contracts can result in large accumulations or deficits.

In the process of delivery, it is usually the short position that notifies the clearing corporation that delivery of the physical commodity will be forthcoming. This takes place on the *intention to deliver day*. Each commodity has its own rules with respect to last trading day, intention to deliver day, notification of delivery day, and delivery day. The exchanges widely disseminate this information. All of these housekeeping transactions are part of the role played by the clearing corporation of each exchange. The rules are designed to provide for orderly execution of obligations by both longs and shorts and to provide a mechanism that maintains fair pricing between direct placement markets and futures markets for each commodity traded.

As distinct from a cash contract, the ending of a futures contract position does not necessarily result in delivery of the physical commodity. Ending a futures contract obligation also can be done either by liquidating the position or by engaging in an *exchange of physicals*. A position is liquidated by buying back (or selling) the futures contract that had been sold (or purchased) before the delivery or expiration data of the contract in question. Because the futures contract is made with the exchange and not an individual, the process of ending or *unhooking* a position is greatly facilitated through the clearing house function that each exchange provides. An exchange of physicals also can close a position on a futures exchange. This procedure is as follows: Before delivery has to be taken (made), if the trader with a long (short) position can find another buyer (seller) on the exchange with physical inventory to accept (make) delivery, then the trader can end his delivery obligation. This obligation is transferred to the other participant. Typically, a premium is paid to the acceptor of the obligation in the form of a price discount or premium on the commodity relative to the going contract price. Regardless of how positions are closed, each particular contract must be acted upon before contract maturity if contracting in the physical commodity is to be avoided. Among the reasons for not taking delivery are the following:

1. The delivery locations are too far away for production efficiency.
2. Physical inventories are sufficient for current planning.
3. The trader has no physical facilities for making or taking delivery and has no need of using exchange-designated warehouses.
4. Futures trading was done for price protection and not quantity protection.
5. The fixed maturity (delivery) date of the futures contract does not match the timing requirements of the trader for the use of the physical commodity.
6. Storage insurance and financing costs may be excessive in relation to the trader's wealth and credit position.

The futures exchanges make available information on the total amount of contracting done. The two items reported are volume and open interest. *Volume* defines the number of contracts traded daily. *Open interest* is a number that represents the net open (i.e., unliquidated), positions on the exchange. While it is true that for every buyer there is a seller, it is also true that a futures transaction either creates a new long and short position or liquidates an existing long and short position. Open interest represents the total number of contracts long or the total number of contracts short since both are the same number. This number represents the amount of contracts that are potentially deliverable. Typically, only a small percent of open interest actually ends up in delivery; approximately 5 percent of the average open interest during the life of a futures contract is delivered.

6 OPTIONS, FORWARD AND FUTURES CONTRACTS:
Complements and Substitutes

As noted above, an option can be exercised or not, at the holder's discretion, sometime during the life of the contract. A forward contract commits the buyer to purchase or sell a given quantity and quality of a commodity at a precise time in the future. These commitments typically are made by direct placement between buyer and seller and not through an organized exchange. A futures contract is traded on an organized exchange and requires settlement, that is, financial adjustment, at the end of each day, unlike a forward contract which is settled only at maturity. That is, a futures contract may be viewed as a sequence of one-day forward contracts. Both the forward and futures contracts differ from the option contract in that they *require* a purchase or sale at a specified time. The option contract holder has the right to these purchases or sales but not the obligation.

Futures contracts traded on organized exchanges require little margin and most of that can be met by treasury bills instead of cash. This enables manufacturers, processors, and others to hedge their operation in the futures market with little more financial drain than hedging through direct placement in the forward market. Hence, the forward and futures markets may be viewed as substitutes to these buyers and sellers. Moreover, the forward and futures markets offer opportunities for arbitrage between them. For example, the direct placement of a sale of three-month forward gold may have a price that is above a corresponding three-month forward gold futures price. The skillful consummation of both the direct placement sale and the purchase of the futures contract would offer the trader an arbitrage profit. Here, futures and forward contracts are complementary financial instruments. Options, also, may be viewed as substitutes and complements to either forward or futures contracts. Instead of using a forward or futures contract to hedge a business commitment, the prospective hedger could substitute the purchase of an option to be exercised if needed. Options also may be written against a forward or futures contract position in order to limit possible losses or to capture arbitrage opportunities. This complementarity may go in the other direction as well: Futures contracts and forward commitments may be used to hedge options contracts as, for example, the use of the financial futures markets to hedge standby commitments.

The optimal mix of options, forward commitments, futures contracts, and physical inventories is a difficult issue addressed in detail in subsequent chapters where various methods of optimization have been set forth. At this juncture it can be said that an optimal mix depends on (1) the business objective of the trader e.g., hedging, (2) the constraints imposed by the different contracts e.g., cash reserves and other commitments and (3) the costs of the different contracts e.g., borrowing or opportunity costs for margin.

7 SELECT COMPARISONS BETWEEN COMMODITY
AND SECURITY EXCHANGES

Although it is not the purpose of this book to explore the securities markets, some comparisons between organized commodities exchanges and organized securities markets are worthwhile. Organized securities markets have several operational characteristics that are unlike those of the organized commodities markets. First, securities markets have higher margins. That is they require more money backing a position than do futures markets. Commodities exchanges rarely require more than 20 percent initial margin whereas securities markets often require 50 to 100 percent margin. This, of course, means differences in the leverage and risk of loss between securities and commodities trading. Second, commodity futures contracts, unlike equities, have finite lives. Consequently, if the commodity trader's position matures, he must either take or make delivery or "switch" the position forward; that is, he must liquidate the position and take a similar position in a contract maturing further into the future. These circumstances can result in losses to the commodity trader that the securities trader may not incur. Often the securities trader can hold the equity position until the market prices improve, or hold bonds or notes until maturity and receive full face value of the securities. In short, a securities trader can often ride out the storm. Commodities traders do not have the same degree of luxury. Third, futures contracts have *daily trading limits* (maximum price change) whereas the securities markets do not. This can have dramatic effects on liquidity. A limit move in either direction in the commodities markets brings with it the de facto ending of trading. This can be an advantage to some, some of the time, and a disadvantage to others some of the time. Fourth, futures contracts, unlike securities, are marked to market each day. This can be a disadvantage for commodities traders relative to securities traders when prices move adversely to the position. Once again the securities trader can wait until prices improve. The commodities trader does not have this opportunity. Finally, the prices of base commodities often respond more strongly and with greater speed to events in other commodity markets than securities do in response to the same events or to events in neighboring industries and securities. This simply places a much greater information burden on the commodities trader than on the securities trader.

8 DIRECT PLACEMENT AND OPEN OUTCRY MARKETS:
A Comparison

Direct placement markets refer to direct communication and agreement between the buyer and seller. The open outcry markets are more convoluted. Here, the buyer enters into a contract with the exchange or its representative clearing house as does the seller. The exchange is responsible for clearing and matching the contracts and ensuring their compliance. Proponents of the direct placement markets are quick to point out the increased flexibility in the timing of cash market contracts. Futures contracts trade for specific maturity dates in specific months. Direct placement markets can accommodate maturities on a daily basis. Nevertheless, certain months are heaviest in each commodity, and timing anomalies between futures contract maturities and business needs can be handled through discounts, loans, and borrowing that cover the timing gaps. Moreover, the ability to enter into a contract without having the other side of the contract requiring (in a legal sense) the absolute delivery of the physical commodity gives to futures contracting a great commercial benefit. Since delivery need not be taken in futures contracting, the role of such activity is geared towards price protection. Futures markets are not typically used by commercial interests to secure or distribute supplies of commodities. However, to the surprise of some traders, commercial interests sometimes do use the futures markets for these purposes.

Table 2.1 summarizes the distinctions between direct placement and open outcry exchange placement contracts. At the risk of oversimplification, the basic distinction is the difference between a standardized contract and a nonstandardized contract: One is "off the rack"; the other one is tailor-made. The tailor-made contract fits a specific need. If the individual wants out of his contract, he must find somebody who wants to pick up that contract. A standardized contract provides much greater liquidity and transferability. In short, the trade-off is between fit and greater transferability. Both are important and for this reason both markets flourish side by side.

Table 2.1

COMPARISON OF DIRECT PLACEMENT AND EXCHANGE PLACEMENT CONTRACTS

TYPE OF CONTRACT	CONTRACT FEATURES					
	Physical Delivery	Price	Contract Horizon	Quantity	Place of Delivery	Quality
Direct Placement	Legally required	Fixed or variable	Fixed or variable	Variable	Variable	Variable but specified in advanced
Exchange Placement	Not legally required/ monetary settlement	Fixed	Fixed	Fixed	Fixed alternatives	Fixed minimum

9 SUMMARY

The problem of achieving both spatial and intertemporal price equilibrium revolves around trading in both direct placement and exchange markets. Combinations of contracting in the spot cash, forward cash, options, and futures markets can fit the myriad needs of the various participants, be they hedgers, arbitragers, or speculators. Pricing in these markets is generally determined by the exchange of bids and offers, either by direct or brokered two-party negotiation or open outcry on an organized exchange. Options pricing presents special problems owing to the inherent nature of the contingent claim. This valuation is explored in Chapter 5.

The elements of contracting in the direct and exchange placement markets have been presented to highlight their commonality and differences. These markets do not exist in isolation. Rather, they can be complements to or substitutes for one another.

10 BIBLIOGRAPHY

ARTHUR, H. B., *Commodities Trading as a Business Tool.* Cambridge, Mass.: Harvard University Press, 1974.

BLACK, F., "The Pricing of Commodity Contracts," *Journal of Financial Economics,* No. 3 (1976), pp. 167–179.

CHICAGO BOARD OF TRADE, *Commodity Trading Manual.* Chicago: Chicago Board of Trade, 1982.

GALI, D. "Pricing of Options and the Efficiency of the Chicago Board of Options Exchange." Ph.D. dissertation, University of Chicago, 1975.

KRUZENGA, R. J., "Put and Call Options: A Theoretical and Market Analysis." Ph.D. dissertation, Massachusetts Institute of Technology, 1956.

PECK, A. E., ed., *Selected Writings on Futures Markets,* Vol. 2. Chicago: Chicago Board of Trade, 1977.

3

AMBIENT PERSPECTIVES ON ASSET AND LIABILITY MANAGEMENT

||||||||||||||||||||||||||||||||||||||||||||||||||||||||||||||||||||||||||||||||||||||||||||||||||||||

1 INTRODUCTION

A systematic approach to commodities investment decisions has three prerequistites: (1) the correct formulation of the business objective(s), (2) an information structure that provides relevant information on all alternative courses of action, and (3) a decision process designed to use relevant information so as to identify actions that will lead to the achievement of the objectives. These prerequisites, of course, are no less true in commodities than they are in more well traveled areas. This chapter focuses on the business objectives of commodities trading. The information structure and decision process to achieve these objectives are the subjects of subsequent chapters.

In general, there are three basic trading objectives: hedging, speculation, and arbitrage. Each can occur in many forms and a single definition of each would be inadequate. Nevertheless, a general definition of each is essential. *Hedging* is a means of defense and, in our case, a means of defense against financial loss and/or at times against supply shortages. *Speculation* is the act of engaging in an investment with an element of risk and a chance of profit. Thus, buying IBM stock and buying gold bullion are speculative albeit the technical details are different. *Arbitrage* is the purchase (sale) of an item in one market for immediate resale (purchase) in another in order to capture a profit. Each of these objectives can be approached from some combination of three distinct vantages: over time, between markets, and across commodities. While each is similar, each is different and requires different information and decision processes. For example, one may hedge flour in the wheat market, or arbitrage between money rates and commodity rates, or speculate on the price difference between two markets.

The purpose of this chapter is to spell out these objectives and their similarities and differences from different vantages. In Section 2 hedging, speculation, and arbitrage are explored in the context of intertemporal decisions. In Section 3 these objectives are discussed for applications across commodities and between markets. Investment decisions that simultaneously consider different markets, commodities, and time are explored in Section 4. Finally, the chapter is summarized in Section 5.

2 OBJECTIVES OF FORWARD CONTRACTING

The objectives of forward contracting in direct placement and organized exchange markets are the following:

1. To reduce risk while maintaining an adequate return (i.e., hedging).
2. To attempt to secure profits from market disequilibria (i.e., arbitrage).
3. To bet and win against the expectations of the consensus of market participants (i.e., speculation).

What distinguishes one participant from another is more often the intent of the transaction than the outcome. Indeed, there are participants who, in a world of changing expectations and prices, may employ trading strategies and tactics that are geared to all three objectives.

2.1 Intertemporal Hedging and Risk Transference

Hedging over time, that is, *intertemporal hedging*, is done by processors, producers, and financial intermediaries in order to lock in a selling price and/or costs in order to help assure a profit from their operations. For example, the hedger can have forward (cash) commitments to deliver some commodity at the going but as yet unknown market price at the time of delivery. In this case, the hedger would sell forward in the futures market with the intent of capturing profits in the futures market as an offset to losses on the cash commitments if prices fall. Naturally, the hedger would liquidate the futures position just before delivery of the physical commitment or the maturity of the futures contract, whichever comes first. Otherwise, the hedger may be forced to make delivery without adequate supplies or become a de facto speculator. Alternatively, the hedger can have fixed forward commitments in the cash market, but must hedge either to protect against a shortage of supplies to meet these commitments or to lock in the prices of base commodities required for delivery. In short, hedging over time stems from the need to remove uncertainty. This uncertainty is about future prices or supplies. The financial incidence of these risks can be on the cost and/or selling-revenue side of profits.

Three features of hedging, intertemporal or otherwise, warrant special comment; First, the preeminence of futures contracts as hedging complements and substitutes: second, the notion of risk transference as insurance: and third, the fact that, while some hedgers may be long and others short, total hedging tends to have a net position.

2.1.1 Contract Substitutes and Complements

For any hedger there exists a commitment in the direct placement markets and hedging is the process of taking an offsetting *complementary position* to that commitment in an alternative market to reduce the risk of loss. Insofar as futures contracts are used to hedge a commitment, they are an obvious financial complement to that commitment: They reduce the risk of the investment and are an integral part of its risk-return profile. Futures contracts also are *substitutes* for other commodity contracts. Options and offsetting cash commitments also can be used as hedging vehicles. However the popularity of futures contracts for hedging, where they are available, is a result of two unique attributes: They are highly liquid and require little margin.

To illustrate the complementarity and substitutability of futures contracts as a hedging vehicle, consider a U. S. corporation that is committed to purchasing an item six months forward and the price of the item is denominated in deutschemarks. Because the deutschemark/dollar rate of exchange could change so as to raise the value of deutschemarks relative to the dollar, that is, raise the dollar cost of the item six months forward, the company might hedge the dollar value of the purchase commitment. This could be accomplished by entering into an offsetting transaction of buying deutschemarks in the futures market. The hedge will be a "perfect one" if the dollar amount of the forward contract and the timing of the forward contract just matches up with that which can be obtained in the futures market. The offset or hedge characteristic of this transaction is "definitional": What will be gained in one market from exchange rate fluctuations will be lost or offset in the other market. Since the variability of the deutschemark/dollar exchange rate is eliminated by the construction of the so-called *perfect hedge*, risk is reduced for that particular individual transaction. In this sense, the futures contract is complementary to the cash transaction and is a substitute for a forward foreign exchange transaction. Which alternative will be chosen, futures, forward or, in some cases, an option, depends on their costs and market liquidity. For every sale of a deutschemark futures contract there has to be someone who purchases a deutschemark futures contract. Both parties enter into the transaction with the clearing corporation of the exchange and not with one another. Hence, there will exist either another hedger or arbitrager who will be delivering deutschemarks in six months or a speculator who is willing to take an uncovered position for that period.

2.1.2 Hedging, Correlation, and Insurance

It has often been stated that hedging is a form of price insurance. However, this comparison is inappropriate since the principle that justifies insurance is the *principle of independent events*. That is, the death of one person will be independent of the death of another person. Or a fire in one factory will not consume all factories insured by a particular carrier. If, in fact, claims have a chance of bunching up, the insurance carrier will lay off such risks by entering the reinsurance market. Because the events being insured against are independent, risk can be spread among the large group of policyholders. The underlying nature of insurance is risk spreading through the independence of events and not the fact that risk spreading is created. All risk reduction is not insurance. While risk reduction is the objective of hedgers, the concept of insurance through independent events has little to do with the concept of hedge contracting. It is because events are *not* independent that hedge contracting becomes economically viable and, in the process, risk shifting is attained. It is, in fact, when events, that is, prices, in one market are "perfectly correlated" and hence not independent with the hedger's underlying business that the "perfect hedge" or "perfect risk spreading" is attained.

The theoretical criterion that defines a market to be a *good hedging market* is one where the prices of the hedge instrument are highly correlated with the price of the commodity being hedged. However, the attribute of being correlated in terms of price may not correspond to the attribute of being a physical substitute for the commodity in question.

2.1.3 Net Hedging

It must be noted that hedgers need not always be on one side of the market. Some hedgers can be long a cash contract and short a futures contract, while others may have just the opposite position for the same commodity. The side of the market they are on depends, of course, on their business. A producer (e.g., a wheat farmer) may go short a futures contract to protect against a fall in prices while a processor (baker) may go long in order to protect against a rise in prices. To a large extent, hedgers' positions offset one another. Nevertheless, for the market there are *net hedging* positions and these must be offset by other market players. Here the players on the other side of the net hedge position are speculators. It is in this sense that risk is transferred from hedgers to speculators.

2.2   Intertemporal Arbitrage: The Mechanics of Efficiency

Arbitrage in its purest form is the simultaneous sale and purchase of a commodity in two separate markets at two separate prices. That is, to effect an arbitrage one buys in the cheaper market and sells in the more expensive one simultaneously. Arbitrage over time, that is, *intertemporal arbitrage*, simply trades money borrowing and lending rates against the implicit interest rates in the cash or futures commodity markets. In short, one compares borrowing or lending rates on money for different time horizons against the rates of interest implied between different futures or forward commodity prices.

2.2.1   Cash and Carry Examples

A common form of intertemporal arbitarge is the so called "cash and carry." Table 3.1 illustrates three time arbitrage opportunities: a "cash and carry," a "forward cash and carry," and a "reverse forward cash and carry."

Table 3.1
MARKET OPPORTUNITIES

TIME HORIZON (months)	COMMODITY RATE (percent per annum)	BORROWING RATE (percent per annum)	LENDING RATE (percent per annum)
0–6	10	12	12
3–9	14	12	12
6–12	13	13	13
9–15	13	15	15
12–18	14	14	14

Suppose the trader had inventories scheduled for the next six months. The above illustration reveals an intertemporal arbitrage opportunity: Sell the commodity now and buy it back six months forward at a cost of 10 percent per annum, but invest the proceeds from the sale (e.g., a six-month bankers acceptance), at the indicated return of 12 percent per annum, yielding a 2 percent per annum arbitrage profit. This is an elementary example of a transaction known as a *cash and carry*. A *forward cash and carry* arbitrage also is revealed in Table 3.1. This entails selling nine months forward now and buying back the commodity fifteen months forward at a cost of 13 percent per annum and simultaneously lending the proceeds at a profitable rate of 15 percent per annum from nine months forward to fifteen months forward. Another example also presents itself—a *reverse forward cash and carry*. Table 3.1 reveals that it would be profitable to borrow money three months forward for six months and invest those proceeds in the commodity for that same period. This would cost 12 percent per annum but reap 14 percent per annum for a gross trading profit of 2 percent per annum.

2.2.2 Arbitrage and Speculation: some gray areas

The question of delineating arbitrage from speculation is not an easy one. The reason for this is that arbitrage trading is often done with the intent of liquidating the arbitrage positions before they mature. For example, one may buy CBT gold at $645 an ounce and sell COMEX gold at $650 an ounce, a small profit that would be a net loss owing to the delivery costs. The intent here is to liquidate the positions at a profitable price differential before delivery has to be made. Owing to price volatility the liquidation could be done, for example, by selling the CBT gold at $640 and buying the COMEX gold at $640, yielding a $5 an ounce gross trading profit. While some players may consider this an arbitrage trade, in effect, it is truly a speculation. It is based upon the prediction of what will happen to the CBT-COMEX price differentials. Another example would be to sell wheat futures nine months forward and buy them twelve months forward, if the price difference between them is very small. Here the intent is to carry the position until the price difference between the two contracts widens and the more distant maturity carries a significantly higher price than the nearer maturity. If this occurs, the trader can liquidate the position at a profit by buying back the near contract and selling the forward contract. Once again, the price levels are irrelevant: The profits or losses are determined by the difference in the price differentials. Here also, the trade is a speculation and not a true arbitrage.

2.2.3 Returns to Arbitrage

Returns to arbitragers can be viewed as the price that markets pay to those individuals who, through their hard work and diligence, help bring about spatial and temporal equilibrium between markets. The theory of transactions costs suggest that these returns may not, in fact, be small. The fact that a producer can purchase copper in either New York or London and not worry about whether one market has a distorted price in comparison to the other is something worth paying for. From whose pockets the arbitragers earn their returns may be difficult to ascertain, but everone who uses commodities for whetever reason benefits from the actions of this group of traders. Their efforts help guarantee equilibrium in prices among different markets. Here we have an example of Adam Smith's oft-related idea that when individuals pursue their own best interests, everyone benefits.

2.3 Speculation

Speculation is derived from the latin word *speculari* which means "watchtower" or "to seek out." *Speculation* in commodities entails taking a position, that is, betting on the future path of prices which the marketplace does not anticipate. In a sense, all speculation involves the passage of time. There are two aspects of speculation in the commodities or financial markets. First, it is done either with concentration or diversification; second, the speculative position may be an outright long or short position or, on a price differential as in the gold example noted above.

2.3.1 Concentration and Diversification

Speculation entails taking an unhedged position. An obvious speculative position is to go long or short a commodity. Here, the investor's funds are concentrated on a single "bet." In some cases, a speculator may go long or short some combination of commodities. This collection or *portfolio* of positions may be selected in order to *concentrate* funds in those commodities and positions that promise the greatest speculative returns. Alternatively, the portfolio may be selected not only with the intent of capturing a speculative gain but also of reducing the risk of loss by diversifying the invested funds among the various commodities. The act of *diversification* takes advantage of offsetting movements among the prices of the commodities. The trends of each commodity will dictate the position taken in each: long if prices are expected to rise or short if prices are expected to fall. However, the prices of the commodities may fluctuate around their expected trends. Here, the selection, that is, diversification, among commodities is made so as to minimize the net variation in the return on the entire portfolio, subject to some minimally acceptable return on the portfolio. The concept of portfolio selection in commodities is covered in Part 2 and Part 5. Suffice it to say that diversification per se is not speculation. Indeed, it is entered into with the express purpose of reducing the variability of return from a portfolio of investments and in this context is an act of risk reduction not risk taking. Risk reduction, of course, is not the same as an absence of risk and the portfolio, whether diversified or not, will have some variability of return and therefore some risk; that is, it will involve speculation.

2.3.2 Outright Positions and Spread Trading

When people think of a speculator, they more often than not think of a trader that takes an *outright position*, that is, net long or short one or more commodities. When a speculator is *net long*, that is, has the physical commodity or a commitment to buy the commodity, the hope of the speculator is that prices will rise so that the physical commodity or purchase commitment can be sold at a profit. Similarly, when a speculator is *net short* a commodity, that is, has a commitment to sell the commodity, he or she is betting on a fall in prices in order to buy back the sale commitment at a profit. It is the net position that defines the degree of speculation. Speculation is not confined to outright positions. Spread trading also can be speculative.

In simple terms, speculative *spread trading* is betting upon the price differential between commodity contracts. The spread can be between markets or maturities for the same commodity or between commodities such as a spread between treasury bills and treasury bonds. Indeed complex spreads can pair different commodities, markets and maturities. These cases are discussed in Section 3.

Speculating on the spread for a commodity takes the form of buying the commodity with one delivery date and selling the same commodity with another delivery date. The intent is to sell (buy) a wide (narrow) spread, that is, to sell (buy) a wide (narrow) price differential and then, at some time in the future before the maturity of either contract, buy back (sell) the spread at a narrower (wider) differential and in so doing capture a profit. When one buys the cash or near maturity and sells forward it is called being *long the basis*. Similarly, when one sells the near maturity and buys the further forward maturity it is called being *short the basis*. If a hedger is long the basis, the hedger will profit (lose) if the basis narrows (widens). When one is long the basis and the basis narrows (widens), any loss (gain) on the cash (futures) side is offset by the gain (loss) on the futures (cash) side. For example, suppose one is long the basis in gold with a long cash position at $650 an ounce and short a futures contract at $680 an ounce—a spread of $30 an ounce. If the cash and futures prices change to $620 and $640 an ounce, respectively, the trader could short the basis at these prices by selling cash gold at $620 an ounce (a cash loss of $30 an ounce) and buy back the futures contract at $640 an ounce, a profit of $40 an ounce. Taken together, the liquidation yields a net $10 an ounce profit.

It should also be noted that while this individual is long the basis and may be "speculating" on a narrow basis, he or she is defined nevertheless to be a *short hedger*. That is, whether a person is a long or short hedger depends upon the position that is taken in the futures market and not the cash market. The person is a hedger because of the "offsetting" positions in the two markets. Clearly, speculating on the basis casts a new light on hedging.

2.3.3 Unintentional Speculation: the imperfect hedge

There are, of course, cases where every intent is made to hedge a cash position but a net speculative position evolves despite the trader's best efforts. That is, the hedger becomes an *unintentional speculator*. For example, suppose an insurance company attempts to hedge the value of their treasury bonds by going short in the futures markets. Initially they may be able to hedge the exact dollar amount. However, subsequent price movements in the cash and futures markets for treasury bonds may not be perfectly correlated and the insurance company may end up with a net short position in the futures market. That is, owing to subsequent price movements, the value of the futures contracts may exceed the value of the underlying assets being hedged. The insurance company now would be considered a speculator to the extent of the excees short position. If the amount of the excess is not equal to an interger number of futures contracts, then the insurance company would not be able to enforce the hedge by liquidating the excess short position: Some fraction would be left over. While the net position may be a small fraction of the amount being hedged, it nevertheless may be a large dollar value. Like a chameleon, the hedger can become a speculator and, as noted in Section 2.3.2, the speculator may be disguised as a hedger.

3 CONTRACTING ACROSS COMMODITIES OR BETWEEN MARKETS

There are, of course, many types of speculation, hedging, and arbitrage across commodities and between markets. They are common for commodities that have some production or financial linkage between them. Among the commodities with close technical linkages are soybeans and their byproducts soybean oil and soybean meal; feeder cattle and live (ready for slaughter) cattle; live hogs and pork bellies; the oil group including corn oil, cotton-seed oil, and soy oil; copper ingots and copper wire bar; gold and gold coins; and many of the financial instruments including T-bills, T-bonds, T-notes and GNMAs. Most of these commodities have both futures and cash markets. While the specific trades across commodities or between markets vary depending on the commodity combination and markets involved, the essential elements are the same. These elements are presented in the following paragraphs.

3.1 Hedging for Price and Supply

Trading between markets for the reduction of financial risk from possible adverse price movements is not uncommon. Indeed most hedging entails operations in two different markets: the cash and futures markets or the cash and options markets. These operations have been noted above and need not be repeated. *Hedging across commodities*, that is, *cross-commodity hedging*, occurs when a futures contract or option contract does not exist in the same asset of reference as the commitment in the cash markets. For example, an importer-exporter may need to hedge the value of a contract in a currency that is not liquid and for which there is no corresponding futures or options contract. Here, the importer-exporter may still be able to hedge the value of the contract by taking a position in a combination of futures contracts in foreign currencies that are highly correlated with the currency to be hedged. The precise currencies are an empirical question and, as shown in Part 4, statistical estimation methods such as multiple regression may be used to determine the weighting scheme. The maturity structure of the futures contracts in a cross-commodity hedge is determined by the maturity of the underlying commitment to be hedged and the liquidity of the futures contracts. The maturity of the futures contracts should be as close to the underlying commitment as possible, and preferably not earlier than the underlying commitment, to provide full-period coverage. The futures contracts also should be active contracts in order to ensure liquidity when it comes time to liquidate the hedge. To be sure, the extent to which the proxy hedge does not move in lock step with the underlying commitment is a speculative risk. Moreover, the trader in this case would be a speculator owing to the net futures position despite the hedging intent.

Hedging between markets, that is, *cross-market hedging*, for supply purposes is not as straightforward as hedging between markets for financial purposes. Often a producer will hedge needed supplies by taking a long position in the futures markets. If the supplies cannot be obtained in the cash markets at a better price, then the futures market may be used as a source of supply. If the delivery points of the futures market are at distant locations to the production or processing site, the transportation costs from the futures market warehouse to the producer or processor can be prohibitive. One way of getting around these transportation costs is to perform an exchange of physicals. An *exchange of physicals* can be done in direct placement or on a futures exchange. In direct placement it is an exchange of warehouse receipts between the trading parties. For example, one may hedge their U.S. copper supplies by taking a position in London on the London Metal Exchange. If delivery is taken, the transport cost can be prohibitive. However, if the trader is large and has stocks around the world, then the London stocks could be exchanged for warehouse receipts in the United States at a much closer point to the ultimate destination with a lower transportation cost.

An exchange of physicals on a futures exchange involves the settlement of a cash transaction between two trading parties on the exchange. The transaction is arranged between the buyer and seller and done by brokers on the futures exchange. The brokers transactions are done outside the ring, i.e. ex-pit, but are recorded as if done in the ring or pit. There are two equivalent ways the price is affixed to the exchange of physicals in a futures market. In some cases the cash to futures spread i.e. the basis, is established first and then the futures transaction is made and the cash price derived as the futures price less the basis. In other cases the futures transaction is consummated first and then the basis is established and used to derive the cash price. In either case the futures transaction is ex-pit and both the buyer and seller must be settling a cash transaction.

3.2 Arbitrage and Speculation

While the definitions of a speculator, hedger, and arbitrager are straightforward, the distinction by trading intent is not always clear-cut. The cross-commodity hedge is a case in point: The intent is to hedge but by definition the trader would be a *cross-commodity speculator*. The distinction between arbitrager and speculator is perhaps even less clear-cut than the distinction between hedgers and speculators when trades are made across commodities and between markets. Consider, for example, a processor that typically hedges the profitability of forward sales of soybean oil and meal by going short soybean oil and meal futures. The same processor may arbitrage between beans and oil and meal. This usually takes the form of buying beans and selling oil and meal at a differential that exceeds the cost of processing and shipment. This is known as *trading the crush*. While a *cross-commodity arbitrage* by intent, it also offers opportunities for speculation. Suppose the differentials suddenly change and offer the processor a liquidation profit much greater than the profit that could be made if deliveries were taken. The processor may liquidate the position and take the profit—provided the remaining production was sufficient to maintain market share and satisfy customers. Here the processor would have entered into an arbitrage and completed a speculative trade.

The technical details in cross-commodity arbitrage or speculation are formidable. To illustrate, consider the "crush" example given above. The meal-oil content changes depending on the time of harvest and the corresponding moisture content of the beans. Moreover, soybeans, soybean oil, and soybean meal all trade in different quantities and in order to trade the crush one may trade 10 bean contracts against 12 meal contracts and 9 oil contracts or some variation of this weighting scheme. Furthermore, the prices of each element do not move in lock step with one another because oil and meal have different uses, substitutes, and complements. These considerations taken together make trading the crush an exercise for the extremely skilled and those who can take or make delivery in the event of an error. Similar complexities exist for each of the other commodity groups mentioned above.

There are, of course, arbitrage and speculative opportunities that combine different markets, different time periods, and different commodities. One such example is an "arbitrage" between three-month forward London copper cathodes (a forward market) and COMEX copper wire bar (a futures market) in the nearest active contract corresponding to three months forward. The London price in dollars may be above the COMEX price when both are three months forward, but this price position may reverse as the contracts mature.

In this market situation, the objective is to sell London three months forward and buy COMEX and then, after the passage of time, to liquidate the positions when their relative prices have narrowed or reversed. Here, rates of interest in the two countries and exchange rates as well as the premia of wire bar to cathodes all play an important role in determining the evolutionary profile of these prices and the resulting "arbitrage." While it is called an arbitrage, the trade is in spirit a speculation; the prices between the markets may widen as the positions mature.

Another type of speculation, often referred to as *intermarket arbitrage*, is the attempt to capture price differentials between two different commodity markets in the same commodity and the same time horizon, for example, buying and selling gold between the CBT and COMEX. Here, the trader works closely with floor brokers on both exchanges. The bids and offers are reported to the trader as they are made in each market. As soon as a profitable price discrepancy emerges, such as a high bid in one and a low offer in the other, the bid is sold and the offer is bought and a position is established. The trader could let the position mature but this could erode profits owing to the costs of delivery. Indeed, the price differential may not be profitable if deliveries have to made and taken. Typically, such an "arbitrage" requires liquidation before the positions mature. But this liquidation is not a sure thing. For example, suppose one went long CBT December gold at a price of $630 an ounce and went short COMEX December gold at $680 an ounce. The position could be liquidated at a gross trading profit (i.e., profit before consideration of commissions and other trading costs), if CBT was sold and COMEX was bought back at any price differential less that $50. Such a liquidation would occur is the trader could sell CBT at $660 and buy back COMEX at $660. To be sure, this liquidation is speculative: The prices between CBT and COMEX must narrow in order to capture the profit before delivery. If for some reason the price differential between CBT and COMEX does not narrow, deliveries may have to be made and taken or the trader may have to liquidate at a loss. To be sure, the very act of "arbitrage" in this case helps ensure the price differentials will not be large or long-lasting.

There are, of course, many variations on all of the themes mentioned above and to explore each is beyond the scope of this book. The examples given here, nonetheless, provide some insight into the major types of intermarket and intercommodity hedging, arbitrage, and speculation in the commodities markets. However, there are some special considerations worth noting. These are presented next.

4 TRADING ACROSS COMMODITIES, MARKETS, AND TIME

When the determination of price relationships become complicated, fewer traders participate in the market. Those who remain are usually more astute and fleeter of foot. So it is with the coterie of individuals who simultaneously trade across commodities, markets, and time. While many such cases of this multidimensional trading exist they are especially common among financial instruments. Few commodity transactions are more involved or offer better examples of these complexities than foreign exchange, bond, and money market instruments. The following paragraphs offer a few illustrations from these markets.

4.1 Multidimensional Equilibrium: the case of foreign exchange

In a world of eight major currencies—the dollar, deutschemark, sterling, Swiss franc, French franc, guilder, Canadian dollar, and Japanese yen—there are 28 different pairs of spot foreign exchange prices. These prices are pushed into equilibrium through the actions of arbitragers. For example, if it takes $2 to buy £1 and £1 buys 4 deutschemarks (DM) then $1 cannot buy 3 DM. For if $1 could buy 3 DM then an individual would make a certain profit by simultaneously buying 6 DM for $2, taking the deutschemarks and buying £$1\frac{1}{2}$ and taking the £$1\frac{1}{2}$ and converting them into $3. This would be a state of affairs equivalent to discovering a perpetual money machine. If this situation existed, the demand for deutschemarks would become great at the price of 3 DM to the dollar and this increased demand would force up the price of deutschemarks in terms of dollars, that is, fewer deutschemarks per dollar could be purchased. This process would continue until the profitable arbitrage differential was eliminated.

The arbitrage process also implies that prices of foreign currencies be in equilibrium over time as well. The mechanism that relates the price of money today to the price money at some date in the future is the rate of interest. The rates of interest that link the present with the future also help determine the forward rates of foreign exchange.

4.1.1 The Multinational and Interest Rate Parity

To see how interest rates tie together the forward foreign exchange rate with the spot rate, consider the following illustrative example. A German concern negotiates to purchase a division of a U.S. corporation located in Chicago, Illinois. A cash payment of $100,000,000 is to be made in six month's time to the U.S. parent corporation by the German concern. The German concern has several alternatives. It can pay deutschemarks six months hence for dollars or it can borrow today a sum of deutschemarks in Germany that, when converted into dollars and invested in the United States or Eurodollar market today, will grow to $100,000,000 in six months. Given an existing spot exchange rate in Germany of 1.6667 DM per $1.00 ($0.60 per 1 DM) this is equivalent to a discount loan with a maturity value of 166,670,000 DM. The deutschemark cost of the loan is 166,670,000 DM divided by the six-month U.S. interest factor. If the 6 month Eurodollar rate or annual bond equivalent rate on T-bills is 12.36 percent so that the actual six-month rate is 6 percent, then 166,670,000 DM/1.06 is equal to 157,235,840 DM that can be converted at today's foreign exchange rate into $94,339,617 which, when invested at a 6 percent return for six months, will accumulate to $100,000,000, the sum that is needed to effect the purchase of the division. At the end of the six-month period, the German concern receives $100,000,000 in the United States

$$(1 + .06) \frac{166,670,000 \text{ DM}}{(1.06)(1.6667 \text{ DM}/\$1)} = (1.06)(\$94,339,617) = \$100,000,000$$

and pays off the deutschemarks loan in Germany of $(1 + r_{G6})(166,670,000 \text{ DM})/1.06$ where r_{G6} is the six-month rate of interest in Germany. Since the transaction was financed with a loan, the alternative is equivalent to paying deutschemarks later for dollars later. That is, the German concern, by entering into the deutschemark loan, buys dollars in six months by paying deutschemarks in six months. This is the same as contracting at present for forward delivery dollars. The ratio of the German and U.S. loan rates times the spot deutschemark-dollar exchange rate gives the forward deutschemark-dollar exchange rate

$$\frac{1 + r_{G6}}{1 + r_{US6}} \text{ (Spot DM per \$1 rate)} = \text{Forward DM per \$1 rate.}$$

Rearranging the above terms and simplifying notation yields

$$r_{DM} - r_\$ = \frac{\text{F.DM.R} - \text{S.DM.R}}{\text{S.DM.R}} + r_\$ \frac{(\text{F.DM.R} - \text{S.DM.R})}{\text{S.DM.R.}},$$

where FDMR is the forward DM per $ rate, SDMR is the spot DM per $ rate, and r_{DM} and $r_\$$ are the corresponding German and U.S. rates of interest. Since the last term on the right hand side of the above equation is small, it is often restated for approximation purposes as

$$r_{DM} - r_\$ = \frac{\text{F.DM.R} - \text{S.DM.R}}{\text{S.DM.R.}}.$$

This is the formulation of the *interest rate parity theorem*. It states that the percentage change between the forward and spot exchange rates will be approximately equal to the difference in interest rates between the two countries.

4.1.2 Euromoney Rates

It is often thought that money is invested in the country with the highest rate of interest in order to earn a higher rate of return. Making such an investment without considering the implied forward exchange rate can lead to actual returns that may not meet expectations. Seemingly high profit opportunities between interest rates in different arbitrage networks often are a "will o' the wisp" after exchange rate conversion at the future date. The following example illustrates two possible investment routes by a German investor and the parallelism of returns that are available in the U.S. and German Euromoney·markets after exchange rate conversions. At the same time the example reveals the complexity of the calculations involved in forward foreign currency arbitrage.

Figure 3.1 depicts two three-month *Euromoney rates* from spot to forward. The Euromark rate is $8\frac{11}{16}$ percent per annum and the Eurodollar rate is $14\frac{7}{16}$ percent per annum, a seemingly large differential. The spot and 91 day forward exchange rates are 1.7310 and 1.7065 DM to the \$, respectively.

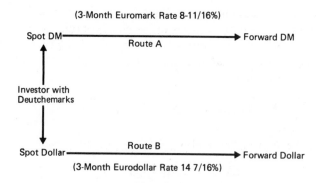

Figure 3.1

ALTERNATIVE EUROMONEY RATES FOR GERMAN INVESTOR
WITH DEUTSCHEMARKS AS OF 1/21/80

With the linkage between money markets offered by the foreign exchange market, the holder of funds has two investment routes:

Route A: Invest funds in the domestic German money market.

Route B: Invest funds in the "overseas" U.S. money market.

If the German investor has a 1,000,000 DM investment, route A can be summarized as follows:

ROUTE A

Invest DM on 1/21/80 at Euromark rate of $8\frac{11}{16}$ for 91 days	1,000,000 DM
Interest earned (1,000,000 DM @ $8\frac{11}{16}$ for 91 days)	21,960 DM
Principal plus interest on 4/21/80	1,021,960 DM

On the other hand, if the German investor follows Route B, the transaction and results would be as follows:

ROUTE B

Sell DM on 1/21/80 for $ spot (1,000,000 DM ÷ 1.7310) and invest in Eurodollar market for three months @ $14\frac{7}{16}$%	$577,700
Interest earned ($577,700 @ $14\frac{7}{16}$% for 91 days)	21,083
Principal plus interest on 4/21/80	$598,783

A comparison of these two alternatives reveals which is the most profitable for the German concern and the possibility of arbitraging between them. In this case it is more profitable for the German investor to invest in DM at the Euromark rate of $8\frac{11}{16}$ than to convert to dollars and invest in Eurodollars at $14\frac{7}{16}$ and then convert back to DM at maturity. This can be seen in two ways. First, the $598,783 captured in the Eurodollar market converted to DM at the current forward rate of 1.7065 is equivalent to 1,021,823DM at maturity on 4/21/80. Alternatively, an investment in Euromarks at $8\frac{11}{16}$ over the same period produces a principal plus interest of 1,021,960DM. That is, investing in DM at $8\frac{11}{16}$ is better for the German firm than investing in Eurodollars at $14\frac{7}{16}$ after exchange rate conversions are taken into account. Second, one can use the interest rate parity relationship to determine the most profitable investment alternative. The difference between the Eurodollar rate and the Euromark rate is $5\frac{12}{16}$ or 5.75%. The right side of the interest rate parity relationship given above using the values in this example yields a value of 6.4076% on an annualized basis. That is, the exchange rate conversions outweigh the simple interest rate differential by 6.4076% − 5.7500% = .6576%. In the context of an interest rate arbitrage the above results imply a profit opportunity from borrowing in the Eurodollar market to lend in the Euromark market assuming, of course, the brokerage and other transaction costs do not outweigh the arbitrage differential.

4.1.3 A Foreign Exchange Hedge and Speculative Gain

The second example involves basis trading in Japanese yen by a U.S. corporation that routinely hedges its holdings of yen. In this example, the company not only hedges against an adverse move in the exchange rate on yen, but also makes a speculative gain in the difference between the cash and futures prices, that is, the basis, on the yen.

As of November 5, 1979, the Corporation is long 200 million yen and wants to protect against a fall in the exchange rate for the next six to seven weeks. The spot rate for yen on this date is $0.00420/Y. A short hedge is put on in March '80 yen futures on November 5, 1979, at $0.00433/Y by selling 16 yen futures contracts. The basis on November 5, 1979, is $0.00420/Y − $0.00433/Y = −$0.00013/Y.

On December 21, 1979, spot yen is $0.00418/Y, the March '80 future is $0.00422/Y and the basis is −$0.00004/Y. Closing the trade on December 21, 1979, results in the following gains and losses:

1. A loss in spot yen of $0.00002/Y
2. A gain in yen futures of $0.00011/Y
3. Hence, a basis gain of $0.00009/Y
4. A resulting basis gain of $18,000 ($0.00009/Y × 200 million Y),

Here the intent of hedging has led to speculative gains. To be sure it could have led to losses if the basis had moved the other way. In short, to the extent a hedge is not perfect, the outcome of the "hedge" is speculative. Whether a futures contract of reference exists or not, for the asset to be hedged, a hedge is rarely perfect: almost all hedges contain some risk, albeit only a fraction of the risk without the hedge. In this case the risks were between markets and over time.

4.2 Multidimensional Equilibrium: spread trading

A spread is the price difference between two commodity contracts. A spread can be constructed for any two contracting positions. These include between-market spreads for a commodity, called intermarket spreads; between-maturities spreads on a market for a commodity, called simple spreads; and between-commodities or intercommodity spreads. Among the most common spreads are spot cash/futures (the basis), spot cash/forward, futures/futures, forward/futures, forward/forward, cash/option, option/forward, and option/future. Each of these, of course, can be for the same commodity or for different commodities, markets or time horizons.

4.2.1 Objectives and Risks

Whether one is long the nearest maturity and short the farthest or just the opposite is not important per se. It is the change in the spread as the positions mature that determines if a profit or loss is achieved. Hopefully, the position will anticipate the true trend in the spread. But even this is not necessary for some forms of spread speculation. In some cases, all that is necessary is that the spread varies: One can either buy or sell the basis and capture a profit if the spread will subsequently vary around the position taken.

4.2.2 A Speculative T-Bond-GNMA Example

Financial instruments have special characteristics compared to other commodities and trading in them is somewhat more complex than trading in gold or wheat. The following example highlights trading across financial instruments and/or time. The illustration in Figure 3.2, is a *futures/futures*

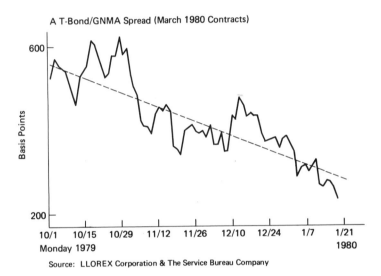

A T-Bond/GNMA Spread (March 1980 Contracts)

Source: LLOREX Corporation & The Service Bureau Company

Figure 3.2

AN INTERCOMMODITY DIFFERENTIAL

price differential between March '80 T-bonds and March '80 GNMAs: an intercommodity futures-futures spread. As can be seen, if one went short T-bonds and long GNMAs on 10/1/79, a profit of almost 400 basis points or $12,500 (400 × $31.25 = $12,500) per contract pair could have been captured over a four-month holding period. While this "trend" is not typical, it cogently reveals the opportunity of capturing large gains (or losses) from what is considered a conservative trading tactic: shorting one instrument and going long a different instrument where both have similar time horizons and quality ratings.

5 SUMMARY

There are three basic perspectives to commodities trading: hedging, speculation, and arbitrage. The operational distinctions between them are not always as clear-cut as their definitions might imply, regardless of the original intent. A position in the futures market may originally be for hedging purposes. However, if the spread between the cash and futures prices subsequently changes in some unanticipated way, the hedger may liquidate the position and take a speculative profit or capture an arbitrage profit against the cost of money covering the period between the cash price and the futures delivery date. The complexities and changing perspectives of commodities trading are exacerbated when trading simultaneously across commodities, markets, and time. These complexities notwithstanding, the ultimate dimensions of commodity trading decisions are profit and risk. Essential to both of these are prices and their fluctuation. The next chapter touches on elements of commodity price formation.

6 BIBLIOGRAPHY

CHICAGO BOARD OF TRADE, *Selected Writings of Holbrook,* Working Vol. 1. Chicago: Chicago Board of Trade, 1977.

COOK, T. Q., ed., *Instruments of the Money Market.* Richmond. Va.: Federal Reserve Bank of Richmond, 1977.

GOSS, B. A., and B. S., YAMEY, *The Economics of Futures Trading.* London: 1972.

HEYWOOD, J., *Foreign Exchange and The Corporate Treasurer.* American Management Association, 1979.

HOBSON, R. B. *Futures Trading In Financial Instruments.* Washington Commodity Futures Trading Commission, October 1978.

JAFFE, N. L. and R. B., HOBSON, *Survey of Interest-Rate Futures Markets.* Commodity Futures Trading Commission, Washington, December 1979.

SHARPE, W. F., *Investments,* 2nd ed. Englewood Cliffs, N. J.: Prentice-Hall, Inc., 1981.

WORKING, H., "Futures Trading and Hedging," *The American Economic Review,* June 1953, pp. 314–41.

4

ELEMENTS OF PRICE FORMATION

||||||||||||||||||||||||||||||||||||||||||||||||||||||||||||||||||||||||||||||||||||||||||||||||||||

1 INTRODUCTION

Regardless of one's trading objectives, prices influence the priorities of alternative actions. This chapter discusses elements of price determination. It focuses on market efficiency, changes in prices, and select relationships between spot and future prices. Operational distinctions between the forward and futures markets are set aside to highlight general relationships in and between the spot and future (forward) markets. Section 2 touches on market equilibrium and efficiency and the role they play in price determination and the implications for price forecasting and trading systems. Section 3 discusses differences between spot and future prices with special emphasis on carrying costs, contango and backwardation, and the covergence of spot and futures prices. The risks surrounding differentials between two futures prices and between the spot and some future price are summarized in Section 4. The identification of hedgers and speculators in the price formation process is discussed in Section 5.

2 MARKET, PRICES, ADJUSTMENTS, AND FORECASTS

2.1 Markets, Linkages, and Equilibrium

A *market* is said to exist whenever individual members of a society are in sufficiently close contact to be aware of opportunities for exchange and are free to take advantage of them. In general the direct participants in a market for some commodity may be separated into two groups: those who demand (seek to buy), and those who supply (seek to sell) the commodity. There are, of course, many indirect participants in a market for a commodity who in turn are direct participants for other commodities. Among the most important of these indirect participants is the broker.

The *broker* acts as a catalyst enabling buyer and seller to come in sufficiently close contact to be aware of opportunities for exchange and helps facilitate their transactions. The broker, of course, is a direct participant in another commodity. Specifically the broker sells a "commodity" made up of market communication, trade facilitation, and record keeping. Buyers and sellers of other commodities both demand brokering services to effect their primary business. Brokers' commissions, of course, are accounted for by those using their services and are reflected in the bids and offers and resulting trade prices. Similar perspectives on direct and indirect market participation can be made for banks and other financial intermediaries. Ultimately, all participants in all commodity markets are linked indirectly.

If no market participant in any market for any commodity could improve his position through a change in actions then a state of *general equilibrium* would exist. If just one individual in one market could improve his position then at best partial equilibrium may exist. *Partial equilibrium* is said to exist when all the participants in a particular market are in equilibrium. This state of affairs may come about because the disequilibrium in some other market has not yet reached this market through the various indirect channels. That is to say, partial equilibrium is a temporary state of affairs.

2.2 Market Process, Stability, and Efficiency

The *market process* refers to the adjustments that are made by individual market participants owing to their disappointments in a disequilibrium market. These adjustments are reflected in new bids or offers and new trade prices. In general there is a tendency for bids and offers to be revised until all bids and offers are successfully accepted at the market. As long as there are discrepancies between prices bid and offered for a given quantity or as long as their are discrepancies between the quantities demanded and supplied at a given price there will be disappointments among buyers and/or sellers. These disappointments cause subsequent changes in their bids and offers.

The market process is said to be *stable* if the process of revising bids and offers converge on a uniform market price and uniform quantities are offered and demanded in the market at that price.

A market is said to be *efficient* if the participants have achieved a minimum of waste, expense, and dissatisfaction to the best knowledge of the participants. Efficiency in this context also implies consistency among goals and their decisions. Each market participant may wear many hats: a buyer of one commodity and a seller of another; a seller today and a buyer tomorrow. To the extent the multiple positions of one or more participants are inconsistent the market is said to be inefficient. The market process will reflect inconsistencies in new bids and offers intended to achieve consistency and efficiency. Insofar as market prices fully reflect the decisions and goals of the participants, and those decisions and goals in turn fully reflect all available information, the market prices are said to be *efficient market prices*.

2.3 Market Efficiency and Price Forecasting

It is argued that in an efficient market, past prices have limited relevance for speculative trading systems. Indeed, in an efficient market, where investors are concerned only with expected rates of return, some academics claim that past prices have no relevance at all and that trading systems cannot be more profitable than the opportunities revealed in current prices.

This conclusion simply observes that if all the available and relevant information is used by the market in assessing all possible future returns, an investor cannot use that same information as the basis of a trading system that has expected returns in excess of what the fully knowledgeable market already knows and expects. Why? Because there is no net new information on which to base any improvements: If there were, the market would not be efficient by definition. Consider the following representation of the price formation process as embedded in the class of *expected return* models of efficient markets:

$$P_{jt} = \frac{E(\tilde{P}_{j,t+1} : I)}{1 + E(\tilde{R}_{j,t+1} : I)}.$$

That is the expected one-period-ahead price of commodity j given information I,

$$E(\tilde{P}_{j,t+1} : I),$$

discounted by 1 plus the expected one-period-ahead return for that commodity using the same information, $E(\tilde{R}_{j,t+1} : I)$, determines the equilibrium price at time t, P_{jt}. Here, the symbol E denotes the expected value operator, I denotes the available information, $\tilde{P}$ denotes an alternative future price and $\tilde{R}$ denotes an alternative future return. Both $\tilde{P}$ and $\tilde{R}$ are assumed to contain a random component that cannot be forecast with perfect confidence. For any given set of information, I, the expected value operator, E, weights each of the possible returns or prices by their probability of occurrence. The sum of these weighted prices is their weighted average or "expected value."

While empircal tests tend to support the existence of efficient markets there are several possible shortcomings. One criticism is the assumption that the market uses a simple expected value to summarize a distribution of returns. Many argue that higher-order characteristics of the distribution of prices may influence the determination of investment decisions and in turn influence prices (Friedman and Savage 1948; Farrar 1962). Here the variance and kurtosis, as well as the possibility of bi- or multimodal distributions are especially noteworthy. Furthermore, what may be true for one period ahead may not be true for two periods ahead owing to complex interdependencies between the two forward periods.

The *random walk* model may be regarded as a version of the expected return model that makes a more detailed statement about the stochastic process that generates the returns. In essence the random walk model assumes that the distribution of the returns repeats itself through time. This additional assumption allows one to explore some of the shortcomings of the simple expected value models. However, the random walk model gives a strong measure of importance to past prices for the development of trading systems. Because return distributions are assumed to be the same throughout time, past returns are the best source of information about the character of the distribution. However, the random walk model does say that the sequence or order of the past returns is random and that the past cannot be used to forecast future returns.

The work of Labys and Granger (1970) suggests that random walk models are appropriate for short periods of time of up to two weeks but that for longer periods of time, say two months or longer, commodity price changes exhibit patterns that cannot be considered random with a high degree of confidence. Moreover, even a casual analysis of commodity price data reveals distributions of prices that are not easily dealt with by statistical theory: The distributions are often bi- or multimodal and their variability changes over time. Furthermore, there is evidence to suggest that "runs" of price changes of a similar sign are randomly distributed. This observation may contradict the assumption that each price change is random. Indeed, the fact that two near-contradictory assumptions can both be supported by empirical tests and observation strongly suggests that the last word in the debate about the randomness of commodity price movements has not been written.

As regards the "full use" of all available information, one need only consider the failures of the Russian wheat harvests in 1974 and 1979 when the

Russians and select U.S. government agencies had accurate estimates of the size of the shortfall but the information was not released outside a small inner circle until after Russian orders were placed at prices reflecting ignorance of this information. While crop failures may occur randomly and the corresponding fluctuations in prices may therefore appear random, this does not prevent those with "inside" information from taking advantage of the random occurrence a moment or two before the rest of the world learns of the same information. Tests that support the time series randomness of commodity prices notwithstanding, trading systems may be developed that are based on a monopoly "edge" over some information.

Nevertheless, efficient market models appear to have substantial empirical support as a description of price patterns but the conclusion cannot be made to apply to all commodities all of the time with perfect certainty. Distributions of past prices may be useful in developing profitable trading systems. Moreover, real-world price distributions do not always fit precisely into the assumptions of statistical theory needed to test the randomness of price movements. Finally, randomness notwithstanding, players with an informational edge over the rest of the market can capture profits and there is evidence to suggest that such players exist and have captured consistent speculative profits.

3 PRICE DIFFERENTIALS BETWEEN DELIVERY DATES

The example in Chapter 1 of the sixteenth-century Italian vintner revealed the business implications of uncertainty about future prices. While future prices are uncertain they nevertheless influence current prices. This linkage of anticipated future prices to current prices is a reflection in part of *inventory decisions*. These decisions are based in part on anticipated prices, storage costs, borrowing costs, current prices, and the ability to buy and sell between the spot and forward markets. Often, future prices are above current prices but sometimes they are below them. In both cases the inventory decision process and intertemporal arbitrage are essential factors in determining these differentials as shown in Chapter 24.

Although the precise differential between spot and future prices, that is, the *basis*, may be impossible to forecast perfectly, there are logical bounds within which this differential must lie.

3.1 Contango and the Basis Upper Bound

Because of the ability to contract in either the cash or forward (or futures) markets the price at a future date cannot exceed the cash price today plus the resource and financial costs of carrying physical inventory to make delivery at that future date. This argument has two parts, First, if the price at a future date were greater than the cash price plus the costs of carrying the commodity then it would be possible to enter into a transaction that would generate a sure profit without incurring any risk. Second, the presence of sure profits will attract traders who will buy spot and sell forward. In so doing, they will increase the demand for spot and, in turn, the price for the spot commodity. Moreover, the increase in the supply of forward commodities will reduce the price of the forward commodity. But raising the spot price and reducing the forward price lowers the profit differential. This will continue until profits are so low that arbitrage is no longer worthwhile.

For example, suppose in May cash soybeans sell for $7.00 per bushel and storage costs including insurance and deterioration are 5¢ per bushel per month. Moreover, suppose November soybeans on the Chicago Board of Trade were to trade at a price of $7.50 per bushel. It would pay an individual to sell November soybean futures on the CBT at $7.50 per bushel, enter the *cash* markets and pay $7.00 per bushel for soybeans and *carry* them (forward) to November, at an additional cost of 30¢ per bushel and satisfy the contract by delivering the soybeans at the end of November. The short sale generated $7.50 per bushel and the cost of the soybean "cash and carry" for November delivery was $7.30 per bushel: a profit of 20¢ per bushel. This is equivalent to a 28.5 percent return over a six-month period, on an investment requiring 10 percent margin. When such an opportunity arises it does not last for long. Traders will seize the opportunity and sell November soybeans futures and buy cash soybeans. This increase in the supply of November soybean futures will depress its price while the increase in demand for cash soybeans will raise their price. Together these forces of "arbitrage" will reduce the profit potential. Thus, it is the cost of storage, the rate of interest, and arbitrage that together ensure the futures price cannot rise above the current cash price plus the costs of carry, insurance, and "decay." When these future prices are above the cash price the market is said to be in *contango*.

3.2 Backwardation and the Basis Lower Bound

There is nothing to prevent the future price from being below the current spot price, a situation referred to as *backwardation*. Indeed, backwardation is considered "normal" by some. Market conditions are said to be "normal" when spot demand and supply conditions and the spot price are not expected to change. Under these conditions speculators on average will be buyers in the futures market only if the futures price lies below the spot price. This is required if speculators are to capture an expected return from their long positions. The reason for speculators to be net long, and not net short, in the futures markets is a delicate argument explored in Section 5. As regards the basis lower bound, the amount of backwardation is viewed as a return speculators must receive in order to bear risk. This return will be no lower than the return the speculator can receive from bearing equivalent risk in other markets.

3.3 Arbitrage and the Convergence of Cash and Futures Prices

The limits placed upon the relationship between the futures price and the current spot price have no implications for what level the future spot price will be. However, if there are no restraints on arbitrage one thing is certain: At the maturity date of the futures contract, the futures contract will trade at the same price as the cash, or spot, commodity save adjustments for any quality or delivery charges. A differential between the markets would be arbitraged away by selling in the high-priced market and buying in the low-priced market. The increased supply in the high-priced market and the increased demand in the low-priced market would lower and raise their prices, respectively, until a profitable arbitrage differential no longer existed. Hence, if there are no impediments to arbitrage, there will be a *convergence* between the futures contract price and spot or cash price as the maturity of the futures contract shortens.

4 SPREAD TRADING AND RISKS

A spread, or straddle, refers to the simultaneous purchase of one position and the sale of another. The differences in the positions may be in the commodity, the location, the time of maturity, or some combination of these characteristics. Spread trading is pursued by hedgers, arbitragers, and speculators. The hedger may safeguard the value of a cash position by taking an opposite position in futures contracts in the same or similar commodity with a corresponding delivery date. Here the intent is to offset losses in the cash market from unanticipated changes in prices with gains in the futures market. An arbitrager trades spreads with the intent of profiting from temporary differentials between the same commodity. For example, if in July the December price of gold is higher in Chicago than it is in New York, the arbitrager would sell the Chicago contracts and buy the New York contract knowing that by December the two prices will come into parity and a profit will be captured. Indeed the prices may come into parity before December and the arbitrager may then liquidate and take a profit before December. Speculators trade spreads on the assumption that a narrow spread now will widen in the future and vice versa. For example a speculator may think in July that the spread between July wheat and July corn is narrow and bound to widen because the price of wheat is too low and likely to increase more rapidly than the price of corn. In this case the speculator would buy the spread in anticipation of selling it at a profit. That is, the speculator would buy July wheat and sell July corn with the hope of being able to subsequently sell the July wheat and buy the July corn and end up with a profit.

4.1 Speculative and Arbitrage Spread Risks

There are, of course, risks associated with spread trading. These risks are obvious for the speculator: The spread may not move in a profitable direction and losses from liquidation may occur.

In general, speculating on the direction of intracommodity spreads can be less risky than taking an outright position in the same commodity. The reason is twofold. First, the absolute dollar volatility measured in terms of margin requirements is much smaller for a spread than an equivalent number of contracts, held outright. Second, the relative intraday volatility typically is much larger than an outright position. That is, the percent change in the basis during a single day can range over 100 percent and often from positive to negative. The commodity price levels do not, indeed cannot, exhibit this degree of volatility. To the extent that basis positions are more volatile, the trader has more opportunities to capture a profitable liquidation.

The risks for the pure arbitrager are also obvious: There are none. The arbitrager only puts on a spread position that contains a profit if all the contracts are held to maturity and deliveries are made and taken. If an arbitrager takes a spread position that is profitable in terms of the purchase and sale prices but not when delivery costs are considered then the arbitrager is implicitly betting that the spread will change, allowing a profitable liquidation before either of the contracts mature. In this case the arbitrager is in fact a speculator, and subject to the same risks. The risks facing the hedger are not as obvious as in the previous cases.

4.2 Hedger Spread Risks

There are two types of hedges: short and long. A *short hedge* involves the sale of futures contracts with the intention of liquidating them later by buying futures contracts for the same instrument with the same delivery date. Such a hedge is used to protect the value of assets and/or to lock in costs. Here, the cash market losses, owing to an unanticipated rise in prices or interest rates, are "offset" by gains captured in the futures market over the same period. A *long hedge* involves the purchase of futures contracts to guard against losses in the cash market from a fall in prices or interest rates.

Whether short or long, a hedge is said to be perfect if every dollar change in the cash market is exactly offset by a change in the futures market. A perfect hedge requires identical and stable delivery conditions, an exact value correspondence between the markets, *and* that the markets move in lock step with one another. Frequently perfect value correspondence and stable delivery conditions can not be reached and, almost assuredly, the different markets will not move in lock step with one another. Insofar as a hedge is not perfect it contains a residual element of risk. This risk has several parts: (1) basis-yield curve-risk, (2) correspondence risk, and (3) delivery risk. In addition, the futures markets, unlike the cash markets, are marked to market every day and settlements are made through margin payments. Because the cash market position being hedged is not settled every day, but at the end of the hedging period, the hedger is subject to (4) interim cash flow margin risk. Each of these risks are described in the context of a short hedge example.

4.2.1 A Short Hedge Example

Suppose as of January 2, 1980, a savings bank commits to originate $1 million in mortgages by April 1980 based on a current cash price of 98-24 (98.75) for GNMA-11's. If rates were to rise (prices fall) between January and April the value of the mortgage pool would fall. To hedge this exposure the savings bank could sell a "corresponding" amount of June 1980 CD GNMA-8's futures contracts (12 contracts). This is a "cross-hedge" because the GNMA-11's are hedged with a near but different asset of reference—GNMA-8's. As of January 2, 1980, these futures contracts were selling for 78-07 (78.2187). The difference between the cash price and the futures price is called the *basis*. In this case the initial basis would be 98-24 minus 78-07 or 20-17 (20.5313). It must be noted that this "basis" calculation entails the comparison of two different assets of reference. Hence, the dollar value of a 32nd in this basis is not the same as the dollar value, $31.25, of a 32nd in the futures market. If by mid-April the savings bank sold $1 million GNMA-11's in the cash market at 90-27 (90.8625), the loss would be $78,875. However, in the futures market the price of CD GNMA-8's dropped to 70-03 (70.0937). Buying back these futures contracts at the same time the GNMA-11's were sold would result in a futures market gain of $96,000. The net result of having hedged the cash market commitment in the futures market would have been a gain of $17,125, a considerable improvement over the unhedged loss of $78,875. This example is summarized in Table 4.1.

It must be noted that as of April 15, 1981, the basis was 90-27 less 70-07 or 20-20 (20.6437): a widening of $\frac{3}{32}$. This change in the basis was to the advantage of the savings bank. Had the basis remained the same the purchase of the June 1980 CD GNMA-8's would have been done at a higher price and therefore produced a lower profit in the futures market and less of a counterbalance against the loss in the cash market. To be sure, the basis could have moved in the opposite direction, that is, narrowed and weakened the financial value of the hedge. This uncertainty in the basis is called *basis risk*.

Table 4.1

ILLUSTRATIVE SHORT CROSS-HEDGE

DATE	CASH	FUTURES	TWO-MONTH BASIS
1/2/80	Commit to originate $1 million in mortgages based on current price of 98-24 (98.75) for GNMA-11's by mid-April.	Sell (short) 12 June 80 CD GNMA-8 futures at 78-07 (78.2187).	20–17
4/15/80	Sell $1 million in GNMA-11's at 90-27 (90.8625).	Buy (liquidate) 12 June 80 CD GNMA-8 futures at 70-07 (70.2187).	20-20
Financial Summary 4/15/80	$78,875 loss if unhedged.	$96,000 gain in futures hedge position. $17,125 net gain from short cross-hedge.	

4.2.1.1 Yield curve risk. The short hedge example given above illustrates a basis between a cash April price and a June futures price. In terms of time differences this is a two-month basis. However, this two-month basis was established in January with an April maturity. That is, the two-month basis was established three months forward. As the hedge came to maturity the three-month forward—two-month basis became a spot two-month basis. While still a two-month basis the two months are covering a different time interval. This "ride on the yield curve" may be unpredictable owing to unpredictable changes in the slope of the yield curve as well as unpredictable shifts in it. The change in the yield curve in the short hedge example is shown in Figure 4.1.

4.2.1.2 Correspondence risk. The short hedge example in Section 4.2.1 also illustrates the problem of correspondence risk. This risk emerges when a cash market asset may not be translated into an integer multiple of futures contracts and consequently the value of the hedge position is not in correspondence with the cash market position. The $1 million in GNMA-11's at 98-24 converts to more than $1,200,000 of GNMA-8's futures. Since CD GNMA-8's are traded in contract sizes of $100,000, the savings bank would take a $1,200,000 or 12 contract position as the nearest corresponding hedge value. It must be noted that the correspondence difference is not a constant dollar amount or proportion of the hedge value with regard to interest rate changes. That is, as interest rates change the correspondence differential will change and this may contribute to a change in the basis.

4.2.1.3 Delivery risks. Delivery risk reflects unanticipated changes in the "quality" of the asset of reference used for delivery against a contract.

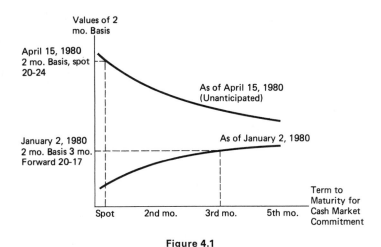

Figure 4.1

TWO-MONTH BASIS FOR DIFFERENT TERMS TO MATURITY
FOR CASH MARKET COMMITMENT

With regard to the short hedge example the price of the CD GNMA-8's futures contracts are based on the GNMA contract that is least expensive to deliver. When the yield curve shifts, the least expensive GNMA contract may change from one coupon to another. Thus the least expensive GNMA to deliver may not be the least expensive at the time of delivery owing to interim shifts in the yield curve. As discussed in Chapter 7, these changes in the optimal delivery asset are different for a yield maintenance contract and for a price maintenance contract. To be sure, delivery on the futures contracts may not have to be made or taken for a hedge. However, the pool or distribution of different GNMA contracts that qualify for delivery is not uniform. These differences in supply can be reflected in the basis as changes in rates cause changes in the optimal deliverable GNMA. Analogous problems can occur in other commodities, for example, shrinkage in livestock or spoilage of potatoes.

4.2.1.4 Interim cash flow margin risk. Futures contracts are bought or sold on margin. When a position is established some margin must be paid. This margin is referred to as original margin. Because the futures exchanges mark to market every day, the hedger may have to make subsequent margin payments should the market price move against the original position price. These subsequent margin payments are called maintenance margin. These interim margin payments pose a potentially serious cash flow drain on the hedger: The cash markets settle only on the maturity date and any offset in this market is deferred to maturity.

In the short hedge example given above, the hedger receives margin owing to the fall in final prices well below the original short position price. If the price on GNMAs had gone up instead of down, the hedger would have been subject to large margin calls. These margin calls pose a serious threat to the cash reserves of the hedger and in turn may trigger a default or a costly liquidation of other assets.

5 PRICE FORMATION AND THE IDENTIFICATION OF HEDGERS AND SPECULATORS

Price determination, of course, depends on the forces of supply and demand. In the context of commodities trading, taking a short position adds to supply and taking a long position adds to demand. While the forces that determine the desire for short and long positions are many and complex, it is nonetheless true, or at least accepted, that hedgers comprise the net short side of the futures markets while speculators are net long. Accounting constraints guarantee that if hedgers are net short, then speculators are net long, since the market must balance.

The reason hedgers are typically thought to be short in the futures markets is they are typically thought to be long in the physical or cash markets. For speculators to be net long in the futures markets they must expect returns on their positions over and above the return on a riskless investment. For this to be the case the net long speculators must expect futures prices to rise. In a stable spot market this implies that the futures prices must be below the spot market price by an amount at least equal to the riskless rate of interest. In this case the futures prices will rise over time and converge on the stable spot market price. The condition where futures prices are below spot prices is called *backwardation* or *normal backwardation*. It is argued that backwardation is an indication that hedgers are net short in the futures markets and that speculators are correspondingly net long.

Similarly, if hedgers are net long in the futures markets then speculators must be net short. For speculators to be net short in the futures markets the futures prices must be above the stable cash price and expected to converge on it from above. The situation when futures prices are above cash prices is called *contango* or a normal carrying charge market. The carrying charge reflects the costs of storage and insurance as well as the riskless rate of interest. It is argued that when a market is in contango, hedgers are net long and speculators are net short.

Unfortunately backwardation, or contango, does not necessarily imply hedgers or speculators are net long or short. The reason for the ambiguity is twofold. First, the markets are not always stable. That is, expected future cash prices fluctuate owing to changes in the best available information.

Second, many hedgers can take positions with a dual objective in mind: hedging and speculation. To see how this might be done, consider the following example: A baker may wish to hedge the profitability of forward commitments to sell bread at a contracted price by locking in the cost of wheat for the product. Here, a long position may be taken in the futures market as a means of ensuring delivery at a fixed future price. The futures contract, of course, would have a maturity corresponding most closely to the date before which production must begin in order to meet the production commitment. Suppose further, the price differential per bushel between the selling price and the cost of wheat after adjustment for processing is $1.00. Now suppose the price of forward wheat remains unchanged but the spot price drops by 20¢ per bushel and the cost of carrying the wheat to the beginning of production is only 10¢ per bushel. The baker would seize this profit opportunity and sell (liquidate) the futures contract, buy the physical wheat and carry it to production and reap a 10¢ per bushel addition to profits. Alternatively, suppose the spot price went up by 10¢ per bushel but the futures price went up by 30¢ per bushel. Here, also, the baker can capture a profit opportunity by selling the futures contracts, buying spot, and carrying to production. This would also yield a 10¢ per bushel addition to profit. In either case, the basis changed in favor of the hedging baker, enabling the baker to liquidate the old hedge and capture a net profit. To be sure, the basis could have moved against the hedger. In this case, the hedger would hold the original position to maturity. This fluctuation in the basis enables commerical interests to hedge their physical commitments and gives them the opportunity to capture unexpected profitable shifts in the basis.

6 SUMMARY

Regardless of the commodity, there exists at any moment in time a spot price for a commodity, f.o.b. a common warehouse location. At the same time, there exists a price for the same commodity, f.o.b. the same location, for delivery at some future date. These two different prices are determined in both auction and direct placement markets and are known by all participants.

Then there exists a crucial third price, which unfortunately is not known today. That price is the spot price that will exist in the future. The relationship among these three prices determines who will be the winners and losers in the allocation of the physical commodity and financial risks among speculators, hedgers, and arbitragers. The future spot price will be determined by the future supply and demand for immediate delivery at some future date.

To be sure, no one can truly see what the future cash price will be.

Nevertheless, there are best collective estimates of what the future price will be. These estimates are quoted in the forward and futures markets on any given day. The efficient market hypothesis contends that the market estimates of future cash prices, if based on all relevant information available at the time, are the best possible estimates of those prices. Statistical tests based on the mathematical notion of an expected value (an average) tend to accept the further hypothesis that efficient markets prevail and therefore that reliance on past prices to try to beat the market is a futile effort. The evidence supporting these conclusions while imposing is not absolute. Not all market participants have the same accuracy of information or have it on the same timely basis. Moreover, price changes appear to occur frequently as runs where there are several successive price changes in the same direction. This, in turn, implies that past prices may frequently play a predictive role and that the markets are not efficient. Regardless of the tests, speculators are not in short supply and many have played successfully for a long time.

Regardless of the predictability of future cash prices and the efficiency of the markets, there are price relationships that fall within logically predictable bounds. The contango upper bound is such a limit on price differentials.

In general, the difference between two commodity prices is called a spread. The difference can be predicated on timing, type of commodity, location, or some combination of these attributes. The difference between the cash price of some commodity and its future price is called the basis. The basis as well as other spreads are subject to unanticipated changes or risks. Among the most important of these risks are yield curve risk, correspondence risk, delivery risk and, where futures markets per se are involved, interim cash flow margin risks.

Finally, the often dual objectives of the hedger and the unintentional speculation of the hedger, make the theoretical distinction between speculator and hedger more academic than practical. The empirical distinction between hedger and speculator is even more difficult. While logic dictates bounds on forward or future prices in relation to spot prices, owing to the roles of hedgers and speculators, the mixed role of hedgers and the swings of prices from contango to backwardation make empirical observation and identification extremely difficult. Without the aid of a thorough model of the commodity market in question and without ample supporting data, the quantification of the effect of hedgers as opposed to the effect of speculators on prices is a near-impossible task, if it is possible at all.

The elements of price formation presented above apply to cash and futures markets for both outright and spread positions. While the cash markets include options, and the above comments apply to them in general, there are features of options that require special consideration. These topics are the subject of the next chapter.

7 BIBLIOGRAPHY

FAMA, E. F., "Efficient Capital Markets: A Review of Theory and Empirical Work," *Journal of Finance*, 35, (May 1970), 383–417.

———— and M. H., MILLER, *The Theory of Finance*. New York: Holt, Rinehart & Winston, 1972.

FARRAR, D. E., *The Investment Decision under Uncertainty*. Englewood Cliffs, N.J.: Prentice-Hall, Inc., 1962.

FRIEDMAN, M., and L. J. SAVAGE, "The Utility Analysis of Choices Involving Risk," *Journal of Political Economy*, 56, No. 4, (August 1948), 279–304.

HICKS, J. R., *Value and Capital*. New York: Macmillan, 1946.

HOUTHAKKER, H. S., "The Scope and Limits of Futures Trading," in *Allocation of Economic Resources*, ed. M. Abramovitz et al., pp. 136–61. Stanford, Calif.: Stanford University Press, 1959.

————, "Normal Backwardation," in *Value, Capital and Growth: Papers in Honour of Sir John Hicks*. Edinburgh: Edinburgh University Press, 1968.

KALDOR, N., "A Note on the Theory of the Forward Market," *Review of Economic Studies*, No. 7, 1939–40, pp. 196–201.

KIRZNER, I., *Market Theory and the Price System*, Princeton, N.J.: D. Van Nostrand, 1963.

LABYS, W. C., and C. W. J. GRANGER, *Speculation, Hedging and Commodity Price Forecasts*. Lexington, Mass.: Heath 1970.

SAMUELSON, P. A., "Proof That Properly Anticipated Prices Fluctuate Randomly," *Industrial Management Review*, 6 (Spring 1965), 41–49.

5

THE PRICING AND APPLICATION OF CONTINGENT CLAIMS

||||||||||||||||||||||||||||||||||||||||||||||||||||||||||||||||||||||||||||||||||||||||||||||||||||||||

1 INTRODUCTION

A contingent claim or option is the right, but not the obligation, to buy or sell something. It is defined by the price at which the purchase or sale can be made, the quantity and quality of the commodity in question, the delivery conditions, and the period over which the option is valid or exercisable. Options have been used in business since biblical times and virtually every commodity has its own version of them. In the financial markets "standby commitments" made directly between the writer and buyer are a form of option as are warrants, a liability of a company, that give the buyer the right to purchase securities over some time period according to some price schedule.

While the applications and analyses of contingent claims are almost without end, only a handful of considerations are common to them all: the factors that influence the value of options, the valuation formulae, and the pitfalls of option valuation. The purpose of this chapter is to summarize these aspects of contingent claims together with select applications of options contracting in commodities.

Section 2 summarizes the factors that influence the value of an option. Included here are general assessments of how these factors influence options valuations. Section 3 summarizes the option valuation formulae for the eight major variations of options together with a relative ranking of these option values. Select applications of options in commodity trading are given in Section 4. Included here are hedging applications, reductions in operating costs, and financial instrument standby commitments. The chapter is summarized in Section 5.

2 TYPES OF CONTINGENT CLAIMS AND FACTORS INFLUENCING THEM

As noted in Chapter 2, contingent claims can fall into one of eight catagories depending on whether they are puts or calls, American or European, or spot or forward commitments. A put option gives the buyer the right to sell and a call option the right to buy. American options can be exercised at any time during the life of the option contract. A European option can be exercised only on the last day of the life of the contract. Regardless of the commodity the contingent claim can be either for the spot, that is, for the physical item for immediate delivery upon exercising the option, or for a forward claim on the commodity, for example, an option to buy a claim for silver 30 days forward from the date the option is exercised. Regardless of the type of option the value of each is influenced by only a few basic factors. These factors and their general effect on the value of an option are as follows:

Rate of Interest: For all options except options on futures, the higher the rate of interest the higher the option value. Options on futures decrease with increases in the rate of interest.

Price Volatility of Underlying Item: For all types of options, the greater the price volatility of the underlying item the higher the value of the option.

Term to Maturity: Options increase in value when the term to maturity is lengthened.

Striking Price: For call options, the higher the striking price the lower the value. For a put option the higher the striking price the higher the value.

Market Price: The higher the market price, the higher the value of a call and the lower the value of a put.

The specific impact of these factors varies depending on the type of option. The linkages defining these impacts are considered next.

3 OPTION VALUES

The conceptual foundations of option values are presented in the references at the end of this chapter. The relationships noted here draw on these foundations.

3.1 Option Valuation Formulae

Drawing on the results of Black and Scholes (1973), Merton (1973), Black (1976), Parkinson (1977), and Rendleman and Bartter (1977), the valuation formulae for European and American options on spot and futures contracts are summarized in Table 5.1 together with their respective hedging ratios. s and f denote spot and futures, respectively. E and A denote European and American, respectively, and c and p denote call and put respectively. V denotes the option value and H denote the hedge ratio.

The derivation of these formulae are set forth in the references cited above and are not repeated here. However, the nature of their derivation gives rise to several practical considerations and warrants brief comment. In general they all require the invocation of stochastic calculus to arrive at the value of an option. This expression takes the form of a second-order partial differential equation with boundary conditions and, as will be shown in Section 2.4, can lead to operating problems for the uninitiated trader.

For European puts and calls on both spot and futures contracts and for American calls on spot contracts, closed-form solutions have been derived and are given in the summary in Table 5.1. The valuation of American puts on spot contracts and American put and call contracts on futures contracts requires a numerical approximation such as the binomial distribution approximation procedures developed by Parkinson (1977) and Rendleman and Bartter (1977). As with any numerical approximation, the degree of accuracy depends on the parameters assigned and different markets may require different minimum degrees of accuracy.

One of the benefits from the closed-form valuation of an option is the extent to which the option should be hedged in order to achieve a "perfect hedge." This percent value can be derived from the valuation formula and is equal to the change in the option value brought about by a change in the market price of the asset holding all other factors constant. For options with closed-form solutions this ratio is specified. For those options requiring numerical solution techniques the hedging ratio is indicated by the appropriate (partial derivative) rate of change that also must be calculated numerically.

3.2 Comparative Values of Options on Spot and Futures Contracts

As noted earlier, futures contracts are settled at the end of every day and the value of the contract at this time is zero. Moreover, futures contracts do not effectively require an investment: Original margin can be met by T-bills. These differences between futures contracts and their physical or spot counterparts give rise to differences in their option values. The differences

Table 5.1

COMPENDIUM OF
VALUATION FORMULAE FOR
CONTINGENT CLAIMS

		EUROPEAN	AMERICAN
Call	Spot	$EV_c^s = {}^mPC(g_1^s) - {}^ePe^{r(t-t^*)}C(g_2^s)$ $EH_c^s = C(g_1^s)$	$AV_c^s = EV_c^s$ $AH_c^s = EH_c^s$
	Future	$EV_c^f = e^{r(t-t^*)}[{}^mPC(g_1^f) - {}^ePC(g_2^f)]$ $EH_c^f = e^{r(t-t^*)}C(g_1^f)$	$AV_c^f = A\pi_c^f(r, {}^mP, {}^eP)$ $AH_c^f = \dfrac{\partial AV_c^f}{\partial {}^mP}$
Put	Spot	$EV_p^s = {}^ePe^{r(t-t^*)}C(-g_2^s) - {}^mPC(-g_1^s)$ $EH_p^s = C(-g_1^s)$	$AV_p^s = A\pi_p^s(r, {}^mP, {}^eP)$ $AH_p^s = \dfrac{\partial AV_p^s}{\partial {}^mP}$
	Future	$EV_p^f = e^{r(t-t^*)}[{}^ePC(-g_2^f) - {}^mPC(-g_1^f)]$ $EH_p^f = e^{r(t-t^*)}C(-g_1^f)$	$AV_p^f = A\pi_p^f(r, {}^mP, {}^eP)$ $AH_p^f = \dfrac{\partial AV_p^f}{\partial {}^mP}$

Mnemonics for Contingent Claim Formulae

^mP = Market price

^eP = Exercise price

$$g_1^s = \frac{\ln({}^mP/{}^eP) + (r + .5\sigma^2)(t^* - t)}{\sigma\sqrt{t^* + t}}$$

$$g_2^s = \frac{\ln({}^mP/{}^eP) + (r - .5\sigma^2)(t^* - t)}{\sigma\sqrt{t^* - t}}$$

$$g_1^f = \frac{\ln({}^mP/{}^eP) + .5\sigma^2(t^* - t)}{\sigma\sqrt{t^* - t}}$$

$$g_2^f = \frac{\ln({}^mP/{}^eP) - .5\sigma^2(t^* - t)}{\sigma\sqrt{t^* - t}}$$

e = Base of the natural log

r = Rate of interest (risk free)

ln = Logarithm operator

σ = Instantaneous standard deviation of return

t^*, t = Terminal date and value date, respectively

$C(\ )$ = Cumulative normal density function

V = Value of the option

H = Ratio of the amount of an item to the amount of options in the hedged position, that is, the "hedge ratio."

$\pi(\ )$ = An operator denoting a numerical valuation procedure as developed by Parkinson (1977) or Rendleman and Bartter (1977)

$\partial V/\partial {}^mP$ = Rate of change in V brought about by a change in ^mP holding all other factors constant

SOURCE: F. Black, "The Pricing of Commodity Contracts," *Journal of Financial Economics*, 3 (*1976*), 177. New York: North Holland Publishing Co.; F. Black and M. Scholes, "The Pricing of Options and Corporate Liabilities," *Journal of Political Economy*, 81 (May-June 1973), 644 (reprinted by permission of The University of Chicago Press); and R. C. Merton, "The Theory of Rational Option Pricing," *The Bell Journal of Economics and Management Science*, 4, No. 1 (Spring 1973), 144, 157, 159.

are more than simple numerical adjustments: They result in different valuation structures.

European options on futures admit to closed-form solutions that are similar but distinct from their spot or physical counterparts. American call options on spot also have a closed-form solution. They are equal to European call options with the same attributes. However, the value of American puts and calls on futures contracts do not yet have closed-form solutions. Nevertheless, relative comparisons can be made between options values on spot and futures contracts for both European and American options. These comparisons are summarized below.

3.2.1 European Options on Spot and Futures Contracts

The value of European options on spot and futures contracts closely parallel one another. The European call on spot has "ideal conditions" analogous to those for stocks (Black and Scholes 1973) and tends to have a higher value than a European call on a futures contract when both are "in the money." This reflects the different impact of interest in the valuation formulae. Because the investment in a futures contract is effectively zero, an interest rate term drops out of the valuation formula. These differences are summarized in Table 5.1 and are illustrated in Figure 5.1. The put option

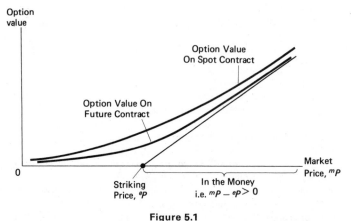

Figure 5.1

COMPARISON OF EUROPEAN CALL OPTIONS ON SPOT
AND FUTURES CONTRACTS

formulae also are summarized in Table 5.1 and are shown in Figure 5.2. As can be seen, the spot values lie below the futures options values for a put—just the opposite of the call option values shown in Figure 5.1.

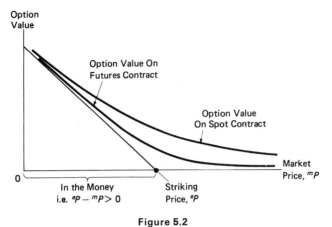

Figure 5.2

COMPARISON OF EUROPEAN PUT OPTIONS ON SPOT
AND FUTURES CONTRACTS

3.2.2 American Options on Spot and Futures Contracts

Although American options on futures contracts do not have closed-form solutions like their European counterparts, some comparative relations present themselves. The American call on the cash or physical commodity has a premium equivalent to a European call option on spot and this premium converges on the risk-free interest payment as the market price becomes larger as shown in Figure 5.3. Consequently, the American call on a futures contract converges on the intrinsic value, (i.e., the value when

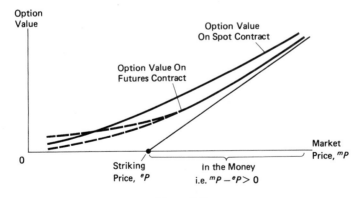

Figure 5.3

COMPARISON OF AMERICAN CALL OPTIONS ON SPOT
AND FUTURES CONTRACTS

exercised), as the market price becomes larger. However, the value of an American call option on a futures contract may exceed its value on a spot contract over some domain of market prices. This is an empirical issue and also is illustrated in Figure 5.3. American put options on spot and futures contracts both converge on the intrinsic value of the option as the market price falls below the striking price. The put option on a futures contract may carry a higher premium than its spot contract counterpart. Such a case is illustrated in Figure 5.4. Once again this is an empirical issue and little can be said about their precise relative positioning when they are "out of the money."

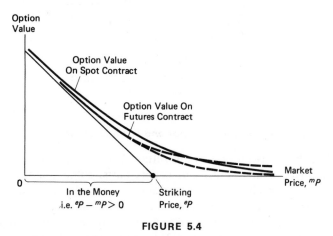

FIGURE 5.4

COMPARISON OF AMERICAN PUT OPTIONS ON SPOT
AND FUTURES CONTRACTS

3.3 Value Rankings of American and European Puts and Calls

The above relationships can be summarized in terms of the relative rankings of American and European puts and calls. The results are as follows:

OPTION VALUE

PUT	CALL
$APF \gtreqqless APS$	$ECS = ACS$
	$\vee$ $\wedge$
$EPF \gtreqqless APS$	$ECF < ACF$
$\vee$ $\vee$	
EPS EPS	

Here the first letter, *A* or *E*, denotes American or European option respectively, the second letter, *P* or *C*, denotes a put or call, respectively, and the last letter, S or F, denotes a spot or futures contract, respectively. The value of an American put on futures exceeds the value of a European put on futures which in turn exceeds the value of a European put on spot. The American put on spot also exceeds the value of the European put on spot but its value relative to the other put options cannot be stated in general. The value of the European and American call options are equal and both exceed the value of the European call on futures. The American call on futures also exceeds the value of the European call on futures but its positioning relative to the European call on spot also cannot be stated in general.

4 PITFALLS OF OPTIONS VALUATION

There are several practical problems associated with the valuation of options. Among the most important are the assumption of log normally distributed prices, forecasts of the future rate of interest, the forecast of the future standard deviation of the rate of return, and the lack of invariance.

4.1 Log Normality and Binomial Approximations

Regardless of the particular type of option, their valuation formulae all depend on the invocation of several assumptions. Many of these were noted earlier such as efficient markets and all that they imply. In addition, there also is a technical assumption that may not always be valid. Specifically, the above formulae assume that prices are log normally distributed or approximated by a binomial distribution of changes in price. These distributions are designed to accommodate the essential economic property that prices cannot be negative. However, nonnegativity is not the same thing as log normality or a binomial approximation. While it has been shown that properly anticipated prices fluctuate randomly, it also is true that empirical results cannot be obtained by deduction from a nonempirical base of axioms (Samuelson 1965). To the extent that prices follow some other distribution, the above formulae, though approximately right, will nevertheless be precisely wrong.

4.2 Forecasting Volatility and Rates of Interest

The valuation of an option also requires the prediction of future economic activity. The standard deviation of return for the underlying item must be forecast for the period of the option. To be sure, the prediction of price volatility is not an easy task. These volatilities can change dramatically in response to simple business decisions—for example, when organized exchanges alter their trading limits (the maximum allowable price range within a day). In fact, trading limits can impinge on the log normality assumption and changes in them can both reflect and influence price volatility.

The prediction of interest rates is an equally difficult problem. Three-month options written in August 1979 with an interest rate assumption of 9 percent per annum were off the mark two months later when the federal funds rate exceeded 17 percent and 90-day treasury bills hit 13 percent per annum.

These problems of prediction suggest an operational paradigm: Options valuations should be simulated for a variety of interest rate and price volatility assumptions. Here the writer or buyer of an option can assess options values and make decisions from the point of view of worst-case interest rate and price volatility scenarios.

4.3 The Lack of Invariance

Owing to the character of the options valuation formulae, options values are not invariant to linear or stochastic transformations of the price of the item. Simply stated, the option valuation formulae would be price invariant if the value of an option denominated in one particular unit of measure could be translated into the value of an option on the same item denominated in some other price unit of measure. For example, if the value of an option on gold denominated in dollars after translation into British pounds at the going exchange rate equaled the option value, calculated from the same formula for an equivalent option on gold but denominated in British pounds with the same rate of exchange, the options valuation formula would be invariant under the simple transformation (magnification or contraction) from dollars to pounds and vice versa. Unfortunately this is not the case when the interest rates also are changed owing to the interest rate parity relationship. It is also true that owing to the mathematical character of the option valuation formula, simple linear transforms of the price unit of measure may not be "passed through" to the option value with exactly the same transformation. That is, the option valuation formulae are not invariant under an affine transform. Moreover, stochastic transformations also can be troublesome. For example, if London prices of silver in sterling are log normally distributed and the pound-dollar exchange rate is log normally distributed, then their ratio is a Cauchy distribution and does not have finite moments; the variance is infinite. In this case the corresponding option value in dollars cannot be calculated.

The practical problems of the lack of invariance are hard to overstate. Translating London options to U.S. equivalents or hedging T-Bill options with T-Bill futures indices are not simple artithmetic transformations. Indeed, such translations can be misleading and therefore costly.

5 TRADING APPLICATIONS

Commodity options trading is a large business that has gone unrecognized because the trading, for the most part, is done directly between buyer and writer. The major exception to this rule is the London Commodity Options Exchange. In this section several types of options trading examples are set forth. The examples are not exhaustive but illustrative. They proceed in difficulty or financial complexity from simple hedging and speculative operations to more intricate business applications. The first example is an application of options to reduce the financial risk to a manufacturer owing to possible adverse price movements. The next example illustrates the use of options in conjunction with futures contracts to reduce the cost of inventory. The third application focuses on the financial markets, and the use of futures contracts to hedge directly placed standby commitments. The fourth example addresses the problem of securing supplies and hedging against cost increases from the point of a processor. The last case explores the use of options valuations to set stop-loss orders in speculative futures trading.

These examples cover the major applications of options trading:

1. Protecting against an increase in "raw material" prices or protection against a fall in the value of inventory (Example 5.1).
2. Reduction of operating costs (Example 5.2).
3. Securing a source of supply (Examples 5.1, 5.2, 5.3, and 5.4).
4. Speculation (Example 5.5).
5. Arbitrage (Example 5.1, 5.2, 5.3, 5.4, and 5.5).

For each of the problems presented, indeed for any operation requiring options trading, the following issues must be given full consideration:

1. The amount to be hedged
2. The timing of the options contract
3. Long- and short-term forecasts of prices, interest rates, and price volatility
4. Desired profit margins
5. Excess inventory calculations
6. Differences in price units of measure between an object and its corresponding option
7. Operating costs
8. Delivery conditions including location and quality

Finally, to recapitulate, call buyers and put writers are both potential buyers of the physical commodity and put buyers and call writers are potential sellers of the commodity.

5.1 Hedging Inventory Value: lumber prices and future building commitments

A builder needs large stocks of lumber to meet business commitments. These commitments value lumber prices as of the date of construction. The builder has 200,000 board feet of lumber at the current market price of $230 per 1,000 board feet. The lumber is to be used in one month. If prices rise by this time the builder will make inventory profits and if they fall the builder will incur inventory losses. In order to limit downside risk, that is, to limit losses, the builder considers the purchase of a put option with a striking price of $230 per 1,000 board feet and a cost of $3 per 1,000 board feet per month. The schedule of profits and losses, with and without the put option, excluding carrying costs that are common to both alternatives are as follows: Here the builder has probability expectations about the future price

PROFIT(+) AND LOSS(−) PROFILES
$ PER 1,000 BOARD FEET

		UNHEDGED		HEDGED	
PRICE IN ONE MONTH($)	PROBABILITY OF OCCURRENCE	Outcome($)	Expected Outcome($)	Outcome($)	Expected Outcome($)
240	.10	10	1.00	7	0.70
235	.10	5	.50	2	0.20
230	.15	0	.00	−3	−0.45
225	.25	− 5	−1.25	−3	−0.75
220	.40	−10	−4.00	−3	−1.20
Expected Outcome			−$3.75		−$1.50

of lumber and, on the basis of these anticipations, the expected outcome of the unhedged and hedged positions clearly favor the hedging alternative.

To be sure, the use of futures contracts to hedge the builder's position is another alternative. Here the use of stop-loss orders and the possibility of whipsawing through them several times would have to be taken into account. This analysis and comparision to an option is done in the next example.

5.2 Reduction of Operating Costs through Options and Futures Contracts

Options and futures can be used in manufacturing to help reduce operating costs by increasing profits through the combined use of options on inventory and futures contracts to meet replacement needs should the options be exercised. There are many varaitions on this theme and the one presented here is not unsophisticated from a trading point of view.

A copper fabricator currently has 100,000 pounds of copper inventory scheduled for the next three months. The combined costs of storage, insurance, and interest (on this inventory investment) is 1.5¢ per pound per month. During this period the firm must have no less than 50,000 pounds on hand at any given time and must have the full 100,000 pounds at the end of the three-month period. At present, the value of a three-month call option in the direct placement market is 2.5¢ per pound per month. The firm could offset some of the inventory costs by writing three-month call options for 50,000 pounds of copper and purchasing futures contracts with an appropriate maturity as a supply hedge if the options are executed. However, if the futures contracts (2@ 25,000 lb each) are bought immediately along with the writing of the options, then the firm runs a financial risk if prices fall and the options are not exercised. In this case the firm would have to sell off the futures at a loss. One way to try to cut down on this potential loss is to buy the futures only when the price rises to a point that makes the option profitable. Since the options are call options the writer need only consider the futures price just before expiration since the call options always have more value alive than exercised when the option has not yet reached maturity. This strategy has the following outcomes.

Case 1: Price rises no more than 2.5¢. The call options are not executed and the futures contract is not purchased. The firm captures 2.5¢ per pound per month for three months on 50,000 pounds of copper for a total profit of $3,750.

Case 2: Price rises more than 2.5¢ and does not recede. The call options are exercised and two futures contracts are purchased at 2.5¢ per pound over the price of the inventory (the baseline price). The firm receives 2.5¢ per pound per month for three months on 50,000 pounds of copper but loses 2.5¢ per pound on the 50,000 pounds of copper it had to purchase through the futures market to meet end of period inventory needs. Total profits here are $2,500.

Case 3: Price oscillates (whipsaws)—options may or may not be exercised. This case requires a trading strategy decision. On the last day the price may momentarily exceed and then fall back below the 2.5¢ price rise that makes the options worth exercising. Owing to timing, the options may not be exercised. One hedging rule would require the firm to buy the futures contract when the futures price rises more than 2.5¢ over the baseline inventory price and liquidate when the price falls back to the baseline if the options have not been exercised. This causes a 2.5¢ loss for each such whip-saw. A second hedging strategy would have the firm buy the futures if the price rises 2.5¢ or more, hold it all day, and sell on the close if the options are not exercised. Here the firm runs the risk of losing more than 2.5¢, but only once.

For either trading strategy the options may be exercised. If this occurs following the first strategy the cost would include the whipsaw costs incurred up to the time the options are exercised plus the 2.5¢ cost associated with the final purchase of the futures contracts. In the second hedging strategy the costs would be limited to the 2.5¢ per pound loss to cover the exercised options.

Because of 3¢ trading limits on copper the firm decides to follow the second hedging strategy. With this decision the third case would capture profits of at least $3,750 - (5.5¢ \times 50,000) = $1,000$.

If the numbers were "narrower" the firm would have to make a detailed decision analysis based on the costs of each strategy for each "state of the world," that is, for each alternative price pattern and option exercise alternative. Several criteria could be invoked to select a strategy. These criteria include the least costly of the worst possible outcomes, and the lowest expected monetary loss.

5.3 Standby Commitments to Buy GNMAs and Futures Contract Hedging Strategies

This example considers the sale of a put option in the financial markets and the corresponding hedging strategy of the writer. Here, the option may be executed at any time, assuming the standby commitment (the option) is of the American put variety. The market conditions as of July 6, 1978, and the risk-profit profiles of the trading operation are summarized below.

As of July 6, 1978 the firm takes the following actions:

1. Sells 150-day standby commitment to buy GNMA 8 percent contracts from XYZ Inc. at 89-00 for a premium of $\frac{24}{32}$ or $750 per contract. Gross receipts are $7,500.
2. Sells ten December GNMA futures at 89-00. Round turn commissions are $10 \times $65 = 650. Original margin is $10 \times $1,500 = $15,000$.
3. Enters buy stop order for ten December GNMA futures at 89-08.

The possible outcomes as of December 1978 are:

1. Rates remain unchanged and the option is not exercised. Buy ten December GNMA futures at 89-00 and receive original margin of $15,000. Gross profit is $6,850.

2. Rates rise more than $\frac{24}{32}$ and the option is exercised. Deliver ten GNMAs against GNMA futures sale and receive original margin of $15,000. Maximum gross profit is $6,850 (less cash and carry costs for execution before the 150th day).

3. Rates fall and the option is not exercised. Buy back ten December GNMA futures when market hits 89-08 and take a trading loss of $2,500. Receive original margin of $15,000. Maximum gross profit is $4,350 (less possible whipsaw costs).

5.4 Options as a Source of Supply and Futures to Hedge Profits

A cocoa processor buys cocoa beans and processes them into final products. To meet forward commitments for the final products and capture desired profit margins the processor needs 300,000 pounds of beans at $1.40 per pound in the period from July 1980 to September 1980. Owing to storage constraints the processor purchases the beans "on differential" from dealers through the purchase of a 300 point (3¢ per lb) "buyers call." This instrument requires the purchaser to buy cocoa at a fixed differential (of 3¢ per lb) above the market price at the time of execution. The purchaser must buy the cocoa within a certain period but can do so at any time within that period. This type of instrument is sometimes referred to as a "reverse option": The buyer has the obligation to buy but the right to exercise at any market price during the exercise period instead of the right but not the obligation to buy at a fixed exercise price. Given the source of supplies, the cocoa processor can hedge its profits by taking a long position in ten September futures contracts at the current price of $1.37. As the processor exercises portions of the "buyers call," an equivalent number of futures contracts would be liquidated. If prices rose, the profit on the futures contracts would offset the potential loss in profits the processor would have incurred if the "buyer's call" went unhedged. The buyer, of course, could use stop-loss sell orders on the futures contracts to try to capture profits if prices fell over the purchase period. Here the problem of whipsawing can arise once again. The use of options valuation methods to set stop-loss orders is discussed in the next example.

5.5 Stop-Loss Determination for Day-Trading through Options Valuation

A hedged investment in a commodity future may consist of being long the future and short on an appropriate number of options. Here the value of the equity in the position within the day (because futures are settled at the end of each day) would be the price of the future less the ratio of the value of the option to the hedge ratio. For a short interval of time, such as a day, the change in the value of the equity would be the change in the price of the commodity less the ratio of the change in the value of the option to the hedging ratio. This implies that for a zero change in equity, the change in the price of the future times the hedge ratio would have to equal the change in the option value.

To a speculator seeking to make a given price change objective, the zero change in equity criteria can be used to determine the stop-loss differential to the position price. In brief, this differential would be equal to the price change objective times the hedge ratio. For example a day trader in gold may have a $4 price change objective (trading profit objective). If the volatility of the rate of return on the asset of reference (gold) is 20 percent per annum and the short-term rate of interest is 15 percent per annum and the market price is $378 per ounce, the hedge ratio would be .52. This implies a stop-loss buy order at $375.90 on a long position in gold at $378 per ounce with a price objective of $382 (a price change objective of $4). It is interesting to note that the stop-loss order will never be further away from the position price than the price objective and frequently a fraction between .25 and .50. Moreover, surveys of trader rules suggest that markets follow the hedge ratios within a few percentage points. Suprisingly, most of those queried did not use options valuation techniques per se to determine these ratios and stop-loss positions. If the options valuation approach is, in fact, the optimal procedure to use, assuming its caveats hold true, then the marketplace through trial and error has learned enough to converge to within a narrow neighborhood of this rule.

6 SUMMARY

Almost every financial activity has some aspect that may be viewed from the perspective of an option. In commodity trading, options can be used as substitutes or complements to other forms of commodity contracting. In the United States, commodity options are traded in the direct placement markets. Futures markets are often used as a hedging vehicle for writers of options and as an alternative market for arbitragers seeking to capture profits from price discrepancies between the options and futures markets.

Organized options markets exist for select commodities in London. While some U.S. traders may attempt to use this market for hedging purposes, or for arbitrage against U.S. commodity contracts, they run the risk of a serious nonmathematical equivalence between the U.S. contract and the London options contract. This is the problem of invariance. This problem also can effect options writers in the United States. For example writers of options in the form of standby commitments on financial instruments run the risk of nonmathematical equivalence when the futures contracts used for the hedge are priced in terms of an index such as T-bills where the futures contract is a linear transform of the T-bill rate. While options are not easy to value from a mechanical point of view they are an important tool in commodity trading. From a practical perspective, options valuations require the buyer and writer to forecast rates of interest and the price volatility of the market. While these requirements may seem impossible to satisfy, they are less a criticism of option valuation than a recognition of the decision-making environment. The formulae to value options, while demanding, at least provide a mechanism that ties the decision-making parameters into an understandable and simulatable form. This of course takes option valuation out of the realm of guesswork and places it in the realm of an operational tool. The examples presented illustrate the variety of applications of option trading and valuation.

7 BIBLIOGRAPHY

BLACK, F. "The Pricing of Commodity Contracts," *Journal of Financial Economics,* 3 (1976), 167–179.

———, and J. C. COX, "Valuing Corporate Securities: Some Effects of Bond Indenture Provisions," *Journal of Finance,* May 1976, pp. 351–367.

———, and M., SCHOLES, "The Pricing of Options and Corporate Liabilities," *Journal of Political Economy,* 81, (May-June 1973), 637–654.

BRENNAN, M., and E. SCHWARTZ, "The Valuation of American Put Options," *Journal of Finance,* May 1977, pp. 449–462.

COX, J. C., and S. A. ROSS, "The Valuation of Options for Alternative Stochastic Processes," *Journal of Financial Economics,* January 1976, pp. 145–166.

DOTHAN, U., "The Pricing of an American Put Option." Northwestern University, 1977.

GALAI, D., and R. W. MASULIS, "The Option Pricing Model and the Risk Factor of Stock," *Journal of Financial Economics,* January 1976, pp. 53–81.

MALKIEL, B. G., and R. E. QUANDT, *Strategies and Rational Decisions in The Securities Options Market.,* Cambridge Mass.: MIT Press, 1969.

MERTON, R. C., "The Theory of Rational Option Pricing," *Bell Journal of Economics and Management Science,* 4, No. 1 (Spring), 141–183.

———, "On the Pricing of Corporate Debt: The Risk Structure of Interest Rates," *The Journal of Finance,* May 1974, pp. 449–470.

————, "Option Pricing When Underlying Returns Are Discontinuous," *Journal of Financial Economics,* January 1976, pp. 125–144.

————, M. SCHOLES and M. L. GLADSTEIN., "The Returns and Risk of Alternative Call Option Portfolio Investment Strategies," *The Journal of Business* (University of Chicago), April 1978, pp. 183–242.

PARKINSON, M., "Option Pricing: The American Put," *Journal of Business* (University of Chicago) January 1977, pp. 21–36.

RENDLEMAN, R. J., and B. J. BARTTER, "Two-State Asset Pricing: Simplified Valuation of Complex Contingent Claims." Discussion Paper 77–5, Banking Research Center, Northwestern University, 1977.

6

ELEMENTS OF FINANCE

IIIIIIIIIIIIIIIIIIIIIIIIIIIIIIIIIIIIIIIIIIIIIIIIIIIIIIIIIIIIIIIIIIIIIIIIIIIIIIIIIIIIIIIIIIIIIIIIIIIIIII

1 INTRODUCTION

All commodity contracting depends on two parameters that are common to all financial decisions: return and risk. In general, the concept of *rate of return* is straightforward: If one invests V_1 dollars at the beginning of the present period and receives V_2 dollars at the beginning of the next period, then the one-period rate of return is defined as $(V_2 - V_1)/V_1$ or $(V_2/V_1) - 1$. In practice the calculation of rates of return are not always as straightforward as the definition would imply. There are a plethora of complications: The *value dates* (maturity dates) of the borrowing and lending may not be perfectly matched; reinvestment rates may vary over several periods; the investment periods may have to be converted to some other time unit of measurement; different markets may be involved and different conventions may prevail in each, requiring conversion to some common unit of measurement; delivery conditions such as grade and location may carry discounts or premia that must be taken into account; variation margin can change the amount invested as well as the time period of the investment. Separately or taken together, these factors make rate of return calculations an intricate task that belies the intuitive simplicity of the notion.

The concept and assessment of risk is less intuitive and even more difficult to measure than rate of return. Following convention, *risk* is assumed to be directly proportional to the variation in the expected rate of return and measurable by the statistical variance in the expected rate of return. Many of the technical issues that apply to the measurement of the rate of return also apply to the measurement and assessment of risk. There are, of course, some additional concerns. These include the symmetry of the risk measurement that weights a given shortfall the same as an equivalent size excess; the lack of invariability which makes measurement of risk incomparable when the units of measurement are changed by a simple linear transformation; the ways in which risk are weighed against rate of return in the decision-making process; and the differences between single asset and portfolio risk.

This chapter focuses on the measurement of rates of return and risk in the commodities markets. Both the direct placement and organized futures markets are considered. Special attention is given to nonfinancial assets of reference. Financial assets of reference are considered in the next chapter.

The chapter is organized as follows: Rate of return calculations are summarized in Section 2. Included here are conversions from daily to annual rates of return, adjustments for nonmatching value dates, and the effect of intermediate cash flows. Examples are given to underscore the notions presented. In Section 3 a wheat–money market arbitrage, combines several of the considerations covered in Section 2. Investment decisions and risk are considered in Section 4. Here the notion and measurement of risk for a single asset and for a portfolio of assets are given special attention. The chapter is summarized in Section 5.

2 RATE OF RETURN

The rate of return on an investment is the value of the gain or loss from that investment expressed as a percent of the invested capital for the time period of the investment, for example, 10 percent per annum. While a seemingly straightforward concept, its calculation in practice can be very complex. In the following paragraphs the elementary notion of rate of return is formalized and the effects of practical considerations are shown mathematically and through select examples.

2.1 Elementary Holding Period Rate of Return

Regardless of the kind of transaction entered into there is a combination of a purchase and sale that determines the rate of return. In its most elementary form the *holding period rate of return* can be summarized as

$$R_{S_2 - S_1} = \frac{V_{S_2}}{V_{S_1}} - 1$$

where V_{S_1} is the amount invested at time S_1 and V_{S_2} is the amount received at time S_2. S_1 and S_2 are settlement dates for good funds and $S_2 - S_1$ is the length of the holding period.

2.2 Complicating Factors

In practice, the calculation of rates of return is complicated by several factors. Among the most important are the indivisibility of contract size, the conversion to annualized rates, and adjustments for nonmatching value dates. In addition, each commodity has its own special idiosyncrasies that further complicate the calculation of rates of return. Each of these topics is discussed below.

2.2.1 *Contract Size and Indivisibility*

While standardization of size and price within any particular commodity market helps ensure transferability, standardization can limit contracting flexibility. However the standard size of a contract means the sums invested must be an integer number of the contract cost. Because the investable funds may not be an integer multiple of the contract size some funds may be left over. The rate of return on the investable funds equals the rate of return on the invested funds times the percent of total funds invested plus the rate of return on the excess funds weighted by its percent of total investable funds. Typically, the return on the excess funds is taken as the rate of interest on readily available alternative investments such as short-term money rates. If $h = S_2 - S_1$, the h period rate of return on total investable funds, R_h can be denoted

$$R_h = w_I R_h^I + w_x R_h^x$$

where w_I is the percent of total funds invested at rate R_h^I, w_x is the percent of funds "leftover" invested at rate R_h^x and $w_I + w_x = 1$, $w_I \geq 0$, $w_x \geq 0$.

This notion, of course, can be extended to capture the rate of return on a collection (i.e., portfolio), of investments. That is, the h period rate of return on a portfolio of investments as of time t where any "leftovers" are considered as just another investment can be denoted

$$R_h = \sum_{j=1}^{n} w_j R_h^j$$

where n is the number of investments in the portfolio, R_h^j is the h period return on the jth investment $w_j \geq 0$ for $j = 1, \ldots, n$, and $\sum_{j=1}^{n} w_j = 1$.

The differences in contract size between commodities and or markets limit intermarket speculation, hedging, and arbitrage to multiples of common denominators. Unfortunately, closely related commodities often are in quantities that make trading among them the domain of those able to take relatively large positions.

For example, in wheat, oats, corn, and soybeans, the trading unit per contract is uniform: Each of these futures contracts is written for 5,000 bushels. But derivative products such as soybean oil and soybean meal are traded in 60,000-pound and 100-ton contracts, respectively. Since soybeans can be processed into meal and oil, it is common for processors to compare bean prices to oil and meal prices. The technical relationship between one bushel of beans and its derivative oil and meal is 10.6 pounds of oil and 47.5 pounds of meal, and 1.9 pounds of waste. For the processor, the cost of beans plus processing, that is, crushing, is compared to the revenues received for the corresponding sales of oil and meal. For example, if one could buy one bushel of soybeans for $6.00, process the beans into oil and meal for another 50¢ and receive 11¢ per pound of meal and 13¢ per pound of oil the profit differential per bushel of soybeans would be 10¢.

In the futures markets soybeans, soybean oil and soybean meal can not be traded in quantities that parallel their technical relationship of 47.5 pounds of meal and 10.6 pounds of oil per bushel of soybeans. A perfect "crush" would compare 1 bean contract to 1.187 meal plus .8833 oil contracts. A close approximation is 10 bean to 12 meal plus 9 oil contracts.

Depending on the nature of the physical business, similar problems of correspondence and lack of divisibility occur in almost every other commodity. In the meat complex, feeder cattle contracts are for 42,000 pounds, live beef cattle for 40,000 pounds, pork bellies for 38,000 pounds, iced broilers for 30,000 pounds, and live hogs for 30,000 pounds.

In the metals markets, silver futures contracts trade in units of 5,000 troy ounces, gold futures contracts are for 100 troy ounces, and copper futures contracts (COMEX) are for 25,000 pounds. In the direct placement markets, the corresponding contract sizes are 5,000 troy ounces, 1,000 troy ounces, and 50,000 pounds respectively. In London, many commodities are traded in metric ton equivalents, one metric ton being equivalent to 2,204.6 pounds. In short, when one is trading between commodities and or markets, close common denominations require careful calculation.

2.2.2 Annualized Rates of Return from Daily Data

Returns on investments are compared to alternatives and the cost of money. For price purposes a common time unit of measure is used, for example, rate of return per annum. Calculating annualized rates of return can be done in several ways depending on conventions and assumptions. One may calculate annual returns on a 360- or 365-day year and with different corresponding frequencies. The most common relationships are summarized and compared below.

Using daily observations the simple rate of return as defined above is:

$$\frac{V_{S_2} - V_{S_1}}{V_{S_1}} = R_{S_2 - S_1}$$

where

$R_{S_2 - S_1}$ = Holding period return
$S_2 - S_1$ = Number of days in the holding period
V_{S_1} = Value of contract at initial settlement day ex-purchase day
V_{S_2} = Value of the contract at final settlement day ex-sale day.

The *annualized rate of return on a simple interest basis* for a 360-day year is

$$\frac{V_{S_2} - V_{S_1}}{V_{S_1}} \times \frac{360}{S_2 - S_1} = R_{360}$$

and for a 365-day year is

$$\frac{V_{S_2} - V_{S_1}}{V_{S_1}} \times \frac{365}{S_2 - S_1} = R_{365}.$$

The *annualized rate of return with compounding* for a 360-day year is

$$\left(1 + \frac{V_{S_2} - V_{S_1}}{V_{S_1}}\right)^{360/(S_2 - S_1)} = \tilde{R}_{360}$$

and for a 365-day year is

$$\left(1 + \frac{V_{S_2} - V_{S_1}}{V_{S_1}}\right)^{365/(S_2 - S_1)} = \tilde{R}_{365}.$$

For example, suppose $V_{S_1} = \$900{,}000$, $V_{S_2} = \$950{,}000$, and $S_2 - S_1 = 180$ days. The returns using each of the above methods are given in Table 6.1.

Table 6.1

TYPE OF RETURN	TIME UNIT OF MEASUREMENT (days)	RATE OF RETURN (percent)
Simple	180	5.555
Annual		
No compounding	360	11.111
No compounding	365	11.265
Daily compounding	360	11.419
Daily compounding	365	11.580

Which rate of return is appropriate depends on the reinvestment rates and the accounting and decision rules of the firm. The *simple rate* is always calculated on the 360-day rate without compounding as in a standard bank loan. Indeed it is so defined in the General Regulations Governing United States Securities, Treasury Department Circular No. 300.

2.2.3 Adjustments for Different Value Dates

For any investment there is either an actual cost of borrowed funds or an opportunity cost of invested funds. Regardless of the type of cost, the rate of return on an investment must be compared to it in order to assess different investment and borrowing alternatives that together determine the profit rate of the investment. This is no less true when the period over which monies are borrowed differs from the period over which they are invested. For example, actual debiting of a checking account for an investment may be delayed by a weekend, giving rise to a short period the borrowed funds in the checking account may not be used. These monies "in float" may be invested over the weekend. Similarly, there may be timing anomalies at the maturity of the investment and borrowing periods. Here, the return can end on or before the repayment of the loan. Once again, this timing anomaly must be taken into consideration when calculating the rate of return on the investment.

To demonstrate the calculation consider the case where a loan matures on or after the maturity of an investment and begins on or after the initiation of the investment. Let S_1 denote the settlement date upon initiating the investment, S_2 the settlement date for beginning the loan, S_3 the settlement date and the end of the investment, and S_4 the settlement date for ending or repaying the loan. Furthermore, let $R^I_{S_3-S_1}$ be the annualized rate of return per dollar of investment for the period from S_1 to S_3 and let $R^B_{S_4-S_2}$ be the simple annualized rate of interest per dollar of loan for the period from S_2 to S_4. Then the annualized *net rate of return* over the period from S_1 to S_4 is

$$R^N_{S_4-S_1} = R^I_{S_3-S_1}\left(\frac{S_3-S_1}{S_4-S_1}\right) - R^B_{S_4-S_2}\left(\frac{S_4-S_2}{S_4-S_1}\right) + R^R_{S_4-S_3}\left(\frac{S_4-S_3}{S_4-S_1}\right).$$

$R^R_{S_4-S_3}$ is the annualized reinvestment rate per dollar of return from S_3 to S_4. If there is no reinvestment then $R^R_{S_4-S_3}=0$.

2.2.4 Margin Calls, Reinvestment Rates, and Rates of Return

When positions are taken in futures contracts *initial margin* has to be put up. If prices do not change during the life of the position, no additional margin is required. Upon liquidation of the contract or delivery, the original margin is returned. However, if prices change subsequent to the taking of the position, then additional margin may be called from or paid to the investor. This additional margin is referred to as *variation margin*. If the investor has a long (short) position and prices rise, then the position is earning (losing) money and margin payments (calls) are made to (by) the investor. The first day of the position these payments are equal to the difference between the position price and the day's *settlement price* on the exchange. The margin payments thereafter are equal to the difference between the previous day's settlement price and the present day's settlement price. This daily *mark to market* helps preserve the financial integrity of the exchange: All credits and debits are balanced at the end of the day. It must be noted that some leeway is provided in that margin payments are not made if the price change is less than some fraction of the original margin. This fraction varies by exchange and commodity. Be that as it may, price changes can lead to changes in the amount of capital invested in a futures position and these changes in turn influence the rate of return on the investment.

The correct equation to calculate the rate of return on an investment in a futures contract where margin calls or payments must be considered is not universally agreed upon. The problem lies in the assumptions made about the opportunity costs of the additional margin payments and the reinvestment rates of variation margin receipts. While many schemes are used for assessment purposes, two are most common: the internal rate of return and the average direct rate of return.

2.2.4.1 Internal rate of return: yield to maturity. The *internal rate of return* assumes that all intermediate payments and receipts earn or cost the same as the rate of return that just equates the discounted present value of the cost stream to the discounted present value of the earnings stream where the discount rate is the internal rate of return. In terms of a futures position with margin payments and/or calls, the internal rate of return per contract is that value of r that satisfies the equation

$$\sum_{j=0}^{h} - M_{t+j}(1 + r)^{h-j} + (P_{t+h} - P_t) = 0$$

at the time of liquidation, $t + h$, where M_t is the margin payment per contract by, or to ($-$) the investor at time t, P_{t+h} is the price of the futures position as of the maturity date or liquidation date of the futures position, P_t is the original price at which the position was taken, and r is the internal rate of return that satisfies the above equality. This rate of return assumes that all reinvestment rates or opportunity costs of money are equal to r.

2.2.4.2 Average direct rate of return. The *average direct rate of return* uses actual intermediate rates of return or costs, r_t, for the intermediate margin borrowings, M_t, or investments and then solves for the rate of return for the full period h given by

$$r_h = \sqrt[h]{\frac{(P_{t+h} - P_t)Q}{M_0} - \frac{1}{M_0} \sum_{t=1}^{h} \frac{M_t}{(1 + r_t)^{t-h}} + \sum_{t=0}^{h} \frac{M_t}{M_0}} - 1$$

where M_0 denotes the original margin and Q is quantity.

3 SELECT RETURN CALCULATIONS IN NONFINANCIAL COMMODITIES

3.1 A Wheat Example

The following example illustrates the difference between the two assessment schemes. Suppose a long position is taken in wheat and the original margin is $10,000 for 50,000 bushels or ten contracts of wheat. The position is held for 30 days and liquidated at that time. The price differential between the original position price and the liquidation price is 10¢ per bushel or gross profit of $5,000. A margin call of $2,000 was incurred 15 days after the position was taken and prices did not change until the day of the liquidation. That is, an additional $2,000 in margin was put up for the last 15 days the position was held. The opportunity cost of this additional margin is 24 percent per annum or, for simplicity .002 percent per day. The internal rate of return would be that value of r that satisfies the condition

$$-10,000(1 + r)^{30} - 2,000(1 + r)^{15} + (.10)50,000 + 12,000 = 0$$

where the $12,000 represents the margin reimbursements on liquidation.
The internal rate of return on this 30-day investment would be

$$r = .0125 \times \frac{360}{30} = .15 \text{ or 15 percent}$$

on a 360-day annualized basis without compounding.
The corresponding average direct rate of return for the 30-day investment would be

$$r^{ADR} = \sqrt[30]{\frac{(.10)50,000}{10,000} - \frac{1(2,000)}{10,000(1 + .002)^{18}} + \frac{12,000}{10,000}} - 1$$

$$= \sqrt[30]{1.5071} - 1$$

$$= 1.0137 - 1$$

$$= .0137$$

or

$$r^{ADR} = .1644 \text{ or 16.44 percent}$$

on an annual basis without compounding.

3.2 Wheat–Money Market Arbitrage

A large processor of wheat has 53,000 bushels in excess inventories for the next three months. At present, the wheat market offers $4.50 per bushel for spot and $4.60 per bushel for delivery three months forward. The money markets at present are offering 10 percent per annum for three-month money (a loan of three months). The cost of carrying the inventory is 8 percent per annum. The processor has to evaluate the opportunity of selling wheat spot, buying it back three months forward, and investing the proceeds for three months in the money market. The relevant return and cost calculations in percent per annum are summarized below.

$$\text{Cost of borrowed funds (sell spot and buy three months forward)} = \frac{\$4.60 - \$4.50}{\$4.50} \times \frac{360}{90}$$

$$= 8.88\% \text{ per annum.}$$

$$\text{Net return on invested funds} = 10\% - 8.88\%$$

$$= 1.12\% \text{ per annum.}$$

$$\text{Net economic return (net return plus cost of carrying inventory)} = 1.12\% + 8.00\%$$

$$= 9.12\% \text{ per annum.}$$

4 INVESTMENT DECISIONS

The discussion of rate of return considered thus far has been from the vantage of certainty. The rate of return measures have either been ex-post, that is, after the investment matured, or on the assumption the investment would be held to maturity. The discussion of margin calls revealed the intrinsic uncertainties that surround all commodity investments. Investment decisions, of course, are made ex-ante—they are based on anticipations. Indeed, decision making under uncertainty is a topic that pervades almost every aspect of commodity trading and analysis. For this reason, almost every chapter in this book includes some aspect of it and a detailed discussion is presented in Chapter 12. Nevertheless, the present discussion would be incomplete without some elementary discussion of risk and its measurement. In particular the following concepts and measurements are considered: expected rate of return, the measurement of risk for individual investments, the measurement of risk for a portfolio of investments, and a preview of criteria for decision making under risk and uncertainty.

4.1 Uncertainty, Expected Return, and Risk for a Single Asset

Any outcome of an experiment that is not known beforehand is said to be *uncertain*. We have seen that, even when the investor's intent to is hold a commodity futures contract to maturity or to arbitrage in some way, the rate of return is nonetheless uncertain by virtue of possible margin calls. The uncertainty of speculative positions in either the direct placement or futures markets is obvious to all: The price at which the position will be liquidated cannot be forecast with perfect certainty. If the probabilities of the possible outcomes are not known or estimable the decision-making problem is said to be one under conditions of *perfect uncertainty*. For most commodity investment decisions, the probabilities of the possible investment outcomes can be estimated. In this case, the decision problem is said to be one under *conditions of risk*.

For investments under conditions of risk, the cash flows at the end of each period $C_0, C_1, \ldots, C_n$ are viewed as random variables. That is the C_j are assumed to have a purely indeterministic element. Insofar as the cash flows are random variables, their discounted present value also is a random variable. This randomness, together with the definition of internal rate of return, implies that the internal rate of return or yield on an uncertain investment also is a random variable. The intent of the following paragraphs is to set forth the linkage between uncertain cash flows, their expected values and variances, and the correspondence between the probability of a discounted cash flow and the probability of the associated internal rate of return or yield.

4.1.1 Expected Present Value

The *discounted present value* of an n period investment can be denoted

$$PV = C_0 + \frac{C_1}{1+k} + \frac{C_2}{(1+k)^2} + \cdots + \frac{C_n}{(1+k)^n}$$

where k is the discount rate and C_j is the cash flow for the jth period. If the C_j are random variables they may be viewed as the sum of two parts: a fixed value U_j and a purely random element e_j. In general, the expected value of a variable is the sum of each possible outcome for that variable times its respective probability. That is, the expected value is a weighted average of the possible outcomes where the weights are the probabilities of those outcomes. If the random elements have an expected value of zero, that is, $E(e_j) = 0$, then the *expected value of the discounted present value* of the cash flows can be denoted

$$\overline{PV}^* = E(PV) = U_0 + \frac{U_1}{1+k} + \frac{U_2}{(1+k)^2} + \cdots + \frac{U_n}{(1+k)^n}$$

where $E(\ )$ denotes the expected value operator, that is, the calculation of the expected value. It must be noted that the assumption that $E(e_j) = 0$ follows from the assumption that the estimates of the futures cash flows are unbiased. That is not to say the estimates are always correct but that on average the overestimates and underestimates cancel out. This is a reasonable assumption since biases can be recognized in assessments of past performance and can easily be corrected.

4.1.2 Probability of a Given Rate of Return or Better

The present value of the discounted cash flow $\overline{PV}$ will equal or exceed $\overline{PV}^*$ only if the internal rate of return equals or falls below the discount rate k. Thus given the discount rate k, the probability the present value will equal or exceed $\overline{PV}^*$ is equal to the probability that the internal rate of return r^I, will equal or falls below the *discount rate k*. That is

$$P(\overline{PV} \geq \overline{PV}^* \mid k) = P(r^I \leq k).$$

This probability, P, of course, is for a single value of k given the cash flows and may be estimated from past experience or from subjective estimates. By varying the value of k and repeating these probability calculations, one can derive a complete probability distribution for the internal rate of return. Each different discount rate produces a different discounted present value and each of these has a different probability of being equaled or exceeded. These probabilities, in turn, imply corresponding probabilities that the internal rate of return will equal or exceed the different discount rates. The resulting distribution of the rate of return on the investment then can be used to assess the expected return and risk associated with that investment.

4.1.3 Risk for a Single Asset of Reference

Risk is said to exist if an individual is willing to make decisions based on probability distributions of expected outcomes. The focus here is on risk. By convention based on intuitive appeal the risk associated with an uncertain outcome is asumed to parallel the variability of the outcome. That is, for any expected outcome the greater the dispersion around that expected outcome the greater the risk. For example, an investment with an expected payoff of $100 and a 99 percent probability of lying between $90 and $110 is said to be less risky than an investment with the same expected value but a 99 percent probability of lying between $50 and $150.

The variability of an investment is most often measured by the statistical variance of the outcome. This measure can be written

$$V(x) = \sum_{i=1}^{n} P_i[x_i - E(x)]^2$$

where P_i is the probability of the ith outcome and x_i is the value of the ith possible outcome.

In the context of the cash flows noted above, where the cash flows are neither perfectly correlated or strictly independent but consist of an independent part and an interdependent part the variance can be written

$V(PV)$

$$= \sigma_{I_0}^2 + \frac{\sigma_{I_1}^2}{1+k} + \frac{\sigma_{I_2}^2}{(1+k)^2} + \cdots + \frac{\sigma_{I_n}^2}{(1+k)^n} + \left[\sigma_{D_0} + \frac{\sigma_{D_1}}{1+k} + \frac{\sigma_{D_2}}{(1+k)^2} + \cdots + \frac{\sigma_{D_n}}{(1+k)^n}\right]^2$$

where $\sigma_{I_j}^2$ is the variance of the independent part of the jth cash flow and σ_{D_j} is the standard deviation of the interdependent portion of the jth cash flow.

If the outcomes are normally distributed then for a given discount rate, k, one may calculate the probabilities associated with different interval outcomes. These results, in turn, imply different interval outcomes and associated probabilities for the internal rates of return. The variance in the resulting distribution of internal rates of return also can be used as a measure of risk. In short, one may consider expected return and risk measured in dollars or in terms of internal rates of return. For comparison between different investment alternatives the expected internal rate of return and its variation are most common.

4.1.4   The Decision Perspective: a risk-return criterion

When two or more investments are competing for the same funds, the investment decision between them typically rests on two statistical measures. These measures are the expected return which represents the most likely or "average" return and the variance or standard deviation of that return which measures the degree of risk associated with the investment. Deferring detailed considerations of alternative decision criteria to Chapter 12, three different decision problems can emerge and the investor's decision-making process must accommodate each of them. First, if the competing investments each have the same expected rate of return the decision to allocate funds between them will rest on their relative degrees of risk. Second, if the alternative investments have the same degrees of risk the investment decision will rest on their expected rates of return. Finally, if both the expected rates of return and degrees of risk are different, the investment decision will have to weigh and compare some combination of return and risk for each investment. In general, the first and second cases are variations of the third.

While various schemes have evolved to distinguish between investments where their expected returns and risks are allowed to vary they all have one thing in common: They require some formal trade-off between return and risk in the decision maker's criterion. That is, the decision to invest in one alternative or another will be based on a criterion defined as some weighted combination of return and risk. From an operational point of view the precise nature of the criterion must be specified. This is no trivial task as the discussion in Chapter 12 will reveal. Unfortunately there is no substitute for the construction of such a criterion except for the most trivial cases where returns or risks are always the same across alternative investments.

To illustrate the need for such a criterion, consider two investments. One has an expected rate of return of 10 percent per annum and a standard deviation in its return of 4 percent per annum. The other has an expected return of 12 percent per annum but a standard deviation of return of 7 percent per annum. The latter has the highest expected return but also has more risk. The question facing the investor is a difficult one—is two percent per annum more in the expected rate of return worth three percent per annum more in the standard deviation of that return? The answer to this question requires some formal tradeoff between return and risk.

4.2 Portfolio Investment Decisions

The above discussion of return and risk considerations in the investment decision process was from the vantage of selecting a single unit from two or more investment alternatives. The same principles apply to cases where the decision is between two or more collections or portfolios of investments.

The selection of a portfolio from among the set of possible portfolios also involves return and risk considerations. The tasks confronting the investor in this regard are several fold. First, the return and risk of the portfolio must be defined. Second, the set of efficient portfolios must be identified. That is, the portfolios that have the lowest variability for any given return or the highest return for a given level of variability must be identified. Third, the portfolio must be selected from the efficient set that has the most suitable combination of return and risk according to the investor's preferences. Here, the most suitable portfolio depends in large part on the investor's risk preference. Each of these issues is discussed below.

4.2.1 Expected Return and Risk

The *expected rate of return for a portfolio* of n assets can be denoted

$$R = w_1 r_1 + w_2 r_2 + \ldots + w_n r_n = \sum_{i=1}^{n} w_i r_i$$

where n_i is the fraction of total funds invested in asset i, and r_i is the expected return of asset i. The expected return r_i of asset i can be determined as described in Section 4.1 above. Since the r_i's are random variables, R also is a random variable and contains an element of risk.

Paralleling the case for the individual asset selection case, the risk in the portfolio return is measured by the variability in its return. Using the *variance of R as the measure of risk* this variability can be written

$$V(R) = \sum_{\substack{i=1 \\ i \neq j}}^{n} \sum_{j=1}^{n} w_i w_j \sigma_{ij} + \sum_{i=1}^{n} w_i^2 \sigma_i^2$$

where w_i denotes the fraction of resources invested in asset i, σ_i^2 is the variance of the ith asset's return, and σ_{ij} is the covariance between the ith asset's return and the jth asset's return.

4.2.2 Covariability and Diversification

It must be noted that portfolios of investment have a unique attribute in comparison to the selection of a single asset for investment: Portfolio risk includes covariance terms between the different investments. The *covariance of returns* between different assets offers the investor the opportunity to combine assets with positive expected returns but negative covariances. That is, the investor may be able to reduce risk without reducing return by *diversifying investment funds* between assets with negative covariances. Briefly stated, covariability offers the possibility of reducing risk for the portfolio to levels below that of any individual asset in the portfolio save a risk-free asset if one indeed exists. In general it has been shown that diversification pays (Samuelson 1967).

4.2.3 Efficient Portfolios

A particular portfolio is defined by the specific weighting scheme, that is, by the values of the w_i. Different weighting schemes can alter either or both the expected return and risk of the portfolio. Assuming the investor is rational, the portfolio selected will be from among the *efficient set of portfolios*. These include only those combinations of assets that have the lowest variability for a given expected rate of return and the highest return for a given degree of variability. While the efficient set of portfolios is but a small fraction of all possible portfolios the number of efficient candidates to chose from nevertheless can be enormous. Moreover, a selection requires some criterion or objective function on the part of the investor.

4.2.4 Portfolio Selection

The basic problem of portfolio selection is to combine risk, return, and operational constraints into a sensible criterion from which a satisfying combination of investments can be derived. A common criterion, or objective function, is to find the weights, w_i, that maximize $Z = R - \lambda V(R)$, subject to $L_i \leq w_i \leq U_i$, $i = 1, \ldots, n$, where $\sum_{i=1}^{n} w_i = 100$ and R and $V(R)$ are defined in 4.2.1. Here, Z is the value of the objective function and λ is the coefficient, or degree, of risk aversion that translates risk into the same unit of measure as return. The constraint $\sum_{i=1}^{n} w_i = 100$ simply denotes that the percent of investable funds assigned to each investment alternative, w_i, when added together must total 100 percent. The constraints $L_i \leq w_i \leq u_i$ prescribe the percent upper, u_i and lower, L_i, bounds the indicated asset weights must lie within. These bounds may come from legal and/or policy constraints.

The solution of this problem and examples are deferred to Chapter 24. Suffice it to say for now that several factors influence the selection of a portfolio based on this objective function. Clearly, the given returns, risks, constraints, and degree of risk aversion are important. In addition, the accuracy of the risk and return information and the operational ability to achieve the indicated portfolio, owing to differences in the liquidity of the different assets, also are important factors. As is shown in Chapter 24 the specific weight of each asset in the portfolio can change as any one, or any combination, of these factors change.

5 SUMMARY

Commodity investment decisions are based in part on rates of return. While the notion of rate of return is straightforward, its measurement can be exceedingly complex owing to a variety of practical considerations. Among the most important are the indivisibility of contract size, different pricing conventions, different value dates, and the conversion to annualized rates of return depending on the assumed reinvestment rates.

Investment decisions also are based in part on risk. Typically the risk associated with an investment decision is measured by the variability surrounding the expected outcome. This is a statistical measure and its value is in part subjective and exposed to measurement errors embedded in the calculation of the rates of return from which their variability is calculated. The most common measures of risk are the variance and standard deviation of the expected return. However, other measures of risk can be used, such as the range of possible outcomes. Regardless of the specific risk measure used, the value of each is influenced by the way in which the rates of return are calculated. This is especially important when investments in different commodities are considered and those commodities have different terms to maturity, different units of measure, and so forth.

The examples presented to highlight return calculations under operating conditions focused on nonfinancial commodities of reference. This was done because financial commodities such as securities and foreign exchange have special attributes that further complicate the calculation of return and risk. These topics are considered in the next chapter.

6 BIBLIOGRAPHY

MAO, J. T. C., *Quantitative Analysis of Financial Decisions,* New York: The Macmillan Company, 1969.

SAMUELSON, P. A., "General Proof that Diversification Pays", *Journal of Financial and Quantitative Analysis,* vol. 3. March 1967, pp. 1–13.

SHARPE, WILLIAM F., *Investments,* 2nd ed. Englewood Cliffs, N.J.: Prentice-Hall, Inc. 1981.

VAN HORNE, *Financial Management and Policy,* 6th ed. Englewood Cliffs, N.J.: Prentice-Hall, Inc., 1983.

7

THE CASH AND FUTURES MARKETS
FOR FINANCIAL ASSETS OF REFERENCE

|||||||||||||||||||||||||||||||||||||||||||||||||||||||||||||||||||||||||||||||||||||||||||||||||||||||||||||

1 INTRODUCTION

For agricultural commodities, metals and manufacturing items, and foreign exchange, the prices and values of commodity contracts in the cash and futures markets are directly related. While differences in contract size and/or pricing convention may exist, their correspondence is not a complex task, just a detailed one, However, trading financial instruments in the cash and futures markets is both detailed and complex. A financial instrument, unlike another "commodity," is explicitly valued according to some rate of interest or time rate of discount and some specified maturity. To be sure, changes in rates of interest influence the price of wheat or gold in the forward and futures markets insofar as they influence the cost of the funds invested. While changes in rates of interest influence the cost of invested funds for financial commodities, they also have a direct effect on the intrinsic value of the underlying asset of reference, a sensitivity that nonfinancial commodities do not share. To complicate matters further, different financial instruments can have different maturity horizons and different discount or interest-bearing schemes that can make direct comparison erroneous. Furthermore, pricing conventions differ for some financial commodities between the cash and futures markets. These differences are not just trivial unit transformations but may include more convoluted index numbers.

The purpose of this chapter is threefold: to set forth the special characteristics of financial futures contracts, to provide a correspondence between financial futures and their underlying assets of reference, and to illustrate trading opportunities for speculators, hedgers, and arbitragers. Section 2 summarizes the special difficulties of trading financial commodities. Section 3 presents a summary of price and value correspondences between cash and futures instruments and between cash prices and their rates of interest. Differences in contract size, price quotation, and timing anomalies between different markets and instruments are discussed in Section 4. Several trading examples are given in Section 5. Included here are a liquidity arbitrage and a diversification of the yield curve ride. Gresham's Law is discussed for select financial futures in Section 6 and the chapter is summarized in Section 7.

2   DIFFICULTIES OF TRADING FINANCIAL COMMODITIES

In general, the special difficulties of trading financial commodities arise from any combination of the following factors or considerations. First, similar instruments such as commercial paper and treasury bills can have different terms to maturity. These differences must be accounted for in the calculation of annualized rates of return. Moreover, for long-term instruments with earnings streams, such as a coupon bond, differences in term to maturity can alter the present value of the instrument and its rate of return.

Second, different financial instruments may be quoted in different terms, and comparisons between the instruments require the establishment of a correspondence between the different quotations. Among the most common methods of measurement are the bank discount rate and the bond equivalent yield. The correspondence between these measures is not intuitively obvious.

Third, financial instruments with different coupons, maturities, cash flows, prices, and discounts can be compared on a uniform basis through their annualized yield to maturity. The yields to maturity typically are different for different terms to maturity, for example, 3 months versus 12 months, and for different catagories of instruments, for example, governments versus private paper. These yields can shift owing to market expectations, credit risk and liquidity preference, and the shifts may not be parallel over time or between classes of instruments.

Fourth, the futures market prices of financial instruments have implicit yield curves that offer a new dimension to yield curve analysis: a futures yield curve. For comparison to their cash market counterpart the futures market yield curves must be discounted to the present. Here the appropriate discount rate is specific to the trader.

Fifth, the price units of measure for the treasury bill futures contract is an index that is a linear transformation of the discount rate on the instrument, and treasury bond futures are priced assuming an 8 percent coupon. These conventions complicate the comparison of financial futures to their cash counterparts as well as to other instruments.

Sixth, different financial instruments have different degrees of market volatility and corresponding differences in their financial consequences from a change in interest rates. For example, a 50 basis point move in long-term government bonds has a much larger financial impact than a 50 basis point move in a 90-day treasury bill. While both instruments are linked to interest rates their response to a given change in rates can be much different.

Finally, some instruments have a call feature and the method of evaluating this "option" is not universally accepted. Some use a "yield to call" calculation while others use the discounted value of the call in their yield calculations.

3 SELECT PRICE, RATE, AND YIELD RELATIONSHIPS

Among the most popular financial instruments with corresponding futures contracts are 90- to 92-day treasury bills, one-year treasury bills, $3\frac{1}{2}$-to-10-year treasury notes, long-term treasury bonds, GNMA collateralized depository receipts, GNMA certificates, 90-day certificates of deposit, and Eurodollar CDs. The exploration of all the possible combinations of the above problems for, and between, each of these financial instruments traded in the cash and future markets is a book in itself. However, there are several basic relationships that can help facilitate these analyses. These relationships include: the *linkage of yield, rate of interest, and price* and the *correspondence between cash market and futures market pricing conventions*; the relationship between the bank *discount rate* and the *bond equivalent yield*; the T-bill index, actual and futures market yield curves; and the calculation of yields for GNMA and long-term treasury bonds using alternative call feature valuation methods. Each of these topics is presented below.

3.1 Cash and Futures Market Price and Rate Relationships

Table 7.1 summarizes the relationships between the cash market yield and price of each of the above instruments as well as the correspondence of pricing conventions for the same instruments in the cash and futures markets.

3.2 Bank Discount Rate and Bond Equivalent Yield

Treasury bills are one of the most popular securities and are often traded for other securities with different maturities and cash flows. In order to trade T-bills and especially to assess swaps of T-bills for other longer-term

Table 7.1

CASH AND FUTURES MARKET PRICE AND RATE RELATIONSHIPS

	CASH MARKET			FUTURES MARKET	
		Price/Quoted Rate Correspondence			
Instrument	Price	Quoted Rate	Instrument	Price Quote	
91-Day T-bill (91 days to maturity)	$P = F - dF \times t/360$ ex: $1,000,000 - .10 \times 1,000,000 \times 91/360$ $= \$974,722.23$	d	90 Day T-bill	$P_I = 100.00 - d \times 100.00$ (Price adjustment made for different maturity dates)	
		$d = .10$			
30-Day Commercial Paper (30 days to maturity)	$P = F - dF \times t/360$ ex: $1,000,000 - .10 \times 1,000,000 \times 30/360$ $= \$991,666.67$	d $d = .10$	30-Day Commercial Paper (A1 or P1)	$P_I = 100.00 - d \times 100.00$	
90-day Commercial Paper (90 days to maturity)	$P = F - dF \times t/360$ ex: $1,000,000 - .10 \times 1,000,000 \times 90/360$ $= \$975,000.00$	d $d = .10$	90-Day Commercial Paper (A1 or P1)	$P_I = 100.00 - d \times 100.00$	
At Issue Date 6-Year Note (6 $\times$ 365 Days to maturity + 1 or 2 days depending on leap years)	$P = \dfrac{1/2cF}{(1 + r/2)} + \cdots + \dfrac{1/2cF}{(1 + r/2)^{12}} + \dfrac{1/2cF}{(1 + r/2)^{12}} + \dfrac{F}{(1 + r/2)^{12}}$	$r_s = \left[\left(1 + \dfrac{r}{2}\right)^2 - 1\right]$	$3\frac{1}{2}$-to-10-Year T-Notes	Price percentage of par based on a fixed coupon. Accrued interest is excluded from price calculation and number of semiannual periods is based on rounding down to nearest quarter. (Pricing of futures geared to cheapest notes deliverable.)	
After Issue: 6 year Note	$P = \displaystyle\sum_{j=b}^{12} \dfrac{1/2cF}{(1 + r/2)^j} + \dfrac{F}{(1 + r/2)^{12}} - I r^{/365}_a$ $I r^{/365}_a = $ Number of days interest from last interest payment to settlement $\times$ corresponding daily rate of interest	r_s, but price and rate quoted is without accrued interest			

GNMA[a]	$$P = \sum_{j=1}^{144} \frac{m - s(m - p_j)}{\left(1 + \frac{r}{12}\right)^{j+\delta}}$$ $$+ \frac{F\left[\left(1 + \frac{r}{12}\right)^{360} - \left(1 + \frac{r}{12}\right)^{144}\right]}{\left[\left(1 + \frac{r}{12}\right)^{360} - 1\right]\left[\left(1 + \frac{r}{12}\right)^{144+\delta}\right]}$$ where $$\delta = \frac{\Delta - 31}{30}$$ [a]Based upon an assumption of 12-year prepayment of principle. In effect the GNMA is a self-amortizing continuously callable bond with a variable coupon.	GNMA (CDR)	Price percentage of par determined from 30-year, 8% coupon pass-throughs (CBT) with assumption of 100% prepayment of principle in 12 years; quoted in 32nds. CDRs (collateralized depositary receipts, formerly known as due bills) can be converted to actual GNMAs within 15 business days. (Pricing of futures geared to cheapest GNMAs deliverable.)
	$$r_s = 2\left[\left(1 + \frac{r}{12}\right)^6 - 1\right]$$		
Long-term Gov'ts (15 years to first call)	$$P = \sum_{j=b}^{T'} \frac{1/2cF}{(1 + r/2)^j} + \frac{F}{(1 + r/2)^{T'}} - Ir_a^{r/365}$$	Long-term T-bond (at least 15 years to first call)	Price percentage of par based on an 8% coupon. (CBT contract). Accrued interest is excluded from price calculation and number of semianuual periods is based on rounding down to nearest quarters; quoted in 32nds. (Pricing of futures geared to cheapest bonds deliverable.)
	$$r_s = \left[\left(1 + \frac{r}{2}\right)^2 - 1\right].$$ Price and rate quoted is without accrued interest		

Table 7.1—Continued

P	= Price (theoretical)
P_I	= Price index
F	= Face value
t	= Number of days
d	= Bank discount rate
r_s	= Annual rate of interest with semiannual compounding or bond equivalent yield
r	= Annual yield
$I r/365$	= Accrued interest
a	
c	= Annual coupon rate
m	= Monthly mortgage payment based on 30 year mortgage
p	= Monthly principle payment based on 30 year mortgage
s	= Monthly service fee as a percent of interest paid
$r/12$	= Monthly rate of interest
δ	= Actual payment penalty in months
Δ	= Pass-through delay in days
b	= Number of semiannual periods since issue
T'	= Number of full semiannual periods until first call date

securities the intricacies of T-bill pricing conventions must be well understood.

When one purchases a treasury bill whose duration or term to maturity is one year or less, the price paid is less than (i.e., at a discount to) the face value of the treasury bill. At maturity, the government pays the owner of the bill the face value. For example, if the discount rate quoted is 10.5 percent and the bill will mature in exactly one year, then the discount on a $1 million treasury bill will be $105,000 and the purchase price will be $895,000. If held to maturity, the investor would receive $1 million at the end of one year. The simple bank discount rate is the difference between the purchase price and maturity value divided by the maturity value of the instrument. This rate then is annualized, that is, converted to an annual rate equivalent, as noted in Section 3.1. In the above example, the conventional bank discount rate is 10.5 percent. However, since only $895,000 was initially invested, the return of $105,000 implies a "holding period" rate of return different from the bank discount rate. The holding period rate of return in this case would be 11.732 percent.

The relationship between the bank discount, d, and the bond equivalent yield, r^*, depends on the term to maturity for the T-bill. For T-bills with six months to maturity or less, the relationship is

$$r^* = \frac{365 \times d}{360 - td}$$

where t is the number of days to maturity (365 in our example) and 360 represents the number of days in the bank calendar year (an institutional anomaly). A 13 week T-bill with a bank discount rate of 10.5 per cent would have a bond equivalent yield of 10.936 per cent.

Treasury bills with more than six months to maturity are quoted so as to reflect an imaginary coupon payment paid on a coupon security of the same maturity. The coupon is paid six months from settlement date. For a long discount bill, the bond equivalent yield is given by

$$r^* = \frac{-(S_2 - S_1) + \sqrt{(S_2 - S_1)^2 - (730(S_2 - S_1) - 365^2)(1 - FV/V_{S_1})}}{(S_2 - S_1) - 365/2}$$

where the S's and V's are investment dates and amounts, respectively. For a 270-day bill with a discount quote of 10 percent the bond equivalent yield is 10.773 percent.

3.3 Treasury Bill Index

To avoid confusion of a decreasing rate as the equivalent of a decreasing price, the Chicago Merchantile Exchange instituted treasury bill trading on a price index basis. The index is designed in such a manner that when rates go up the index goes down and when interest rates go down, the index goes up. The *treasury bill index* results from subtracting the bank discount rate quoted on an annual basis from the index value of the T-bill at maturity, namely 100. An index of 100 is equivalent to $1,000,000 face value. For example, with an annual bank discount rate of 10.5 percent the index would be 89.50. If there is a 100 basis point decrease in interest rates the index will increase from 89.50 to 90.50. In this case, a long position in a treasury bill futures contract would benefit from a 100 basis point decrease in interest rates and the investor's account would be ahead by the value of 100 basis points movement in the index. Since a basis point move is the equivalent of $25, the long position would be ahead by $2,500. The annual return of one basis point, .01 per cent or .0001, on $1,000,000 is $100. The 90-day T-bill has one quarter of the 360-day (annual) interest days, hence, $25 per basis point.

3.4   Actual and Futures Market Implicit Yield Curves

One of the interesting aspects of the interest rate futures markets is the ability to have auction-determined rates of interest for various maturity financial instruments that are to be delivered in future periods extending out over a horizon of more than two years. That is to say, a set of forward interest rates are generated for each financial futures instrument that is traded upon the organized exchanges.

The traditional *yield curve* relates *spot* prices of risk-free securities for different maturing instruments. The yield to maturity is typically plotted on the vertical axis and the time to maturity is plotted on the horizontal axis. Yield curves can be upward sloping, level, or downward sloping over various portions of the maturity horizon. Various theories have been put forth that explain the shape of the yield curve and also suggest trading strategies that many aggressive money managers implement in dealing with their short-term liquid portfolios. However, arbitrage opportunities help ensure there is a close relationship between rates of interest in the cash market and the implicit rates in the organized futures market. These opportunities can be uncovered by examining the relationship between the yield curves in these separate markets.

Comparisons between futures yield curves and current cash market yield curves are complicated by mismatched value dates. Interest rate futures are only traded for fixed periods for delivery and these dates do not always correspond to their cash market counterparts. These timing anomalies vary from exchange to exchange and by type of instrument.

It must be noted that as long as the timing gaps are taken into account, the correct forward rates can be identified. The spot yield curve implied by the set of futures prices is called the *strip yield curve*, and it is comparisons between the spot yield curve and the strip yield curve that reveal arbitrage opportunities.

The following example illustrates the construction of forward rates from spot prices on the treasury bill market and their comparison with rates of interest implied by existing futures contracts. For simplicity, the date is assumed to be the last delivery date of a 90-day T-bill futures contract.

Let r_1 = Future bond equivalent rate for a 90-day T-bill (in this case, the rate implied by the index on the last delivery date of the contract)

r_i = Future bond equivalent rates for 90-day T-bills for subsequent maturing contracts (3 months, 6 months, 9 months, etc., from today)

R_1 = Spot rate for a 90-day T-bill (same day as above)

R_2 = Spot rate for a 180-day T-bill or note (same day as above)

R_i = Spot rate for a $(90 \times i)$-day T-bill or note (same day as above)

If equilibrium is to exist, that is, if arbitrage opportunities are to be eliminated, spot and futures rates must correspond according to the following.

$$R_1 = (1 + r_1) - 1$$
$$R_2 = \sqrt[2]{(1 + r_1)(1 + r_2)} - 1$$
$$R_n = \sqrt[n]{(1 + r_1)(1 + r_2) \dots (1 + r_n)} - 1.$$

Solving for r_n

$$r_n = \frac{(1 - R_n)^n}{(1 + R_n - 1)^{n-1}} - 1$$

For example, if a spot 270-day note yields 12.5 percent and a 360-day note yields 11.5 percent then the 270-day forward 90-day rate should equal 8.553 percent. Since the bank discount rate d can be defined as $d = \dfrac{360r}{365 + tr}$, the discount will be 8.26 percent and T-bill futures above or below 91.74 will give rise to arbitrage profits.

3.5 Yield to Call and Yield to Call With Option

Some financial instruments are callable such as long-term government bonds and GNMAs. That is, they may be redeemed prior to maturity at the issuer's option. This contingency makes the cash flow uncertain and in turn makes the yield uncertain. In order to provide a measure of yield for comparison to the yield to maturity of noncallable bonds, the marketplace typically computes the "yield to call." The yield to call is calculated the same way as the yield to maturity but on the assumption that the bond's cash flow is terminated on the earliest call date and the principal is redeemed at the specified call price at that time.

The *yield to call* is calculated as that semiannual rate r^{yc} that satisfies the following condition:

$$\frac{C}{r^{yc}} + \left[\frac{1}{(1 + r^{yc})^T}\right]\left[Z - \frac{C}{r^{yc}}\right] - P = 0$$

where P is the market price of the bond; r^{yc} is the yield to call; T is the number of time periods, typically half-years, to the earliest call date; C is the coupon rate in dollars per \$1,000 face value per time period, and Z is the call price of the bond. The yield to call assumes away the value associated with the call feature: The call may not be exercised and the stream of earnings may continue until the maturity date. An alternative approach values the call option and includes it in the yield calculation. Deferring the valuation of an option to Part 5, let the value of the call feature be denoted

$$V(\sigma, r^{xo}, M - T)$$

where σ is the standard deviation in the yield of the underlying asset measured in semiannual terms, r^{xo} is the yield of the underlying asset including the option, and $M - T$ is the length of the option in half-years, that is, the difference between the maturity date M less the earliest call date T.

The value of the call can be used together with "yield to call" or "yield to maturity" calculations to obtain adjusted yields to maturity with and without the call feature. The two approaches are similar, but different owing to the discounting scheme employed. In either case the value of this call option is valued as of time T and must be discounted back to the present.

The *yield to maturity with the option adjustment* is that rate r^{mo} that satisfies the condition

$$\frac{C}{r^{mo}} + \left[\frac{1}{(1 + r^{mo})^M}\right]\left[1{,}000 - \frac{C}{r^{mo}}\right] - \frac{V(\sigma, r^{mo}, M - T)}{(1 + r^{mo})^T} - P = 0.$$

The *yield to call with the option adjustment* is calculated as that rate, r^{co}, that satisfies the condition

$$\frac{C}{r^{co}} + \left[\frac{1}{(1 + r^{co})^T}\right]\left[Z - \frac{C}{r^{co}}\right] + \frac{V(\sigma, r^{co}, M - T)}{(1 + r^{co})^T} - P = 0.$$

Regardless of the method used, the yield on callable bonds is an estimate based on assumptions and conditions not found in noncallable bonds. Changes in market rates of interest or bond prices will have different effects on the "yield" of the two types of bonds, all other characteristics being equal.

4 SIZE, QUOTATION, AND TIMING ANOMALIES

4.1 Contract Size and Quotation Differences

In the financial futures markets the standard contract size varies with the commodity. For long-term treasury bonds and GNMA CDRs the size unit in $100,000 principal, but for U. S. T-bills the unit of the contract is $1 million. In foreign exchange, British pounds futures contracts are traded in quantities of £25,000; Canadian dollars, $100,000; West German marks, 125,000 DM; Swiss francs, 125,000 francs; and Japanese yen, 12.5 million yen. For some contracts, the price, especially in the financial futures markets, are not quoted in dollar terms but in reference to an index that is established by the exchange. This has been done to facilitate marketing of the particular contract so that traditional long and short price movements in the financial futures instruments would be similar to those already existing in the grains and metals.

Not all financial instruments are traded in the same units. GNMAs and long-term government bonds are quoted in 32nds with an indicator for 64ths. Treasury bills and CDs are traded in percent. Not all these conventions are paralleled in the futures markets. These differences mean that effective hedging in the futures markets requires careful correspondence with cash positions.

4.2 Timing Anomalies

A major pitfall and opportunity for profit is the timing differential that may arise between financial instruments. Here, three considerations are most important: mismatched value dates, the cost of carry, and the idiosyncrasies between payments mechanisms. Each of these are discussed below.

4.2.1 Mismatched Value Dates and the Cost of Carry

The holding of two different positions in two different markets may result in contract value dates not being identical. For example, a long position in 30-day forward deutschemarks and a short position in the current deutschemarks futures contract on July 14, 1980, has a one-day difference in value dates. The 30-day forward contract has a value date of Thursday, August 14, 1980, and the August deutschemark contract has a value or maturity date of Wednesday, August 13, 1980. Hence, if delivery were to be taken on the futures contract on August 13, 1980, then it would have to be carried one day if it were to be used to satisfy the commitment in the forward market.

4.2.1.1 A foreign exchange example. For illustrative purposes the cost of carry on the 30-day Eurocurrency rate is presented in Table 7.2.

Table 7.2

MISMATCHED VALUE DATES AND THE COST OF CARRY–INTERNATIONAL MONETARY MARKET (IMM) NEAREST FUTURES CONTRACT VERSUS 30-DAY FORWARD INTERBANK RATE

CURRENCY	INTERBANK FOREIGN TERMS	IMM FOREIGN TERMS	DIFFERENCE IN PIPPS[a]	INTERBANK U.S. TERMS	IMM U.S. TERMS	DIFFERENCE IN CENTS	COST OF CARRY	DAYS OF CARRY
Deutschemarks	1.7633	1.7661	+28	.5671	.5662	-.09	2.65	1
Swiss francs	1.6147	1.6239	+92	.6193	.6158	-.35	1.57	1
Canadian dollars	1.1554	1.1527	-27	.8655	.8675	+.20	3.58	1
Yen	216.30	216.78	+48	.004623	.004613	-.0010	3.50	1
Sterling	2.3172	2.3195	+23	2.3172	2.3195	+.23	4.68	1

[a]*Pipps* are the last two digits of the quote. They are also called points, or basis points.

Here the cost of carry for deutschemarks is 2.65 basis points per day. Any financial transaction involving a mismatched value date in deutschemarks would have to account for this cost of carry in order to obtain a true estimate of the return on the transaction.

4.2.1.2 The cost of carry and repurchase agreements. The financing cost for debt instruments is often determined by the repurchase agreement rate. For example, if financing $1 million, $10\frac{3}{8}$ coupon 20 year government bonds costs $12\frac{3}{8}$ percent then the 2 percent financing cost is equivalent to a carry cost of $55.55 per day or twice the 1 basis point daily cost of carry of $27.78. This is equivalent to a price loss of almost $\frac{6}{32}$ percent per month. Because of the ability to borrow and lend assets, the cost of carry affects the relation of future prices to current prices. This arises since the choice always exists between buying today, financing the purchase through a repurchase agreement, and simultaneously selling a futures contract.

4.2.2 Value Dates and Delivery Dates

Trading in foreign exchange highlights the need for special attention to value date identification. *Value date problems* arise for several reasons:

1. Different national holidays
2. Different clearing mechanisms
3. Requirements to confirm trades in writing

These market anomalies give rise to the use of conventions for value dating.

Spot currency value date for dealing in a foreign currency against the U. S. dollar is usually two business days from transaction date in the currency traded provided that day is also a business day in New York. If there is a holiday in either of the countries, the value date is moved forward until there is a business day in both countries. If, however, one deals in Canadian dollars, the "spot date" is taken to be one rather than two business days forward.

The same is true for *forward value dates* in foreign exchange. A 2 month forward transaction may not have a value date 60 days ahead of the transaction date. The value date must be a business day in both countries. If moving forward the value date would change the month of the contract, then the value date is moved backward to allow the fixing of a date for settlement.

When trading foreign exchange in the direct placement market, it is important to know the exact dates of settlement as prices are quoted to reflect the time period from settlement.

Futures contracts do not have uniform delivery dates. Precious metals on COMEX and T-bonds on the CBT do not have unique delivery dates. A long may receive notice of intention to deliver from the first to last deliverable day of the maturing month contract. To further complicate value comparisons between cash and futures pricing procedures can create an additional option valuation premium or discount that must be taken into account. For example, notice to deliver T-bonds does not have to be made to the clearing house until 5:00 pm, several hours after settlement and, hence, after delivery prices have been fixed. Under these delivery conditions the short, in effect, owns a put option whose expiration period is a half day. The anomalies discussed point out the pitfalls that can be encountered and are most important for those traders who end up making or taking delivery.

5 SELECT TRADING EXAMPLES IN FINANCIAL INSTRUMENTS

The following examples illustrate some of the issues raised in Section 2. Although not exhaustive they are representative of trading analyses and operations specific to financial futures. The examples include a liquidity arbitrage, and the diversification of a yield curve ride.

5.1 Liquidity Arbitrage

Since futures contracts in treasury bonds are substitutes for cash bonds, arbitrage opportunities present themselves that allow long bond investors to improve the performance of their portfolios and at the same time reduce liquidity risk. Pursuing these arbitrage opportunities helps attain market efficiency and helps the bottom line.

Transactions. The transactions using actual market data and alternative outcomes are as follows.

Step 1. Initial Position, July 27, 1978

1. Sell $1,000,000 face value of long-term U.S. governments 8s 1996–01 for 94-00. Receive $940,000.

2. Buy ten June 1979 long-term U.S. bond futures at a price of 92-09. Put up margin of $10,000 and pay round turn commissions of $650.

3. Buy $930,000 face value T-notes $7\frac{3}{4}$s at a price of 99-18 for a cost of $925,932.

4. Position at end of July 27, 1978:
   a. long ten June futures
   b. long T-notes
   c. long cash of $3,418.

Step 2. Liquidation, June 27, 1979

1. Receive $66,068 interest on T-note.

2. Receive $930,000 from U.S. government.

3. Pay $922,813 for delivery of U.S. T-bonds with at least 15 years to call or maturity closing out the futures position.
4. Receive margin of $10,000.
5. Position at end of June 27,1979: long U.S. treasury bonds.

Alternative cash returns

A. Being long U.S. governments 8s 1996–01

By June 27, 1979, received $80,000 interest with no reinvestment of intermediate interest payments. After-tax cash returns $80,000 × (1 − .46) = $43,200.

B. Doing the liquidity arbitrage

1. Maintained 11-month cash position of $3,418.
2. Received $66,068 11 months' interest on T-note.
3. Received $7,187 difference from closing out futures position with proceeds from T-note.
4. Received margin of $10,000.
5. Can add $650 commission to cost basis of the bond position.

By June 27, 1979, received $86,673 with no reinvestment of intermediate interest payments. After-tax cash returns $66,068 × (1 − .46) + $20,605 = $56,281. On June 27, 1979, both alternatives are long U. S. government bonds. Since delivery was taken there is no tax liability on the futures contract. There must be an equivalent "purchase and sale" of the same asset. The 11 months that the futures contract was held can be added to the holding period of the long-term bond position for determining gains and losses when the bond asset is liquidated.

5.2 Treasury Bill Parity: diversifying the yield curve ride

An interesting arbitrage arises from the comparison of equivalent risk-free instruments that can be constructed from a set of shorter-term instruments or contracts. Consider a six-month T-bill that spans two three-month bills.

	The Spanning Horizon	
0	91 Days	182 Days
First Settlement Day	Maturity Day of Bill 2	Maturity Day of Bill 1 and Bill 3
S_1	Bill 1	
	Bill 2	S_2
		Bill 3 S_3

Bill 1 and bill 2 are spot bills and bill 3 is a forward bill, that is, its first settlement date is 91 days hence. Given the spot prices and rates what should one pay for bill 3? This problem is known as the bill parity problem. Since owing bill 2 and bill 3 is equivalent to owning bill 1 the *T-bill parity discount rate* on bill 3 is the equilibrium rate that eliminates arbitrage profits and is given by

$$d^3 = \left(1 - \frac{V_{S_1}^1}{V_{S_1}^2}\right)\left(\frac{360}{S_3 - S_2}\right)$$

or

$$V_{S_2}^3 = FV^3 - \left(1 - \frac{V_{S_1}^1}{V_{S_1}^2}\right)\left(\frac{S_3 - S_2}{S_2 - S_1}\right)FV^3.$$

where the superscripts denote the bill e.g. d^3 for bill 3.

Alternatively, given that futures prices imply discount rates for bill 2 and bill 3, then the discount rate on the longer bill that spans bill 2 and bill 3 is

$$d^1 = \left\{\left[1 - d^2\left(\frac{S_2 - S_1}{360}\right)\right]\left[d^3\left(\frac{S_3 - S_2}{360}\right) - 1\right] + 1\right\}\frac{360}{(S_3 - S_1)}.$$

If T-bill 1 does not span T-bill 2 and T-bill 3 then daily borrowing or lending opportunities arise. These opportunities are conveniently measured by market quotes for repurchase agreements.

It is often said that it sometimes pays to buy a longer bill and convert it to a shorter bill by not holding it to maturity. This is often referred to as *riding the yield curve*. With equivalent instruments constructed from a *strip* or set of futures contracts different opportunities can arise that compare favorably to holding the cash instrument. The calculations shown in Tables 7.3 and 7.4 were done for two different time periods with different market characteristics and, not surprisingly, with different results. The interesting point to note in both cases is the cash and futures markets are not in equilibrium and the arbitrage opportunities can be substantial.

Another more intricate example is shown in Table 7.5. This table compares a longer-term cash T-bill (the "far cash" T-bill) against a composite made up of shorter-term cash T-bill (the "near cash" T-bill) and successive T-bill futures contracts that collectively span a similar time interval as the "far cash" T-bill. The "differential" indicates how much more profitable (or less, if negative) it is to buy and hold to maturity the "near cash" T-bill and each of the successive futures contracts that make up the "composite" than it is to buy and hold to maturity the "far cash" T-bill. The profit of $7,507 in this case includes adjustments for intermediate interest payments and receipts summarized in the section entitled "Composite Cash Flow."

Table 7.3

DIVERSIFYING THE YIELD CURVE RIDE

MARKET CONDITIONS ON JULY 6, 1978

Instrument	Maturity	Days Held	Discount Rate (percent per annum)	Price
T-bill	12/21/78	168	7.34	$965,796
T-bill	9/21/78	77	6.94	985,161
September T-bill future	12/21/78	91	7.43	979,124

ACTIONS

Alternative 1
  Buy 12/21/78 maturity T-bill and hold to maturity — Gross profit $34,204

Alternative 2
  Buy 9/12/78 maturity T-bill and hold to maturity — Gross profit $14,839
  Buy September T-bill future and hold to maturity — Gross profit $20,876

Total gross profits $35,715

Gross benefit of Alternative 2 over Alternative 1 — $ 1,311

Table 7.4

DIVERSIFYING THE YIELD CURVE RIDE

MARKET CONDITIONS ON SEPTEMBER 19, 1979

Instrument	Maturity	Days Held	Discount Rate (percent per annum)	Price
T-bill	12/27/79	98	10.13	$972,423
T-bill	4/1/80	194	10.08	945,680
December T-bill future	3/21/80	90	9.67	975,825

ACTIONS

Alternative 1
  Buy 6-month T-bill and hold to maturity — Gross profit $54,320

Alternative 2
  Buy 3-month T-bill and hold to maturity — Gross profit $27,577
  Buy T-bill future and hold to maturity — Gross profit $24,175

Total gross profit $51,572

Gross benefit (loss) Alternative 2 over Alternative 1 — $(2,748)

But with Alternative 2 there
  is $1,000,000 available to invest for
  9 more days to match April 1
  value date on 6-month bill. Since
    9 days @ 10% is $2,500,
  Alternative 1 is still better.

Table 7.5

"FAR CASH" T-BILL COMPARED AGAINST "NEAR CASH" AND/OR
FUTURES COMPOSITE

	T-BILL MATURITY DATE	PRICE($)	RATE (%)	DAYS TO MATURITY
Far Cash	8/12/82	868,275	14.370	330
Composite	9/16/82	861,218	13.688	365
Near Cash	4/22/82	912,618	14.430	218
March 82 T bill future	6/17/82	965,774	13.540	274
June 82 T bill future	9/16/82	966,229	13.360	365
Differential		7,057	−0.682	35

COMPOSITE CASH FLOW

DATE	AMOUNT ($)	ITEM	INTEREST ($)
9/16/81	−912,618	Buy near cash	0
9/16/81	868,275	Sell far cash	0
3/18/82	−965,774	Futures delivery	−3,052
4/22/82	1,000,000	Near cash mature	−13,337
6/17/82	−966,229	Futures delivery	−551
6/17/82	1,000,000	T-bill matures	0
8/12/82	0	Far cash matures	209
9/16/82	1,000,000	T-bill matures	135

6 GRESHAM'S LAW: TREASURY BONDS, GNMAs, AND YIELD TO MATURITY

Gresham's Law states that for any market the physical good used to satisfy the delivery requirements of the contract will be that which is cheapest to deliver. For nonfinancial commodities, the delivery grade will be the lowest grade acceptable for delivery, all other factors being the same. For example, COMEX gold futures contracts require .995 pure gold bullion. Any grade above .995 can be exchanged for .995 plus a value differential. For a financial futures contract, especially those with a long-term maturity such as long-term U. S. treasury bonds and GNMAs, the selection of what is the cheapest deliverable instrument is not as easy to ascertain. The reason for this is that price adjustments based on maintaining some fixed price or yield can make some financial instruments cheaper than others for satisfying contractual obligations.

To illustrate this point, consider the list of bonds that qualify for delivery against the long term bond futures contract, in Table 7.6. These bonds trade in the cash market and reflect the shape of the yield curve on

Table 7.6

THE CHEAPEST BOND ON MARCH 21, 1979

DELIVERABLE TREASURY BOND	CASH OFFER PRICE	÷	MARCH '79 FACTOR	=	FUTURES EQUI-VALENT PRICE
3% of '95	77-06		.5566		138-22
$3\frac{1}{2}$% of '98	77		.5593		137-22
$8\frac{1}{4}$% of '99	95-06		1.0432		91-08
$7\frac{7}{8}$% of '00	89-10		.9887		90-11
$8\frac{3}{8}$% of '00	93-24		1.0336		90-22
8% of '01	90-10		.9998		90-11
$8\frac{1}{4}$% of '05	92-20		1.2052		90-11
$7\frac{5}{8}$% of '07	86-16		.9608		90-01
$7\frac{7}{8}$% of '07	90-21		.9868		91-28
$8\frac{3}{8}$% of '08	93-22		1.0397		90-04
$8\frac{3}{4}$% of '08	97-06		1.0800		90-00

Final price of deliverable future is based on settlement price.

that date, March 21, 1979. The futures contract, however, is priced to reflect the cheapest deliverable bond; hence the prices of the deliverable cash bonds have to be adjusted on the basis of yield equivalency with an 8% bond selling at par. This is accomplished by using price factors that discount the prices of the bonds whose coupons are above 8 percent. These factors are taken from bond tables selected by the exchange. Because of the shape of the yield curve one bond may have the least costly equivalent futures price. For example, on March 21, 1979, the cheapest bond was the $8\frac{3}{4}$ percent of 2008 whose cash price was 97-06 or \$918.75. This kind of contract and price conversion is called a price maintenance contract. Alternative price conversions are based on yield maintenance. For example, for yield maintenance contracts the settlement price on the last trading day determines the yield to maturity of the traded bond. This bond has a fixed coupon such as 8 or 9 percent, and its yield to maturity will be greater or less depending on market conditions in the cash market on delivery date. All deliverable bonds are then priced to yield this fixed yield to maturity determined by the settlement price and fixed coupon of the expiring future.

The differences in prices, shown in Table 7.6, highlight the relationship among prices, coupons, yield to maturity, and the term structure of interest rates. These relationships are not entirely transparent.

6.1 Price, Term Structure, and Yield to Maturity

The following calculation shows the *change in yield to maturity, dR_{TM}*, as a function of changes in the forward rates of interest for a zero coupon discount bond. If $r_i, i = 1, 2, \ldots, n$ is the set of forward rates of interest and R_{TM} is the yield to maturity, then since

$$1 + R_{TM} = \sqrt[n]{\prod_{i=1}^{n} (1 + r_i)},$$

the change in the yield to maturity is

$$dR_{TM} = \sum_{i=1}^{n} \frac{1}{n}\left[\prod_{j=1}^{n} (1 + r_j)^{1-n/n}\right] \prod_{j \neq i}^{n} (1 + r_j)dr_i.$$

where dr_i is the change in the rate of interest at time i.

For a coupon bond with semiannual payments with T years to maturity the change in yield to maturity as a function of changes in the forward rates of interest is

$$dR_{TM} = \frac{\sum_{j=1}^{2T} \frac{jc}{(1 + r_j)^{j+1}} dr_j + \frac{2T \times 1000}{(1 + r_{2T})^{2T+1}} dr_{2T}}{\sum_{j=1}^{2T} \frac{jc}{(1 + R_{TM})^{j+1}} + \frac{2T \cdot 1000}{(1 + R_{TM})^{2T+1}}}.$$

where c is the semiannual coupon payment. Since some dr_j may be positive and some negative and the relationship is nonlinear in R_{TM}, the change in the yield to maturity is not intuitively obvious.

7 SUMMARY

Financial analyses of investment opportunities among different financial instruments and between the cash and futures markets are complicated by the different pricing conventions for those instruments and markets. The relationships and correspondences between prices and rates in the cash and futures markets were presented along with select market anomalies that influence the calculation of prices and rates. In addition several examples were given to demonstrate calculations for comparative investment and arbitrage purposes. Included among them was an application of Gresham's Law for treasury bonds.

To be sure, investment in financial instruments also has an element of risk. As for other commodities, this risk is measured typically by the variation around the expected rate of return. No effort was made here to outline the various forms of this measurement. This issue was considered in the previous chapter and the relationships noted there apply with equal weight to financial commodities.

Regardless of the type of commodity, there are accounting conventions and regulations that dictate the calculation of returns as well as the tax treatment of commodity investments. To be sure, accounting and tax considerations can strongly influence expected returns and risks and subsequent investment decisions. Tax considerations and accounting conventions are the subject of the next chapter. The estimation of hedge ratios for financial assets are discussed in the Appendix to this book.

8 BIBLIOGRAPHY

EINZIG, PAUL, *Textbook of Foreign Exchange*. New York: Macmillan, 1966.

Federal Reserve Bank of New York, "Interest Rate Futures," *Quarterly Review*, Winter, pp. 33–46, 1979–80.

HOMER, SIDNEY, and MARTIN L. LEIBOWITZ, *Inside the Yield Book*. New York: Prentice-Hall, Inc., and New York Institute of Finance, 1972.

JAR, FRANK C., and JAMES E. WEST, "The Effect of Call Risk on Corporate Bond Yields," *The Journal of Finance*, 22 (December 1967), 312–325.

LOOSIGIAN, ALAN M., *Interest Rate Futures*. New York: Dow Jones–Irwin, 1980.

New York Futures Exchange, *Regulations of the New York Futures Exchange*. New York: New York Futures Exchange, 1980.

SANDOR, RICHARD L., "Trading Mortgage Interest Rate Fortunes," *Federal Home Loan Bank Board Journal*, 8, No. 9 (September 1975), 14–22.

SCHWARTZ, EDWARD F., *How To Use Interest Rate Futures Contracts*. New York: Dow Jones–Irwin, 1980.

SENFT, DEXTER E., *Pass-Through Securities*. Boston: First Boston Corporation, March 1978.

SHARPE, WILLIAM F., *Investments*, 2nd ed. Englewood Cliffs, N.J.: Prentice-Hall, Inc., 1981.

SMITH, C. W., JR., "Options Pricing: A Review," *Journal of Financial Economics*, January-March 1976, pp. 3–51.

SWISS BANK CORPORATION, *Foreign Exchange and Money Market Operations*. New York: Swiss Bank Corporation, July 1978.

8

REGULATION

‖‖‖

1 INTRODUCTION

In order to understand the commodities markets it is necessary to know the operating structure of the markets. This includes the steps involved in a trade, the role of different players along the route, and the regulations, reports, and accounting rules that shape their actions and define their responsibilities.

The purpose of this chapter is to summarize the major elements of these procedures, rules, and regulations. Primary emphasis is placed on the futures markets where regulatory authorities and regulations abound. The cash markets are governed by the laws of contracts and are not repeated here except for select tax aspects of trading. Section 2 describes the network of an illustrative commodity futures transaction. Included here are a description of the various stages of the trade, the participants at each stage, and their role. Section 3 summarizes the major rules and regulations that define the activities and responsibilities of the various market participants. In this section special emphasis is given to the reporting requirements set by the Commodities Futures Trading Commission (CFTC). Selected rules and regulations of the self-governing bodies of the various commodity exchanges are presented in Section 4. While these rules vary from exchange to exchange a common thread of intent exists for all of them. This section summarizes the common characteristics of these rules and objectives. Commodity trading rules and regulations of the Internal Revenue Sevice (IRS) are presented in Section 5. The rules and regulations of other regulatory authorities including state insurance commissions, state banking commissions, and pension fund authorities also are highlighted. Once again these rules and regulations vary in technical detail from state to state and only their common intents are summarized. The chapter is summarized in Section 6.

2 THE NETWORK OF A FUTURES TRADE

In order to get a better understanding of the role and incidence of regulation, it is worthwhile to understand the network through which orders are brought to the floor of an exchange and executed. Figure 8.1 illustrates

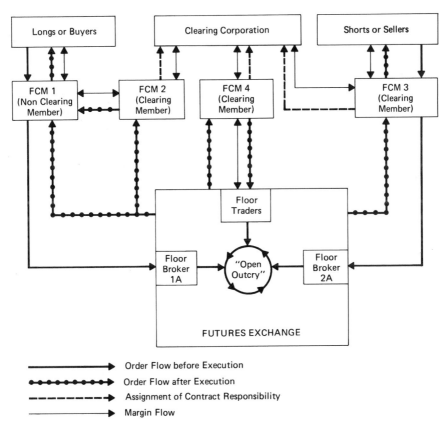

Figure 8.1

THE NETWORK OF A FUTURES TRADE

the basic network of a trade, for a ring or pit system as opposed to an electronic exchange.

Let us turn, first, to the participants. In Figure 8.1 the buyers and sellers are nonmembers of the exchange. Hence their orders must be brought to the floor by an approved member. An approved member is one who can deal with the public. There are two kinds of individuals who can deal, that is, solicit and accept orders, from the public. They are *futures commission merchants* (FCMs) and *associated persons* (APs) of the FCM. The distinction between an FCM and an AP is that an FCM must also accept margin payments. It should be noted that the customer representative or typical commodities broker who is an employee of an FCM must be an AP.

The FCM who is also a member of the clearing corporation transmits the order to the floor where a *floor broker*, a member of the exchange, will attempt to execute the order by open outcry in the pit or ring. The floor broker executes orders for others and earns a commission for each trade done. In the network the FCM is an agent for the customer and the floor broker is an agent for the clearing corporation. The clearing corporation assumes the responsibility of guaranteeing to each customer, both buyer and seller, that the contract will be satisfied according to the rules of price and delivery. Hence, the agent for the customer, the FCM, and the agent for the exchange, the floor broker, are relieved of responsibility as a guarantor of the futures contract.

The *floor traders* who also participate in the open outcry trading are exchange members, or nominees of members, who trade for their own account and cannot deal with the public. But they too must *clear* their trades with a clearing member FCM as shown in Figure 8.1. While all FCMs can receive orders from the public and receive margin payments not all FCMs are clearing members: It may not pay to be an FCM clearing member. Clearing member FCMs handle the margin responsibility for open trades. Consequently, their financial requirements are greater than those of nonclearing member FCMs. These financial requirements can be costly or otherwise difficult to meet for small FCMs. Hence, an FCM who is not a clearing member FCM, for example, the FCM 1 in Figure 8.1, will first funnel the trade to a clearing FCM who will assume responsibility of meeting the margin and accounting requirements set by the clearing corporation and the CFTC. The FCM 1 does not deal with the clearing corporation. When the order is finally executed by open outcry in the commodity ring or pit, only the price, bid or offer, is hit or taken. When this is done a contract is created.

Given the role of the participants in this network, bids and offers can be initiated by both members and nonmembers as illustrated by the network flows in Figure 8.1. Floor traders are not only "scalpers," looking to take advantage of short-term, intraday or intrahour price patterns. They can be representatives of large commercial firms, traditionally trading as hedgers.

Since the futures contract is standardized as to kind and delivery only the price is considered on the trading floor. When a price is hit an executory contract is created. An executory contract is a contract that has not been fully performed. In this sense a futures contract represents a promise to perform over some fixed horizon extending to the maturity date of the contract. The executory nature of an open futures contract has tax and accounting implications as discussed in Section 5.

An electronic exchange differs from the ring or pit system in two major ways. First, the ring or pit is replaced by an electronic trading system that records, assembles, and disseminates bids and offers and confirms trades for each participant. Although the bids and offers are available for all market participants to see, the confirmations only go to the parties in the trade. (The parties in the trade are recognized by their member identification codes.) Second, there are no floor brokers or floor traders. As with all futures exchanges all trades must be cleared through a clearing member and the contracts are made with the clearing corporation.

3 CFTC REGULATIONS AND THOSE REGULATED

The need for regulation arises from two concerns: assuring that the fiduciary responsibility of those who deal with customer funds is upheld and that the integrity of commodity prices as reflecting "normal" supply and demand conditions is maintained. The latter concern is directed to controlling the degree of speculation and controlling the extent to which any individual can participate in commodity futures trading.

The imprint of regulation in the commodities industry is nonexistent in the direct placement market, except for that embodied in the law of contracts and taxation. In contrast, futures trading in the United States can only be done on organized commodity exchanges that are regulated by the Commodity Futures Trading Commission (CFTC).

The CFTC was authorized by Congress in the Commodity Exchange Act of 1974 to replace the Commodity Exchange Authority. Its five commissioners are appointed by the president. Besides regulating all futures trading in the United States, it has jurisdiction over commodity options and gold and silver *leverage contracts* (off exchange futures contract) that are presented to the public through brokerage services.

By statute, the CFTC appoints an executive director and a general counsel. The executive director is responsible for the management and coordination of operations in accordance with the general policies of the commission. The general counsel is chief legal officer of the commission, and represents the commission in various legal capacities and performs other legal and review functions for the commission.

The CFTC is organized functionally in three operating divisions: Enforcement, Economics and Education, and Trading and Markets. It is the intent and purpose of the commission that such functional structuring will facilitate a responsiveness to the public without unnecessary bureaucracy and regulatory delay. *Enforcement* handles customer complaints and reparations, allegations of fraud or manipulations, and all other enforcement proceedings. *Economics and Education* conducts economic research, education, and market surveillance. *Trading and Markets* performs contract market analysis and designation functions that includes which exchange(s) will be allowed to trade what commodities and contract maturities, and supervises audit and registration procedures.

An *Office of Hearings and Appeals* is responsible for implementing adjudicatory hearings required by the Commodity Futures Trading Commission Act, and usually heard by administrative law judges or hearing officers. It is also responsible for adjudicating reparation controversies.

Other staff offices are *Congressional Relations, Intergovernmental Affairs, Policy and Planning, Public Information,* and *Secretariat.*

From the authority granted in the Commodity Exchange Act come the regulations that govern all who deal in futures.

3.1 Individuals

Individuals are regulated in the following manner by the CFTC:

1. Futures contracts are only legal when done on an organized exchange, and cannot be struck by two individuals.
2. Large traders are required to report their open positions. For example, for interest rate and foreign currency futures 25 open contracts is a minimum reportable speculative position.
3. The CFTC restricts the size of a position that can be taken depending on the commodity and the intent, speculative versus hedge, of the transaction.
4. The CFTC may require disclosure of trading identity of a foreigner.
5. Individuals cannot purchase or sell gold and silver leverage contracts.
6. Individuals must satisfy maintenance margin requirements or the FCM can liquidate the open position.
7. The CFTC can restrict liquidation of a futures contract in other than the spot futures contract month when price limit moves are exceeded since trading must be done on the exchange.
8. The CFTC can force the exchanges to increase margin requirements.
9. The CFTC can suspend trading in any contract as well as order trading for liquidation purposes only.

10. The CFTC restricts FCMs and floor brokers from disclosing customers' orders and trading ahead of customer orders as well as trading against customer orders. These rules are known as the "dual trading" rules.

While the objective of individual regulation is protection, the objective of exchange member regulation is performance.

3.2 Futures Commission Merchants and Associated Persons

Since the futures commission merchant (FCM) solicits and accepts orders from the public, FCMs and their associated persons (APs) must register and be approved by the CFTC. Moreover, the CFTC requires that the FCM not only screen his APs but also take pains to determine that individuals who are the clients of FCMs and their APs are "qualified" to trade futures contracts. Considerations that an FCM must make with respect to customer eligibility revolve around the financial status and character of the customer. The FCM will or should assess each customer as to:

1. Net worth
2. Family structure
3. Employment history
4. Personal traits
5. Ability to understand and take risk

Because of the nature of leverage inherent in futures trading, the CFTC requires that customer protection rules be satisfied before orders can be solicited from the public. Hence, the CFTC requires that every FCM notify his customers in writing that futures trading is risky. This written disclosure statement must be given to customers before trading can commence and be updated periodically. Furthermore, it is the responsibility of the FCM to make sure that the customer can comprehend the risks that a commodity futures position entails and the position must continually be appropriate to the financial character of the investor. Since customers deal with the FCM through the typical "broker," the AP, it is the responsibility of the FCM to screen his agents.

As part of dealing with the public, the FCM accepts customer margin payments. In order to maintain the integrity of customers' funds the CFTC regulates the financial requirements of FCMs including minimum capital requirements. As a further safeguard, the CFTC requires the segregation of customer margin payments. An FCM receives margin payments prior to initiating a trade, these funds must be segregated from the funds or working capital of the FCM: no commingling of funds is allowed. However the FCM may use the margin funds to buy treasury bills. While the T-bills purchased with margin funds must go into the segregated accounts the interest on them goes to the FCM.

Upon initiating a trade, margin must be deposited with the clearing corporation since it assumes responsibility for performance. An FCM who is not a clearing FCM must make an intermediate margin transaction with an FCM who is a clearing member. Upon establishing a position, *initial margin* must be posted with the clearing corporation. This margin payment may be made in cash, T-bills, or a letter of credit. Subsequent margin payments, owing to price movements against the position, are called *maintenance margin* and are made in cash. (This allows the daily marking to market of futures contracts to be done on a good funds basis.)

In complying with these regulations several reporting requirements have to be satisfied by an FCM. Among the more common reports are the following:

1. Audited annual and unaudited quarterly financial reports
2. Segregation of funds records to ensure the integrity of margin deposits
3. Transactions records of customers
4. Financial ledger record for each customer
5. Daily trade journal for the FCM
6. Monthly point balance that reconciles customers' open positions
7. Large trader reports
8. Reports by hedgers

3.3 Commodity Trading Advisors

The commodity trading advisor (CTA) is an individual or corporation who advises the public with respect to commodities. While the nature of the services provided by a CTA are advisory and typically directed towards trading, that is not the sole guideline for CTA status. Information services about commodities, regardless of whether they provide specific trading advice and regardless of whether they are in a printed form, can require CTA classification if compensation in some form is anticipated. In this sense the CFTC's jurisdiction expands beyond the limits of commodity futures trading. CTA regulations, reporting requirements, and registration can apply if the information deals only with cash commodities except foreign currencies and government debt instruments.

In dealing with the public, CTAs are required to make available their written communications that constitute their advice. They must also include a risk disclosure statement and schedule of fees for their advice. If CTAs trade for their own account in commodities for which they give advice to others the CTA is required to notify clients that the principals of the CTA intend to trade for their own accounts the same commodities that may enter into the trading decisions of the managed account. However, CTAs are not required to list all of their trades nor are they required to allow clients to examine their books with respect to their own trades.

Many CTAs develop their own trading algorithms based upon select technical analysis. These "secret" trading rules become proprietary and clients do not have the right to have free access to the foundations of, and trading rules emanating from, such systems. Such trading systems can be used by a CTA to manage individual discretionary accounts. For this the CTA receives a fee. This fee can comprise both a service charge and a share of the profits. A CTA, however, cannot pool funds of individual clients, but a CTA can be the advisor to a commodity pool or an FCM. It should be pointed out that individual accounts managed by a CTA, whether on a discretionary (CTA controlled) or nondiscretionary (client controlled) basis, must assume all risk inherent in the positions created.

Being a CTA means that formal registration with the CFTC must be made and renewed every year. The CFTC reserves the right to reject an application for CTA status.

3.4 Commodity Pool Operators

Just as mutual funds satisfy the need for diversification with respect to securities, many individuals have a desire to diversify commodity investments. The brokerage industry has responded to these needs by providing various commodity pools geared to the small investor. The individual who solicits and brings together funds to share risk and return is known as a *commodity pool operator* or CPO.

Many commodity pools are organized as limited partnerships and the commodity pool operator is the general partner. This structure is for tax purposes to avoid any double taxation of profits. Moreover, most pools hire a CTA who is responsible for the trading decisions.

While a CPO may manage more than one pool, a CPO is restricted from commingling funds from any pool with the property of another person, including any personal account of the CPO. However, in order to take advantage of discounts emanating from trading volume, pool orders may be combined.

Commodity pool operators, like CTAs must apply for and be accepted for registration with the CFTC.

The question of whether commodity pools are securities and, hence, whether their offering must be registered with the SEC is still open to debate. The characteristics of a security that may be associated with a futures commodity pool are (1) there exists a common enterprise attribute and (2) one derives profit solely from the enterprise of others. However, the fact that profits only accrue from price changes in commodity futures positions may not be considered as being derived from the enterprise of others.

In this regard the SEC has declared that it will not seek jurisdiction or attempt to exercise its regulatory authority over a limited partnership that restricts its investments to financial futures. However, most commodity pools offered to the public do register under the federal and state security laws to avoid conflicts over jurisdictional authority between the SEC and CFTC. Hence, most pools are offered through a prospectus that may include registration information sent to the CFTC and must include a risk disclosure statement.

4 EXCHANGE REGULATION

Since all futures trading done in the United States must be carried out on a regulated organized exchange, the first line of defense for maintaining trading integrity is self-regulation imposed by the exchanges themselves. The exchanges are private membership organizations geared to providing the trading arena, setting the professional standards of trading, and maintaining the integrity of the markets. The main thrust of exchange regulation is in the following areas:

1. Determining contracts to be traded
2. Defining the delivery conditions for the underlying asset of reference.
3. Setting flexible margin requirements that are responsive to underlying market price movements
4. Providing buyers and sellers with the clearinghouse function
5. Fixing the settlement price upon which open positions are marked to the market at the close of each day
6. Providing a mechanism for arbitration of both customer and trader disputes
7. Processing price and commodity information to both members and the public through both printed and electronic means
8. Fixing floor rules and procedures to guarantee uniform trading
9. Fixing the hours of trading and setting qualifications for trading upon the floor by members

4.1 Delivery

A major objective of exchange rules is to help ensure delivery as the futures contracts mature in the spot month. Without adequate supplies the specter looms that deliveries will not be made and the markets will be thrown into disarray. In order to minimize such a problem the exchanges have regulations that allow monetary settlement if the underlying asset of reference cannot be delivered.

4.2 Speculative Position Limits

Another major objective of the exchange rules is to prevent one individual or a group of individuals from capturing a large proportion of the open contracts, thus enabling them to control market prices. Here, the exchanges have established, in conjunction with the CFTC, limits on the number of open speculative contracts held for select commodities. These limits do not apply to individuals or corporations who qualify as bona fide hedgers, that is, to those with an equal but opposite position in the cash market. To establish bona fide hedging status the exchanges require all members acting as FCMs to obtain evidence that all hedging trades are in fact hedges.

4.3 Reporting of Trades

The exchanges also have strict rules dealing with the reporting of trades. These rules are directed to accuracy and precision as well as to timing of the price and quantity information. As part of this reporting process some exchanges require time stamping of all trades within a minute of receiving them and a minute of execution.

4.4 Settlement Prices

Another important area of exchange regulation is the determination of settlement prices. This problem of regulation stems from the open outcry process itself whether physical or electronic. The last trade may not occur at the close of trading and the bid and asked for prices during the close may be far different from the last traded price. The position of the exchanges in this regard is that the settlement price should reflect the bids and offers currently in the market and not necessarily those that transpired before the close. A common but not universal rule is to take the lowest bid as the official settlement price if no trades are executed on the close. When several trades are executed on the close the average of the last trade prices are often used to establish the settlement price. The importance of fixing the settlement price at a fair market level stems from the accounting importance of the settlement price. It is the settlement price that is used to mark to market the traders' positions and determine the variation margin calls.

4.5 Limit Price Moves

Another aspect of price regulation carried on by the various exchanges is the setting of price limit moves for various commodities. Exchanges have the right to change the price limits depending upon previous day's activities.

For example, if all contracts traded in a commodity have three successive days of limit up or down moves, then trading on the subsequent day may be subject to a price limit move of 150 percent of the previous limit. And this cycle can be repeated for subsequent limit moves. If, through the surveillance procedures of the various exchanges, it is discovered that price aberrations unconnected to supply and demand patterns exist, the exchanges do have the authority to suspend trading. This, of course, is a drastic action but nevertheless exists in the arsenal of exchange regulations.

In sum, the intent of exchange regulations is to foster professional trading and provide orderliness in trading and integrity for the pricing process. There is no self-interest for any exchange to do this job poorly. To the contrary, there is self-interest for the exchanges to control themselves.

5 IRS AND OTHER REGULATIONS

5.1 IRS Regulations

As everyone knows, living in a world of taxation is different from living in a world where decisions can be made independent of tax laws.

Today, commodity investments take place in a world of taxes, and gains or losses from investments in the futures markets are taxed at different rates than if they occurred in the cash markets. Among the factors influencing IRS tax treatment are (1) the definition of the taxable event, (2) the holding period of a long or short position, (3) whether one is a hedger or dealer or speculator and, (4) the economic justification of the trade.

5.1.1 The Taxable Event

The first thing that must be determined in trying to assess tax implications of futures trading is to establish a taxable event. First of all, futures transactions are not the same as buying and selling the underlying commodity. Hence they are taxed differently. When initial margin is posted with a broker and any subsequent maintenance margin payments are made, they have nothing to do with establishing the cost basis of the transaction.

Upon initiating a futures position an executory contract is created. Hence, as long as the position is held open, nothing is "bought" or "sold." However, since futures contracts are marked to the market daily upon fixing of the settlement price after the close of trading, money does change hands. This results in accumulations and withdrawals of good funds into the accounts of shorts and longs through the daily clearinghouse mechanism.

In this sense the futures contract has a value of zero at the opening of each day's trading. From a cash viewpoint profits and losses are realized. However, from a tax viewpoint there has not been established a taxable event. The taxable event occurs only upon closing out the position by either buying back or selling the futures position or by marking the contracts to market on the last trading day of the year, whichever comes first. (The difference in the initial price and closing or settlement price determines the gain or loss, and not the intermediate margin payments.)

5.1.2 The Holding Period

The holding period is the length of time the commodity is held. The commodity can be held in the form of a futures contract as well as physically. Indeed, if a futures contract is held to maturity and delivery is taken, the holding period will be the sum of the length of time the futures contract was held plus the length of time the physical commodity was held. However, if a long futures position was liquidated before maturity and the physical commodity was purchased and held for some period before being sold, the holding period of the commodity would not be the sum of the two holding periods but two distinct holding periods: one period for holding the futures position and another period for which the physical commodity was held.

If the closing of the contract results in the actual making or taking delivery of the physical contract then the holding period is adjusted by the time that the physical commodity is in the possession of the trader. For example, if ten July 1980 wheat contracts are purchased on January 2, 1980, and sold on July 15, 1980, then the holding period will be six months and two weeks. If delivery of the maturing July 1980 wheat contracts is taken and held until September 2, 1980, whereupon the wheat is sold in the cash markets, then the holding period for tax purposes is eight months. Likewise, if the commodity is one that is deliverable and is owned prior to entering a short futures position on January 2, 1980, the holding period associated with the futures position is extended by the duration of ownership of the physical commodity prior to January 2, 1980.

If the futures contracts are not closed on the last trading day of the year then they must be marked to market on that day and the resulting gain or loss is calculated as follows: 40 percent short term capital gain or loss and 60 percent long-term capital gain or loss. Hence, the maximum effective tax rate is 32 percent. These allocations apply to both outright and straddle positions. The commodity gains or losses are considered short-term capital gains or losses if the holding period is less than six months and long-term capital gains or losses if held for six months or longer.

5.1.3 Investors: long and short

The IRS treats non-cash settlement futures contracts as capital assets. Hence, for investors, profits and losses are broken down between either short-term or long-term capital gains depending upon the length the position was maintained and whether the initial transaction was a long or a short.

For example, if a futures trade initiated by a long position registers a capital gain or loss and it was held for less than six months, then the gain will be short term. If the gain or loss accrued over a period extending more than six months, then the gain or loss is considered long term. Since agriculture is a favored industry, especially among legislators, the six-month definition of long-term capital gain was maintained for gains and losses arising from trading futures contracts as opposed to the twelve-month definition which was imposed upon other capital assets during the Revenue Act of 1978. Hence, for an outright long position in a futures contract, only half as much time is necessary to lock in a capital gain in the futures market as opposed to the cash or forward markets. This favored treatment has not been given to stock index futures.

To further complicate matters for investors, the IRS does not take a symmetrical view of initial positions. The IRS views the unhedged short sale of a futures contract by an investor to be the sale of an asset which doesn't yet exist. In this sense the short sale is viewed as the placing of a bet and, hence, all short positions result in short-term gains or losses regardless of the duration of the contract.

For example, if on January 2 an investor sold ten November soybean contracts at a price of $9 per bushel and held that open position until September for a period of nine months and closed that position by buying them back at a price of $7 per bushel, the investor would net for tax purposes a profit of $2 per bushel or $100,000 for the ten contracts over the nine-month period minus transactions costs. This gain would be taxed as a short-term gain. Whereas, if the position were reversed in the sense that a speculator purchased ten November soybean contracts at a price of $7 per bushel in January and held them until September when the price increased to $9 per bushel, the same monetary gain would be made. However, in this case the investor would be taxed as having made a long-term capital gain and the gain would be taxed at the maximum rate of 20 percent.

The only effect of this taxation rule is to discriminate between long speculators and short speculators. Another interesting anomaly is the way income is now treated from investing in treasury bills.

Before the Economic Recovery Act of 1981 treasury bills were not capital assets. Treasury bills, because they are purchased at a discount, were considered to have earned income, that is, interest income over their holding period, rather than generating a capital gain. Hence, if one bought a six-month treasury bill in the cash market and held it to maturity, interest income was earned. Whereas, if a futures contract in treasury bills was purchased and held for a period longer than six months before it was closed out, the gain on the futures contract would have been classified as a long-term capital gain rather than as the earning of interest. However, if a long-term gain was obtained in a T-bill futures contract and delivery was taken, then the subsequent sale of the cash T-bill might have converted a long term capital gain into ordinary income.

The holding of the physical commodity for more than six months prior to a short sale may result in a long-term capital loss if the commodities are used for delivery upon closing out a short futures position even if the short futures contract was held for less than six months. Since T-bills are now capital assets no ordinary gains and losses can be captured from combinations of cash and futures T-bill positions. As discussed in the next section, the intent of the transaction plays a role in determining its tax status.

5.1.4 Hedgers and Dealers

The holding period determines one of the conditions for fixing tax consequences but it is not the only one. The intent of the trade likewise has tax implications. Intent depends on the definition of the trader. Gains and losses that accrue as part of the ordinary course of doing business distinguish a hedger from a speculator. Hedgers do not make capital gains and losses upon positions in the futures markets since hedging is done in the ordinary course of business to offset their physical exposure.

This tax treatment holds even though hedgers may have different business characteristics when dealing in the cash commodity. For example, while a dealer in plywood buys and sells plywood, a builder, seeking to hedge building material costs, is typically only a purchaser of the commodity. Nevertheless, dealers and builders are treated as hedgers with respect to the tax status of futures trading. Hence, gains and losses become classified as income lost or made and do not usually qualify for a capital gain treatment. While there exists no clear definition of a hedge transaction, the following characteristics should generally be maintained:

1. There should be price correspondence between the futures transaction and the underlying commodity.
2. The timing of the closing of the futures contracts should match the closing of the cash transaction.
3. The underlying commodity should be used in the business of the hedger.
4. The trading activity among and across contracts should be minimized over the life of the hedge transaction.
5. The crossing of tax years by rolling over futures contracts should be avoided.
6. The motive for the hedge should be to stabilize profit and not lock in a loss.

While cross-hedging can be justified from a statistical point of view, the tax laws may not allow such transactions to be identified with allowable hedges. Hence, hedging a cash Brazilian cruzerios position with a linear combination of Japanese yen, deutschemarks, and soybeans awaits an IRS ruling.

5.1.5 Short Sale Rules and Straddles

One tax advantage in trading futures contracts as opposed to securities is that the short sale rule does not apply. That is, if the identical futures contract, other than in an identified straddle, is purchased within 30 days, a loss or gain can still be established. However, all transactions should have a business rather than just a tax purpose.

Before the Economic Recovery Act of 1981 one of the most controversial areas of taxation and its involvement with trading in futures contracts, was the controversy surrounding the so-called "tax straddle." The idea behind the "tax straddle" was to generate a sequence of losses and gains that crossed tax years in such a way that losses against income were incurred in the current tax year and equal long-term capital gains were established that matured in the following tax year. The most common forms of tax straddles are cash and carry transactions and so-called double-spread tax straddles sometimes referred to as butterfly straddles. Each of these types of transactions is discussed below. However, there are IRS perspectives and issues of risk that are common to both.

The IRS position against tax straddles is based on the philosophy that the transactions should not be purely tax motivated. That is, if there is no chance for profit before taxes and no risk of loss but only an after-tax benefit then the transactions have no real economic justification. The IRS views tax straddles as riskless and therefore does not allow them.

Straddles in general, and not just tax straddles, have risk characteristics that are less extreme than outright positions. Nevertheless, they are not without risk. Indeed, apparent tax straddles may have significant risk of loss or gain depending on how the positions are held. In the *Smith* vs *The IRS* case noted below, if the futures positions had been held to the spot month when the trading limits are removed from the maturing contracts, the risk profile could have been much different. Under these conditions the prices on the spot contracts could fluctuate without restriction while the prices on the more distant contracts would still be subject to limits on their price movements and significant risk could have been encountered. The specific details of the trades that distinguish tax-straddles from legitimate trades can slip by the unsophisticated observer.

5.1.6 The Cash and Carry

A cash and carry transaction is typically the purchase of the cash commodity, the sale of a futures contract, and the carrying or inventorying of that cash commodity for delivery against the short futures contract. Cash and carry strategies involve not only the leverage inherent in the futures contract but also the leverage from financing the cash position by using the physical commodity as collateral. These leverages make it easy for many non-dealers and non-professionals to engage in these trades. Some seeking only tax benefits have used cash and carry transactions to generate commission and interest charges against current income and a deferred capital gain. Another variation on this theme is to generate a long-term capital gain to offset a long-term capital loss and generate short-term interest and commission charges in the same amount but taxed at income rates.

If the trades are done from the posture of a dealer, then any interest costs are considered financing charges and can be deducted as expenses. If the intent of trading is that of a speculator or investor then any interest or financing charges may be subject to the investment interest expense limitation, in which case the scale of cash and carry transactions become restricted.

In sum, while tax avoidance and planning is a vital concern of business decision making, the tax authorities take a dim view of transactions that have no other purpose but to convert short-term gains or income into long-term gains or to freshen up loss carry-overs. Being on safe ground means that commodity futures and cash transactions must be economically justified.

5.1.7 Economic Justification

Many types of commodity trades can lead to short-term losses and longer-term rewards that may be taxed at different rates. For example, when a short-term loss is incurred and a near-offsetting long-term gain is established, as a consequence of the same trade(s), both the gains and losses may be taxed as an integrated set of transactions rather than two separate transactions unless economic justification can be given for the trade(s). Here, economic justification means an underlying business activity that offers a possible and probable net gain before consideration of tax differentials. The purpose of demonstrating economic justification, of course, is to show there is more than just tax advantage to the trade(s) and thereby establish economic intent.

The case of *Smith* vs. *The IRS* (1981) illustrates one application of the rule of economic justification. Here, Smith entered into combinations of straddle trades that simultaneously established short-term losses at the end of one year and long-term gains at the beginning of the next tax year. The losses incurred from the commodity futures trading were used to offset short-term capital gains received earlier from an independent event. The deferred gains from the commodity futures trading activity that offset the losses were claimed as long-term capital gains. The trades conducted by Smith were done in the futures market and are referred to as butterfly straddles. These straddles consist of two simple straddles that share a common short position, for example, long March '74 silver and short July '74 silver in one straddle and short July '74 silver and long December '74 silver in the other straddle. Taken together these two straddles make up a single straddle with a "near" and "far" long position and an intermediate short position. Subsequent to establishing this type of straddle position Smith changed the maturity profile of the straddles. In particular the March '74 long position was switched to a May '74 long position and the December '74 long position was switched to a September '74 long position. The result of these switches was to create a loss from the March '74 and December '74 contract liquidations, that was a taxable event in 1973, and created a deferred gain in the futures market that was claimed in 1974 when the open contracts were liquidated in February 1974.

In this case, the evidence against any economic justification was strong and was not counterbalanced by evidence supporting any economic justification. In particular, the prices affixed to the spread trades were set at values that maximized the short-term loss but could have been affixed at prices that would have greatly reduced the claimed loss. Furthermore, the switch trades establishing the claimed short-term loss and long-term capital gain did not have any historical probability of improving the speculative nature of the commodity trading. Since the trades could not be justified from an economic perspective the *futures* gains and losses were netted one against the other and the advantages from using the differential tax rates were eliminated. That is, the short-term capital loss in the futures market could not be netted against the short-term capital gain obtained from an independent transaction.

5.2   Other Regulations

Institutional participants in the commodities markets and particularly in the financial future markets are subject to regulatory restrictions and control from several sources. For example, banks are regulated by the Federal Reserve Board, the Comptroller of the Currency, the Federal Deposit Insurance Corporation, and state banking commissioners, the extent depending on their charter and membership. Insurance companies are regulated by state insurance commissioners, and pension funds come under the aegis of the prudent man rule and the Employment Retirement Income Security Act.

5.2.1   Banks

In November 1979 the Comptroller of the Currency formally pronounced that forward contracting in both the cash and futures markets as well as in the options or standby commitments markets were complementary. Hence, bank participation in them could be viewed as effective means of controlling risk exposure. Trading or hedging strategies and tactics did not require any approval by the Comptroller. However, the board of directors became responsible for setting the guidelines under which participation in the various contracting markets took place. Furthermore, exact matching of cash versus futures or forward instruments was not required in order for a transaction to be considered a hedge. However, in order to highlight any risk that might ensue from trading in leveraged futures contracts, the Comptroller requires that all forward or futures contracts be carried on the accounts of the bank on a mark-to-market basis. While this procedure records futures losses on a daily basis, any offsetting gains from a hedged cash position may be carried at historical values, thereby, causing accounting profit and loss accruals that do not reflect the value of the hedged position. Certain segments of the banking industry, for example, mortgage bankers that have instituted accounting procedures geared to forward trading, are excluded from the mark-to-market reporting requirement.

While no specific guidelines have been set with respect to banks acting as agents for others in doing both direct placement and exchange forward contracting, banks do take security interest in futures contracts that arise from contractual obligations in a loan agreement. Hence, financing processors and manufacturers can lead to acquiring the rights to a futures contract if default occurs. In such a case the bank can liquidate the futures position to obtain funds that are due. Under such circumstances the CFTC has ruled that this transaction is neither a sale nor a purchase since it was created by the actions of a third party. This kind of transaction can create the only form of off-exchange trading of futures contracts.

Since banks act much like a dealer with respect to financial instruments, there are no restrictions on banks being members of organized commodity exchanges. Many banks, especially those with large multinational branch networks, have become members of futures exchanges and contribute to the liquidity of the futures markets especially in financial instruments, foreign exchange and precious metals.

5.2.2 Insurance Companies

Regulation while being even-handed in one area may be completely discriminatory in another. Insurance companies in many states have been denied the authority to trade futures contracts. Moreover, the prospect of uniform participation independent of location is complicated by having separate insurance company regulation for each state. However, recent fluctuations in the prices of financial instruments have heightened the need for such participation, and restrictions are being removed.

What is interesting is that while futures trading by the large insurance companies was prohibited, trading in exchange traded options was considered a prudent policy. Consider the following statement by the New York State Insurance Department issued in 1974.

Previously the sale of an option could result in an insurer losing control
of the underlying stock upon which the option was written, as the seller
had little choice but to await either the exercise of an option by the
holder or its expiration. With the advent of regulated option exchanges,
this objection is no longer present.[1]

Why futures trading is disallowed to a group of corporations who have
need to hedge financial exposure can only be understood by a view that
overemphasizes the specter of overspeculation by people who have a fiduciary
responsibility. Unfortunately, not to hedge is to speculate, and too narrow
a regulatory view may cause less rather than more prudence.

5.2.3 Pension Funds

As fiduciaries, pension funds have legal obligations to their benefi-
ciaries. They are accountable for being loyal and exercising care and diligence in their investment decisions. The regulation of such behavior is
embodied in the laws of trust and the Employee Retirement Income Security
Act (ERISA) of 1974. ERISA provides a firmer foundation from which a
"prudent man" may participate in futures trading. This comes about because
of the implicit concentration of the returns to the portfolio of investments
as an entity rather than judging each individual investment in isolation.
This is an important distinction when examining the returns of a hedge
transaction, since, by its nature, one side of a hedge will typically show a
gain and the other a loss. But again, since futures trading exhibits a high
degree of leverage, explicit rules should be laid out describing the strategies
of futures trading that the fiduciary can assume. Otherwise, exposure to
liability may come about for the plan manager.

Given the following prudent man guidelines under ERISA, there
appears to be no economic basis to prohibit their trading in commodities
including futures and direct placement option markets.

The prudent man shall consider:

1. The overall portfolio mix of return and risk and diversification
2. Comparable volatility of the portfolio returns to market returns
3. The ability to earn returns commensurate with funding objectives
4. The ability to have sufficient liquidity to satisfy plan payments to bene-
   ficiants
5. The underlying economics of the investments undertaken

None of these criteria should prove a barrier to the alternative forms of
contracting that are available.

[1](11 NYCRR 174 1974); Regulation No. 72.

5.2.4 National Futures Association (NFA)

In September of 1981, Congress sanctioned the NFA as an industry self-regulatory body. All FCM's, CTA's and CPO's that deal with the public must join the NFA. The purpose of such regulation is to provide more timely control and improve the integrity of commodity trading on organized exchanges.

6 SUMMARY

The modes of regulation come from government agencies such as the CFTC, from the common law of contracting and trusts, and from the tax agencies of governments and private associations such as the regulatory bodies of the commodity exchanges. The purpose of such regulation is geared toward maintaining integrity of contracting in commodities markets and to afford customer protection against misrepresentation, inadequate business performance, and inappropriateness of risk taking.

7 BIBLIOGRAPHY

ARTHUR ANDERSEN & CO., *Accounting and Control Techniques for Banks,* Chicago: Chicago Board of Trade and Chicago Mercantile Exchange, 1978.

ARTHUR ANDERSEN & CO., *Federal Tax Implications,* Chicago: International Monetary Market, CME, 1979.

The Business Lawyer, 35 (March 1980). Entire issue devoted to commodity futures trading.

Commodity Exchange Act as Amended and Regulations Thereunder. Chicago: Commerce Clearing House, 1977.

Commodity Exchange Incorporated., *Regulations of the Commodity Exchange Incorporated,* New York: Commodity Exchange Incorporated, 1981.

INTERNAL REVENUE SERVICE, Internal Revenue Service, Revenue Ruling 77–185; Washington D.C., 1977.

OPPENHEIM, APPEL, DIXON & CO., *Interest Rate Futures Trading Accounting and Control,* New York: Amex Commodities Exchange, Inc., 1979.

1979 Report of the Secretary of the Treasury, Washington D.C., Department of Treasury. pp. 283–93.

9

ACCOUNTING PERSPECTIVES ON FUTURES CONTRACTING AND FORWARD AND STANDBY COMMITMENTS

▮▮▮

1 INTRODUCTION

The existing accounting literature on futures transactions, forward and standby commitments is unsettled. Indeed, the accounting principles recommended by different sources are often at odds with one another and all have been applied in practice. This diversity of accounting treatments understandably has caused concern among businesses, the U. S. Congress, financial institutions, supervisory agencies, and the accounting profession.

As a result of the divergence in practice, various organizations are seeking clarification of existing accounting literature to eliminate diversity in financial reporting. While a consensus has not yet been reached, one is emerging. This chapter discusses some of the issues surrounding the accounting treatment of common types of forward commitments, futures transactions, and standby commitments that financial institutions and other business enterprises are entering into.

Section 2 focuses on accounting considerations that are unique to futures trading on organized exchanges. Section 3 reviews some of the major accounting issues surrounding the treatment of futures, forward, and standby commitments from the perspective of the firm or individual entering into these transactions. Section 4 presents several examples of the accounting treatment of hedging transactions. These examples represent recent recommendations and illustrations of the American Institute of Certified Public Accountants (AICPA). The chapter is summarized in Section 5.

2 ACCOUNTING CONSIDERATIONS FOR FUTURES MARKET INTERMEDIARIES

Since futures are marked to market daily there are accounting procedures that impact the various participants. For futures commissions merchants (FCMs) and the clearing corporation, the books must reconcile daily price changes to accommodate margin payment requirements.

2.1 The Clearing Corporation

At the end of the day the clearing corporation provides a trade sheet for each commodity contract month traded for each FCM. This lists all open trades, longs and shorts, the price at execution, the settlement price, and the resultant gain or loss for each trade for that day.

The clearing corporation then aggregates the months traded for each commodity, for each FCM, to come up with a recapitulation sheet that exhibits the cash flows that are owing to the FCM from the clearing corporation or to the clearing corporation from the FCM. Each clearing corporation establishes its own rules with respect to net or gross cash flows due from each of its FCMs.

2.2 The Futures Commissions Merchant

Futures commission merchants must segregate customer margin funds. When margin is deposited, a general ledger entry is made crediting the customer's account. Prior to a trade, however, margin funds must be deposited with the clearing corporation. Upon execution of a trade no general ledger entry is made to record the value of the position. Since gains and losses accrue daily, an off-line entry in a difference account is created. The Commodities Futures Trading Commission (CFTC) requires the FCM to reconcile the difference accounts with the general ledger. This is called point balance reconciliation. Through point balance reconciliation the FCM monitors customer accounts with respect to credit lines, size of trading, risk position and margin requirements. It should be noted that the FCM may require more than the minimum margin, both initial and maintenance, from their customers.

When a futures trade is closed, then the profits accrued in the difference sheets and any residual margin are posted to the general ledger and the customer is sent a statement of profit and loss. At this time the full round turn commission is charged. With respect to the latter, competition sets the price and quantity discounts are common.

Just as FCMs have daily cash obligations with respect to trading so do their clients. While there are no fixed accounting rules for all commodities transactions, aside from tax considerations, mark-to-market procedures will limit accounting exposure and allow better control of trading procedures. This is often done more than once a day. For example, FCMs of floor traders, will check intraday positions to control the risk that a floor trader may pass on to the FCM if too large an overnight position is carried.

3 ACCOUNTING FOR FORWARD PLACEMENT, FUTURES CONTRASTING, AND STANDBY COMMITMENTS[1]

3.1 Some Preliminaries

Regardless of the type of trader or corporation involved, the following list of auditing and control problems and procedures need to be addressed to assure integrity of commodity trading:

1. The bonding of employees, brokers, and traders

2. Monitoring private trading of employees

3. Maintaining adequate frequency of reports and positions

4. Setting limits on trading authority

5. Distinguishing account positions when trading across markets (e.g., some London futures do not mark-to-market and no variation margin must be made)

6. Protecting against unauthorized trading, whether for the house or going beyond explicit discretion granted

7. Establishing parallel audit trails

8. Monitoring the risk position for determining adequate coverage

3.2 Issues to Be Resolved

Although firm rules for the treatment of futures, forward, and standby commitments have not yet been achieved, the American Institute of Certified

---

1. American Institute of Certified Public Accounts, "Accounting for Forward Placement and Standby Commitments and Interest Rate Futures Contracts," Issues Paper (Washington, D.C.: AICPA, December 16, 1980), pp. 38–51.

Public Accountants has studied the major issues and made recommendations for each. Briefly the major issues are:

1. Should the accounting treatment for forward, futures, and standby transactions be consistent?
2. Should the assets and liabilities underlying forward, futures, and standby contracts be recorded in the accounting records before the settlement date?
3. If the assets and liabilities underlying forward, futures, and standby contracts are not recorded in the accounting records before settlement date, how should business enterprises account for changes in market price of the contracts between the trade and settlement dates?
4. Are criteria needed for ascertaining whether forward and futures contracts are entered into as hedges?
5. If the cash transaction does not occur when an anticipatory hedge is closed out, when should gains and losses on the forward and futures positions be recognized?
6. If an anticipatory hedge is extended or rolled over, should gains and losses be recognized currently or deferred to maturity of the extension or rollover?
7. When should an enterprise recognize gains and losses on forward and futures contracts used to hedge assets?
8. If hedged securities are deliverable under the terms of forward and futures contracts, should "locked in" gains and losses be amortized over a period ending with the maturity of the contracts?
9. If a series of futures contracts (referred to as a strip) is entered into for successive delivery months, how should gains and losses relating to each component of the strip be accounted for?
10. What financial statement disclosures should be made for open forward and futures positions?

3.3 AICPA Recommendations

Based on AICPA task force reports and other related position papers and standards, the AICPA has issued recommendations regarding each of ten issues listed above.

3.3.1 Consistency

The accounting treatment for financial futures and forward placement transactions should be consistent. They are alternative transactions similar to foreign exchange futures and forward transactions. However, in forward transactions under which a standby commitment is sold, the transaction should be accounted for as a "put" option. The premium received (standby commitment fee) on the sale of the option should be recorded as a liability representing the market value of the standby commitment on the trade date. Thereafter, the liability should be accounted for on a market value basis. The writer (seller) of the option should report the option in the liability section of the balance sheet and subsequently adjust it to its current market value (payment required to close out the open standby commitment). Unrealized gains or losses should be credited or charged to current income. For example, if the current market value of the option exceeds the premium received, the excess is a loss; if the premium exceeds the current market value of the option, the excess (limited to the amount of the premium received) is a gain. The higher of cost and market valuation for standby commitments should be followed rather than the mark-to-market method when an entity uses the lower of cost and market value for similar types of short-term or other trading positions. Obtaining the market value of a stand-by commitment may sometimes be difficult, thereby necessitating a fair value determination. Among the many factors to be considered in determining the fair value of a standby commitment are the price of the underlying asset, the liquidity of the market, and the time remaining to the settlement date.

In contrast, the purchase of a standby commitment is a transaction similar to a purchase of a forward placement contract (except for the premium paid), and the buyer should account for the transaction as a forward placement contract. Standby commitments not purchased for hedging should be accounted for on a market value basis. Premiums paid on standby commitments purchased as a hedge of an asset should be deferred and included in the determination of the gain or loss on the standby commitment.

3.3.2 Recording on the Balance Sheet

Assets and liabilities underlying a forward and futures contract should not be recorded in the balance sheet on a trade date basis, except as prescribed for investment companies and municipal bond funds. The accounting treatment recommended is consistent with the accounting treatment for other types of commitments, including foreign exchange forward commitments.

3.3.3 Presettlement Recording

Changes in market values of forward and futures contracts should generally be recognized currently in the income statement. This basis of accounting (commonly referred to as "mark-to-market") should be used when (1) the forward and futures contracts are entered into for speculation: (2) forward and futures contracts represent hedges of asset positions, contemplated asset purchases, or short positions, all of which are, or will be, carried at market value; or (3) the criteria for hedge accounting for specific hedging transactions are not met. However the lower of cost and market valuation for forward and futures contracts should be followed rather than the mark-to-market method when an entity uses the lower of cost and market method for similar types of short-term or other trading positions.

3.3.4 Hedging Criteria

Criteria should be established to distinguish hedge from nonhedge situations. The following are the recommended criteria:

1. At the time the forward commitment or futures contract is entered into, its purpose should be specifically identified and documented as part of the accounting records. The dollar amount and description of the asset or liability for which the hedge is intended should be specified.

2. The price of the forward commitment or futures contract and the hedged assets or liabilities should have a high degree of positive correlation, that is, the tendency to move in the same direction with similar magnitude.

3. For an anticipatory hedge, the anticipated transaction should reasonably be expected to be fulfilled in the ordinary course of business.

If these criteria are met, a specific hedge is entered into and hedge accounting should be followed.

The establishment of criteria to identify specific hedging situations in which hedge accounting is to be applied is based on the presumption that in the absence of evidence to the contrary, the intended cash transaction will occur and will conform to the timing originally contemplated and documented as part of the accounting records. Failures to complete transactions as originally intended may indicate that the activity is a speculative trading activity. For example, if an enterprise repeatedly closes out anticipatory hedges and recognizes gains, stating that the original intended cash market transactions will not occur, then market value accounting should be followed for subsequent futures and forward transactions.

3.3.5 Anticipatory Hedging

A forward or futures contract entered into as an anticipatory hedge should extend at least to the anticipated transaction date. The intended use of successive futures contracts satisfies this condition if the futures market precludes a single contract covering the entire period. However, if a forward or futures contract previously considered as a hedge of an anticipatory transaction is closed out, paired off, or otherwise terminated before the cash transaction date, the deferred gain or loss, if any, should continue to be deferred and included in the measurement of the dollar basis of the asset acquired or the liability incurred. If it becomes known that the anticipated cash market transaction will not occur, the deferred gain or loss on the forward or futures contract should be recognized immediately in income.

3.3.6 Rollovers

If an anticipatory hedge is extended or rolled over and such extension or rollover was not previously contemplated in the original anticipatory hedge transaction, the extension or rollover should be accounted for as a completed transaction. The deferred gain or loss, if any, should be recognized immediately in income. For example, if a forward commitment to purchase securities is entered into as an anticipatory hedge with the anticipated transaction date being the maturity of the forward commitment and it is extended or rolled over, any unrealized gain or loss on the forward commitment should be recognized in income on the extension or rollover date.

3.3.7 Recognition of Gains and Losses

The deferred gain or loss on a forward or future contract used to hedge an asset accounted for on a cost basis should be recognized when the hedged asset is sold. However, if the short forward or futures position is closed out before the hedged asset is sold, the carrying amount of the asset should be adjusted for deferred gains or losses. The carrying amount of the asset, however, should not be adjusted to an amount in excess of the fair market value of the asset at the date the hedge position is closed out. A premium or discount resulting from the adjustment to the carrying amount should be amortized over the remaining life of the asset as interest income. It should be noted that the Economic Recovery Act of 1981 does not allow open positions to be carried over tax years without tax consequences unless one is a dealer or hedger.

3.3.8 Amortization of Loss

If a hedged security is deliverable under a forward or futures contract used as a hedge, and if a loss is attributable to the hedge, the loss should be amortized to income over the life of the forward or futures contract; a gain attributable to the hedge should not be recognized until the forward or future contract is closed out or the hedged asset is sold.

3.3.9 Strip Ratability

A futures strip should be viewed as one security transaction bearing a composite yield to be recognized ratably over the life of the strip.

3.3.10 Disclosure

In specific hedging situations the amount of long and short forward and futures positions as well as the nature of the hedging activity should be disclosed in an enterprise's financial statements. Further, gains and losses deferred under hedge accounting for open positions should also be disclosed.

4 EXAMPLES OF HEDGE ACCOUNTING[2]

Because the nature of a hedge is not always clear-cut, the following examples from the AICPA (1980) illustrate the offset of the recomendations. The assumptions used in the examples:

- Margin requirement on futures contract is $1,000 per contract.
- Daily settlement is made in cash with the broker for all interest rate futures gains and losses.
- Commissions and fees are ignored.
- Premium amortization and discount accretion are ignored.
- All accounting journal entries are made on a pretax basis; that is, income tax effects of transactions are ignored.

4.1 Short Hedge of Investment Security Accounted for on a Cost Basis

Summary of hedge transaction. On October 12, 1979, an institution purchased $10 million 8¾ percent U. S. treasury bonds due August 1994, at a price of 89.30 or a cost of $8,993,750. Having funded the investment with short-term deposits and fearing an increase in interest rates, management decides to hedge this investment by selling short 100 December '80 U. S. treasury bond futures contracts on the XYZ Exchange at a price of 83.16.

The hedge is maintained until March 31, 1980, when the U. S. treasury bonds are sold at a price of 74.10, and the futures position is closed out by buying 100 December '80 U. S. treasury bond futures contracts on the XYZ Exchange at a price of 67.27. (See Table 9.1.)

4.2 Anticipatory Hedge of Purchase of GNMA Pass-Through Certificates

Summary of hedge transaction. On January 1, 1980, an institution, currently funding its home mortgage loan portfolio with fixed rate, long-term deposits, anticipates reinvesting its expected mortgage repayments of $900,000 over the next six months in GNMA pass-through certificates. Fearing interest rates will fall before such a reinvestment can take place,

---

2. Ibid.

Table 9.1
ACCOUNTING JOURNAL ENTRIES

	DEBITS	CREDITS
October 12, 1979		
Investment in U.S. treasury bonds	$8,993,750	
Cash		8,993,750
(To record purchase of $10 million $8\frac{3}{4}$% U.S. treasury bonds due August 1994 @89.30.)		
Margin Deposit with Broker	$100,000	
Cash		$100,000
(To record margin deposit for short sale of 100 December '80 U.S. treasury bond futures contracts @ 83.16.)		
October 13–31, 1979		
Cash	$312,500	
Deferred Gain/Loss on Short Hedge of Investment Security		$312,500
(To record cash settlements with broker for gain on futures position. Futures price is 80.12 on October 31, 1979. $31.25 × $(83\frac{16}{32} - 80\frac{12}{32})$ × 100 = $312,500.)		
Month Ended November 30, 1979		
Deferred Gain/Loss on Short Hedge of Investment Security	$265,625	
Cash		$265,625
(To record cash settlements with broker for loss on futures position. Futures price is 83.01 on November 30, 1979. $31.25 × $(83\frac{1}{32} - 80\frac{12}{32})$ × 100 = $265,625.)		
Month Ended December 31, 1979		
Deferred Gain/Loss on Short Hedge of Investment Security	$62,500	
Cash		$62,500
(To record cash settlements with broker for loss on futures position. Futures price is 83.21 on December 31, 1979. $31.25 × $(83\frac{21}{32} - 83\frac{1}{32})$ × 100 = $62,500.)		
Three months Ended March 31, 1980		
Cash	$1,581,250	
Deferred Gain/Loss on Short Hedge of Investment Security		$1,581,250
(To record cash settlements with broker for gains on futures position. Futures price is 67.27 on March 31, 1980. $31.25 × $(83\frac{21}{32} - 67\frac{27}{32})$ × 100 = $1,581,250.)		
Cash	$100,000	
Margin Deposit with Broker		$100,000
(To record return of margin deposit from broker upon closing out of short futures position by buying 100 December '80 U.S. treasury bond futures contracts @ 67.27.)		
Deferred Gain/Loss on Short Hedge of Investment Security	$1,565,625	
Gain on Sale of Investment Securities		$1,565,625
(To recognize deferred gain on short hedge at time it is closed out.)		
Cash	$7,431,250	
Loss on Sale of Investment Securities	1,562,500	
Investment in U.S. treasury bonds		$8,993,750
(To record loss on sale of $10 million $8\frac{3}{4}$% U.S. treasury bonds due August 1994 @ 74.10.)		

management decides to protect the institution against the risk of falling interest rates by entering into a forward placement contract to purchase a $1 million $9\frac{1}{2}\%$ GNMAs pass-through certificate for delivery on June 1, 1980, at a price of 88. The institution and the seller (brokerage firm) agree that "good delivery" of $9\frac{1}{2}\%$ GNMAs will be within $2\frac{1}{2}\%$ ($\pm$) of the $1 million principal balance. (See Table 9.2.)

Table 9.2

ACCOUNTING JOURNAL ENTRIES

	DEBITS	*CREDITS*
January 1 through May 30, 1980 (No entries are necessary as forward placement contracts require no margin deposit or daily cash settlements for market value fluctuations over the holding period. Recorded as a memo item.)		
June 1, 1980 Investment in GNMA $9\frac{1}{2}\%$, Pool No. XXXXX	$874,654	
Cash		$874,654
(To record purchase of $9\frac{1}{2}\%$ GNMA, Pool No. XXXXX delivered with a current face amount of $993,975, within the $2\frac{1}{2}\%$ range for "good delivery.")		

4.3 Anticipatory (Long) Hedge of Purchase of Investment Security to Be Accounted for on a Cost Basis

Summary of hedge transaction. A company owns $5,000,000 of securities maturing on May 1, 1980. On October 1, 1979, management decides to hold these securities to maturity and then reinvest the proceeds upon maturity in four-year U. S. treasury notes. Having funded the existing securities with long-term, fixed-rate liabilities and fearing a decrease in interest rates, management decides to hedge this anticipated transaction by buying 50 May '80, four-year U. S. treasury note futures contracts on the ABC Exchange at a price of 92.18.

The anticipatory hedge is maintained until April 30, 1980, when it is closed out by selling 50 May '80, four-year U. S. treasury note futures contracts on the ABC Exchange at a price of 89.50.

On May 2, 1980, the company buys $5,000,000 $9\frac{1}{2}$ percent U. S. treasury notes due May 1984, at a price of 98.17. (See Table 9.3.)

4.4 Anticipatory Hedge of Debt Issuance

Summary of hedge transaction. On January 15, 1980, a company finalizes its plans to issue $25 million, ten-year notes in late March 1980. On that date management decides to hedge against the risk of rising interest

Table 9.3

ACCOUNTING JOURNAL ENTRIES

	DEBITS	CREDITS
October 1, 1979		
Margin Deposit with Broker	$50,000	
Cash		$50,000
(To record margin deposit for purchase of 50 May '80 U.S. treasury note futures contracts @ 92.18.)		
Three Months Ended December 31, 1979		
Deferred Gain/Loss on Long Hedge of Investment Security	$182,754	
Cash		$182,754
(To record cash settlements with broker for loss on futures position. Futures price is 88.40 on December 31, 1979. $15.62 \times (92\frac{18}{64} - 88\frac{40}{64}) \times 50 = \$182,754$.)		
Three Months Ended March 31, 1980		
Deferred Gain/Loss on Long Hedge of Investment Security	$402,996	
Cash		$402,996
(To record cash settlements with broker for loss on futures position. Futures price is 80.36 on March 31, 1980. $15.62 \times (88\frac{40}{64} - 80\frac{36}{64}) \times 50 = \$402,996$.)		
Month Ended April 30, 1980		
Cash	$460,790	
Deferred Gain/Loss on Long Hedge of Investment Security		$460,790
(To record cash settlement with broker for gain on futures position. Futures price is 89.50 on April 30, 1980. $15.62 \times (89\frac{50}{64} - 80\frac{36}{64}) \times 50 = \$460,790$.)		
Cash	$50,000	
Margin Deposit with Broker		$50,000
(To record return of margin deposit from broker upon closing out of long futures position by selling 50 May '80 U.S. treasury note futures contracts @ 89.50.)		
May 2, 1980		
Investment in U.S. treasury notes	$5,051,522	
Deferred Gain/Loss on Long Hedge of Investment Security		$ 124,960
Cash		$4,926,562
(To record purchase of $5,000,000 $9\frac{1}{2}$ U.S. treasury notes due May 1984 @ 98.17, and to include deferred loss on anticipatory hedge in the measurement of the dollar basis of the treasury notes purchased.)		

rates, between January 15 and the date the debt is to be issued, by selling short 350 June '80 U. S. treasury bond futures contracts on the XYZ Exchange at a price of 80.16.

As feared by management, interest rates increase; however, on March

14, 1980, management believes that interest rates have stabilized and may begin to fall. Therefore, on March 14, management decides to close out the short futures hedge position by buying 350 June '80 U. S. treasury bond futures contracts on the XYZ Exchange at a price of 69.08. The $25 million, ten-year notes are issued on March 28, 1980. (See Table 9.4.)

Table 9.4

ACCOUNTING JOURNAL ENTRIES

	DEBITS	CREDITS
January 15, 1980		
Margin Deposit with Broker	$350,000	
Cash		$350,000
(To record margin deposit for short sale of 350 June '80 U.S. treasury bond futures contracts @ 80.16.)		
January 16–31, 1980		
Cash	$1,881,250	
Deferred Gain/Loss on Hedge of Debt Issuance		$1,881,250
(To record cash settlements with broker for gain on futures position. Futures price is 75.04 on January 31, 1980. $31.25 $\times$ $(80\frac{16}{32} - 75\frac{4}{32}) \times 350 = \$1,881,250$.)		
Month Ended February 29, 1980		
Cash	$2,143,750	
Deferred Gain/Loss on Hedge of Debt Issuance		$2,143,750
(To record cash settlements with broker for gain on futures position. Futures price is 69.00 on February 29, 1980. $31.25 $\times$ $(75\frac{4}{32} - 69) \times 350 = \$2,143,750$.)		
March 1–14, 1980		
Deferred Gain/Loss on Hedge of Debt Issuance	$87,500	
Cash		$87,500
(To record cash settlements with broker for loss on futures position. Futures price is 69.08 on March 14, 1980. $31.25 $\times$ $(69\frac{8}{32} - 69) \times 350 = \$87,500$.)		
Cash	$350,000	
Margin Deposit with Broker		$350,000
(To record return of margin from broker upon closing out of short futures position by buying 350 June '80 U.S. treasury bond futures contracts @ 69.08.)		
March 28, 1980		
Cash	$25,000,000	
Deferred Gain/Loss on Hedge of Debt Issuance	3,937,500	
Notes Payable—Principal		$25,000,000
Notes Payable—Unamortized Hedge Gain		3,937,500
(To record issuance of debt and establish an unamortized gain account to be amortized over twenty-five years.)		

5 SUMMARY

While this chapter addressed accounting issues related to transactions in forward and standby commitments as well as futures contracting in commodities, the emphasis was not placed on issues of storage cost, spoilage, or transportation costs. These considerations are well established in the accounting literature and their treatment is not diverse or unclear. Rather, the discussion focused on those issues that have not yet found a consensus and are likely to be a problem after one is found. Among the most important of these is the definition of a hedger, and the monitoring and accounting treatment of hedging transactions. Another important issue is the treatment of futures, forward, and standby commitments on the books of firms both before a liquidation has occurred and after. Although several generalities can be found, the principal task still facing the accounting profession is to establish rules that can accommodate the idiosyncrasies of the various types of commodities. As familiarity with the different commodities markets grows accounting rules will evolve to meet them with consistency and precision. The AICPA recommendations summarized here are a major step in this direction and provide guidelines for future variations on these themes.

6 BIBLIOGRAPHY

AMERICAN INSTITUTE OF CERTIFIED PUBLIC ACCOUNTANTS, "Accounting Practices in the Mortgage Banking Industry," Statement Position 74–12.
———, "Audit and Accounting Guide for Savings and Loan Associations," S&L Guide.
———, "Inventory Pricing," *Accounting Research Bulletin,* No. 43, Ch. 4.
ARTHUR ANDERSON & CO., "Interest Rate Futures Contracts—Accounting and Control," Chicago, September 1978.
FINANCIAL ACCOUNTING STANDARDS BOARD, "Accounting for the Translation of Foreign Currency Transactions and Foreign Currency Financial Statements," Statement of Financial Accounting Standards (SFAS) No. 8. Connecticut.
MORTGAGE BANKERS ASSOCIATION, "Accounting for GNMA Mortgage Interest Rate Futures Market Transactions," Accounting Opinion No. 2.
OPPENHEIM, APPEL, DIXON & CO., "Interest Rate Futures Trading Accounting and Control," *CPA Journal,* April and May 1980.

II

ELEMENTS OF OPERATIONS RESEARCH AND TIME SERIES ANALYSIS

One cannot proceed in commodity analysis without at least a heuristic understanding of several important concepts in time series analysis, probability and statistics, decision theory, and mathematical programming. The objective of Part 2 is not to educate the reader in each of these disciplines but, rather to provide an introduction to them. Its purpose is one of correspondence: to set forth essential concepts in probability, statistics, time series analysis, decision theory and mathematical programming in the context of commodity analysis to provide a perspective for all that is to follow.

Even a cursory review of commodity analyses and trading operations reveals a "discipline" that is "engineered" to meet the special needs of its environment. While the term employed to describe these characteristics are at times inconsistent and/or seemingly arbitrary they nevertheless reflect an important fact: The empirical characteristics of commodity prices do not always adhere to the tenents of mathematical statistics and well-behaved time series that are necessary to perform rigorous scientific analyses. This observation is not presented to give license to every wandering effort. On the contrary, it has been raised to better segregate that which is known and proven from that which is unknown and untestable. Without this distinction, the gap between knowledge and understanding cannot easily be bridged.

Despite the limited objective of these chapters is it nevertheless difficult to select those concepts that are most important for commodity market analysis and trading operations. No doubt the selection made here omits topics that some consider crucial and includes topics that others consider unnecessary. In addition to "artistic license," our selection of topics is as much dictated by experience as it is by theory.

10

ELEMENTS OF PROBABILITY
AND STATISTICS

IIIIIIIIIIIIIIIIIIIIIIIIIIIIIIIIIIIIIIIIIIIIIIIIIIIIIIIIIIIIIIIIIIIIIIIIIIIIIIIIIIIIIIIIIIIIIIIIIIIIIIIIIIIIIIII

1 INTRODUCTION

Probability and statistics are of special importance to the commodity analyst and trader. Indeed they live with them everyday. Future (as well as past) commodity prices, unlike the path of a planet, cannot be estimated without encountering unexplainable disturbances. Yet, the commodity trader must make decisions despite this veil of uncertainty. The material presented here covers select topics in probability and statistics that are especially useful to measure this uncertainty and pave the way for improved decision making. The intent is to introduce terms, concepts, and procedures in the context of commodity trading and analysis, not to explore their theoretical heritage. For a more rigorous and general discussion of the concepts introduced in this chapter the reader is referred to the supplemental readings provided in the bibliography.

2 PROBABILITY

Because the future price of a commodity cannot be determined exactly and forecast prices can strongly influence current trading decisions the analyst and trader necessarily encounter the notion of likelihood that a certain outcome may or may not occur. In general, this likelihood may be referred to as a *probability:* a number less than or equal to 1 and greater than or equal to 0 that expresses the relative frequency of occurrence of an outcome of an experiment that together with the probabilities for all other possible outcomes for that experiment sums to 1.

To the commodity trader the next business day may be viewed as the *experiment* and the price the commodity takes on that day is the *outcome*. The question "Where will price be tomorrow?" is an imprecise rendition of the question "What is the probability the price will be greater than (or less than) or equal to some specific value x?" Symbolically this probability may be denoted

$$P \text{ (price} \geq x)$$

for the greater than or equal to case.

2.1 Mutual Exclusivity and the Law of Addition

Outcomes or events are said to be *mutually exclusive* if only one of them can occur on any one trial or experiment. If A and B are two mutually exclusive events, then the probability of either of them occurring is the sum of their respective probabilities. Symbolically,

$$P(A + B) = P(A) + P(B).$$

If A and B are not mutually exclusive events, then the probability of either occurring is equal to the sum of their respective probabilities less the probability of both happening. That is,

$$P(A + B) = P(A) + P(B) - P(AB).$$

For example, a trader may have positions in two different commodities and may be interested in the probability that the price of either one will go up. Here event A may be viewed as the price increase in the first commodity and event B as the price increase in the second commodity. Clearly A and B are not mutually exclusive. Because both prices could increase, the probability that either will increase is the sum of their individual probabilities less the probability that both may occur.

2.2 Independence

The probability that both A and B might occur depends in part on whether they are *independent events* or not. If they are, the probability that both commodities will increase in price is equal to the product of their respective probabilities of occurrence. That is,

$$P(AB) = P(A)P(B).$$

If *A* and *B* are not independent, the probability that both may occur is equal to the probability of one event times the probability of the other event conditioned on the occurrence of the other event. Symbolically,

$$P(AB) = P(A)P(B|A)$$

where $P(B|A)$ denotes the probability of event *B* given, that is, conditioned on the occurrence of event *A*. If events *A* and *B* are independent then $P(B|A) = P(B)$.

2.3 Joint, Marginal, and Conditional Probabilities

The consideration of joint events gives rise to the notions of joint, marginal, and conditional probabilities. The relationships between these probabilities are easily shown in the following example. Consider four possible joint events or outcomes of price changes over two consecutive days: (up, up); (down, down); (up, down); (down, up). Suppose these joint events have *joint probabilities* of .40, .10, .25 and .25, respectively. By definition, the *marginal probability* of a price rise on the first day is the sum of the joint probabilities of getting a price increase the first day followed by a price increase the second day and getting a price increase the first day followed by a price decrease the second day. This *relationship between joint and marginal probabilities* is shown in Table 10.1, together with other marginal probabilities.

Table 10.1

JOINT AND MARGINAL PROBABILITIES
OF SUCCESSIVE WHEAT PRICE CHANGES

	CHANGE IN PRICE OF WHEAT DAY 2		
CHANGE IN PRICE OF WHEAT DAY 1	Up 20¢	Down 20¢	*MARGINAL PROBABILITY*
Up 20¢	.40	.25	.65 (up Day 1)
Down 20¢	.25	.10	.35 (down Day 1)
Marginal Probability	.65 (up Day 2)	.35 (down Day 2)	1.00

Often the commodity analyst is interested in the probability of an outcome "conditioned" on the occurrence of another event. In the context of the above example an analyst may seek the *conditional probability* of an increase in price the second day, given that the price dropped the first day. The probability of this conditional outcome is denoted *P* (up Day

2|down Day 1), where the vertical line is read "conditioned upon." By definition the conditional probability of an outcome is the joint probability of the outcome divided by the marginal probability of the condition. From Table 10.1 the conditional probability would be

$$P(\text{up Day 2}|\text{down Day 1}) = \frac{\text{Joint probability of (down Day 1, up Day 2)}}{\text{Marginal probability of (down Day 1)}}$$

$$= \frac{.25}{.35}$$

$$= .714.$$

With regard to Table 10.1 the probability of *either* a price increase in Day 1 *or* a price increase in Day 2 is

$$P(\text{up Day 1 or up Day 2}) = P(\text{up Day 1}) + P(\text{up Day 2}) - P(\text{up Day 1 and up Day 2})$$

$$= .65 + .65 - .40$$

$$= .90.$$

Table 10.1 can also be used to illustrate another important property of joint, marginal, and conditional probabilities. In general, consider two events, A and B. The probability of event A conditioned on event B, $P(A|B)$, is equal to the joint probability of both events occurring divided by the marginal probability of event B occurring. Similarly, the probability of event B occurring conditioned on event A occurring, $P(B|A)$ is equal to the joint probability of both events happening divided by the marginal probability of event A. That is,

$$P(A|B) = \frac{P(A \text{ and } B)}{P(B)}$$

and

$$P(B|A) = \frac{P(A \text{ and } B)}{P(A)}$$

respectively. With a little rearranging these relationships imply

$$P(A)P(B|A) = P(B)P(A|B),$$

or

$$P(B|A) = \frac{P(B)P(A|B)}{P(A)}.$$

The practical importance of this result far outweights its simplicity: Given one set of marginal and conditional probabilities one may be able to calculate other conditional probabilities of more pressing importance. This lies at the heart of Bayesian analysis. Deferring that topic for the moment, the application of the above result can be shown with regard to Table 10.1. Suppose event *A* corresponds to a 20¢ price increase in Day 1 and event *B* corresponds to a decrease in price of 20¢ on Day 2. Moreover, suppose an analyst only has the following probabilities: the marginal probability of event *A*, $P(A) = .65$, the marginal probability of event *B*, $P(B) = .35$, and the conditional probability of event *A* given that event *B* occurs (perhaps based on past information), $P(A|B) = .714$. The analyst then could calculate the probability of a price decrease in Day 2 given that that price increased in Day 1. From Table 10.1 these probabilities are

$$P(B|A) = (.35) \frac{.714}{.65}$$

$$= .385.$$

2.4 Bayesian Analysis

Commodity analysts and traders almost always are confronted with the problem of revising their estimates of commodity price moves owing to the occurrence of some other event. This other event may be viewed as an indicator of the price movement and has a certain degree of reliability. Here, *reliability* is a pseudonym for the conditional probability that the indication will occur given that a particular price movement or some other event occurs. Before the additional information is available the analyst will have "*prior*" *probability* estimates of the commodity price outcomes. Subsequent to the new information, that is, after the occurrence of the indication, the analyst can revise the prior probabilities of the commodity price outcomes and obtain "*posterior*" *probabilities* estimates of their occurrence.

The infusion of the new probability information with the prior probabilities to obtain posterior or revised probabilities is the essence of Bayes Theorem. In general, Bayes Theorem is nothing more than a restatement of the relationships between conditional, marginal, and joint probabilities. For two events *A*1 and *A*2 and a third conditioning event *B* the conditional probability of *A*2 given *B* can be written as the ratio of the (joint) probability of the joint event (*A*2, *B*), $P(A2, B)$, divided by the marginal probability of event *B*, $P(B)$:

$$P(A2|B) = \frac{P(A2, B)}{P(B)}$$

where, of course, $P(B) = P(A1, B) + P(A2, B)$ and events *A*1 and *A*2 are assumed to be mutually exclusive.

If these joint and marginal probabilities are not known, the desired conditional probability may still be obtained if other related marginal and conditional probabilities are available. According to Bayes Theorem the above conditional probability may be derived alternatively from the formula,

$$P(A2|B) = \frac{P(A2)P(B|A2)}{P(A2)P(B|A2) + P(A1)P(B|A1)}.$$

2.4.1 A Trading Example

For example, suppose the prior probability that the price of wheat will increase tomorrow is $P(\text{up}) = .3$ and the prior probability that the price of wheat will drop (tomorrow) is $P(\text{down}) = .7$. Suppose the analyst surveys select floor brokers after the close of business on the first day but before the opening of business on the second day and gets their opinions as to the price move expected the second day. This survey has shown itself to be .90 reliable. That is, 90 percent of the time the survey will indicate a forthcoming price increase (decrease) when in fact a price increase (decrease) does occur. Ten percent of the time the test will indicate a price decrease (increase) when in fact a price increase (decrease) took place the following day.

If the survey indicated a price rise for tomorrow the analyst's revised or posterior probability of a price rise tomorrow would be calculated from Bayes Theorem as follows:

$$P(\text{up}|\text{sur.ind.up}) = \frac{P(\text{up})P(\text{sur. ind. up}|\text{up})}{P(\text{up})P(\text{sur. ind. up}|\text{up}) + P(\text{down})P(\text{sur.ind.up}|\text{down})}$$

$$= \frac{(.3)(.9)}{(.3)(.9) + (.7)(.1)}$$

$$= \frac{.27}{.34}$$

$$= .794.$$

One must bear in mind that the reliability of the floor broker information in the above example is not the same as the conditional probability of the price going in a certain direction given that the floor broker information indicated the price was going in a certain direction. These are two different conditional probabilities: While both share the same joint probability, one is normalized by the marginal probability that a certain price movement occurs and the other is normalized by the marginal probability that the floor brokers will give a certain indication.

2.5 Objective and Subjective Probabilities

While important properties of probabilities have been noted, nothing has been said about the origin of their numerical values. Probabilities may be quantified in either of two possible ways: objectively or subjectively. *Objective probabilities* are determined through estimation in the form of relative frequencies based on recorded data or as some logical consequences of the underlying mechanism and the experiments related to it. *Subjective probabilities* are reflections of the analyst's belief or degree of confidence in the occurrence of an event based on whatever information is available. As is true for so many researchers, the commodity analyst frequently encounters the need to invoke both types of probability quantification.

The following sections are intended to provide some insight into the estimation and use of probabilities in statistical analyses.

2.6 Random Variables and Expected Values

Commodity analysts and traders must base their decisions or recommendations on outcomes that may assume a number of values owing in part to chance. In such cases, the outcomes of concern are referred to as *random variables*. For example, the price of wheat tomorrow may be considered a random variable insofar as its outcome may assume a number of different possible values based in part on chance. Typically, the analyst or trader will be interested in several characteristics of these random variables. Two of the most common are the *mean* and *variance*. These are measures of central tendency and dispersion around that measure of central tendency, respectively. The *expected value* of a variable when its possible outcomes are grouped, for example, from 0 to 49.99 . . . , 50 to 99.99 . . . , is the weighted average of the possible group outcomes where the weights are the probabilities of occurrence of the respective outcomes; that is, the expected value of X can be denoted $E(X) = \sum P_m X_m^*$ where P_m is the probability (relative frequency) of outcome m and X_m^* is the mid-value of discrete outcome m and $\sum$ denotes summation over all groups. If the expected value of X is a measure of *central tendency* and is equal to some constant u, then the *variance* of X can be defined as the expected value of the squared differences between the possible values of X_m^* and u weighted once again by the probabilities of those deviations occurring. That is,

$$\text{var } X = E(X - u)^2 = \sum P_m(X_m - u)^2.$$

Alternatively, if the data are not grouped, $E(X)$ and var X could be calculated as

$$E(X) = \sum_{i}^{n} X_i/n$$

and

$$\text{var } X = \sum_{i}^{n} (X_i - u)^2/n$$

respectively, where i denotes the ith individual outcome and n is the number of outcomes.

While the notion of expected value applies to an entire *population* as well as a *sample* from that population, the expected values of a sample need not, and often do not, equal their population counterparts. For now, the population mean and variance will be denoted by *u* and σ^2, respectively; the *sample mean and variance* will be denoted by $\bar{X}$ and S^2, respectively. The sample mean and variance are defined as

$$\bar{X} = \sum_{i=1}^{n} \frac{X_i}{n}$$

and

$$S^2 = \sum_{i=1}^{n} \frac{(X_i - \bar{X})^2}{n}$$

respectively.

2.7   Random Walk and the Probability of Ruin

Commodity prices fluctuate over time. Starting at a given date the price at this time—time 0—is at its initial value or "position." At subsequent times 1, 2, . . . the price will move a step either in the positive or negative direction. If the direction of each step is random, that is, not correlated with its previous steps, then the path of prices over time is said to follow a *random walk*. When a trader takes a position in the commodity markets either the price wanders until it reaches a point where the trader has lost all of his or her capital or a desired profit objective has been reached. At either of these two times the speculative "trials" terminate, that is, the game is over. Such a "game" is often referred to as a random walk with two absorbing barriers: one at zero (the loss of capital) and another at a value equal to the original capital plus desired winnings. This variation of the random walk is referred to as the *classical ruin problem*. For any given constant probability of a profitable price move or step, fixed initial capital, and fixed bet size, the probability of ultimate ruin can be determined. To determine the probability of ultimate ruin let

p = Probability of a profitable price move in a single step

$q = (1 - p)$

C = Initial capital

b = Betting size

π = Desired profit

A = Players advantage over the market: $A = p - q > 0$.

q_k = Probability of ruin

$k = C/b$; the number of initial betting units

$z = C + \pi$, trading goal

$a = \pi/b$, profit in terms of number of trading units

$f = z/b$, trading goal in number of trading units

Following Feller[1] the outcome of the first trial in terms of the number of betting units is either $k + 1$ or $k - 1$. Therefore, after the first trial the probability of ruin may be written

$$q_k = pq_{k+1} + qq_{k-1}$$

where q_{k+1} is the probability of ruin if the first trial is a success (i.e., a profitable move), and q_{k-1} is the probability of ruin if the first trial is a failure. The boundary conditions on this difference equation are $q_0 = 1$; that is, when the capital has been exhausted the player is ruined and the probability of ruin is therefore 1, and $q_f = 0$; that is, when the player has won the probability of ruin is 0. The solution to this bounded difference equation is

$$q_k = \left(\frac{q}{p}\right)^k$$

for $q < p$. Since $A = p - q$, $2p = 1 + A$, and $2q = 1 - A$, and since $(q/p) = (2q/2p)$, the probability of ruin can be written

$$q_k = \left(\frac{1 - A}{1 + A}\right)^k.$$

For example if the player had \$10 in capital and the bets were \$2, the number of trading units would be $10 \div 2 = 5$. Moreover, if the probability of winning was $p = .55$ then the advantage of the player would be $A = p - q = .10$, and the probability of ruin would be

$$q_k = \left(\frac{.9}{1.1}\right)^5$$

$$= .366.$$

A variation on the above theme is the probability of ruin before reaching the trading goal when starting from any accumulated position. For example, what is the probability of ruin after accumulating \$50,000 in profits starting with an initial capital of \$10,000 but desiring a trading goal of \$100,000, that is, \$50,000 more profit? It has been shown by Coolidge[2] that this probability can be written

$$q_{k,a} = \frac{1 - (p/q)^a}{1 - (p/q)^{a+f}}$$

$$= \frac{[(1 + A)/(1 - A)]^a - 1}{[(1 + A)/(1 - A)]^{a+k} - 1}$$

where $a = \pi/b$ and $f = a + k$.

1. William Feller, *An Introduction to Probability Theory and Its Applications*, Vol. 1, 2nd ed. (New York: John Wiley, 1957), pp. 313–15.
2. Julian Lowell Coolidge, *An Introduction to Mathematical Probability* (New York: Dover, 1962), pp. 53–54.

Finally it must be noted that for a given probability of winning, p and initial capital C, the probability of ruin decreases when the size of the bet is increased.

2.8 Probability Distributions

A *probability distribution* of a discrete random variable, X, that can assume values $X_1, \ldots, X_n$ with associated probabilities $p_1, \ldots, p_n$ has the following properties:

$$p_i \geq 0 \text{ for all } i$$

and

$$\sum p_i = 1.$$

Frequently, commodity analysts are interested in the probability that a price will lie above (or be less than or equal to) some value, X^*. Here the *cumulative probability distribution* provides this measure. For example, the probability that a price is greater than or equal to X^* is

$$P(X^*) = 1 - \sum_{X_i < X^*} p_i.$$

This notion can be extended to consider the probability that X lies in a given interval. For example, the probability that X lies at or above value X_1 but less than or equal to X_2 is

$$P(X_1 \leq X \leq X_2) = 1 - \sum_{X < X_1} p_i - \sum_{X > X_2} p_i.$$

For a continuous probability distribution, sometimes referred to as a *probability density function*, $f(x)$, the corresponding properties are

$$\int_a^b f(x)\, dx = 1,$$

$$P(x - x^*) = 1 - \int_{x^*}^b f(x)\, dx,$$

and

$$P(x_1 \leq x \leq x_2) = \int_{x_1}^{x_2} f(x)\, dx,$$

where $\int$ denotes integration, b and a are the upper and lower bounds of the values x can take and dx denotes the differential of x. It can be shown that the probability of a specific outcome x^* is equal to zero.

There are several well-explored types of probability distributions that are commonly used by commodity traders and analysts. Some of them are listed in Table 10.2 together with select comments on their application and character.

These distributions have many business applications in commodity trading and several of them are spelled out in this and subsequent chapters. Among the most important applications are hypothesis testing and confidence interval construction. The binomial and normal distributions also are used in the valuation of options discussed in Chapter 5.

Table 10.2

SELECT PROBABILITY DISTRIBUTIONS
USED IN COMMODITY ANALYSIS

Binomial

$$f(x) = \frac{n!}{x!(n-x)!}(1-P)^{n-x}P^x$$

where n is the number of experiments, x is the number of "successes," p is the probability of a "success," $(1-p)$ is the probability of a failure, and ! denotes factorial.

Normal (Limit of the Binomial as $n \longrightarrow \infty$)

$$f(x) = \frac{1}{\sqrt{2\pi}\sigma}e^{-1/2(x-u)/\sigma^2}$$

Here x may be arithmetic or the log value of some number greater than zero.

t-Distribution

$$f(t) = c\left(1 + \frac{t^2}{v}\right)^{-(v+1)/2}$$

where $t = (\bar{x} - u)/s_{\bar{x}}$, c is a constant, $v = n - 1$, n is the sample size, $\bar{x}$ is the sample mean and $s_{\bar{x}}$ is the standard deviation of $\bar{x}$. If $(\bar{x} - u)/\sigma$ is normally distributed, replacing σ with the estimate $s_{\bar{x}}$ results in the t-distribution.

F-Distribution

$$f(F) = cF^{(v_1/2)-1}\left(1 + \frac{v_1}{v_2}F\right)^{-(v_1+v_2)/2}$$

where $F = \hat{\sigma}_c^2/\hat{\sigma}_r^2$, $\hat{\sigma}_c^2$ is the between-column sample variance, $\hat{\sigma}_r^2$ is the between-row sample variance, c is a constant depending on v_1 and v_2, v_1 is the number of degrees of freedom for $\hat{\sigma}_c^2$ and v_2 is the number of degrees of freedom for $\hat{\sigma}_r^2$.

χ^2

$$f(\chi^2) = c(\chi^2)^{v/2-1}e^{-\chi^2/2}$$

where c is a constant depending on v, v is the number of degrees of freedom, e is the base of the natural logarithm, and $\chi^2 = \sum(f_o - f_b)^2/f_b$ where f_o = observed frequency and f_b a theoretical or specified frequency.

---

3 STATISTICS

Statistics can be defined as the mathematics of the collection, organization and interpretation of numerical data; especially the analysis of population characteristics by inference from sampling. As with most definitions, this one only scratches the surface. There are many types of sampling, different ways of estimating characteristics, multiple criteria for assessing estimators and of course, linkages and applicators to probabilities and decisions. Each of these issues are touched in the following sections.

3.1   Elements of Sampling

In most circumstances, sampling is the only practical method of obtaining desired information available to the commodity analyst since it may not be possible to investigate every member of the population. Moreover, where surveys of other traders and brokers are concerned, questioning all of them may be self-destructive; the analyst's or trader's hand may be "tipped." Given the need for a sample, the problem arises of how to select the sample in such a way that the sample data are representative of the population about which inferences and decisions are to be made. Although volumes exist on sampling theory and procedure, two types of sampling are practical and theoretical cornerstones:

3.1.1   *Nonrandom and Simple Random Sampling*

Nonrandom sampling uses judgment to select which elements of a population to sample. For example, some floor brokers may be better informed than others and discrete in their discussions with the investigator. Here there is no substitute for experience in selecting the sample.

Simple random sampling is a sample drawn from the population in such a way that every possible combination of elements in the sample has an equal chance of being in the sample. For commodity-related problems the sampling typically is done without opportunity for replacement. That is, once an element has been drawn from the population it is not replaced for possible reexamination, for example, asking the same floor broker the same question twice adds no more information to the sample than asking the question once—assuming it was answered correctly and completely the first time.

3.1.2   *Stratified and Sequential Sampling*

Variations of simple random sampling that may be useful include *stratified sampling* and *sequential sampling*. Each can be used to advantage by commodity traders and analysts. Briefly, stratified sampling partitions the populations into groups and simple random samples are drawn from each group. This is particularly useful when the analyst must survey each major market participant, for example, hedgers, speculators, and arbitragers. Moreover, stratification reduces the variance of the overall estimate. Sequential sampling involves the selection of a sample that is observed one at a time and a decision is made after each observation whether or not to continue the sampling. This decision may be based on factors such as the risk of exposing one's trading intentions and its associated costs.

3.1.3 *Use of Random Numbers*

Regardless of the type of sampling, the way in which the random sample is drawn is not always obvious. One of the most popular methods is the use of random numbers. Here, the elements in the population of size N to be sampled are assigned numbers from 1 to N. This list of elements and numbers constitutes the sampling frame from which a sample of size M will be drawn. The actual drawing is done from a table of *random numbers* where M numbers will be selected in any systematic manner. The numbers selected, of course, must not exceed N. Other methods are available for the drawing of samples. The reader is referred to Deming (1960) for examples and further theoretical discussion.

3.1.4 *Sample Size*

Given a certain size sample one can estimate the precision with which a hypothesis can be rejected or accepted. The *determination of a sample size* is the obverse of this issue: Given a desired degree of precision, how large a sample is required? In subsequent sections the degree of precision is estimated for several tests of hypotheses using several different probability distributions. Each depends on the sample size and number of degrees of freedom. Without further elaboration these examples can be "inverted" to solve for the appropriate sample size in each case given the desired degree of confidence.

3.2 Estimates and Estimators

The commodity analyst frequently must make trading recommendations based on estimated price levels or price differentials. Regardless of whether these are *direct estimates* and obtained, for example, from survey data on the anticipated price of the commodity, or *indirect estimates* from an equation that required its coefficients to be estimated, the estimates are statistical inferences of population parameters from incomplete information. In general, two types of estimates are of interest to the commodity analyst: point estimates and interval estimates. A *point estimate* of a price or price differential is a single number, that is, a point, used to represent the value of an unknown population parameter. An *interval estimate* consists of two numbers between which there is a certain degree of confidence that the population or "true" parameter will lie. These intervals sometimes are referred to as *confidence intervals*. For example, there may be 95 percent confidence that the spread between two commodity prices will lie between

20¢ and 40¢ per unit or a 67 percent confidence that the price of some commodity will lie between $4.10 and $4.60.

It is important to distinguish between the notion of an estimate and that of an estimator. Simply stated, an *estimate* is the numerical outcome: point or interval. The *estimator* is the method of estimation such as the use of a sample mean for an estimate of the population mean. Here the sample mean may be viewed as both an estimator and an estimate. Least squares, described below, is an estimation method and a specific value of the equation estimated is an estimate—a regression estimate.

3.3 Unbiasedness, Consistency, and Efficiency: the quality of an estimate

Having obtained sample estimates of a mean and/or variance the analyst must, of course, assess their "quality" before these estimates are to be used: They may require modification to improve their accuracy. Here three criteria are most important: unbiasedness, consistency, and efficiency. If the expected value of a sample statistic is equal to its population value then the estimate is said to be *unbiased*. It can be shown that the sample mean, $\bar{X}$, is an *unbiased estimate* of the population mean, u; that is,

$$E(\bar{X}) = u.$$

However, the expected value of the sample variance, $E(S^2)$, is not equal to its population value but a multiple of it. In particular, where $S^2 = \sum_{i=1}^{n} \frac{(X_i - \bar{X})^2}{n}$,

$$E(S^2) = \sigma^2 \frac{(n-1)}{n}.$$

Consequently, an unbiased estimate of the population variance can be obtained from the sample variance by multiplying it by $n/(n-1)$. That is $(S^2)n/(n-1)$ is an unbiased estimate of the population variance σ^2.

The fact that the expected value of a sample statistic is unbiased does not mean it is equal to the population value. Indeed, one can expect differences or variations to occur. If this variation between the sample estimate and the population becomes smaller as the size of the sample becomes larger, then the sample estimate is said to be a *consistent* estimate of the population parameter. For example, the variance of the sample mean around the population mean is

$$E(\bar{X} - u)^2 = \frac{\sigma^2}{n}$$

and therefore the sample mean is said to be consistent since σ^2/n becomes smaller as the sample size n becomes larger.

An estimate is said to be *efficient* if, in relation to another estimate, the variance of the estimate is smaller. For example, a larger sample would provide a more efficient estimate of a population mean than a smaller sample estimate of that mean.

Even if an estimate is unbiased, efficient, and consistent, these properties per se do not tell the analyst whether to accept or reject a particular hypothesis or specify the precise interval around an estimated outcome the true value can be expected to fall a certain percent of the time. To address these questions one must know something about the entire distribution of outcomes of an experiment.

3.4 Degrees of Freedom

In the previous section the term "degree of freedom" was introduced. Its technical definition is straightforward but its intuitive notion is more elusive. Technically, the number of *degrees of freedom* is equal to the number of observations in the sample less the number of parameters estimated from those sample data. If, for example, there are n observations in the sample and two parameters are being estimated from these data, then there would be $n - 2$ degrees of freedom. Intuitively, one may consider the number of observations as bits of information and one cannot extract more information from the sample than the sample contains: that is one cannot have negative degrees of freedom. The mean of a sample is one bit of information taken from the sample and leaves $n - 1$ bits of information within the sample. In a multiple regression, the estimated parameters constitute drains on the information in the sample. If m parameters were being estimated, including the constant, the number of degrees of freedom would be $n - m$.

3.5 Probability Estimates, Hypothesis Testing, and Confidence Intervals

There are several types of probability assessments a technical analyst must perform based on knowledge of the probability distribution of the random variable(s) in question. Among the most important are estimating the probability of an outcome, testing the significance of the difference between two values, and testing the goodness of fit.

3.5.1 Speculation, the Random Walk, and Probability Estimates

The normal and t-distributions in Table 10.2 may be used to assess the probability of commodity price movements. For example, suppose a particular commodity price follows a random walk; that is, suppose the price at time t, P_t, is equal to its previous value plus some random disturbance e_t where e_t is normally distributed with a mean of zero and a standard deviation of \$0.10. Here the standard deviation is assumed to be known. The probability that tomorrow's commodity price will be $0.25 or more above today's price is

$$P(P_t - P_{t-1}) \geq .25 = P(e_{t+1} \geq .25)$$

$$= P\left(z \geq \frac{.25 - 0}{.10}\right)$$

$$\approx .005.$$

Now if the standard deviation was not known but estimated then a "t" statistic would be used instead of the z variate.

3.5.2   Arbitrage, the "t" Statistic, and Hypothesis Testing

The "t" statistic is also used to assess the *statistical significance* of regression coefficients, the significance of differences between two sample means, and other similar applications.

For example, an arbitrager may desire to buy and sell the same forward commodity in two different markets with the intent of liquidating the positions at a profit before either the purchase or sale mature. Moreover, the arbitrager may perform this operation in either of two commodities—say silver or gold. Based on past data the expected returns for each commodity over several three-month sample periods are as follows:

	GOLD G	SILVER S
Average return: $\bar{X}$	5.36%	4.62%
Standard deviation: S	0.51%	0.43%
Sample size: n	10	12

The arbitrager would like to trade the commodity that offers the greatest opportunity of capturing a profit. While gold appears to have a higher return, its variation in that return is larger. But in each case the differences appear to be small. One *hypothesis to test* is whether the average returns are significantly different or not. The t-test can be used to accept the hypothesis that the sample means are the same (the null hypothesis) or reject that hypothesis. The t-statistic for this test is

$$t = \frac{\bar{X}_G - \bar{X}_S}{S_{\bar{x}_G - \bar{x}_S}}$$

where $S_{\bar{x}_G - \bar{x}_S}$ is the estimated standard error of the difference between $\bar{X}_G$ and $\bar{X}_S$. Because the sample sizes are small it is common to assume the population variances of the rates of return are equal. An estimate of this variance is

$$S^2 = \frac{(n_G - 1)S_G^2 + (n_S - 1)S_S^2}{n_G + n_S - 2}$$

and the corresponding estimated error between the two means is

$$S_{\bar{x}_G - \bar{x}_S} = S\sqrt{\frac{1}{n_G} + \frac{1}{n_S}}.$$

The *t*-value is

$$t = \frac{(5.36 - 4.62)}{(.47)\sqrt{\frac{1}{10} + \frac{1}{12}}}.$$

$$= 3.7$$

With a 2 percent chance of being wrong the *t*-value for 20 degrees of freedom is 2.528. Since the observed *t*-value exceeds this value one must reject the null hypothesis that the means are equal. This in turn would suggest the arbitrager should allocate his resources to gold arbitrage and not silver.

3.5.3 Portfolio Assesments, χ^2, and Hypothesis Testing

Tests of goodness of fit typically are used to determine if two population proportions or means may be considered equal with a given degree of confidence. These tests of hypotheses also have many applications of importance to the commodity analyst. One application would be to test if one investment portfolio achieved significantly different distribution of returns from some other portfolio's distribution of returns. Here one could use a χ^2 test.

Whether one accepts or rejects a hypothesis depends on the degree of confidence the tester is willing to accept. For example, suppose the observed portfolio and the baseline portfolio against which it is being compared have the following probability distributions of returns over $k = 5$ intervals.

RETURN (percent per annum)	OBSERVED PORTFOLIO, f_o	BASELINE PORTFOLIO, f_b
5	8.5	15
7	21.5	20
9	30	35
11	22	20
13	18	10

The χ^2 statistic is $\chi^2 = \sum(f_o - f_b)^2/f_b = 10.24$. With $v = k - 1 = 4$, the null hypothesis that the distributions are equal could be accepted with 95 percent confidence. For 98 percent confidence one would have to reject the null hypothesis.

3.5.4 Arbitrage and Confidence Intervals

Confidence intervals are closely related to hypothesis testing in terms of their computation. One of the most common applications of confidence interval estimation is in forecasting and these applications are considered in detail in Part 3, along with technical trading rules. However, commodity traders and analysts also can use confidence intervals in other ways. For example, consider an arbitrager that takes long and short positions in a forward commodity traded in two different markets, for example, forward foreign exchange through direct placement and the corresponding futures contract on the IMM. On the basis of past trading, suppose the following basis point gross trading profits were captured: 68, 70, 89, 100, 56, 66, 48, 80, and 65. Because gross trading profits of 60 basis points or less are not profitable, the trader may wish to know the range in which he can expect to trade 90 percent of the time.

The average of these results is 71.33. A *t*-statistic could be used to construct the 90 percent confidence interval around this mean. The interval would be

$$71.33 \pm t_{.05, \, 8}\left(\frac{s}{\sqrt{n}}\right)$$

or

$$71.33 \pm 1.86\left(\frac{16.1}{3}\right) = 71.33 \pm 9.98$$

where $t_{.05, \, 8}$ represents a *t*-statistic for 5 percent in each of the two tails of the *t* distribution with 8 degrees of freedom. Similarly, the trader could ask the percent of the trades that would be profitable, that is, above 60 basis points. Here one must solve for the appropriate *t*-statistic and then obtain the associated probability. In this case the *t*-statistic is $(71.33 - 60)3/16.1$ and the probability of a basis point profit of more than 60 basis points is approximately 92.5 percent.

3.5.5 Market Fundamentals and The "F-Test"

One application of the *F*-test is the *test for linear restrictions in a multiple regression equation*. Such an equation may be used by a commodity analyst to estimate and predict commodity prices. Typically, the equation is estimated over some time in the past and then extrapolated into the future. Frequently, the structure of the equation may change owing to some socioeconomic events. That is, the coefficients in the regression may be different for different estimation periods. An *F*-test developed by Rao (1952) and explored in econometrics by Chow (1960) can be used to test the null hypothesis that the coefficients are equal in both data sets. Briefly, consider two data sets of size n_1 and n_2, respectively. The regression equation estimated in the first data set is

$$y = b_1 + b_2x + b_3z + e$$

and the equation estimated in the second data set is

$$y = a_1 + a_2x + a_3z + e.$$

Here y is the dependent variable, x and z are independent variables, and e is a random element.

The null hypothesis that the coefficients are the same in both estimation equations is equivalent to the linear restrictions $a_1 = b_1, a_2 = b_2$, and $a_3 = b_3$. The F-statistic for this test is

$$F = \frac{(RRSS - URSS)/(k + 1)}{URSS/(n_1 + n_2 - 2k - 2)}$$

where k is the number of independent variables, $RRSS$ is the restricted residual sum of squares obtained from the residuals from a regression on the pooled data, $URSS$ is the unrestricted residual sum of squares obtained from estimating the equation on each data set separately and adding their individual residual sum of squares.

3.6 Parametric and Nonparametric Statistics

In order to test a hypothesis or construct a *confidence interval* the analyst may know, or invoke assumptions about, the character of the underlying probability distribution of the population, for example, the population is log normally distributed. When this knowledge is available, or an assumption such as this is made, the method of interval estimation and hypothesis testing is said to be *parametric*. Methods of interval estimation or hypothesis testing that do not make these assumptions and are valid regardless of the population distribution are called *nonparametric* or *distribution-free* methods. Among the most common nonparametric methods in commodity analysis are the sign test, runs tests, serial correlation, and spectral analysis (to identify oscillations).

3.6.1 *The Sign Test: Durham and Red No. 2 Wheat*

The *sign test* can be used to test whether two unknown frequency functions are identical. One common application in commodity analysis is the exploration of the spread between two commodity prices, for example, Chicago and Minneapolis wheat. Some may argue that these prices fluctuate for slightly different reasons since one represents Durham wheat and the other represents Red No. 2. Suppose Durham wheat is thought to carry a premium of c cents per bushel over Red No. 2. Regardless of the distribution of these prices the following variable may be constructed:

$$z_i = \begin{cases} 1 \text{ if } x_i - y_i - c > 0 \\ 0 \text{ if } x_i - y_i - c < 0. \end{cases}$$

The variable z_i is a binomial corresponding to a single experiment for which the probability of occurrence $z_i = 1$ is .5. If n pairs of prices are compared, the sum z_i will be a binomial variable corresponding to n independent trails. The binomial distribution then may be used to assess the degree of confidence in the null hypothesis that the distributions are the same for Durham and Red No. 2 wheat save the constant difference of c cents per bushel. If this hypothesis were accepted, the researcher would be able to explore the distribution of one of the prices and apply the results to the other, bearing in mind the difference in their mean value. If the null hypothesis were rejected the researcher would have to investigate the distribution of each price and develop separate hypothesis testing and confidence interval procedures for each.

3.6.2   *The Runs Test: an essential of technical analysis*

The *runs test* is most often used to test for the randomness of consecutive commodity price movements or runs in order to establish with some degree of confidence if the run is a random occurrence or a nonrandom movement that may be taken advantage of. The test is based on the notion that if there are n_1 occurrences of one type, say upward price movements, and n_2 occurrences of another type, say downward price movements, and r is the number of sequences of identical occurrences (i.e., the number of runs), the distribution of r has a mean of

$$\bar{r} = \frac{2n_1 n_2}{n_1 + n_2} + 1$$

and a variance of

$$\text{var}(r) = \frac{2n_1 n_2 (2n_1 n_2 - n_1 - n_2)}{(n_1 + n_2)(n_1 + n_2 - 1)}.$$

If the sample sizes are above 20, the distribution of r can be approximated by a normal distribution. From these results one may estimate the probability that a run of a certain length will occur in a certain sample period.

3.6.3   *Serial-Correlation: the foundation of time series analysis*

Serial correlation can be used to test for patterns of nonrandomness that cannot be detected by the runs test except under rare conditions, for example. Friday's price is dependent on Thursday's price and last Friday's price. This topic is discussed in the next chapter on Time Series Analysis. *Spectral analysis*, also described in the next chapter, investigates serial correlation within and between variables but does so in the frequency domain as opposed to the time domain. That is, it can be used to reveal the amount of price variability attributable to an oscillation within a certain frequency band, that is, within a certain range of periods. Moreover, the method can be used to measure the amount of variation common to two different time series within a given frequency band, the degree of angle coherence (analogous to correlation) and the phase (i.e., timing difference) between the series at that frequency band. The applications, of course, are most common in univariate and multivariate model building where these insights can be used to help select explanatory variables and the transformations they require to be most informative.

3.7 Correlation and Regression

Regression analysis is a method of estimating the values of a variable (the dependent variable) from one or more other variables (the explanatory or independent variables). *Correlation analysis* is a method to assess the degree of association of statistical strength of a relationship between variables. Correlation and regression are closely related and their mutual purposes are fourfold:

1. To obtain a quantified relationship between the dependent variable and the independent variables
2. To obtain a measure of the error involved in using the regression relationship for estimation
3. To obtain a measure of the amount of variability in the dependent variable explained by the independent variables as arranged and quantified in the regression "equation"
4. To obtain measures of the statistical significance of the explanatory relationship and each of its independent variables

When only a single independent and dependent variable are related and compared one speaks of "simple" regression and correlation analysis. When more than one independent variable is used to "explain" the dependent variable one speaks of "multiple" regression and correlation analysis.

3.7.1 Select Relationships and Measures

Without elaboration some of the essential relationships and measures in regression and correlation analysis are:

Multiple Linear Regression Model

$$Y_j = a_0 + a_1 x_{1j} + \ldots + a_m x_{mj} + E_j, j = 1, \ldots, n$$

where $a_0, \ldots, a_m$ are coefficients to be estimated, Y_j is the jth observation of the dependent variable, $x_{1j}, \ldots, x_{mj}$ are the jth observations of the independent variables and E_j is a random error as of the jth observation and $n > m + 1$ is the sample size.

Variance Around the Regression Equation

$$S^2_{Y:1\ldots m} = \frac{\sum (Y - \hat{Y})^2}{n - (m + 1)}$$

where $Y = a_0 + a_1 x_1 + \ldots + a_m x_m$ and $\hat{Y}$ is the estimate of Y, and Y: $1, \ldots, m$, denotes the regression of Y on variables 1 through m.

Standard Errors of the Estimating Equation

$$S_{Y:1\ldots m} = \sqrt{S^2_{Y:1\ldots m}}$$

Simple Correlation Coefficient Between Y and X

$$r^2_{Y:x} = 1 - \frac{S^2_{Y:x}}{S^2_Y}$$

where S^2_Y is the variance of Y and $S^2_{Y:x}$ is the variance of Y explained by x.

Coefficient of Multiple Determination

$$R^2_{Y:1\ldots m} = 1 - \frac{S^2_{Y:1\ldots m}}{S^2_Y}$$

Standard Error of a Regression Coefficient

S_{a_j} = Square root of element in jth column, jth row of $S^2_{Y:1\ldots m} (X'X)^{-1}$

where X is the n by $m + 1$ matrix of observations on the m variables plus the constant; the observations of the constant are represented as a vector of n 1's. It must be noted that correlation analysis can be used above as a nonparametric method: It does not require assumptions as to the distribution of the underlying relationship.

3.7.2 Limitations

The practical limitations and problems of regression and correlation analysis are many. Among the most frequently encountered are nonlinearities, constraints, multicolinearity, and serial correlation.

A relationship is said to be *intrinsically nonlinear* if it cannot be transformed mathematically into a linear one, and is said to be *intrinsically linear* otherwise. When a regression equation is intrinsically nonlinear, one must employ some form of nonlinear estimation procedure, such as the Marquart (1963) or variable metric approach (see Lootsma 1972). This is necessary in order to estimate the coefficients in the regression equation which are non-lineary related to one another and not amenable to linear regression methods.

The coefficients in regression equations frequently must be constrained to certain values or ranges of values by virtue of knowledge of the market process being estimated. Accordingly, *constrained estimation* procedures must be employed. Here constrained least squares (see Theil 1971), which may be viewed as a quadratic programming problem (see Chapter 13), is often very useful. Other constraints such as the binary character of the variables can be accommodated by some combination of transformation of variables and the equation model to be estimated, for example, probit models (Theil 1971; Finney 1964) or logit models (Theil 1971).

Multicolinearity exists when the so-called independent variables are not in fact independent of one another. When this condition occurs it is difficult if not impossible to estimate the statistical significance of the independent variables which in turn makes it difficult to determine which variables should occupy the analyst's attention. Here, mechanical methods may be used to reduce the problem (Kmenta 1971) or the problem may be reduced by a more knowledgeable selection and construction of the variables in the relationship under consideration (Kmenta 1971).

Serial correlation is said to exist when past values of variables are correlated with their present values. This correlation can be particularly troublesome when the dependent variable is correlated with its past. Here methods developed by Box and Jenkins (1970) and Kalman (1969) are especially important. They are discussed in Chapters 16 and 17.

4 SUMMARY

Probability and statistics surround almost every aspect of commodity trading and analysis. Although the topics and examples covered in this chapter are not exhaustive they are indicative of the scope and focus of this discipline in commodities trading and research. Because so much of commodity trading is concerned with investments and outcomes over time, the probability and statistics of time series analysis are of special importance. While some of these elements have been touched on here, the next chapter discusses them in greater detail and, of course, in the context of commodity trading and analysis.

4 BIBLIOGRAPHY

ANDERSON, R. L., and T. A. BANCROFT, *Statistical Theory in Research.* New York: McGraw-Hill, 1952.

CHOW, G., "Tests of Equality between Subsets of Coeffcients in Two Linear Regressions," *Econometrica,* 1960, pp. 590–605.

COOLIDGE, JULIAN LOWELL, *An Introduction to Mathematical Probability.* New York: Dover, 1962.

DEMING, W. E., *Sample Design in Business Research.* New York: John Wiley, 1960.

————, *Some Theory of Sampling.* New York: Dover, 1966.

EDWARDS, A. L., *Expected Values of Discrete Random Variables and Elementary Statistics.* New York: John Wiley, 1964.

FELLER, WILLIAM, *An Introduction to Probability Theory and Its Applications,* Vol. 1, 2nd ed. New York: John Wiley, 1957.

FINNEY, D. J., *Probit Analysis,* 2nd ed. London: Cambridge University Press, 1964.

FISZ, M., *Probability Theory and Mathematical Statistics,* 3rd ed. New York: John Wiley, 1965.

HAMBURG, M., *Statistical Analysis For Decision Making,* 2nd ed. New York: Harcourt Brace Jovanovich, 1977.

HOEL, P. G. *Introduction to Mathematical Statistics,* 3rd ed. New York: John Wiley, 1965.

THEIL, HENRI, *Principles of Econometrics.* New York: John Wiley, 1971.

11

ASPECTS OF TIME SERIES ANALYSIS

||||||||||||||||||||||||||||||||||||||||||||||||||||||||||||||||||||||||||||||||||||||||||||||||||||||||||

1 INTRODUCTION

Most of commodity analysis is concerned with price behavior over time. Here the analyst is concerned with the character of the process that gives rise to a particular series of prices and the extent to which noise (i.e., random errors) corrupts the observations from which a model or description of price behavior may be estimated and forecast. To be sure, much of probability and statistics applies to these issues and several indications of these applications have been given. Nevertheless, there are unique elements and insights to the statistical analysis of time series. Once again, these topics are discussed briefly to acquaint the reader with the essentials and to place them in the perspective of commodity analysis.

2 TIME SERIES: A Definition and Operational Diagnosis

A *time series* can be defined as a set of observations generated sequentially in time. This cryptic definition has behind it several characteristics of special importance to commodity analysts. These include the frequency of observation, the partial indeterminacy of the future, and the possible interconnectedness among time series. Each is discussed below.

2.1 Discrete Snapshots of Continuous Activity: model implications

For the commodity analyst, time series observations are made at regular intervals, for example, daily closing prices. However, these *discrete observations* may be "snapshots" of near *continuous activity* taken (sampled or accumulated) at discrete intervals. Accordingly, the interpretation of many statistical analyses must reflect these origins. In an econometric context the work of Houthakker and Taylor (1970) is of special interest.

In brief, the problem is one of *disguised misrepresentation*. While economic activity may be continuous, the available data are discrete. Consequently, researchers often must use discrete estimation models of continuous activity. Although the estimation model may parallel the underlying "*true*" *model* the closeness may be more apparent than real when the *estimation model* has to be used. To illustrate the problem, consider the continuous model[1]

$$\dot{q}(t) = \alpha\delta + (\beta - \alpha)q(t) + \gamma\dot{x}(t) + \gamma\delta x(t)$$

where α, δ, β, and γ are parameters to be estimated, $x(t)$ is an independent variable, $\dot{q}(t)$ denotes the time derivative of $q(t)$, i.e., its rate of change over an instant of time, and $\dot{x}(t)$ is the time derivative of $x(t)$. The corresponding discrete estimating equation can be written

$$\Delta q_t = A_0 + (A_1 - 1)q_{t-1} + A_2\Delta X_t + A_3 X_{t-1}$$

where A_0, A_1, A_2 and A_3 are the parameters that are estimated, and Δ is a finite difference operator, for example, $\Delta X_t = X_t - X_{t-1}$. It can be shown that the true parameters are related to the estimated ones as follows:

$$\alpha = \frac{2A_0(A_2 - \frac{1}{2}A_3)}{A_3(A_1 + 1)}$$

$$\beta = \frac{2(A_1 - 1)}{A_1 + 1} + \frac{A_3}{A_2 - \frac{1}{2}A_3}$$

$$\gamma = \frac{2(A_2 - \frac{1}{2}A_3)}{A_1 + 1}$$

$$\delta = \frac{A_3}{A_2 - \frac{1}{2}A_3}.$$

The true short-term impact of a change in x on q is $d\dot{q}/d\dot{x}$ and this is equal to γ. Without following the correspondence equations given above the uninitiated researcher may estimate this short-term impact with the estimated coefficient A_2 instead of the correct estimate $2(A_2 - \frac{1}{2}A_3)/(A_1 + 1)$.

So what? If the researcher is interested in the short-term change in the

---

1. H. S. Houthakker and L. D. Taylor, *Consumer Demand in the United States: Analyses and Projections* (Cambridge, Mass.: Harvard University Press, 1970).

178

price of silver owing to a short-term change in world political anxiety and uses the wrong coefficient to estimate this response, the corresponding orders placed in the market will not be where they should have been. This in turn promises the trader either opportunity losses or real losses. In short, mistakes, even precise systematic ones, cost money. While the size of the error may be small when using daily data in technical models, the errors can be dramatic in fundamental models using monthly or quarterly data.

2.2 The Partial Indeterminacy of the Future

If the *future* values of the time series can be exactly determined by some mathematical function, then the time series is said to be *perfectly deterministic*. If, on the other hand, the *future* values of the time series can only be described in terms of some probability distribution, the time series is said to be *purely indeterministic*.

In the context of linear regression, the current value of a purely deterministic time series can be predicted perfectly by a combination of values in the past. Obversely, linear regression cannot predict the current value of a purely indeterministic time series from some combination of its past values. For the most part, economic time series are a combination of both deterministic and indeterministic elements.

2.3 Interconnectedness

A time series may be influenced by and or made up of one or more other time series, and each may be comprised of some combination of deterministic and indeterministic elements. When this occurs the time series are said to be *interconnected*. For example, the time series Y may be influenced by recent and past values of itself, another time series X and some purely indeterministic element. Naturally the various time series in this model must be observed at equispaced intervals for analysis. Here we have transcended the mere definition of a time series to preview the nature *transfer function noise models* described in Chapter 17. Finally, the fact that commodity prices can be viewed as a time series does not necessarily suggest they are amenable to the full weight of formal time series analysis. Here, stationarity and ergodicity are especially important prerequisites.

3 STATIONARITY AND ERGODICITY: Two Important and Related Properties

A time series is said to have *stationarity in the strong sense* if the distribution of observations taken over some time period is the same in all respects as the distribution of observations taken over some other time period. A less strict definition is *stationarity in the weak sense:* This condition is satisfied if the time series has a constant mean and a constant, finite variance and covariance, and if these properties hold at different intervals in time but are not a function of time itself. For example, a history of commodity prices that trend upward (or downward) over time would be nonstationary in the mean (or first moment). If the dispersion of prices around the trend was becoming wider, the time series would be nonstationary in its variance—a property referred to as heteroscedasticity by econometricians among others. If these nonstationarities cannot be accounted for and removed, the nonstationary time series may not be amenable to rigorous time series analysis and model-building efforts. Here the degree of nonstationarity or *rate of evolution* will determine the practicality of these efforts: Slowly evolving nonstationarities may provide acceptable estimation and forecasting tolerances. This issue is discussed in more detail and with application in Part 3.

In order to form good estimates of the mean, variance, and covariances, the time series must be *ergodic.* Simply stated, the time average of the series (as opposed to an average of repeated experiments at a point in time) must be an unbiased and consistent estimate of the population mean as the sample period of observation increases. Similar properties must hold for estimates of its variance and covariances. Insofar as economic experiments are difficult if not impossible to repeat, these ergodic properties are critical.

These properties imply that good estimates of the current value of the time series can be obtained and extrapolated from historical data. Unfortunately economic time series are not always very accommodating in this regard.

One of the most obvious and common maladies of economic time series is nonstationarity in the weak sense. Fortunately this condition is not always hopeless: One may be able to enforce stationarity. Among the most common procedures used to enforce apparent stationarity is that of differencing. Simply stated, the previous value of the time series is subtracted from the current value, and a time series of differentials is constructed from the original series. If the constructed series continues to exhibit nonstationary properties, it is differenced again until a stationary series is constructed. This process combined with appropriate estimation procedures has been popularized by Box and Jenkins (1970) and is reviewed in Chapters 16 and 17. Unfortunately this process tends to remove the long-term (i.e., low-frequency) characteristics of the time series and focus on higher-frequency (shorter-period) movements. This, of course, is not contrary to the objectives of technical analysis but can be troublesome for fundamental analysis. The problem is that transformed data are not easily recognizable, interpreted, or inverted back to an implementable model by the unseasoned practitioner, if at all.

4 SPECIFICATION

Stationarity and ergodicity notwithstanding, the analyst must set forth the factors and general structure that describes the price movements, that is, the relationship must be *specified*. This specification may rely solely on the history of the price series in question or may involve recent or historical values of other time series. Indeed, the relationship in question may be intertwined with other relationships to form some simultaneous description of several time series. For a single relationship the variable being explained is called the *dependent variable* and the explanatory variables are called *independent variables*. When several variables are explained simultaneously in a system of relationships they are called *endogenous* variables and the explanatory variables may include variables that are taken as known or *exogenous* as well as other dependent variable(s). Among the *explanatory* variables often studied by technical analysts are volume and open interest as well as prices, volume, and open interest for related commodities.

5 IDENTIFICATION AND ESTIMATION

The identification of economic time series poses several knotty problems, not the least of which is the use of the term in different ways by economists and time series analysts. To the time series analyst, the problem of *time series identification* is to determine the appropriate lags used in the model. For example, should today's price be related to yesterday's or last week's price or some combination of them? For the economist, the problem of *structural or economic identification* is one of finding a unique quantified description of two or more relationships that are interconnected. For example, estimation of a demand relationship and a supply relationship that together determine the price and quantity recorded in the market.

In the context of a *simultaneous equation model*, the problem of identification facing the economist is to uniquely estimate the coefficients in the demand and supply equations. The identification problem of the time series analyst is to determine the lag structures in each equation. To be sure there is considerable overlap of interest by these two groups and both types of identification are important. Hannan (1970) has explored the conditions to achieve "economic identification" (our term) given the lag structures in each equation. In practice this often requires the analyst to introduce constraints on the structural coefficients dictated by economic theory.

For the technical commodity analyst both problems of identification are critical. With regard to time series identification per se, the analyst must know how long and with what weight current and past events influence current prices. With regard to economic identification the analyst must be able to distinguish between a demand relationship and a supply relationship that together determine price and quantity recorded in the market, if the analyst is to have any hope of understanding the economic fundamentals of that market.

6 ESTIMATION REVISITED

Once the component parts of a time series equation have been specified, including the length of the lags on the various explanatory series, the next step is to obtain estimates of the parameters or coefficients that give weight to the variables. For most time series forecasting models the estimation of the coefficients poses several problems. First, the model(s) almost assuredly will be nonlinear in the coefficients to be estimated and therefore not amenable to simple linear regression methods. This is true for auto-regression—moving average models and more general transfer function models described by Box and Jenkins (1970). Here one must employ some form of nonlinear estimation procedure such as the Marquardt (1963) or variable metric approaches (Lootsma 1972). Second, the estimation may encounter unknown starting values on the "lagged" explanatory variables. This problem may be handled in a variety of ways, for example, by assuming values for the "missing observations" or by estimating these values from sample information. Here, the rule for the technical analyst is to have appropriate estimation capabilities on hand and it is difficult to have too many of them. While volumes have been written about linear and nonlinear parameter estimation, the methods described in Chapters 16 and 17 are among those well suited for technical analysis.

7 CAUSALITY AND FEEDBACK

For the commodity analyst causality and feedback are especially important concepts that are not easy to measure. In order to measure and test the intuitively straightforward notion of *causality* some generally accepted rules must be noted:

1. Anticipations of the future aside, the future cannot cause the past. Causality can occur only from the past to the present or future.
2. The information used to test causality must be selected on the basis of some underlying theory of causal direction (e.g., from open interest to prices).

3. Insofar as all relevant information may not be available, causality may be tested only with respect to the particular collection of information that is available.

With these points in mind it is clear that an operating definition of causality may not be razor sharp or unique. Deferring to common usage, a squared error term (least squares) definition of causality is as follows: If the variance of the estimation error around the estimated time series X_t is smaller when the "lagged" time series Y_{t-s} is included in the information set explaining X_t than it is when Y_{t-s} and only Y_{t-s} has been omitted from the information set, then Y_{t-s} is said to be a cause of X_t with a "causality lag" of s time units.

To be sure, a reduction in the variability of the estimation residual around the estimated, series does not preclude a spurious relationship stemming from the incorrect specification of the model. The only safeguard against this problem is the knowledge the model builder has of the underlying processes, the logical validity of the variables, and their structural relationship. That is not to say the analyst must know the relationship before learning about it. Rather, it is to say it is important to know something about the underlying relationship in order to efficiently learn more about it.

Direct feedback is said to occur if there is causality between Y_{t-s} and X_t and between X_{t-r} and Y_t. That is, direct feedback is said to exist when causality goes both ways with the same or different delays. *Indirect feedback* is said to exist when a third (or fourth) variable enters the linkage. For example, Y_{t-r} causes X_t, X_t causes Z_{t+p} and Z_t causes Y_{t+j}. It should be noted that instantaneous causality cannot be differentiated from instantaneous feedback unless one can bring extra information to bear on the problem; for example, the investigator knows Y_t cannot cause X_t.

8 FILTERS

In a time series context a *filter* is the transformation of a time series with certain characteristics into a time series with at least some different characteristics. For example, if the time series W_t is formed by a linear combination of present and past values of the time series X_t, the constructed series W_t is called the filtered version of the series X_t. If present and past values of X_t are used to construct W_t then the filter is said to be a *backward-looking filter*. The weighting scheme of the filter is called the *transfer function of the filter* or the *distributed lag function of the filter*. Filters often are used in time series analysis to "remove or reduce in importance" characteristics of a time series that are "troublesome," for example, a moving average used to remove seasonal and irregular components. This may be done to reveal a trend for its own rewards or the filtered series may be used to explain yet another filtered series. In the latter case, the unfiltered (unlagged) variable may contain superfluous information and must be filtered (lagged) to better reveal its message and linkage to the time series the analyst is studying.

Filters of various types, such as moving averages, are common to technical analysts and are used in part to differentiate between trends and price oscillations. Technical analysts also are aware that economic responses to some stimulus are not always instantaneous but tend to play themselves out over time. Here also the analyst may use filters to help reveal these impulse-response characteristics in the form of "distributed lags."

9 FORECASTING

Following the definition set forth by Brown (1964) *forecasting* is used here to mean "the routine, objective, computations that (1) throw past data into the future and (2) because they are routine, can be applied to a great many series." The objective of a forecasting model is to find a mechanism such that the error between the actual and forecasted values is as small as possible.

While these notions are almost self-evident, the evaluation of a forecasting mechanism is not as straightforward as it may appear. Insofar as the time series being forecast is not purely deterministic, a zero error forecast has a probability of zero. In an absolute sense, commodity traders consider a price forecasting mechanism "good" if it is accurate enough to make a profit more often than a loss, and "bad" otherwise. How accurate that must be in terms of standard statistical measures depends in part on the market and the type of business the trader represents. In a relative context, one measure of the value of a forecasting model is the comparison between the forecast errors using the model and the errors from a naive "no-change" alternative. For comparisons between two or more forecasting methods that outperform the no-change alternative, their relative accuracy will play a major role in the selection between them. However, other factors may come into play in making the selection. Among the most important are ease of operation, timeliness, and cost. Owing to the changing character of the regulatory environment and evolving business needs, large expensive models are not always the route for the technical or fundamental analyst and trader to follow. These issues of course are answered by each application.

9.1 Forecast Accuracy: analysis and improvement

Some final words on forecasting must be said and they pertain to accuracy. Even though one may obtain unbiased and efficient estimates, the corresponding forecasts may not reveal these properties owing to sampling variation and the absence of estimation constraints that help enforce these attributes. For example, least squares regression constrains estimation residuals to sum to zero but no such constraint exists for forecasts. One popular method of diagnosing the errors between forecasts and actuals and improving the forecasts is the *mean square forecast error* decomposition developed by Theil (1966). Denoting actuals by A_t and forcasts by F_t the mean square error between them is

$$MSE = \sum_n (F_t - A_t)^2 \frac{1}{n}$$

and can be decomposed into the following elements

$$MSE = (\bar{A} - \bar{F})^2 + (S_F - S_A)^2 + 2(1 - p)S_A S_F$$

where $\bar{A}$ and $\bar{F}$ are the means of A and F, respectively, S_F^2 is the variance of the forecasts, S_A^2 is the variance of the actuals and p_2 is the correlation coefficient between the actuals and their forecasts.[2]

The first term on the right is a measure of *error in central tendency*, that is, bias. The second term is a measure of *error in systematic variation*, and the last term measures the contribution of *nonsystematic errors*. The first two terms may be correctable by a simple linear regression adjustment of the forecasts:[3]

$$A_t = a + bF_t + e_t$$

where $\hat{F}_t = a + bF_t$ is the "corrected" forecast.

10 TIME SERIES MODELS, SERIAL CORRELATION, AND SPECTRAL ANALYSIS

The design and estimation of time series models depends in part on the serial correlation characteristics of the time series under consideration. In the context of a multiple regression model one must explore the auto-correlation properties of both the dependent and independent variables as well as their cross-correlation patterns. This information, for example, is useful in determining the length of moving averages to filter certain characteristics from the time series (e.g., seasonal patterns), and/or to help determine the distribution of lags on explanatory variables. These issues are critical to the development of technical trading rules that often must separate short-term oscillations from a long-term trend or cycle and the estimation of economic dynamics in fundamental models.

2. Henri Theil, *Applied Economic Forecasting* (Amsterdam: North Holland Publishing Co., 1966), pp. 29–30, 34–35.
3. Ibid.

Depending on the perspective of a time series model, a researcher may have to focus on the serial correlation properties of individual components of the series such as the trend or seasonal movements. Once these movements have been defined their auto- and cross-correlation properties may be explored. However, this a priori decomposition may not always be accurate or exhaustive: There may be patterns that do not fit any of the ones specified or there may be several variations of a particular type. Rather than decompose a time series into a few components and explore them on a hit or miss basis, one could decompose them into a much larger number of possible components at the outset. In this way one may be able to investigate anticipated properties as well as discover unanticipated ones that otherwise may go undetected. *Spectral analysis* provides such a panorama: It is an efficient method of exploring serial correlation properties within and between time series.

10.1 Spectral Analysis or Correlation Analysis: an analyst's choice

It must be noted that *the spectrum* is a mathematical transform of a correlation function and therefore spectral analysis and correlation analysis are equivalent ways of looking at properties of time series. However, their representation focuses on different aspects of the data and their use can be complementary to one another. Both are especially important for model identification: the variables to be included and their lag structures. Ultimately, the choice between correlation analysis and spectral analysis depends in large part on the nature and use of the models. Commodity analysis and trading tend to be especially aware of various length oscillations, many of which are far shorter than those typically studied by economists.

Moreover, commodity trading models tend to be divided along lines corresponding to the length of certain oscillations, for example, short-term technical models as opposed to long-term fundamental models. In practice, spectral methods can be especially rewarding for this "frequency band" distinction when several years of daily data are available and technical models or simple multivariate models are the order of the day. Accordingly, it is a method that cannot be ignored. The following discussion provides an elementary introduction to spectral methods including a summary of basic formulae, statistics, estimation and testing procedures, and applications. For a thorough discussion the reader is referred to Granger and Hatanaka (1964), Jenkins and Watts (1968) and Box and Jenkins (1970).

10.2 Auto- and Cross-Spectral Analysis: an elementary overview

Auto-spectral analysis looks at a time series as a collection of oscillations of different frequencies. The frequency of each oscillation is reported along with a measure of its importance. The importance of an oscillation (its *power*) is measured by the amount of variation in the series attributable to that oscillation. The *frequency* is the reciprocal of the length of the oscillation. For example, a frequency of zero (the lowest frequency) implies an infinitely long oscillation (e.g., a trend), a frequency of .0833 where months are the time units of measurement corresponds to an oscillation of 12 months, and a frequency of .5 (the highest frequency or shortest length oscillation) corresponds to a period of two months assuming once again that months are the time units of measurement (two weeks if weeks were the time unit of measurement). Some basic formulae in spectral analysis are summarized in Tables 11.1 and 11.2.

Table 11.1

SELECT FORMULAE IN SPECTRAL ANALYSIS

Auto-Spectral Estimate

$$S_x(f) = \frac{\Delta}{\pi}\left[c_x(0) + 2 \cdot \sum_{k=1}^{M-1} c_x(k) \cdot w(k) \cdot \cos\left(\frac{\pi \cdot k \cdot f}{F}\right)\right.$$
$$\left. + c_x(M) \cdot w(M) \cdot \cos\left(\frac{\pi \cdot M \cdot f}{F}\right)\right] \qquad f = 0, \ldots, F$$

where

c_x = Auto-covariance of time series x
M = Maximum lag
f = Frequency
F = Number of frequency points
Δ = Time unit for each lag

Normalized Spectral Density

$$D_x(f) = \frac{\pi}{\Delta \cdot F \cdot c_x(0)} S_x(f) \qquad f = 0, \ldots, F$$

Estimated Cross-Spectrum

$$A_{xy}(f) = \Delta\sqrt{L^2(f) + Q^2(f)} \qquad f = 0, \ldots, F$$

$$L(f) = \frac{1}{\pi}\left[I(0) + 2 \cdot \sum_{k=1}^{M-1} I(k) \cdot w(k) \cdot \cos\left(\frac{\pi \cdot k \cdot f}{F}\right)\right.$$
$$\left. + I(M) \cdot w(M) \cdot \cos\left(\frac{\pi \cdot M \cdot f}{F}\right)\right] \qquad f = 0, \ldots, F$$

$$Q(f) = \frac{2}{\pi}\left[\sum_{k=1}^{M-1} q(k) \cdot w(k) \cdot \sin\left(\frac{\pi \cdot k \cdot f}{F}\right)\right] \qquad f = 0, \ldots, F$$

$$I(k) = 0.5[c_{xy}(k) + c_{yx}(k)] \qquad k = 0, \ldots, M$$
$$q(k) = 0.5[c_{xy}(k) - c_{yx}(k)] \qquad k = 0, \ldots, M$$

Phase

$$P_{xy}(f) = \frac{1}{2 \cdot \pi} \arctan\left[\frac{Q(f)}{L(f)}\right] \qquad f = 0, \ldots, F$$

Coherence Squared

$$C_{xy}^2(f) = \frac{A_{xy}^2(f)}{S_x(f) \cdot S_y(f)} \qquad f = 0, \ldots, F$$

Gain: X to Y

$$G_{xy}(f) = \frac{A_{xy}(f)}{S_x(f)} \qquad f = 0, \ldots, F$$

Gain: Y to X

$$G_{yx}(f) = \frac{A_{xy}(f)}{S_y(f)} \qquad f = 0, \ldots, F$$

SOURCE: G. M. Jenkins and D. G. Watts, *Spectral Analysis* (San Francisco: Holden-Day, 1969) pp. 382–83.

Table 11.2

FORMULAE AND PROPERTIES OF SELECT LAG-WINDOWS FOR SPECTRAL ESTIMATORS

LAG WINDOW		VARIANCE RATIO[a]	DEGREES OF FREEDOM	BAND WIDTH[b]
Rectangular				
$w(k) = 1$	$k = 1, \ldots, M.$	$2\dfrac{M}{N}$	$\dfrac{N}{M}$	.5
Tukey 1 (Tukey–Von Hann)				
$w(k) = 0.5\left[1 + \cos\left(\dfrac{\pi \cdot k}{M}\right)\right]$	$k = 1, \ldots, M$	$\dfrac{3}{4}\dfrac{M}{N}$	$\dfrac{8}{3}\dfrac{N}{M}$	1.333
Tukey 2 (Tukey-Hamming)				
$w(k) = 5.4 + 4.6 \cos\left(\dfrac{\pi \cdot k}{M}\right)$	$k = 1, \ldots, M$	$.7\dfrac{M}{N}$	$\dfrac{8}{3}\dfrac{N}{M}$	1.333
Bartlett				
$w(k) = 1 - \dfrac{k}{M}$	$k = 1, \ldots, M$	$\dfrac{2}{3}\dfrac{M}{N}$	$3\dfrac{N}{M}$	1.5
Parzen				
$w(k) = \begin{cases} 1 - 6 \cdot \left(\dfrac{k}{M}\right)^2 + 6 \cdot \left(\dfrac{k}{M}\right)^3 & k = 1, \ldots, (M/2) \\ 2 \cdot \left(1 - \dfrac{k}{M}\right)^3 & k = (M/2) + 1, \ldots, M \\ 0 & k > M \end{cases}$		$.539\dfrac{M}{N}$	$3.71\dfrac{N}{M}$	1.86

[a] M is the length of the lag and the number of frequency points from zero to .5 for which spectral estimates are made and N is the record (observation) length of the series: Thus if M is 10 percent of the record length N and a Parzen 1 window is used, the variance of the smoothed spectral estimators will be 5.4 percent of the sample spectrum and the number of degrees of freedom will be 37.

[b] The wider the band width the larger the bias tends to be.

SOURCE: Econometrics: Statistical Foundations and Applications, by Phoebus J. Dhrymes 1970, Table 11.1, p. 504, reprinted by permission of Harper and Row Publishers, Inc., N.Y.

An illustrative spectral decomposition of several years of weekly data is shown in Figure 11.1. Here, the series reveals a pronounced peak (i.e., power concentration) at the seasonal frequency of 13 weeks.

As discussed further below these results may be used to assess the accuracy of seasonal adjustment methods or to estimate the distributed lag function (i.e., impulse response function) to capture this oscillation.

Cross-spectral analysis explores the relationship between the same length oscillation within two different time series (measured in the same time units, e.g., months). For example, cross-spectral analysis can indicate how strong a 12-month seasonal pattern in one series is correlated with a 12-month seasonal pattern in another series. The measure of "correlation" is called the *coherence squared* and is reported for each frequency pair, that is, for each pair of common length oscillations.

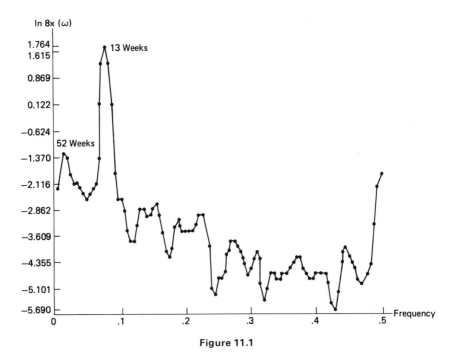

Figure 11.1

NATURAL LOG OF THE POWER SPECTRAL
ESTIMATE OF SERIES X VS. FREQUENCY

The measure of correlation reported between any two series at a particular frequency is the highest correlation obtainable for any lead or lag between those oscillations. That is to say, the coherence squared between two oscillations is given at the coherence maximizing phase.

The phase between the common length oscillation in two series typically is measured as a percent of a circle (a complete oscillation may be viewed as a 360-degree movement after which the oscillation repeats itself). The phase, measured in this way, can be converted into the lead or lag measured in time units by multiplying the length of the oscillation by the phase. For example, if the phase between the two monthly series X_1 and X_2 at frequency .0833 is .25 of a circle, then the 12-month seasonal oscillation (the reciprocal of .0833) in X_1 leads the 12-month seasonal oscillation in X_2 by .25 of 12 months, that is, by three months. Alternatively, X_2 may be viewed as leading X_1 by .75 of a circle, i.e. by 9 months. The direction of causality is a separate issue.

Another important statistic reported in cross-spectral analysis is the gain from one series to another at a particular frequency. The *gain* is an estimate of the "blow-up factor" needed to convert the amplitude of an oscillation in one series into the amplitude of the same length oscillation in another series.

An illustrative lead-lag compendium from cross-spectral analyses of three pairs of series is given in Table 11.3 below. This table only summarizes the cross-spectral properties for a seasonal frequency. A complete cross-spectral analysis of each pair of series would provide similar information for many other frequencies ranging from zero to .5.

10.3   Filter Applications of Spectral Analysis

As mentioned in the introduction, one of the primary uses of spectral analysis is in evaluating methods of estimating trend, cycle, and seasonal movements. Ultimately, this is done by comparing the spectra of a series before and after trend, cycle, and seasonal adjustments (filtering). Here auto- and cross-spectral analyses can reveal the accuracy of the method used to estimate and filter the various movements. For example, suppose one is interested in a series which has trend, seasonal, and irregular components. The spectrum of the unadjusted series will reflect a composite of these components. In general, the trend component represents long periods and will, therefore, display peaks in the spectrum at low frequencies. The seasonal component will show up as peaks in the spectrum at the seasonal frequencies. If contributions at other frequencies are present, these will be represented by peaks over the frequency intervals where they occur. Contributions to the spectrum from the irregular component are spread more or less evenly over the entire range of periodicities.

Suppose the researcher estimates separate trend and seasonal models for long- and short-term trading purposes. The estimates from these models, when removed from the original series, should not reveal any residual trend

Table 11.3

ILLUSTRATIVE LEAD-LAG (PHASE) RELATIONSHIPS BETWEEN
THREE PAIRS OF MONTHLY TIME SERIES

SERIES X_i TO SERIES Y_i	AVERAGE LEAD OR LAG (IN PERCENT OF CIRCLE AND IN NUMBER OF MONTHS)	AVERAGE LENGTH OF ONE COMPLETE SEASONAL OSCILLATION = 1/FREQUENCY	COHERENCE SQUARED (THE "CORRELATION" BETWEEN THE SEASONAL OSCILLATIONS)
X_1 to Y_1	X_1 lags Y_1 by .05 of a circle or .6 months	12 months	.97
X_2 to Y_2	X_2 lags Y_2 by .81 of a circle or 4.86 months	6 months	.82
X_3 to Y_3	X_3 leads Y_3 by .75 of a circle or 9 months	12 months	.84

or seasonal power spectra. The auto-spectrum of the detrended series should resemble the spectrum of the original series except for the absence of power over very low frequencies. Removing seasonality from the series should cause the strong seasonal peaks to disappear from the auto-spectrum of the adjusted series. The remaining auto-spectrum then should represent only the irregular component and should be relatively flat—with no dominant peaks or troughs. The persistence of peaks at the trend and/or seasonal frequencies would indicate maladjustment.

Other criteria for a good seasonal adjustment are the statistics derived from the cross-spectrum of the unadjusted and adjusted series. The coherence squared is a measure of the correlation between two series as a function of frequency. Thus, between the unadjusted and adjusted series, the coherence squared should be low at the trend and seasonal frequencies. As noted earlier, the phase statistic estimates the phase shift between two series, that is, the extent by which one series leads or lags another. The phase shifts between unadjusted and adjusted series should not be significantly different from zero.

10.4 Tests for Significance of Power Spectra

It can be shown (see Jenkins and Watts 1968) that for normally distributed "white noise" the *spectral estimator* is distributed as a χ^2 at each frequency, f, and is approximately distributed as a χ^2 for nonnormal processes when the number of observations, N, is large. For a specific frequency, f, the $100 \, (1 - \alpha)$ percent confidence interval for the true spectral value lies between

$$\frac{\gamma S_{xx}(f)}{\chi_\gamma(1 - \alpha/2)} \quad \text{and} \quad \frac{\gamma S_{xx}(f)}{\chi_\gamma(\alpha/2)}$$

where $S_{xx}(f)$ is the smoothed spectral estimate and χ_γ is the χ^2 statistic for γ degrees of freedom (Jenkins and Watts 1968, p. 254). For example, at a frequency of .0833, corresponding to a 12-month seasonal movement, a smoothed spectral estimate of random noise has a value of 1. Using a Parzen 1 window with a lag, M, equal to 10 percent of the observations, N, a 95 percent confidence interval would lie between

$$(.60)(1.00) \approx .600, \text{ and } (1.51)(1.00) \approx 1.51.$$

If the spectral estimate was above the upper bound it would indicate an oscillation of frequency, f, that cannot be considered the result of random noise with 95 percent confidence: It would indicate a statistically significant oscillation at that frequency. It must be noted that the above interval applies only to a spectral estimate for a single frequency. A confidence interval for h frequencies, at which the estimators are independent, would be $(1 - \alpha)^h$ and for large h will be much smaller than $(1 - \alpha)$. For other tests and a detailed description of them the reader is referred to Jenkins and Watts (1968).

10.5   Assessments of Lead-Lag Relationships

Cross-spectral analysis can be used to assess lead-lag relationships between two variables in a manner similar to that noted above to assess the accuracy of seasonal adjustment or trend estimation for a single series. In the context of a simple regression model a distributed lag on the independent variable may be used to generate an estimate of the dependent variable. These estimates then can be removed from the dependent variable to yield a time series of "residuals." These residuals then can be compared to the original series through cross-spectral analyses to reveal the presence of any remaining significant coherences between the original series and the residuals. If any significant cross-spectral patterns emerge, then the distributed lag structure could be modified to capture these patterns. Moreover, auto-spectral analysis can be used to test for the presence of statistically significant oscillations i.e. auto-correlation in these residuals.

10.6   Cross-Spectral Identification of Distributed Lags[4]

Cross-spectral methods also can be used to specify lag structures directly. Consider a simple linear model of the form

$$y_t = V_0 X_t + V_1 X_{t-1} + \ldots + e_t$$
$$= V(L)X_t + e_t$$

where $V(L)$ is the *distributed lag function* to be estimated and e_t is random noise. It can be shown that the *frequency response function* corresponding to $V(L)$ is

$$V(e^{-i2\pi f}) = \frac{S_{xy}(f)}{S_{xx}(f)}$$

where $S_{xy}(f)$ is the smoothed cross spectral estimator between x and y and $S_{xx}(f)$ is the smoothed auto-spectral estimator of the independent variable x. It also can be shown that

$$V_k = \int_{-1/2}^{1/2} V(e^{-i2\pi f})e^{i2\pi fk} df$$

where v_k is the kth coeficient in the distributed lag model.

For more than one independent variable one obtains a system of relations between cross-spectral estimates and frequency response functions. For

---

4. *Time Series Analysis Forecasting, and Control G.E.P*, Box and G. M. Jenkins, (San Francisco: Holden-Day, 1970), pp. 415–16.

example, for a t linear regression model with two independent variables of the form

$$y_t = V_1(L)X_{1t} + V_2(L)X_{2t} + e_t,$$

the frequency response functions and cross-spectral estimates are related as follows:

$$S_{x_1y}(f) = V_1(e^{-i2\pi f})S_{x_1x_1}(f) + V_2(e^{-i2\pi f})S_{x_1x_2}(f)$$
$$S_{x_2y}(f) = V_1(e^{-i2\pi f})S_{x_2x_1}(f) + V_2(e^{-i2\pi f})S_{x_2x_2}(f).$$

This requires a simultaneous solution for $V_1(e^{-i2\pi f})$ and $V_2(e^{-i2\pi f})$.

10.7 Practical Considerations in Spectral Analysis

The selection of input parameters for performing spectral analysis and the interpretation of the results are discussed in the references, particularly Chapters 7 and 9 of Jenkins and Watts (1968). Nevertheless, a few general guidelines are given here.

First of all, the series to which spectral analysis is applied should be covariance stationary. Therefore, it will sometimes be necessary to perform some form of trend elimination on the raw data such as differencing-prewhitening before applying spectral analysis. Also, it should be noted that the length of the series, N, determines the extent to which peaks in the spectrum may be distinguished. If a series is too short it may be impossible to get satisfactory spectral estimates. For commodity price analyses where daily data are available this is not a serious issue. For fundamental models with quarterly observations spectral analysis may not be worth the effort.

The maximum lag, M, appropriate for the spectral analysis cannot always be determined beforehand. This parameter controls the resolution of the spectrum. One suggested procedure is to choose an initial maximum lag of $N/4$, that is, $1/4$ the number of observations in the series.

It is recommended that the spectra be estimated for several values of M and the results compared. The value of M chosen typically is the lowest value that reveals the "same" spectral structure shown as higher values of M. The smaller M, the larger the degrees of freedom in the spectral estimates. If the spectral estimates change markedly with all values of M it may be necessary to select a small value of M even though some detail may be lost. This often occurs when the data series is too short and ill-suited for spectral analysis.

Because the smoothed spectrum centered around the frequency f represents an "average" estimate over an interval around f, the amount of variance explained by the spectral estimate reflects the amount contributed by all the frequencies in the band. The wider the band, the greater the potential bias and the greater the loss of clarity with which the frequencies can be assessed. For this reason some authors advise smoothing windows with a narrow band around frequencies in which there may be special interest and treating the corresponding increase in variance as a secondary consideration. This, of course, is the users' prerogative.

11   SUMMARY

The analysis of time series and commodity price time series has as its objective the understanding of the underlying process that gives rise to the series observed. The intermediate intent is to model this process which in turn can provide the commodity trader and analyst with the following information:

- Some better idea of the nature of the system generating the time series
- Rules and criteria for selecting and generating forecasting models and forecasts, respectively
- Indications of how two or more time series may be related
- The use of this information to derive improved trading operations

In subsequent chapters the estimation and forecasting of commodity price time series is considered in detail together with the trading rules that complement these estimation and forecasting models.

12   BIBLIOGRAPHY

ANDERSON, T. W., *An Introduction to Multivariate Statistical Analysis.* New York: John Wiley, 1958.

BOX, G. E. P., and G. M. JENKINS, *Time Series Analysis Forecasting and Control.* San Francisco: Holden-Day, 1970.

BROWN, R. G., *Smoothing, Forecasting and Prediction of Discrete Time Series.* Englewood Cliffs, N.J.: Prentice-Hall, Inc., 1964.

GRANGER, C. W. I., and M. HATANAKA, *Spectral Analysis of Economic Time Series.* Princeton, N.J.: Princeton University Press, 1964.

GRANGER, C. W. I., and P. NEWBOLD, *Forecasting Economic Time Series.* New York: Academic Press, 1977.

HANNAN, E. J., *Multiple Time Series.* New York: John Wiley, 1970.

HOUTHAKKER, H. S., and L. D. TAYLOR, *Consumer Demand in the United States: Analyses and Projections.* Cambridge, Mass.: Harvard University Press, 1970.

JENKINS, G. M., and D. G. WATTS, *Spectral Analysis and Its Applications.* San Francisco: Holden-Day, 1968.

KENDALL, M. G., and A. STUART, *The Advanced Theory of Statistics,* Vol. 3.: New York: Hafner Publishing Company, 1968.

LOOTSMA, F. A., *Numerical Methods For Nonlinear Optimization,* New York: Academic Press, 1972.

MARGUARDT, D. W., "An Algorithm For Least-Squares Estimation of Nonlinear Parameters," Journal of the Society of Industrial and Applied Mathematics, 11, 1963, pp. 431–441.

MINCER, J., ed., *Economic Forecasts and Expectations: Analysis of Forecasting Behavior and Performance.* New York: National Bureau of Economic Research, 1969.

THEIL, H., *Applied Economic Forecasting.* Amsterdam: North Holland Publishing Co., 1966.

12

ELEMENTS OF DECISION THEORY

||||||||||||||||||||||||||||||||||||||||||||||||||||||||||||||||||||||||||||||||||||||||||||||||||||||||||||||||

1 INTRODUCTION

The commodity markets often demand and almost always offer opportunities for traders to make investment decisions covering several periods involving more than one commodity and often under conditions of risk or uncertainty. Owing to the stochastic nature of many of these problems, elements of decision theory have found a natural application. To be sure, volumes have been written on each subject and no attempt is made here to survey the literature or provide an introductory course in them. Rather, the intent is one of practical exposure: brief descriptions of the methods and the problems they address, together with commodity trading examples to illustrate their application.

2 DECISION MAKING: Conditions, Elements and Perspectives

Decision making based solely on traditional or classical statistical inference requires the decision maker (e.g., the commodity trader or analyst) to select a degree of confidence in order to determine the values at which trades may take place or hypotheses rejected. For traditional statistical inference the selection of the degree of confidence is arbitrary: For some individuals 95 percent confidence is not enough and for others 80 percent is more than enough. Bayesian decision theory has emerged to overcome this problem. It bases decisions on payoffs in conjunction with whatever statistical information is available. In general, there are two types of decision making in the absence of certainty; decision making under conditions of *uncertainty* and decision making under conditions of *risk*. The former is distinguished from the latter by the absence of probability information about the possible payoffs. For practical purposes decision making under risk, that is, decision making with probability information about the payoffs, will be emphasized. This is not as restrictive as it may seem insofar as the commodity analyst may use subjective probability estimates to transform a decision problem under uncertainty into one of risk.

2.1 Courses of Action, States of the World, and Payoffs

All decision problems under risk have three essential ingredients: the *actions* that may be taken, A_j, for example, buy or sell; the possible *outcomes* of the uncertain variable(s), S_i, for example, the possible ranges in which commodity prices may fall; and the *payoffs* associated with alternative action/outcome pairs, P_{ij}. These characteristics are illustrated in Table 12.1.

Table 12.1
STATES, DECISIONS, AND PAYOFFS

ACTIONS OR DECISIONS	STATES OF THE WORLD $S_1 S_2 S_3 \ldots\ldots\ldots\ldots S_n$
A_1	$P_{11} P_{12} P_{13} \ldots\ldots\ldots\ldots P_{1n}$
A_2	$P_{21} P_{22} \ldots\ldots\ldots$
A_3	$P_{31} \ldots\ldots$
·	$\ldots\ldots$
·	$\ldots\ldots$
·	$\ldots\ldots$
A_m	P_{m1}

2.2 Expected Value Criteria and Nonsequential Stochastic Decisions

When the probabilities of the various states of the world are available, the decision problem is said to be one under conditions of risk. A typical criterion is to select that action that corresponds to the *best expected outcome*, for example, least expected cost or highest expected profit. With regard to the payoff table given above and for probabilities of occurrence P_1, P_2, . . . , P_n, for the n states of the world S_1, . . . , S_n, respectively, the action A_j to take would correspond to the highest or lowest value of

$$V_j = \sum_{i=1}^{n} P_i P_{ij}$$

depending on whether the payoffs are profits or losses, respectively.

2.2.1   An Elementary Decision Problem: buy today or buy tommorow to cover a short

To illustrate a simple decision problem based on the expected value criterion consider the following example: The price of gold today is $550 an ounce and on the basis of past information a firm's research department estimates the price of gold will be $510 tomorrow with a probability of .4 or will be $610 tomorrow with a probability of .6. The firm must cover a short position valued at $575 and due at the close of business tomorrow. Should the firm buy gold today or wait and buy the gold tomorrow. If the firm buys the gold today it will make a trading profit of $25 an ounce with certainty that is, with a probability of 1.00. If the firm waits until tomorrow it has a .4 chance of making a $65 an ounce profit and a .6 chance of losing $35 an ounce. The expected value of buying today is $25 an ounce and the expected value of buying tomorrow is $21 an ounce ($21 = (.4) $65 + (.6) (−$35)). This problem can be illustrated in the *decision tree* shown below in Figure 12.1.

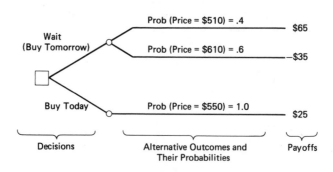

Figure 12.1

DECISION TREE FOR NONSEQUENTIAL ELEMENTARY
STOCHASTIC DECISION PROBLEM

At least two important points must be noted about this problem. First, the decision would be reversed (i.e., wait and buy tomorrow) if today's price was $6 higher, or if the probabilities were reversed, or if the alternative price levels for tomorrow were much lower, or if some appropriate combination of these changes existed. Second, an expected value criterion assumes neutrality toward risk by the decision maker. That is, if the decisions had the same expected outcome the decision maker would be indifferent to which one was chosen regardless of the fact that one has a probability of 1.00, that is, has no possible departure from its expected outcome, and the other has a chance of a higher or lower outcome. This is an important issue and is covered in some depth in Section 3 of this chapter.

2.2.2 The Bidding Problem

Another interesting decision problem that uses the *maximization of expected value* is the bidding problem. This problem may be viewed as a sealed bid auction for a contract that will be awarded to the lowest bidder. The information required to solve the problem includes the cost of the project to the bidder, c, and the probability distribution of the lowest bids on similar contracts, $f(x)$. For example, suppose the bid is for some commodity and is made in cents per unit. Furthermore, assume the cost to the bidder for the project is 50¢ per unit and the probability density function of lowest bids by competitors is

$$f(x) = \begin{cases} .02 & \text{for } 20¢ \leq x \leq 70¢ \\ 0 & \text{elsewhere.} \end{cases}$$

The objective of the bidder is to solve for that bid, y, that maximizes expected profits from the contract. The profit function for the bidder is

$$\pi(y, x) = \begin{cases} 0 & x \leq y \text{ (the bid is lost to competitors)} \\ (y - 50¢) & x \geq y \text{ (the bid is won).} \end{cases}$$

Introducing the probabilities associated with these outcomes yields the expected profit function

$$\hat{\pi}(y, x) = \int_Y^{70¢} \pi(y, x) f(x) \, dx$$

$$= (y - 50¢) \int_Y^{70¢} .02 dx$$

$$= -.02y^2 + 2.4y - 70.$$

In order to maximize this expression the following first order condition must be satisified by the solution value of y.

$$\frac{d\hat{\pi}(y, x)}{dy} = 0$$

$$= -.04y + 2.4.$$

The solution value for y, the corresponding expected profit and the probability of winning are

$$y^* = 60\cent \text{ per unit}$$

$$\hat{\pi}(y^*, x) = 2\cent \text{ per unit}$$

$$\int_{60\cent}^{70\cent} .02 \, dx = 20 \text{ percent,} \quad \text{respectively.}$$

In this example, the decision alternatives are a continuum. That is, there are infinitely many bids that could have been made. In order to "decide" on the optimal value of the bid, elementary calculus was brought to bear to "make" the decision. The previous decision problem had two discrete alternatives and calculus was not called for. But both problems are decision problems and both invoke the maximization of expected value as the decision criterion.

2.3   The Value of Information and Sequential Decisions

The decision maker often is confronted with sequential decision problems, that is, decision problems where a decision necessarily precedes another decision and may influence decisions that follow it. Of particular interest are those sequential decision problems that may reduce uncertainty but at a cost. Here, the notions of *expected value of perfect information* and the *value of perfect information* are especially important. To define and illustrate these notions reconsider the example of a commodity trader faced with a decision of whether to buy gold today or to wait and buy it tomorrow in order to cover a short position due at the close of business tomorrow. If the trader knew tomorrow's price (i.e., had perfect information) the decisions would be straightforward: If the price was going to be $510 per ounce tomorrow, wait and buy tomorrow and capture a profit of $65, and if price was going to rise to $610 per ounce, buy today at $550 per ounce and capture a profit of $25 per ounce. The probabilities of these price outcomes are .4 and .6, respectively. In the context of perfect information these probabilities are viewed as the percent of the time (in decimal fractions) the trader can capture these profits and the corresponding weighted average outcome is a measure of the best possible expected value. This measure is referred to as the expected value of perfect information, *EVPI*, and in this example is

$$EVPI = (.4)\$65 + (.6)\$25$$

$$= \$41 \text{ per ounce.}$$

It has already been shown for this example that without perfect information the highest expected value the trader can achieve is

$$EV^* = \$25 \text{ per ounce.}$$

The difference between the *EVPI* and *EV** is called the value of perfect information, *VPI*. In this case it is

$$VPI = EVPI - EV^*$$
$$= \$16 \text{ per ounce.}$$

This value may be interpreted as the highest value the trader would be willing to pay in order to improve his current state of information to that of perfect information: Surely the trader will not pay more for the added information than it can be expected to add to revenue.

2.3.1 Sequential Decisions and Bayesian Statistics

The decision problems discussed thus far may be regarded as *prior analysis* insofar as the decision-making process was based on expected values calculated from prior probabilities. Simply stated, these *prior probabilities* are the ones originally stated or implied in the problem and unrevised to reflect added information. Indeed, added information has not been considered. However, sequential decisions often involve the introduction of new information that can be used to revise prior probability estimates and in so doing may reduce the level of uncertainty surrounding the decision problem. A common form of this class of problems is one in which a decision to experiment or not precedes a decision to act in some way or another. The experiment provides information that can revise the prior probabilities associated with the outcomes of the alternative actions. Moreover, if the payoffs are available one may assess the value of the experimental information and compare it to its cost in order to decide whether or not the experiment should be conducted. Here the decision rule is straightforward: If the value of the added information from the experiment exceeds its cost conduct the experiment but do not conduct the experiment otherwise. Although these notions are simple their associated calculations are not immediately obvious. The following examples illustrate the procedures involved.

2.3.1.1 A two-outcome, two-stage stochastic sequential decision problem. Using the last example as a point of departure, assume that the trader's research department may perform an additional "test" for the price of gold tomorrow and that this test is 70 percent reliable. That is, on the basis of past performance this test has the following properties: Given that tomorrow's price will be $610 per ounce, the test will indicate a price of $610 per ounce 70 percent of the time; similarly, if the price of gold tomorrow is $510, the test will indicate this price 70 percent of the time; in either case the test will be wrong, that is, indicate the other price, 30 percent of the time. (In keeping with the problem only two price outcomes are possible, $610 and $510; this simplifying assumption is relaxed in the next example.)

The problem now confronting the trader is whether or not to purchase the additional research at its cost equivalent of $5 per ounce. This problem is a sequential decision problem requiring a "*Bayesian*" *revision of probabilities* in order to calculate the expected values needed to answer the problem.

The problem is depicted in the decision tree in Figure 12.2. The problem depicted in the figure has two decisions with one logically preceding the

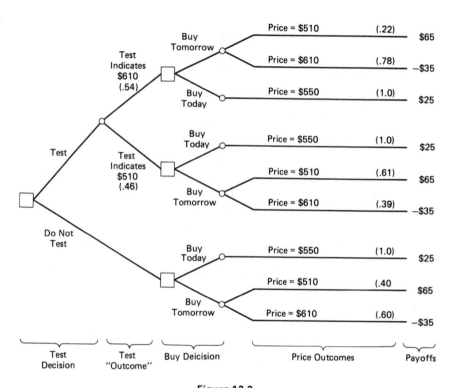

Figure 12.2

ILLUSTRATIVE TWO-STAGE STOCHASTIC SEQUENTIAL DECISION TREE
(PROBABILITIES FROM TABLE 12.2 IN PARENTHESES)

other. The first decision is whether to conduct the test or not. The second decision is whether to buy today or buy tomorrow. If the decision is made not to conduct the test, the subsequent decision to buy today or tomorrow is identical to the simple decision problem discussed in the previous section. If the test is conducted then one must consider the possible outcomes from the test in making the subsequent decision to buy today or tomorrow. Insofar as the test provides additional information and this information may modify the probabilities of the alternative price outcomes, the expected values of the buy decision may differ with regard to the test outcome and these expected values may be different from that calculated for the no-test case. The size of these differences, of course, is an empirical issue.

The calculation of the relevant probabilities for this problem are given in Table 12.2. The table is divided into two parts: One represents the test indication of a $610 price tomorrow and the other represents the test indication of a $510 price tomorrow. In each of these parts the prior probabilities for the $610 and $510 price outcomes are those given in the original problem. The *reliabilities* are conditional probabilities and, when multiplied by their appropriate *prior* (also marginal) *probabilities*, they yield the *joint probabilities* given in the third column of the table. These joint probabilities represent the probability of a joint outcome for the test and tomorrow's price. The sums of these joint probabilities give the *marginal probabilities* of the individual test outcomes. These marginal probabilities when divided into their respective joint probabilities produce the *posterior* (also conditional) *probabilities* given in the last column of the table. In short the table is nothing more than a mechanical representation of the Bayesian probabilities discussed in Chapter 10.

Table 12.2

CALCULATION OF POSTERIOR PROBABILITIES

TOMORROW'S PRICE	PRIOR PROBABILITY	TEST RELIABILITY	JOINT PROBABILITIES	POSTERIOR PROBABILITIES
Test Indicates Price = $510				
$510	.4	.7	.28	.28/.46 = .61
$610	.6	.3	.18	.18/.46 = .39
Marginal Probability Test Indicates Tomorrow's Price is $510			.46	
Test Indicates Price = $610				
$510	.4	.3	.12	.12/.54 = .22
$610	.6	.7	.42	.42/.54 = .78
Marginal Probability Test Indicates Tomorrow's Price is $610			.54	

The probabilities in Table 12.2 together with their associated payoffs produce the following expected values:

```
Conduct Test
   Test Indicates $510
      Buy Today        EV = $25 = (1.0)$25
    **Buy Tomorrow     EV = $26 = (.61)$65 − (.39)$35
   Test Indicates $610
    **Buy Today        EV = $25 = (1.0)$25
      Buy Tomorrow     EV = −$13 = (.22)$65 − (.78)$35
Do Not Conduct Test
    **Buy Today        EV = $25 = (1.0)$25
      Buy Tomorrow     EV =  $5 = (.40)$65 − (.60)$35
```

where the double asterisks indicate the appropriate decision to buy today or buy tomorrow.

The decision to test or not requires a further convolution and comparison of probabilities and expected values. Specifically, the expected value of conducting the test must be calculated and compared to the expected value of not conducting the test. If the test is conducted, the optimal decisions are to buy tomorrow if the test indicates a price of $510 and to buy today if the test indicates a price of $610. The marginal probabilities of these test outcomes are .46 and .54, respectively. These probabilities together with their appropriate expected values produce the following expected value of conducting the test

$$EVT = (.46)\$26 + (.54)\$25$$

$$= \$25.46$$

The optimal expected value of not conducting the test, *EVNT*, is $25 per ounce and corresponds to buying gold today at $550 with certainty. The difference between the expected value when conducting the test and the expected value when not conducting the test gives a measure of the value of the test. This value is

$$VT = EVT - EVNT$$

$$= \$25.46 - \$25$$

$$= \$.46.$$

Because the cost of the test was equivalent to $5 per ounce these results suggest the test should not be conducted: Its cost far outweighs its expected "reward."

2.3.1.2 Prior and posterior probabilities for multiple outcomes: Comex silver. The above example considered a case that only had two possible outcomes: Tomorrow's price would be $510 or $610. Moreover, the test conducted also indicated either of these two outcomes. Often commodity traders can obtain additional information about a single outcome and must adjust their prior probabilities for several possible outcomes from this "test" result. The following example illustrates such a problem. Consider a commodity analyst that has estimated tomorrow's COMEX price of silver as follows:

COMEX PRICE (STATE OF WORLD)	PRIOR PROBABILITY OF OCCURRENCE
8.00	.10
8.05	.25
8.10	.30
8.15	.25
8.20	.10
Expected value = 8.10	

The following morning before the opening of trading on the COMEX the analyst learns that London silver prices opened higher at $8.10. In the past, the morning price of London silver has foretold the closing price of COMEX silver with a certain probability distribution. The London price "test outcome" of $8.10 combined with its past statistical performance gives rise to the following conditional probabilities that morning London silver is $8.10 given alternate COMEX closing prices that afternoon:

$$P(L = 8.10 \mid COMEX = 8.00) = .50$$
$$P(L = 8.10 \mid COMEX = 8.05) = .60$$
$$P(L = 8.10 \mid COMEX = 8.10) = .90$$
$$P(L = 8.10 \mid COMEX = 8.15) = .95$$
$$P(L = 8.10 \mid COMEX = 8.20) = .95.$$

The analyst now must revise the prior probability estimates of COMEX prices based on this London information. The first step would be to calculate the probabilities of the joint events corresponding to a morning London silver of $8.10 *and* an afternoon COMEX closing price of $8.00, of $8.05, and so on. These joint probabilities then may be added to get the marginal probability that a London price of $8.10 would occur. The joint and marginal probabilities then may be used to calculate the revised probabilities associated with alternative COMEX closing prices i.e. the conditional (posterior) probabilities given the London opening price of $8.10. These calculations are summarized in Table 12.3.

Table 12.3

COMEX SILVER PRICE—
ILLUSTRATIVE BAYESIAN PROBABILITY ESTIMATES
BASED ON THE LONDON A.M. PRICE.

STATE OF WORLD	PRIOR PROBABILITIES	RELIABILITIES	JOINT PROBABILITIES	POSTERIOR PROBABILITIES
8.00	.10	.50	.0500	.062
8.05	.25	.60	.1500	.187
8.10	.30	.90	.2700	.336
8.15	.25	.95	.2375	.296
8.20	.10	.95	.0950	.118
Marginal Probability London Price = 8.10			.8025	1.000

The revised probabilities, i.e. posterior, now would be used to calculate expected values. Prior to this revision the expected COMEX close was $8.10. On the basis of the revised probabilities the expected COMEX close is $8.18.

While volumes can be written beyond the material covered in these sections a few additional comments will be made. First, the nature of sequential stochastic decisions is not limited to two-stage problems. Multiple-stage problems would use the posterior probabilities of the previous stage as the prior probabilities in the next stage. Moreover, as the London-COMEX silver example revealed, the number of probability calculations can be large and reliabilities may not be symmetric. Furthermore, the manifestation of a test can take many forms—for example, econometric simulations, surveys of floor brokers, and events in another market—and the costs of these tests can include direct cash outlays and lost business opportunities. The quantification of these costs is an art and science in itself; in the case of lost business opportunities, experience may be the best scale. Finally, the systematic analysis of real-world decision problems often involves large numbers of parameters and alternatives. Here, there is no substitute for mathematical solution procedures. This topic is considered in the next chapter.

Before turning to that chapter, one very important topic must be considered: decision making when the decision maker is not neutral toward risk. Thus far the decision problems considered have assumed risk neutrality; that is, variability in the expected outcome does not influence actions. There are sound theoretical reasons why risk neutrality cannot be considered a satisfactory perspective for all decision problems. More important there is overwhelming empirical evidence and a plethora of practical problems that require the decision process to account for some measure of risk together with return. This topic is considered next.

3 INVESTMENT DECISIONS AND UTILITY

Business decisions are influenced by several factors. Among the most important are:

1. The payoffs associated with the alternative decisions for different states of the world
2. The probabilities of the states of the world
3. The available amount of funds to invest
4. The criterion or preference function on the decision maker

For decision problems under risk where probabilities of outcomes are "known," the expected monetary value of a decision is an important consideration. However, this criterion by itself cannot handle a large variety of business decision problems. First, different decisions may have the same expected monetary value but their payoffs may be dispersed differently around their expected value; for example, one may have a maximum loss of $100 and the other a maximum loss that spells financial ruin. Second, most economic decisions do not offer repeated trails and some apparatus is needed to accommodate *one-time decision making.*

To illustrate the shortcoming with a pure expected monetary value criterion consider the following investments (often referred to as *lotteries* in decision making under risk):

1. Investing $5,000 in silver futures when there is an equal probability of making $10,000 in two weeks or losing $5,000 in two weeks

2. Investing $20,000 in silver futures when there is an equal probability of trebling one's money in two weeks or losing $20,000 in two weeks

3. Investing $5,000 in silver futures when there is an 80 percent chance of making $4,000 in two weeks and a 20 percent chance of losing $3,500 in two weeks

Some investors would prefer the third alternative over the first and second and would prefer the first over the second. While the first and second alternatives have the same probabilities of gain and loss, the dramatic difference in the size of the loss may dominate their decision even though the second alternative has a higher expected monetary value. The third alternative may be preferred to the first even though both have the same expected monetary value because the third has less chance of a loss as well as a smaller maximum loss. Others with different aversions to risk may select otherwise. Consistently making this selection requires that return and risk be weighed against one another on some common scale. Here the notion of utility provides such a scale.

3.1 Maximization of Expected Utility

The criterion of the maximization of expected utility is one way of accommodating these problems in a decision-making context. Its origins date back to Bernoulli's analysis of the St. Petersburg Paradox. A solution was not practical until the path-breaking work of Von Neuman and Morgenstern (1947) led the way to the numerical calibration of utility for an "individual." In brief, the *expected value of an individual's utility* is calculated by adding the utility value of each outcome weighted by the probability of the particular outcome. Although the construction of ordinal utility function along the lines of Von Neuman and Morgenstern initially met with criticism owing to seeming empirical contradictions, these criticisms have been repulsed. The work of Friedman and Savage (1948) showed that the apparent empirical contradictions were in fact consistent with the Von Neuman—Morgenstern approach when the total shape of the utility money curve was considered and not just some segment of the curve. While the theory behind the utility function approach is not trivial, the application of it is far less difficult than one might expect. The following paragraphs illustrate the construction of a numerical utility function and its use in a decision-making context.

3.1.1 Construction of an Individual's Utility Function

A Von Neuman—Morgenstern utility function can be constructed in many ways; the differences are more stylistic than substantive. In general, the information and steps required are as follows:

1. Ascertain largest amounts to be "won" (i.e., the best outcome) or "lost" (i.e., the worst outcome).
2. Assign relative utility values to the best and worst outcomes.
3. Consider alternative probabilities of capturing the best outcome and the complimentary probabilities associated with the worst outcome.
4. Calculate expected utilities according to the formula $U(C) = U(W)p + U(L)(1 - p)$ where $U(C)$ is the utility value of the cash equivalent, C, of the "bet," $U(W)$ is the utility value of the best outcome, W, $U(L)$ is the utility value of the worst outcome, L, and p is the probability of capturing the best outcome.
5. Ascertain the investor's cash equivalent value of a "bet." Here each "bet" is defined by a particular probability of the best outcome.
6. Check and smooth the utility function by redoing the above calculations using new values for the best and/or worst outcomes that do not exceed the range of the original best and worst outcomes.
7. Estimate a continuous utility function from the discrete points calculated above by freehand methods or least squares or some other procedure.

3.1.1.1 An illustrative example. The largest amounts to be won or lost together with their *utility value* and the cash equivalent of a particular "bet" are obtained from the individual with the help of questions such as the following:
Choose between the following:

(a) Receive $0 for certain, or

(b) $\begin{cases} \text{Receive \$10,000 with probability } 1:2 \\ \text{Lose \$8,000 with probability } 1:2. \end{cases}$

Given the response to this question, say (a), the next step is to determine what probability would make the decision maker "just indifferent" between the "bet" and the receipt of $0. To illustrate this process, suppose the utility value arbitrarily assigned to the best payoff, $10,000, is $U(\$10,000) = 1$, and the utility value arbitrarily assigned to the worst payoff, $-\$8,000$, is $U(-\$8,000) = 0$, where $U(\$10,000) > U(-\$8,000)$ must hold. In this case, the expected utility of the "bet" is

$$U(b) = 1 \cdot \frac{1}{2} + 0 \cdot \frac{1}{2}$$

$$= \frac{1}{2}.$$

Since the decision maker prefers $0 for certain to this bet, it follows that the utility value of $0 is greater than $\frac{1}{2}$. In order to determine the utility value of $0 one may change the probabilities in the above bet leaving all other characteristics the same until the probabilities of winning and losing are such that the decision maker is indifferent to taking the bet or receiving $0 for certain. Suppose the decision maker is indifferent between receiving $0 for certain and the bet when the probability of winning is .6 and the probability of losing is .4. In this case, the expected utility would be

$$U(b) = 1 \cdot .6 + 0 \cdot .4$$

$$= .6$$

and would be the utility value of $0.

Now there are three *payoff-utility pairs* (−$8,000, 0), ($0, .6) and ($10,000, 1). In order to find other payoff-utility pairs between these points, the decision maker is asked either (a) at what probability of winning is he or she indifferent between the bet and certain payoff (e.g., $10,000), or (b) for a given probability of winning (e.g., $p = .9$), at what payoff amount is he or she indifferent between the bet and the certain payoff. Doing this for several alternative payoffs between $10,000 and −$8,000 and ascertaining the probability of winning for each payoff at which the decision maker is just indifferent to taking the bet or the certain payoff yields a *utility decision table* as shown in Table 12.4. The utility decision table can be further enhanced by repeating the entire procedure outlined above for different pairs of best and worst outcomes covering segments of the *utility decision schedule* revealed in Table 12.4. For example, one may further resolve the utility decision table and check for its consistency by reconsidering the payoff range from $2,750 to −$6,000 using the same probabilities as before. This effort might result in the utility decision table given in Table 12.5.

This process, of course, is repeated for the upper payoff range, say from $10,000 to −$8,000, as shown in Table 12.6. The utility-payoff pairs from tables 12.4, 12.5 and 12.6 then are used to estimate the decision maker's utility decision curve. An illustrative set of points and the estimated utility decision curve are shown in Figure 12.3. As noted earlier the estimated utility decision curve may be obtained from the data through the use of freehand methods or least squares estimation techniques or some other method. The purpose of

Table 12.4

UTILITY DECISION TABLE: PAYOFF RANGE $10,000 TO −$8,000

UTILITY		PROBABILITY		EXPECTED UTILITY OF BET	
Best Outcome	Worst Outcome	Winning, i.e., Best Outcome (p)	Losing, i.e., Worst Outcome (1 − p)	$U(b) = U(\$10,000)(p) + U(-\$8,000)(1-p)$	UTILITY INDIFFERENT CASH PAYOFF EQUIVALENT
1	0	1.0	.0	1.0	$10,000
1	0	.9	.1	.9	3,250
1	0	.8	.2	.8	2,750
1	0	.6	.4	.6	0
1	0	.4	.6	.4	−2,000
1	0	.2	.8	.2	−6,000
1	0	.0	1.0	.0	−8,000

Table 12.5

UTILITY DECISION TABLE: PAYOFF RANGE $2,750 TO −$6,000

UTILITY		PROBABILITY		EXPECTED UTILITY OF BET	
Best Outcome	Worst Outcome	Winning, i.e., Best Outcome (p)	Losing, i.e., Worst Outcome (1 − p)	$U(b) = U(\$2,750)(p) + U(-\$6,000)(1-p)$	UTILITY INDIFFERENT CASH PAYOFF EQUIVALENT
.8[a]	.2	1.0	.0	.80	$2,750
.8	.2	.9	.1	.74	1,800
.8	.2	.8	.2	.68	1,100
.8	.2	.6	.4	.56	− 400
.8	.2	.4	.6	.44	−1,600
.8	.2	.2	.8	.32	−3,200
.8	.2	.0	1.0	.20	−6,000

[a]From Table 12.4.

obtaining a utility decision curve and the function that generates it is to have a continuum of *utility-payoff points* so that any bet within the payoff range $10,000 to −$8,000 can be evaluated quickly and precisely.

3.1.2 Interpretation of a Utility Decision Curve

The utility decision curve illustrated reveals several different risk-taking postures by the decision maker depending on the size of the dollar payoffs involved. In general, there are three types of risk preference and each

Table 12.6

UTILITY DECISION TABLE: PAYOFF RANGE $10,000 TO −$8,000

UTILIIY		PROBABILITY		EXPECTED UTILITY OF BET	
Best Outcome	Worst Outcome	Winning, i.e., Best Outcome (p)	Losing, i.e., Worst Outcome (1 − p)	$U(b) = U(\$10{,}000)(p) + U(\$0)(1 - p)$	UTILITY INDIFFERENT CASH PAYOFF EQUIVALENT
1 [a]	0	1.00	0	1.00	$10,000
1	0	.95	.05	.95	6,625
1	0	.85	.15	.85	3,000
1	0	.70	.30	.70	1,375
1 [a]	0	.60	.40	.60	0

[a]From Table 12.4.

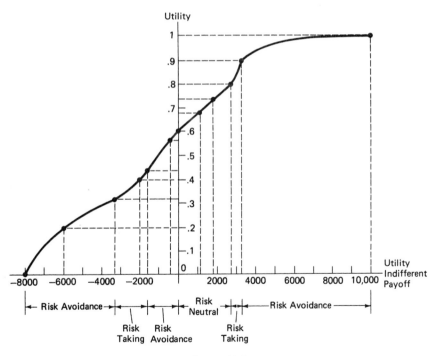

Figure 12.3

UTILITY DECISION CURVE

211

appears in Figure 12.4: risk neutrality, risk avoidance, and risk taking. When utility and payoff have a constant ratio over some range of payoffs, the decision maker is said to be risk neutral over that range. This risk preference is depicted by a straight line as shown in Figure 12.4. When each equal increment in utility requires an increasing increment in payoff over some range of payoffs, the decision maker is said to be risk averse over that payoff range. Analogously, when each equal increment in payoff results in an increasing increment in utility, the decision maker is said to be a risk taker. These cases also are depicted in Figure 12.4.

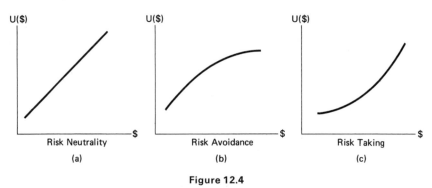

Figure 12.4

ILLUSTRATIVE TYPES OF RISK PREFERENCE

With regard to the utility decision curve constructed in Figure 12.4, the decision maker exhibits all three types of risk preferences depending on the payoff range. For both high payoffs and high losses the decision maker exhibits risk aversion. In the intermediate to small payoff range the decision reveals tendencies toward risk neutrality and risk preference. Once these characteristics are known the information can be put to use in a decision-making context.

3.2   The Exponential Utility Function

A convenient general form of *utility function* that captures each of the three types of utility preference and can be approximated by an equation is called the *exponential utility function*. One of its great virtues is the ease with which the utility indifferent payoff, that is, the risk-adjusted value of the bet, can be calculated when the probability distribution of the payoffs is known.

The exponential utility function can be written

$$U(\$) = \frac{1}{r}(1 - e^{-r\$})$$

where *e* is the base of the natural logarithm and $ is the monetary outcome. Three types of risk preference correspond to the following values of *r*:

$$\text{Risk aversion}: r > 0, U(\$) \text{ is concave}$$

$$\text{Risk taking}: r < 0, U(\$) \text{ is convex}$$

$$\text{Risk neutrality}: r = 0, U(\$) = \$$$

where $U(\$)$ is approximated by the second order expansion $(U)\$ = \$ - \frac{1}{2}r\$^2$. This utility function can accommodate utility decision curves as shown in Figure 12.3 by having different values of *r* for appropriate payoff intervals; for example, $r = 0$ for $\$10,000 > \$ > \$2,000$, $r = 0$ for $\$2,000 > \$ > -\$1,000$, etc.

The *risk-adjusted value* of the bet, *v*, that is, the price for which the decision-maker will be indifferent to holding a bet or selling it, for an exponential utility function, has the general form

$$v = -\frac{1}{r} \ln [E(e^{-r\$})],$$

where *E* denotes expected value. For a wide range of probability distributions the risk-adjusted value of the bet can be calculated from a closed form expression given the value of *r* corresponding to the decision maker's type and degree of risk preference. These results are summarized for several common types of probability distributions in Table 12.7.

3.3 Applications of Utility Analysis to Commodity Decisions Involving Risk

The following decision problems, while not exhaustive, indicate the range of commodity investment problems that are amenable to utility analysis for solution.

3.3.1 Assessing an Outright Position

Suppose an investor has an opportunity to invest $500 in silver with the following payoff schedule for a one-year investment period:

PAYOFF	PROBABILITY
−$1,000	.40
0	.10
1,000	.30
2,000	.10
4,000	.10

Table 12.7

UTILITY INDIFFERENT CASH EQUIVALENT PAYMENT (RISK-ADJUSTED VALUE)
FOR SELECT PROBABILITY DISTRIBUTIONS OF WINNING A BET

DISTRIBUTION	RISK ADJUSTED VALUE V	COMMENTS
1. Binomial $f(X \mid n, p) = \dfrac{n!}{X!(n-X)!} p^X(1-p)^{n-X}$	$-\dfrac{n}{r}\ln(1 - p + pe^{-ra})$	n, the number of trials can be viewed as n inadequate bets with the same v a represents the $ payment per success and X is the number of successes
2. Poisson $f(X \mid \lambda) = \dfrac{\lambda^X e^{-\lambda}}{X!}$	$\dfrac{\lambda}{r}(1 - e^{-ra})$	λ is the mean of the distribution a represents the $ payment per success X is the number of successes
3. Normal $f(X) = (2\pi\sigma^2)^{-1/2}\exp\left[\dfrac{-(X-u)^2}{2\sigma^2}\right]$ $-\infty < X < \infty$	$u - \dfrac{1}{2}r\sigma^2$	X is the payoff and can be any number u is the expected outcome σ^2 is the variance of the outcome $-\frac{1}{2}r\sigma^2$ is called the risk discount
4. Gamma $f(X \mid a, b) = \dfrac{a^b X^{b-1} e^{-aX}}{(b-1)!}$ $X \geq 0$	$\dfrac{b}{r}\ln\left(1 + \dfrac{r}{a}\right)$	X the payoff cannot be negative b/a is the mean b/a^2 is the variance

SOURCE: Gupta, S. K. and J. M. Cozzolino, *Fundamentals of Operations Research for Management*, San Francisco: Holden-Day, Inc. 1975, pp. 250–252.

On the basis of past investment decisions and their relative utility rankings assigned by the investor, the decision maker's utility-payoff curve is summarized in Table 12.8. Should the $500 investment be made or not? On the basis of the above discussion the decision will be to invest the $500 if the expected utility of the investment exceeds the utility value of keeping the $500. In this case the expected utility of the investment is

$$E(U) = .40(.00) + .10(.50) + .30(.53) + .10(.57) + .10(.63)$$
$$= .1859$$

and the expected utility of $500 is

$$E[U(500)] = .52.$$

Accordingly, the investor would not make the investment.

Table 12.8

INVESTORS UTILITY-PAYOFF SCHEDULE

UTILITY	JUST EQUIVALENT PAYOFF
1.00	10,000
.83	7,500
.66	5,000
.63	4,000
.59	3,000
.58	2,500
.57	2,000
.56	1,500
.53	1,000
.52	500
.50	–
.48	–250
.45	–500
.38	–750
.00	–1,000

Now, suppose the same investor could invest \$125 in the same opportunity. Would the investor make the investment or not? In this case, the payoffs would be $\frac{1}{4}$ of the \$500 investment and the expected utility would be

$$E(U) = .4(.48) + .1(.50) + .3(.51) + .1(.52) + .1(.53)$$
$$= .50$$

and the utility value of \$125 would be

$$E[U(125)] \approx .50.$$

In this case, the investor would be nearly indifferent. The different dollar amounts involved change the risk character of the problem. Depending on the size of the investment the investor will fall into different risk preference categories. Different risk categories, in turn, result in different decisions. If the amount invested fell below \$125 the investor would prefer the investment to holding cash.

3.3.2 To Hedge or Not

An investor with an exponential utility function with $r = 2 \times 10^{-4}$ has an opportunity to invest in a commodity that promises a large rate of return. However, the investment is not without risk. There is a .4 probability that a loss will be incurred and, if it is, the loss cannot be predicted. However, statistical analyses suggest strongly that the loss, if incurred, is randomly distributed with distribution

$$f(x) = \lambda e^{-\lambda x}$$

where $x \geq 0$, $\lambda = \frac{1}{4,500}$. The investor can hedge against the loss for a cost of $5,000. Should the investor "put on" the hedge?

The hedge will be placed if the risk-adjusted value of the investment without the hedge, v, corresponds to a loss larger than the cost of the hedge. That is the hedge will be "put on" if $v - \$5,000 > 0$. The risk-adjusted value of the investment is

$$v = -\frac{1}{r} \ln [E(e^{-rx})]$$

$$= -\frac{1}{2} 10^4 \ln \left[.4 \int_0^\infty e^{rx} f(x) dx + .6e^0 \right]$$

$$= -5,000 \ln \left[.4 \int_0^\infty e^{(r-\lambda)x} dx + .6 \right]$$

$$= -5,000 \ln \left[.4 \left(\frac{\lambda}{\lambda - r} \right) + .6 \right]$$

$$= -5,000 \ln (3.4)$$

$$= -\$6,119.$$

Since the risk-adjusted value of the investment without the hedge shows a loss of $6,119 the investor would put on the hedge at the lesser cost of $5,000.

3.3.3 How Much to Invest and What Amount to Hedge

An investor is considering a $10 million project with a normal distribution of payoffs. The project has an expected profit of $3 million and a variance of $15 million. For payoffs in excess of $1 million the investor perfers to avoid risk and has a risk coefficient of $r = .7$.

Investing all $10 million in the project produces a risk-adjusted value of

$$v = u - \frac{1}{2} r \sigma^2$$

$$= 3 - .35(15)$$

$$= -\$2.25 \text{ million.}$$

These results tell the investor not to invest at all. However, the investor may invest in the project by hedging some portion of the project. Here hedging would reduce variation risk more sharply than expected profit and may make an investment attractive. Assuming the investor elects to hedge some portion of the investment, the problem now is to determine how much should be hedged bearing in mind that every dollar hedged has zero profit, one dollar spent on hedging covers $10 of investment, and each dollar spent on hedging is returned at maturity.

To solve this problem the first step is to determine the optimal amount of the available funds ($10 million) to be unhedged. To accomplish this, let

Y = Total available funds ($10 million)

h = Hedge ratio (10 to 1)

B = Funds spent on hedging

U = Amount of funds in unhedged investment

G = Amount of funds in hedged investment.

From these definitions it follows directly that

$$U = Y - G - \frac{G}{h}.$$

Dividing both sides of the equation by Y gives the percent of available funds for the unhedged portion of the investment

$$a = 1 - g(1 + .1)$$

where $a = U/Y$ and $g = G/Y$. The expected return from the investment now is

$$E(x) = a \cdot 3$$

The variance of the payoff now is

$$\text{var}(x) = a^2 15$$

The value of a will be that value that maximizes the risk-adjusted value of the investment. Specifying v as a function of a and setting the first derivative of this expression with respect to a equal to zero yields

$$\frac{dv}{da} = \frac{d\left[a3 - \frac{1}{2}ra^2 15\right]}{da} = 0$$

$$= 3 - ra\,15 = 0$$

$$= 3 - 10.5a = 0$$

Solving the above expression for a produces the percent of $10 million unhedged

$$a^* = .286.$$

The percent of $10 million invested and hedged is

$$g^* = .649$$

and the percent of $10 million spent on hedging is

$$b^* = .065.$$

Following these guidelines the risk-adjusted value of the partially hedged investment would be

$$v = u - \frac{1}{2}r\sigma^2$$

$$= .858 - \frac{1}{2}.7(1.23)$$

$$= \$.428 \text{ million}$$

In this case if the investor would make the investment and hedge it according to the scheme summarized above, the risk adjusted value of the investment would improve dramatically from $-\$2.25$ million to $+\$.428$ million.

4 SUMMARY

This chapter discussed elements of decision making under uncertainty and risk. Special emphasis was given to decision making under conditions of risk. In this case the probabilities of the possible outcomes are known. The use and limitations of the expected monetary value criterion for decision making under risk were set forth.

The notion and measurement of risk as variability around the expected outcome also was given special attention. The concept of utility was used to combine expected monetary value with the measurement of risk. In this regard the construction of Von Neuman—Morgenstern utility functions was demonstrated for commodity decision making. Finally several applications of utility functions to decision making under risk were given.

5 BIBLIOGRAPHY

FISHBURN, P. C., *Decision and Value Theory*. New York: John Wiley, 1964.
FRIEDMAN, M., and L. J. SAVAGE, "The Utility Analysis of Choices Involving Risk," *The Journal of Political Economy*, 56, No. 4 (1948), pp. 279–304.

GUPTA, S. K. and J. M. COZZOLINO, *Fundamentals of Operations Research for Management,* San Francisco: Holden-Day, Inc. 1975.

HADLEY, G., *Introduction to Probability and Statistical Decision Theory.* San Francisco: Holden-Day, 1967.

HAMBURG, M., *Statistical Analysis for Decision Making,* 2nd ed. New York: Harcourt Brace Jovanovich, 1977.

RAIFFA, H., and R. SCHLAIFER, *Applied Statistical Decision Theory.* Cambridge, Mass.: MIT Press, 1968.

RAO, J. C. T., *Quantitative Analysis of Financial Decisions.* New York: Macmillan, 1969.

VON NEUMAN, J., and O. MORGENSTERN, *Theory of Games and Economic Behavior.* Princeton, N.J.: Princeton University Press, 1947.

13

ELEMENTS OF MATHEMATICAL PROGRAMMING

▐▌▌▌▐▌

1 INTRODUCTION

The commodity trader faces the economic problem of allocating scarce resources among competing ends over some time interval. These decisions can involve many commodities, markets, and constraints as well as stochastic elements clouding the possible outcomes and relationships. As the number of parameters and variables grows, the need for efficient solution methodologies becomes imperative. Mathematical programming methods can help achieve these efficiencies for a wide variety of decision problems that arise in commodity trading and investment.

Among the most relevant methodologies are classical programming and nonlinear programming. Emphasis here is placed on those methods that fit the nature of commodity trading problems. In particular the methodologies given special emphasis include dynamic programming, multiperiod-multi-commodity programming, and probabilistic programming. Each of these methods is discussed through their application to commodity trading problems. Preceding these discussions is a brief summary of select elements of classical and nonlinear programming to help set the stage for the subsequent topics.

2 ELEMENTS OF CLASSICAL AND NONLINEAR PROGRAMMING

In general a *mathematical programming problem* is comprised of instruments or controls, constraints that impinge on the value the controls may take, and an objective function that relates the decision maker's criterion to the control variables or instruments.

Such a problem may be summarized as follows;

$$\max F(x_1, x_2, \ldots, x_n)$$

subject to

$$x_i \in X, i = 1, 2, \ldots, n$$

where the x_i, $i = 1, 2, \ldots, n$ are the *instruments*, $F(x_1, \ldots, x_n)$ is the *objective function* and $x_i \in X$ denotes the condition that the x_i's only take on *acceptable values*, that is, are members of the set X of the x_i's that satisfy the *constraints* placed upon them.

The precise type of mathematical programming problem depends on the type of objective function and the type of constraints.

2.1 Classical Programming

When the mathematical programming problem has a differentiable objective function and equality constraints that number less than the number of instruments, the problem is commonly referred to as a *classical programming problem*. This class of problems can be denoted

$$\max_{\substack{w.r.t. x_i \\ i=1,\ldots,n}} F(x_1, \ldots, x_n)$$

subject to the constraints

$$G^1(x_1, \ldots, x_n) = K_1$$
$$G^2(x_1, \ldots, x_n) = K_2$$
$$G^m(x_1, \ldots, x_n) = K_m$$

where $m < n$, $G^j(x_1, \ldots, x_n)$ is a differentiable function in the x_i's, and the superscript j, $j = 1, 2, \ldots, m$ denotes the jth constraint, and w.r.t. means with respect to.

The solution of this type of problem typically invokes the use of a method known as the *Lagrangian multiplier technique*. In essence this method recasts the original problem into a new objective function that includes the constraints. In the above example the *Lagrangian formulation* would be

$$\max_{\substack{w.r.t.\,x_i,\,i=1,\ldots,n \\ \lambda_j,\,j=1,\ldots,m}} Z = F(x_1, \ldots, x_n) + \sum_{j=1}^{m} \lambda_j [K_j - G^j(x_1, \ldots, x_n)]$$

where the λ_j are constants of proportionality whose values are to be solved for along with the optimal values of the x_i's. The solution to this problem ensures the solution to the original objective function and the satisfaction of the m constraints.

While this approach involves the solution of $n + m$ variables and seemingly involves more effort, it is not without redeeming value. The additional m values for the Lagrangian multipliers impart new and useful information. In the context of the above problem the Lagrangian multipliers measure the rate of change in the objective with regard to some small change in the value of the constraint. For example, if one of the constraints was the size of an investment budget and the objective is to maximize profits, then the Lagrangian multiplier for this constraint would measure the rate of change in profits for a small change in the size of the budget constraint; for example, if $\lambda = .25$, and the budget constraint is raised by one dollar, profits go up by 25¢.

From the calculus the necessary conditions to achieve the objective in its Lagrangian form are

$$\frac{\partial z}{\partial x_i} = \frac{\partial F(x_1, \ldots, x_n)}{\partial x_i} - \sum_{j=1}^{m} \lambda_j \frac{\partial G(x_1, \ldots, x_n)}{\partial x_i} = 0 \text{ for } i = 1, \ldots, n$$

and

$$\frac{\partial z}{\partial \lambda_j} = K_j - G^j(x_1, \ldots, x_n) = 0 \qquad\qquad \text{for } j = 1, \ldots, m$$

where $\partial z/\partial x_i$ and $\partial z/\partial \lambda_i$ are the partial derivatives of the constrained objective function with respect to the variables x_i and λ_j, respectively.[1]

An example of classical programming arising in commodity trading is the selection of a portfolio of commodities where the objective is to minimize the variation of the return on the portfolio subject to constraints on the amount of funds available to invest and the level of return provided by the portfolio. The intracacies of commodity portfolio selection are the subject of Chapter 24 and are not repeated here. As a preview of these problems a simple illustrative example would be

$$\max_{w.r.t.\,x_i,\,\lambda_i} z = -A \sum_{i=1}^{n} \sum_{k=1}^{n} x_i x_k c_{ik} + \lambda_1 \left(1 - \sum_{i=1}^{n} x_i\right) + \lambda_2 \left(R - \sum_{i=1}^{n} x_i r_i\right)$$

1. For a more detailed discussion of these conditions and the second order conditions see Courant 1966.

where the c_{ik} are numerically specified covariances between the returns on investments i and k, x_i denotes the percent of available funds allocated to the ith investment, $(1 - \sum_{i=1}^{n} x_i)$ is a constraint that requires the total percent of invested funds adds up to 100 percent as it must, r_i is the expected return on the ith investment alternative, R is the desired rate of return on the portfolio, and A is the coefficient of risk aversion (see Chapter 12).

The *first order conditions* to achieve this objective are

$$\frac{\partial z}{\partial x_i} = -2A \sum_{k=1}^{n} x_k C_{ik} - \lambda_1 - \lambda_2 r_i = 0, i = 1, \ldots, n$$

$$\frac{\partial z}{\partial \lambda_1} = 1 - \sum_{i=1}^{n} x_i \qquad\qquad = 0$$

$$\frac{\partial z}{\partial \lambda_2} = R - \sum_{i=1}^{n} x_i r_i \qquad\qquad = 0.$$

These equations now must be solved simultaneously for values of the x_i's, λ_1 and λ_2 that satisfy the above first-order conditions.

2.2 Nonlinear Programming

Using the notation employed above, the *nonlinear programming problem* may be written

$$\max_{w.r.t. x_i} F(x_1, \ldots, x_n)$$

subject to

$$G^1(x_1, \ldots, x_n) \leq K_1$$
$$\vdots \qquad\qquad \vdots$$
$$G^m(x_1, \ldots, x_n) \leq K_m$$

where now the constraints are of the inequality variety. Once again the functions F and G^j are differentiable, m and n are finite, and the K_j are given constants. In addition to the inequality constraints the difference between this class of problems and the classical programming problem is that m and n do not have any restrictions on their relative sizes: that is $n \lessgtr m$. It also must be noted that the $\leq$ inequality is simply a convention and inequalities of the $\geq$ variety also can be used.

2.2.1 The Kuhn-Tucker Conditions

The nonlinear programming problem given above may be recast as a Lagrangian function by converting the inequality constraints to equality constraints through the use of slack variables. The conversion of the m inequality constraints to equality constraints is accomplished by adding a *slack variable* to each of the m constraints as follows:

$$G^j(x_1, \ldots, x_n) + S_j = K_j$$

where the slack variable s_j is defined as

$$S_j \equiv K_j - G^j(x_1, \ldots, x_n).$$

The Lagrangian function now may be written

$$\max_{w.r.t. x_i, \lambda_i, s_i} z = F(x_1, \ldots, x_n) + \sum_{j=1}^{m} \lambda_j(K_j - S_j - G^j(x_1, \ldots, x_n))$$

where the λ_j are the Lagrangian multipliers noted in Section 2.1. The conditions for the maximization of the above Lagrangian function are known as the *Kuhn-Tucker conditions*[2] and may be written

$$\frac{\partial F(x_1, \ldots, x_n)}{\partial x_i} - \sum_{j=1}^{m} \lambda_j \frac{\partial G^j(x_1, \ldots, x_n)}{\partial x_i} \leq 0, i = 1, \ldots, n$$

$$\left[\frac{\partial F(x_1, \ldots, x_n)}{\partial x_i} - \sum_{j=1}^{m} \lambda_j \frac{\partial G^j(x_1, \ldots, x_n)}{\partial x_i}\right] x_i = 0, i = 1, \ldots, n$$

$$x_i \geq 0, i = 1, \ldots, n$$

$$K_j - G^j(x_1, \ldots, x_n) \geq 0, j = 1, \ldots, m$$

$$\lambda_j[K_j - G^j(x_1, \ldots, x_n)] = 0, j = 1, \ldots, m$$

$$\lambda_j \geq 0, j = 1, \ldots, m.$$

To illustrate a nonlinear programming problem reconsider the portfolio problem in Section 2.1.1 where now the objective function and constraints are

$$\max_{w.r.t. x_i} z = -A \sum_{i=1}^{n} \sum_{k=1}^{n} x_i x_k c_{ik}$$

subject to

$$\sum_{i=1}^{n} x_i = 1$$

$$\sum_{i=1}^{n} x_i r_i \geq R.$$

The principal difference between this problem and the one in Section 2.1.1

2. H. W. Kuhn and A. W. Tucker, "Non-Linear Programming" in *Proceedings of the Second Berkeley Symposium on Mathematical Statistics and Probability*, ed. Jerzy Neyman (Berkeley: University of California Press, 1951), p. 483.

is the inequality constraint on the return from the portfolio. The Kuhn-Tucker conditions for this problem are

$$-2A \sum_{k=1}^{n} x_k c_{ik} - \lambda_1 - \lambda_2 r_i \leq 0, i = 1, \ldots, n$$

$$\left(-2A \sum_{k=1}^{n} x_k c_{ik} - \lambda_1 - \lambda_2 r_i\right) x_i = 0, i = 1, \ldots, n$$

$$x_i \geq 0, i = 1, \ldots, n$$

$$1 - \sum_{i=1}^{n} x_i = 0$$

$$R - \sum_{i=1}^{n} x_i r_i \geq 0$$

$$\lambda_1 \left(1 - \sum_{i=1}^{n} x_i\right) = 0$$

$$\lambda_2 \left(R - \sum_{i=1}^{n} x_i r_i\right) = 0$$

$$\lambda_j \geq 0, j = 1, 2.$$

Owing to the existence of the inequality condition the solution of the above conditions for the optimal values of the x_i's and the λ_j's is not straightforward algebra. Indeed the above conditions may be highly nonlinear and require nonlinear solution methods such as the Newton-Raphson method.[3]

The above conditions, however, happen to be linear and this serves as a useful introduction to linear and quadratic programming which are special cases of the nonlinear programming problem. As will be shown in the next section, the above nonlinear problem is a quadratic programming problem. Its solution conditions are linear and may use linear programming methods to perform the numerical solution.

2.2.2 Linear Programming

A so-called *linear programming problem* is a special case of a nonlinear programming problem. Here all the functions are linear: the objective function and each of the constraints. The primary points in common with nonlinear programming are the inequality constraints and the lack of any restrictions on the relative size of the number of instruments and the number of constraints. Continuing with the same notation used earlier, an illustrative linear programming problem can be written

$$\max_{w.r.t. x_i} z = \sum_{i=1}^{n} x_i r_i$$

3. These and other methods of nonlinear estimation can be found in Marquandt 1963, and Powell 1972.

subject to

$$\sum_{i=1}^{n} x_i b_{i1} \leq K_1$$

$$\cdot \qquad \cdot$$
$$\cdot \qquad \cdot$$
$$\cdot \qquad \cdot$$

$$\sum_{i=1}^{n} x_i b_{im} \leq K_m.$$

where the b_{ij} are known parameters.

For problems with large numbers of variables the problem can be solved efficiently using an iterative technique for solving sets of linear equations known as the simplex method. This method first requires the inequality constraints to be converted to equality constraints. This is accomplished by introducing a slack variable into each inequality constraint. If a constraint is of the less than or equal to variety then a slack variable must be included to enforce the equality. If a constraint is of the greater than or equal to variety then a slack variable must be subtracted to enforce the equality and an artificial variable must be added to the constraint in order to establish an initial basic feasible solution. For example, if one of the constraints in the above problem was

$$\sum_{i=1}^{n} x_i b_{iq} \geq K_q$$

it would require both a slack variable, S_q and an artificial variable a_q:

$$\sum_{i=1}^{n} x_i b_{iq} - S_q - a_q = K_q.$$

The simplex method makes use of the result that if a solution to the problem exists it also exists at a corner point, that is, at a vertex or intersection of the constraints. The *simplex method* moves from vertex to vertex until it finds an optimal solution. An optimal solution is found when a movement to any neighboring vertex does not produce an improvement in the value of the objective function. The selection of the vertices considered follows intuitively simple rules: From an initial "basis" (i.e., vertex) one moves toward that neighboring vertex that has the most dramatic impact on the objective function; for example, if the objective is maximization then the next vertex chosen is the neighboring one that has the greatest positive contribution per unit to the objective function. The starting vertex is that vertex corresponding to the case where all of the slack or artificial slack variables are set equal to their respective constraint values. Each new vertex considered is equal to the previous vertex except one of the variables in the previous vertex has been replaced by a variable heretofore not used to define that vertex. The artificial slack variables are given arbitrarily large and adverse impacts on the objective function: negative if the objective is maximization and positive if minimization. This helps ensure the solution values of the artificial variables will be forced to zero.

2.2.3 Quadratic Programming

A quadratic programming problem is another special case of the non-linear programming problem. Here the objective function is quadratic and the constraints are all linear. This type of problem may be summarized

$$\max_{w.r.t.\,x_i} F(x_1, \ldots, x_n) = \sum_{i=1}^{n} x_i c_i - \frac{1}{2} \sum_{i=1}^{n} \sum_{j=1}^{n} x_i x_j q_{ij}$$

subject to

$$\sum_{i=1}^{n} x_i b_{i1} \leq K_1$$

$$\vdots \qquad \vdots$$

$$\sum_{i=1}^{n} x_i b_{im} \leq K_m$$

where $q_{jk} = q_{kj}$. In general the solution to this type of problem requires the satisfaction of the Kuhn-Tucker conditions noted in Section 2.1.1.

It is important to note that Kuhn-Tucker conditions for a quadratic programming problem are all linear. This was demonstrated in the portfolio optimization example in Section 2.2.1 where the Kuhn-Tucker conditions were derived for a quadratic function subject to linear constraints. This result in turn means that the solution of a quadratic programming problem can be recast as a linear programming solution of the corresponding Kuhn-Tucker conditions. For the above example the derived linear programming problem for the optimization of the quadratic programming problem can be written

$$\min \sum_{i=1}^{n} a_i$$

subject to

$$\sum_{j=1}^{n} q_{ij} x_j + \sum_{k=1}^{m} b_{ij} \lambda_{n+k} - \lambda_i + a_i = c_i, \, i = 1, \ldots, n$$

$$\sum_{i=1}^{n} b_{ij} x_i + S_{n+k} = K_k, \, k = 1, \ldots, m$$

$$x_i \geq 0, \, i = 1, \ldots, n+m$$

$$y_i \geq 0, \, i = 1, \ldots, n+m$$

$$a_i \geq 0, \, i = 1, \ldots, n$$

3 CONTROL PROBLEMS AND PROBABILISTIC PROGRAMMING PROBLEMS

Two other types of problems are especially relevant for commodity trading applications: control problems and probabilistic programming problems. The former involve optimization over time and the latter are designed to contend with stochastic influences on the optimization problem.

3.1 Control Problems

The distinguishing feature of a control problem is its intertemporal perspective. From an economic vantage its objective is to optimally allocate scarce resources over some prescribed interval of time. Here, the objective function is defined over some time interval and the constraints include relationships called equations of motion that describe how the control variables are linked to changes in state variables that describe the system. In general *a continuous control problem* can be summarized as follows:

$$\max_{[u(t)]} J = \int_{t_0}^{t_1} I(x, u, t) \, dt + F(x_1, t_1)$$

subject to

$$\dot{x} = f(x, u, t)$$

$$x(t_0) = x_0$$

$$[x(t), t] \in T$$

$$u(t) \in U$$

where $\dot{x} = f(x, u, t)$ are the *equations of motion*, the x_i's are now *state variables* $\dot{x}_i$ is the time rate of change of x_i, and the u_k's are *control variables* used to "steer" the system optimally over some prescribed time interval from t_0 to t_1 and $F(x_1, t_1)$ is the terminal value of the objective function. Mathematically the problem is one of finding time paths for the control variables that achieve the objective subject to the constraints on the control variable $[u(t)] \in U$, constraints on the state variables $[x(t), t] \in T$, and their relationship over time given by the equations of motion. Among the useful variants of this type of problem are dynamic programming problems and multiperiod-multicommodity programming problems. Examples of each of these problems are given below.

3.1.1 Dynamic Programming

Dynamic programming is designed to handle problems that are multistage, sequential, or dynamic in character, for example, when decisions that are made at one point have consequences for subsequent decisions. Dynamic programming per se is not a specific rule or technique as much as it is a way of approaching or recasting a problem. In essence, it is the decomposition of a large problem into a more manageable sequence of smaller problems. The actual solution at each stage may require calculus, statistics, linear programming, or some combination of all three.

In general, the approach may be summarized as follows:

FIRST: The problem is divided into N stages.

SECOND: Each stage has
  i. Initial state as of stage N: S_N
  ii. Decision variable(s) as of stage N: A_N
  iii. Payoff (loss) function valued as of stage N: $R_N = r_n(S_N, A_N)$
  iv. State adjustment from previous stage to next state $S_{N-1} = s_N(S_N, A_N)$

THIRD: For reasons of efficiency and logic the problem is solved from the end back to the beginning, for example, from stage N to $N - 1$ and then from stage $N - 1$ to stage $N - 2$, and so on.

FOURTH: The objective function is defined in a recursive form covering the entire number of stages; for example

$$F_N(S_N) = \max [r_N(S_N, A_N) + F_{N-1}(S_{N-1})]$$

subject to

$$S_{N-1} = s_N(S_N, A_N).$$

To illustrate the application of the method a sequential stochastic decition problem and a multistage deterministic problem are presented.

3.1.1.1 A sequential stochastic commodity decision problem.

Insofar as the conditions of the market evolve over time the corresponding decisions to buy or sell also are evolutionary in nature. That is not to say that all technical analysis leads to or employs some form of sequential decision making. Rather, it is to say that sequential decision making often is required. As noted earlier, sequential decisions may involve the choice between taking some terminal action immediately or deferring that action and obtaining more information before making the terminal decision. Here the decision to gather more information or not would precede the decision to take some terminal action. This type of problem frequently involves some form of Bayesian statistical analysis and examples of this type already have been given and need not be repeated here.

Other types of stochastic sequential decision problems encountered by commodity traders and analysts also can be couched in terms of a dynamic programming problem. For example, consider the following problem: As of day t a commodity trader has taken a position to sell silver at $9.80 an ounce for delivery at the end of day $t + 4$. As of time t the spot price is $9.60.

Moreover the price changes from day to day with the following probability schedule:

	CHANGE IN PRICE		
	−$.20	0	+$.20
Probability if price decreased yesterday	.50	.30	.20
Probability otherwise	.33	.34	.33

The trader would like to maximize expected profits. This problem can be solved through dynamic programming by setting up the appropriate recursive relations and objective function.

In this problem there are many possible price paths that may emerge from Monday through Friday. Exhaustive enumeration is a time-consuming process and the dynamic programming approach is decidedly more efficient: Instead of evaluating each of the many possible paths at each stage of the process and selecting the one with the *highest* expected payoff one may start from the end of the week (assuming a five-day business week) and optimize at each stage recursively back to the first day. The decision at each stage, of course, is whether to buy that day or wait on the basis of a higher expected reward if one buys the next day. This approach reduces the number of calculations by over 65 percent. The problem may be solved as follows: First, let $t = 1, 2, 3, 4, 5$ denote the days of the week where $t = 1$ is the delivery day and $t = 5$ is the day the short position was taken. Second, let P_{ji} denote the ith price at stage (day) j. Third, let $P(c_j | S)$ denote the conditional probability distribution of price changes c_j conditioned on the stage S that indicates whether a price decrease occurred the previous day $(t + 1)$ or not. That is, when the previous day's price change c_{t+1} is positive or zero

$$P(c_t | S) = \begin{cases} .333 \text{ for } c_t = +20 \\ .334 \text{ for } c_t = \ \ \ 0 \\ .333 \text{ for } c_t = -20 \end{cases}$$

and when c_{t+1} is negative

$$P(c_t | S) = \begin{cases} .20 \text{ for } c_t = +20 \\ .30 \text{ for } c_t = \ \ \ 0 \\ .50 \text{ for } c_t = -20. \end{cases}$$

Fourth, as of the last day Friday (i.e., the first stage), the only possible decision is to buy if one hasn't bought already and the profit function is

$$F_1(P_{1i}) = (\$9.80 - P_{1i})$$

for each of the $i = 1, \ldots, 11$ possible Friday prices ranging from $P_{11} = \$10.40$ to $P_{1.11} = \$8.80$.

Fifth, for all days prior to Friday, that is, for $t = 2, 3, 4, 5$ the decision to buy that day or wait until the next day is determined by the objective function

$$F_t = \max \begin{cases} F_t(P_{ti}) = \$9.80 - P_{ti} \text{ for all } i: \text{Buy} \\ \sum_{c=-20}^{+20} F_{t-1}(P_{ti} + c_{ti}, S)P(c_{ji}|S): \text{Wait.} \end{cases}$$

The solution is to not buy until Friday since the expected outcome of waiting is higher than buying before Friday. This rule offers an expected profit of almost 32¢ compared to the Monday profit of 20¢.

This problem, of course, does not weigh the uncertain 32¢ profit on Friday against the 20¢ profit which is a sure thing as of Monday; that is, the problem assumes risk neutrality. The extension to accommodate risk avoidance can be made and the probability information calculated. Here, the decision maker then must decide whether the extra 12¢ profit is worth the risk of a possible loss measured by the probability of achieving an outcome below a 20¢ profit. This, of course, depends on the risk-return preference of the decision maker; for example, for a probability of loss of 5 percent the decision to wait would be made but for a probability of loss of 10 percent the silver would be bought. These cumulative probabilities may change as the sequence of events emerges and therefore must be recalculated at each stage.

3.1.1.2. A sequential deterministic commodity decision problem. *Deterministic dynamic programming* also has many commodity trading applications. Here, futures market hedging operations are particularly amenable. Consider a processor that sells a commodity such as "city dressed" hogs. As of August 20, 1979, the processor would like to accept three consecutive four-month purchase orders from customers running through August 1980, provided at least $30,000 in profit can be made and the company's cold storage capacity limits are not exceeded. The processor may purchase live hogs on the futures market to cover this period and may sell as much or as little as he has available each period. At present the sales prices of the processor to his customers less processing and delivery costs for each four-month period and their corresponding futures market prices are as follows:

COMPARATIVE PRICE PROFILES
¢ PER POUND

PRICE CATEGORY	FOR PERIOD BEGINNING		
	September '79	January '80	May '80
Sales prices less processing and delivery costs	81	86	84
Futures market purchase prices	82	81	83

Storage capacity is 300,000 pounds, and inventory beginning September '79 will be 30,000 pounds. Selling precedes buying each period so the capacity constraint is on beginning inventory plus net additions each period.

With these conditions one may use dynamic programming to determine the profit-maximizing quantities to purchase in the futures market for each delivery month, the amounts of inventory at the beginning of each period, and total profits. If profits are high enough then the futures market quantities solved for will be purchased and the forward sales consummated.

Using j to denote the decision period the problem can be summarized as follows:

FIRST: Let x_j and y_j denote the quantities purchased and sold respectively in stage j.

SECOND: The next period's beginning inventory is equal to the current period's inventory plus net additions, that is,

$$S_{j-1} = S_j + x_j - y_j$$

where once again j measures the future time remaining in the problem.

THIRD: The inventory constraint is $S_j \leq 300,000$ for any period.

FOURTH: The objective function is to maximize total return for the next n stages beginning with inventory level S_n and subject to the obvious constraints that in period j sales must not be negative or greater than what is available in inventory at the beginning of period j and that purchases cannot be negative or greater than maximum capacity less starting inventory plus sales in any given period. This may be denoted:

$$F_j = \max [p_j y_j - c_j x_j + F_{j-1}(S_j + x_j - y_j)]$$

subject to

$$0 \leq y_j \leq S_j$$
$$0 \leq x_j \leq 300,000 - S_j + y_j.$$

This dynamic programming problem is a sequential linear programming problem. The first-stage solution, that is, the solution for the four-month period beginning May 1980, is

$$F_1(S_1) = \max (84y_1 - 83x_1)$$

subject to

$$0 \leq y_1 \leq S_1$$

$$0 \leq x_1 \leq 300,000 - S_1 + y_1$$

and has solution

$$x_1 = 0$$
$$y_1 = S_1$$
$$F_1(S_1) = \text{maximum profit}_1 = 84S_1.$$

Note that $F_{j-1}(S_j + x_j - y_j)$ is not included in the objective function at this stage because the planning period ends in this stage.

The second stage problem is

$$\max [86y_2 - 81x_2 + F_1(S_2 + x_2 - y_2)]$$

subject to

$$0 \leq y_2 \leq S_2$$
$$0 \leq x_2 \leq 300{,}000 - S_2 + y_2$$
$$S_1 = S_2 + x_2 - y_2$$
$$F_2(S_2) = 86S_2 + \$ 9000$$

The third stage is solved in a similar fashion. The complete solution including profit values is

STAGE	FOUR-MONTH PERIOD BEGINNING	PURCHASES x_j	SALES y_j	BEGINNING STOCK S_j
3	Sept. '79	270,000	0	30,000
2	Jan. '80	300,000	300,000	300,000
1	May '80	0	300,000	300,000
	Total Profit = $45,600			

On the basis of these results the processor would sell the dressed hogs and cover these sales with purchases in the futures market as shown in the above table.

3.1.2 *Multiperiod-Multicommodity Linear Programming*

Not all problems are amenable to a dynamic programming reformulation and not all those that can be reformulated should be: There may be more efficient ways of proceeding. One alternative method that has been found to be useful for commodity-related allocation problems is multiperiod-multicommodity linear programming (MMLP). Typically, a linear programming problem is formulated as one in which an allocation is made across several alternatives so as to maximize or minimize the effect of this allocation measured by some linear criterion provided the allocation adheres to constraints placed on the values of the variables being solved for. The problem is a linear one because the objective function and the constraints ultimately take the form of linear equations. A standard maximization problem can be written

$$\max_{w.r.t. x_i} \ Z = v_1 x_1 + v_2 x_2 + \ldots + v_n x_n$$

subject to

$$\sum_{i=1}^{n} a_{ij} x_i \leq K_j, j = 1, \ldots, m$$

$$x \geq 0, i = 1, \ldots, n$$

where the v_i are per unit contributions of each variable, x_i, to the objective Z (e.g., profits); the a_{ij} are technical coefficients relating the control variables x_i to constraints K_j. The general structure of a MMLP is shown in Figure 13.1.

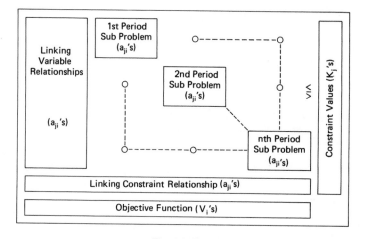

Figure 13.1

GENERAL STRUCTURE OF MMLP PROBLEM

SOURCE: F. S. Hillier and G. J. Lieberman, *Operations Research,* 2nd ed. (San Francisco: Holden-Day, 1974), pp. 150–51.

In the context of a commodity trader an objective function might be the maximization of returns from investments in several different commodities over a several-period time horizon. The constraints might be available funds by source, commodity and time period and accounting relationships. A detailed commodity investment example is given in Chapter 25. Briefly the problem is one of maximizing total returns for a firm that trades three commodities over two time periods by borrowing and investing between the three commodities subject to constraints on their cash availabilities, investment opportunities, rates of return, interest charges, and maturity structures. In this example short sales are not allowed. The problem can be summarized as follows:

$$\max_{\substack{w.r.t. \, l_{ijk}, B_{ijk} \\ i=1,2 \\ j=1,2 \\ i\leq j}} \pi = \sum_{i}^{2} \sum_{j}^{2} \sum_{k}^{3} r_{ijk}l_{ijk} - \sum_{i}^{2} \sum_{j}^{2} \sum_{k}^{3} c_{ijk}B_{ijk}$$
$$\scriptstyle i\leq j \qquad\qquad i\leq j$$

subject to

$$\sum_{j}^{2} \sum_{k}^{3} l_{ijk} - \sum_{j}^{2} \sum_{k}^{3} B_{ijk} = 0 \qquad \text{(Period 1 : Amount invested equals amount borrowed)}$$

$$\sum_{k}^{3} l_{22k} - \sum_{k}^{3} r_{11k}l_{11k} - \sum_{k}^{3} B_{22k} - \sum_{k}^{3} (1+c_{11k})B_{11k} \leq 0 \qquad \text{(Period 2 : Amount invested equals amount borrowed plus net returns Period 1 investments and borrowings maturity at the end of Period 1)}$$

$$B_{ijk} \leq K_{ijk} \qquad \text{(Available funds constraints by time period and commodity)}$$

$$B_{113} + B_{123} + B_{223} \leq K_3 \qquad \text{(Available funds constraints}$$
$$B_{113} + B_{123} \qquad\qquad \leq K_3 \qquad \text{from single source for different commodities over}$$
$$B_{123} + B_{223} \leq K_3 \qquad \text{both time periods)}$$

The numerical solution to this problem also is given and discussed in Chapter 25. Suffice it to say this method is well suited for a common class of investment decision problems arising in commodity trading.

3.1.3 Goal Programming

An interesting variation on multiperiod-multicommodity linear programming is a multiperiod-multicommodity linear programming problem with multiple objectives or goals. Linear programming problems with multiple criteria fall into one of three categories: goal programming, vector maximization techniques, and interactive methods. Each method uses a different conceptual approach to the problem and a different solution methodology. Goal programming treats the objectives as constraints and seeks to satisfy the objectives in the order (i.e., priorities) specified by the problem.

In its simplest form, a goal programming problem would have only one goal and would be a relatively straightforward transformation of the original linear programming problem. For example, suppose the original linear programming problem was

$$\max Z = 5x_1 + 3x_2$$

subject to

$$1x_1 + 2x_2 \leq 10$$
$$2x_1 + 1x_2 \leq 10$$
$$x_1, x_2 \geq 0.$$

The corresponding goal programming problem could be formulated

$$\min L = d^- + d^+$$

subject to

$$1x_1 + 2x_2 \qquad\qquad \leq 10$$
$$2x_1 + 1x_2 \qquad\qquad \leq 10$$
$$5x_1 + 3x_2 + d^- - d^+ = 1,000$$
$$x_1, x_2, d^-, d^+ \geq 0$$

where d^- is the amount by which the goal is underachieved and d^+ is the amount by which the goal is overachieved. The constraint form of the original objective function now includes on the right side an arbitrarily large value of 1,000 against which the overachievement and underachievement are measured; for example, d^+ measures the amount that Z exceeds 1,000. It must be noted that all goal programming models are solved as minimization problems. This is done because goal programming objective function is specified in terms of deviations from some "goal." It also must be noted that for a given goal one cannot solve for both d^- and d^+ at the same time. That is, it is impossible to overachieve and underachieve a goal simultaneously.

Multiple goals take the form of additional constraints in the linear programming formulation. For each of the goals there are a pair of deviation variables d^- and d^+. Depending on the nature of the original objectives constraints and goals either d^- or d^+ or both will appear for each goal in the goal programming objective function. Since multiple goal programming without priorities is equivalent to each goal having the same priority, it may be viewed as a special case of goal programming with priorities. The more general case is illustrated below.

To illustrate a multiple goal linear programming problem with priorities consider the following commodity resource allocation problem: Peoples Savings Bank is to invest in T-bills and GNMAs in period 1 and period 2. T-bills offer .04 return per period and GNMAs offer .03 per period. New deposit forecasts for the next two periods are $80 million per period and are considered to be reliable. Bank policy requires that the amount invested in T-bills in the first period must be at least $10 million and at least $30 million in the second period. Similarly the amounts invested in GNMAs in periods 1 and 2 must be at least \$20 million and \$40 million, respectively.

The bank also will reinvest its first-period earnings in period 2. Moreover the bank wants to hedge its investment against unanticipated increases in the rate of interest. It will do so through the sale of futures contracts in the assets of reference. Because an exact correspondence cannot be achieved in the futures markets with respect to the dollar amount of the assets to be hedged the bank has decided the hedge amount should not fall below the cash market investment amounts. The costs of hedging the T-bills and GNMAs are .02 and .01 per period, respectively.

The priorities for the bank are, first, meet all allocations constraints within and between periods; second, maximize return over the two periods; third, meet the hedge constraints.

The linear programming formulation of this problem without regard to the goal priorities may be written

$$\max Z = .03X_{11} + .04X_{12} + .03X_{21} + .04X_{22}$$

subject to

$$
\begin{aligned}
X_{11} &\geq 10 \\
X_{12} &\geq 30 \\
X_{21} &\geq 20 \\
X_{22} &\geq 40 \\
X_{11} + X_{12} \qquad + .02h_{11} + .01h_{12} &\leq 80 \\
-.03X_{11} - .04X_{12} + X_{21} + X_{22} \qquad + .02h_{21} + .01h_{22} &\leq 80 \\
-X_{11} \qquad h_{11} &\geq 0 \\
-X_{12} \qquad +h_{12} &\geq 0 \\
-X_{21} \qquad +h_{21} &\geq 0 \\
-X_{22} \qquad +h_{22} &\geq 0 \\
X_{11}, X_{12}, X_{21}, X_{22}, h_{11}, h_{12}, h_{21}, h_{22} &\geq 0
\end{aligned}
$$

The goal programming approach would first transform the objective function into the following (11th) constraint—also the 2nd priority:

$$.03X_{11} + .04X_{12} + .03X_{21} + .04X_{22} + d_{11}^- - d_{11}^+ = 100$$

where 100 represents an arbitrarily large profit goal.

Second the inequality constraints would be converted to equality constraints using the deviation variables d^- and d^+. These transformations are, by priority,

Priority 1

$$X_{11} + d_1^- - d_1^+ = 10$$
$$X_{12} + d_2^- - d_2^+ = 30$$
$$X_{21} + d_3^- - d_3^+ = 20$$
$$X_{22} + d_4^- - d_4^- = 40$$
$$X_{11} + X_{12} + .02h_{11} + .01h_{11} + d_5^- - d_5^+ = 80$$
$$-.03X_{11} - .04X_{12} + X_{21} + X_{22} + .02h_{21} + .01h_{22} + d_6^- - d_6^+ = 80$$

Priority 3

$$-X_{11} + h_{11} + d_7^- - d_7^+ = 0$$
$$-X_{12} + h_{12} + d_8^- - d_8^+ = 0$$
$$-X_{21} + h_{21} + d_9^- - d_9^+ = 0$$
$$-X_{22} + h_{22} + d_{10}^- - d_{10}^+ = 0$$

where the subscripts on the d's represent the original sequence of the constraints.

Priority 1 requires the satisfaction of constraints 1, 2, 3, 4, 5, and 6. Because the fifth and sixth constraints were originally of the $\leq$ variety this requires the minimization of d_5^+ and d_6^+. Similarly, because the first, second, third and fourth constraints were originally of the $\geq$ variety the first priority also requires that d_1^-, d_2^-, d_3^-, and d_4^- be minimized. The first priority in total can be denoted $P_1\,(d_1^- + d_2^- + d_3^- + d_4^- + d_5^+ + d_6^+)$ and is to be minimized. In a similar way the second and third priorities can be summarized $P_2(d_{11}^-)$ and $P_3\,(d_7^- + d_8^- + d_9^- + d_{10}^-)$, respectively. Taken together the goal programming model can be summarized as follows:

$$\min J = P_1(d_1^- + d_2^- + d_3^- + d_4^- + d_5^+ + d_6^+) + P_2(d_{11}^-) + P_3(d_7^- + d_8^- + d_9^- + d_{10}^-)$$

subject to

$$
\begin{aligned}
X_{11} \qquad\qquad\qquad\qquad\qquad\qquad\quad &+ d_1^- - d_1^+ = 10\\
X_{12} \qquad\qquad\qquad\qquad\qquad\qquad &+ d_2^- - d_2^+ = 30\\
X_{21} \qquad\qquad\qquad\qquad\qquad\quad &+ d_3^- - d_3^+ = 20\\
X_{22} \qquad\qquad\qquad\qquad\qquad &+ d_4^- - d_4^+ = 40\\
X_{11} + X_{12} + .02h_{11} + .01h_{12} \qquad\qquad\quad &+ d_5^- - d_5^+ = 80\\
-.03X_{11} - .04X_{12} + X_{21} + X_{22} \quad + .02h_{21} + .01h_{22} \quad &+ d_6^- - d_6^+ = 80\\
-X_{11} \qquad\qquad\qquad +h_{11} \qquad\qquad\qquad &+ d_7^- - d_7^+ = 0\\
-X_{12} \qquad\qquad\qquad +h_{12} \qquad\qquad\quad &+ d_8^- - d_8^+ = 0\\
-X_{21} \qquad\qquad\qquad +h_{21} \qquad\quad &+ d_9^- - d_9^+ = 0\\
-X_{22} \qquad\qquad\qquad +h_{22} \quad &+ d_{10}^- - d_{10}^+ = 0\\
.03X_{11} + .04X_{12} + .03X_{21} + .04X_{22} \qquad\qquad\qquad &+ d_{11}^- - d_{11}^+ = 100.
\end{aligned}
$$

It must be noted that the terms P_i are not parameters but instead represent the order of priorities. The solution to this problem involves a modified simplex approach to accommodate the multiple goals. In effect the new simplex tableau would have three objective functions, one for each priority. These objectives would be solved sequentially starting with the first priority. When no further improvement can be made in the first priority the second priority is minimized and so on. In the above example the tableau can be written as shown in Table 13.1. Here one would solve for the first priority, adjust the tableau accordingly and then move on to solve for the second priority and then to the last priority. The solution to this problem is

$$X_{11} = 10, h_{11} = 10, X_{12} = 69.1, h_{12} = 69.1$$
$$X_{21} = 20, h_{21} = 20, X_{22} = 61.9, h_{22} = 61.9$$
$$d^-_{11} = 93.86, \text{ and all other } d\text{'s} = 0$$

where

P_1 is satisfied

P_2 is not satisfied: the shortfall in the profit objective is $^-_{11} d = 93.86$; that is, profit is 6.14

P_3 is satisfied

and all values of the X's, h's and d's are in millions of dollars.

The great practical advantage of goal programming is its ability to accommodate multiple goals that often are not perfectly compatible and in so doing to demonstrate the trade-offs between goals as well as find optimal solutions. For a more detailed discussion Ijiri (1965) and Lee (1972) offer both theory and applications.

3.2 Probabilistic Programming

Probabilistic programming has evolved to meet the special needs of linear programming models owing to the presence of randomness in the parameters. A variety of approaches have evolved to meet these needs depending on the precise character and location of the randomness in the problem. The methods include *chance constrained programming, two-stage programming*, and *stochastic linear programming*, among others (see Sengupta and Fox 1975 and Tintner and Sengupta 1972 for surveys of these and other methods). In general, these methods have much in common: They use knowledge of the probability distribution of the random variables in the problem in order to convert the linear probabilistic problem into a deterministic but typically nonlinear problem. The deterministic problem then is recast as a linear programming problem through appropriate transformations or approximations. Finally, the objective function is redefined to conform with the new problem in such a way that the solution to the new problem also is a solution to the original problem.

Table 13.1

INITIAL GOAL PROGRAMMING TABLEAU

C_B	VARIABLES SOLVED FOR	X_{11}	X_{12}	X_{21}	X_{22}	h_{11}	h_{12}	h_{21}	h_{22}	d_1^-	d_1^+	d_2^-	d_2^+	d_3^-	d_3^+	d_4^-	d_4^+	d_5^-	d_5^+	d_6^-	d_6^+	d_7^-	d_7^+	d_8^-	d_8^+	d_9^-	d_9^+	d_{10}^-	d_{10}^+	d_{11}^-	d_{11}^+	SOLUTION VALUE
P_1	d_1^-	1								1	-1																					10
P_1	d_2^-		1									1	-1																			30
P_1	d_3^-			1										1	-1																	20
P_1	d_4^-				1											1	-1															40
0	d_5^-					.02	+.01											1	-1													80
0	d_6^-	-.03	-.04	+1	+1			+.02	+.01											1	-1											80
P_3	d_7^-	-1				+1																1	-1									0
P_3	d_8^-		-1				+1																	1	-1							0
P_3	d_9^-			-1				+1																		1	-1					0
P_3	d_{10}^-				-1				+1																			1	-1			0
P_2	d_{11}^-	.03	+.04	+.03	+.04																									1	-1	100

Goals

$(Z_j - C_j)$
$\begin{cases} P_3 \\ P_2 \\ P_1 \end{cases}$

		X_{11}	X_{12}	X_{21}	X_{22}	h_{11}	h_{12}	h_{21}	h_{22}	...	d_1^+	...	d_2^+	...	d_3^+	...	d_4^+						d_7^+		d_8^+		d_9^+		d_{10}^+		d_{11}^+	
P_3		-1	-1	-1	-1	1	1	1	1														-1		-1		-1		-1			
P_2		.03	.04	.03	.04																										-1	
P_1		1	1	1	1						-1		-1		-1		-1															

C_1 row (priorities): P_1 P_1 P_1 P_1 P_1 P_3 P_3 P_3 P_3 P_2

Where C_j = Coefficients in the goal programming objective function to be minimized

C_B = Objective function coefficients on the variables in the initial solution (basis)

Z_j = Sum of products of elements in CB column times corresponding element in column j associated with a given priority

$(Z_j - C_j)$ = Rate of net reduction (if negative $Z_j - C_j$ is rate of net increase)

3.2.1 A Stud Lumber Example

To illustrate the approach we will consider a two-stage programming problem patterned after one due to Danzig (1951) but arising in commodity trading.

A stud lumber producer is concerned with the least-cost determination of factory production, x, storage, y, and commodity market purchases, k, to meet client demands. The demand facing the firm, in thousands of board feet, q, is random with a uniform probability density function given by

$$f(q) = \frac{1}{(100 - 50)}$$

The two constraints facing the firm are first, total supply, consisting of production x plus commodity market purchases k, cannot fall below demand q; and second, the amount produced, x, and stored, s, must equal 120. Finally, the cost of production is \$200 per 1,000 board feet and the cost of purchasing it in the commodity market plus transportation, insurance and finance charges is \$250 per 1,000 board feet. This problem may be summarized as follows:

$$\min C = 200x + 250k$$

subject to

$$x + s = 120$$
$$x + k - y = q$$
$$x \geq 0, y \geq 0, s \geq 0, k \geq 0$$
$$f(q) = \frac{1}{100 - 50}$$

Now either production will be greater than demand or it will be less than or equal to it. This fact leads to the following decomposition of the objective function:

$$C = \begin{cases} 200x & \text{if } x > q \\ 200x + 250\,(q - x) & \text{if } x \leq q. \end{cases}$$

That is, if production exceeds demand there is no need to augment supplies from more expensive purchases in the futures market. There is a need otherwise.

There are three cases to consider: $x \geq 100$, $x \leq 50$, and $50 \leq x \leq 100$. In the first case the cost is

$$C = 200x.$$

In the second case the cost is

$$C = \int_{50}^{100} [200x + 250(q - x)]f(q) \, dq$$

$$= \int_{50}^{100} (-x + 5q) \, dq$$

$$= -50x + 18{,}750.$$

Finally, in the last case the cost is

$$C = \int_{50}^{x} 200x \, f(q) \, dq + \int_{x}^{100} [200x + 250(q - x)]f(q) \, dq$$

$$= \int_{50}^{100} \frac{200x}{50} \, dq + \int_{x}^{100} \frac{250(q - x)}{50} \, dq$$

$$= 2.5x^2 - 300x + 25{,}000$$

$$= 2.5[(60 - x)^2 + 6{,}400].$$

On the basis of the last case the total expected cost is minimized at a production level of $x = 60$. The optimal solution for x, $E(q)$, s and k are

$$x^* = 60$$
$$E(q) = 75$$
$$s^* = 60$$
$$k^* = q - 60 \text{ where } y^* = 0$$

respectively.

4 SUMMARY

We have covered select topics in mathematical programming that are of special interest to commodity traders and analysts. In general the large number of commodities, markets, and time periods, along with the often complex nature of the decision problems require mathematical programming methods to assess alternative decisions currently and efficiently. In particular classical, linear, quadratic, dynamic, and probabilistic programming methods are especially useful. The examples given in this chapter illustrate the application of some these methodologies to practical commodity problems. Some of the methods noted here did not include a detailed application. They include multiperiod-multicommodity linear programming and quadratic and linear programming. These methods are intimately tied to special problems such as commodity portfolio selection and integrated commodity trading. These topics are the subjects of entire chapters where their mathematical programming applications are discussed in detail.

5 BIBLIOGRAPHY

Courant, R., *Differential & Integral Calculus,* Vol. 2., New York: Interscience Publishers, 1966.

Dallenbach, H. G., and J. A. George, *Introduction to Operations Research Techniques.* Boston: Allyn & Bacon, 1978.

Dantzig, G. B., "Maximization of a Linear Function of Variables Subject to Linear Inequalities," in *Activity Analysis of Production and Allocation,* ed. T. C. Hoopmans. New York: John Wiley, 1951.

Dreyfus, S. E., and A. M. Law, *The Art and Theory of Dynamic Programming.* New York: Academic Press, 1977.

Fishburn, P. C., *Decision and Value Theory.* New York: John Wiley, 1964.

Gupta, S. K., and J. M. Cozzolino, *Fundamentals of Operations Research.* San Francisco: Holden-Day, 1975.

Hadley, G., *Linear Programming.* Reading, Mass.: Addison-Wesley, 1962.

————, *Nonlinear and Dynamic Programming.* Reading, Mass.: Addison-Wesley, 1964.

Hillier, F. S., and G. J. Lieberman, *Operations Research.* San Francisco: Holden-Day, 1967.

Ijiri, Y., *Management Goals and Accounting for Control.* Chicago: Rand McNally, 1965.

Lee, Sang M., *Goal Programming and Extensions.* Philadelphia: Auerbach Publishers, 1972. (New York: Petrocelli Books, 1973.)

Mao, J. C. T., *Quantitative Analysis of Financial Decisions.* New York: Macmillan, 1969.

Marquandt, D. W., "An Algorithm for Least Squares Estimation of Non-Linear Parameters, *Journal of the Society for Industrial and Applied Mathematics,* 2 (1963), 431–41.

Metzger, R. W., *Elementary Mathematical Programming.* New York: John Wiley, 1958.

Powell, M. J. D., "Some Properties of the Variable Metric Approach," in *Numerical Methods of NonLinear Optimization,* ed. F. A. Lootsma. New York: Academic Press, 1972.

Raiffa, H., and R. Schalifer, *Applied Statistical Decision Theory.* Cambridge, Mass.: MIT Press, 1968.

Sengupta, J. K., and K. A. Fox, *Optimization Techniques in Quantitative Economic Models.* New York: American Elsevier Pub. Co., 1975.

Tintner, G., and J. K. Sengupta, *Stochastic Economics.* New York: Academic Press, 1972.

III

TECHNICAL ANALYSIS

Technical analysis encompasses a wide range of analytical perspectives. While a universal definition of technical analysis may not be easy to find, a perusal of the literature reveals several distinguishing characteristics. First, it tends to focus on "short" time units of measurement, ranging from moment to moment at one extreme to monthly intervals at the other extreme. Second, it covers relatively short investment periods, ranging up to a year. Third, it concentrates on the explanation of price movements. Fourth, it centers on univariate and simple multivariate analysis of price movements. These include "transfer function" models that explain price movements in terms of some combination of their recent past, neighboring circumstances such as volume, episodic events, recent price movements in other commodities and, in some cases, factors seemingly combined in free association.

There is considerable agreement on what technical analysis does not consider. Technical analysis does not attempt to describe long-term movements in commodity prices or the effects of changes in the structural factors that determine the supply of and demand for a commodity. These efforts lie in the realm of fundamental analysis. While market pundits often invoke the terms "upward pressure" for demand and "downward pressure" for supply, technical analysis typically cannot "identify" demand or supply schedules in an economic-econometric context. At best it "identifies" a price series in a time series context and this identification is quite different from that used by economists and loosely invoked by so many market analysts.

Between the boundaries of technical analysis and fundamental analysis lies a gray area where the two overlap and a myriad of hybrids have evolved. To be sure, the two can be pursued rigorously and combined in some consistent integrated framework. Indeed, Part 4 and Part 5 indicate these applications. Nevertheless, some of the hybrids are born as much out of desperation as adherence to discipline and a few of these are discussed.

There is, of course, one fact that all those familiar with technical analysis can agree on: It is not a bromide or talisman for commodity price analysts. Technical analysis, and fundamental analysis for that matter, can at best enhance market judgment. Technical analysis enables the practitioner to systematically study and extract important information from a complex, dynamic, and uncertain world. While objectivity may dominate its intent it is nevertheless highly subjective and an art as much as a science.

In this section several chapters are presented that cover a wide range of technical analyses and their derivative trading rules. Chapter 14 summarizes the language, perspectives, and concepts used in technical analysis. Chapter 15 reviews essential elements of "bar" and "point and figure" chart analyses.

Price trends, oscillations, support levels, resistance levels, reversals, and other price patterns are analyzed using both bar charts and point and figure charts. A collage of technical trading algorithms also is presented. Included here are trend, channel, wave, congestion and N day opposite trading rules.

Univariate estimation and forecasting methods are considered in Chapter 16. Here, special emphasis is placed on moving averages, exponential smoothing, general exponential smoothing, auto-regressive integrated moving average models, and Kalman filtering. Confidence intervals and decision theory are combined to illustrate the trading implementation of these techniques.

Multivariate time series analysis of commodity price movements is presented in Chapter 17. Here, regression methods are emphasized with special consideration given to transfer function models of the Box-Jenkins and Kalman varieties. These procedures also are carried through to trading illustrations.

14

LANGUAGE AND AMBIENT
PERSPECTIVES OF TECHNICAL ANALYSIS

||||||||||||||||||||||||||||||||||||||||||||||||||||||||||||||||||||||||||||||||||||||||||||||||||||||||||||

1 INTRODUCTION

The ultimate objective of technical commodity analysis is to help establish and maintain a profitable trading operation and/or to limit losses while seeking new profit opportunities. This objective, of course, must answer several questions: what to buy or sell, when to take those actions, and at what prices. In an attempt to answer these questions the technical analyst focuses on the price movements of the commodities of interest. While other factors, such as volume and open interest, are often considered, the underlying philosophy is one that might be called "Austrian" after the school of economic thought that considers current prices reflect all the available information in the marketplace. Unlike, but not necessarily inconsistent with, the "Austrian" school, technical analysts rely on past price patterns to estimate future prices and/or to determine the prices at which trades should be made. This approach applies with equal weight to buying or selling a single commodity, or some combination of commodities with the same or different contract maturities.

In pursuit of its objective, technical analysis has generated a collection of terms to describe various market characteristics and trading notions. Unfortunately this language often conflicts with that used in other disciplines. Moreover, these terms and notions take on a widely disparate range of interpretations and applications. This lack of uniqueness stems in part from different trading perspectives and sensitivities, such as profit targets and rates of time preference, that can be as subjective as they are objective and economic. It also stems in part from a real world that all too frequently refuses to accommodate simplifying assumptions. Together these factors have given rise to an "analytical" approach that has great latitude in its inter-pretation and application. Be that as it may, a common language has evolved that captures generic market characteristics, trading objectives, and problems. The following terms are among the most important. Their definitions and correspondence to concepts in other disciplines, if any, are presented in the following sections.

2 TRENDS, SEASONALS, AND RELATED PATTERNS

2.1 The Trend

To the technical analyst the trend is loosely defined as the general direction of a commodity price. It is measured in a variety of ways including (1) a "trend line" connecting the trading tops (bottoms) of peaks achieved when the average direction of prices is down (up); (2) a "trend channel" bounded by trend line connecting the peaks and another trend line connecting the troughs; (3) a line, not necessarily straight, that runs through the mid-point of recent commodity prices.

2.2 Momentum

Technical analysts interpret trends with different slopes as having more or less "momentum"—the greater the slope the greater the momentum. Greater momentum, in turn, is viewed as a trend that is less likely to reverse itself, and if it does reverse it is likely to do so more slowly than a shallower trend with less momentum. The interpretation of momentum, or course, is just that: an interpretation. Its relationship to velocity and acceleration is more apparent than real. Nevertheless models of this type are explored in Chapter 15.

2.3 Reversal and Retracement

A trend is said to be in reversal when the succession of peaks and troughs no longer continue in the same direction as their recent past. When a trend reverses some but not all of its recent movement the reversal is called a retracement. Frequently this retracement is followed by a short period of congestion and the previous trend is reinitiated.

2.4 Trend Length

Despite all the characteristics of a trend the length of a trend is not well defined by technical analysts. What is long for one is often short for another. Several guidelines have emerged. Among the most common are the following: (1) When an oscillation has a period in excess of four years, and (2) when the number of movements in one direction is twice as frequent as movements in other directions. The former definition or guideline is borrowed from time series analysis and methods such as spectral analysis can be useful in uncovering these patterns. The latter definition is borrowed from nonparametric statistics and can be recast in terms of rank correlation tests, sign tests and runs tests. Applications of these tests are given in Chapter 10.

2.5 Seasonal Movements

Consistent with traditional time series and economic usage a "seasonal" movement is one that exhibits an oscillation that completes itself an integer number of times within one year. For the technical commodity analyst seasonal movements from five days to 12 months are monitored. Here spectral analysis may help reveal the character of the seasonal movements, and filters may be designed to remove and isolate them. The work of Granger and Hatanaka (1964), Brown (1963) and Sage and Melsa (1971) are especially useful in this regard.

2.6 Oscillations

Price movements around the trend that are not seasonals but that exhibit a recurring and stable pattern are called oscillations. These movements include cyclical "swings" of one-and-a-half to three years in length as well as other recurring patterns of longer or shorter periodicity.

2.7 Congestion or Consolidation

When prices are fluctuating around a constant price the market is said to be congested, or consolidated.

3 SEQUENCES OF DIFFERENT MOVEMENTS: PATTERN CLASSIFICATION

Technical analysts are prone to interpreting sequences of price patterns in their attempts to recognize an impending price movement. Over the years several patterns have become common language and, despite their lack of precision, are discovered with surprising uniformity among observers. These patterns are summarized below.

3.1 Fulcrum and Inverse Fulcrum

A congestion pattern that follows a downtrend is called a "fulcrum"; one that follows an uptrend is called an inverse fulcrum.

3.2 Resistance and Support

The upper bound or peak price of a congestion pattern is labeled a resistance level. It is said to be "bearish" if it is downward trending and "bullish" if upward trending. The lower bound or lowest price of a congestion pattern is called the support level and is said to be "bearish" if downward trending and "bullish" if upward trending.

3.3 Breakout and Catapult

A breakout is said to occur when the resistance (upside breakout) or support (downside breakout) levels are exceeded. When prices move toward and fluctuate narrowly near the established support or resistance level and then break out, the move is referred to as a "catapult" and prices are believed to continue in the "breakout" direction for some period. It is believed by many and proven by none that the longer the congestion period the more substantial the new trend or "breakout" will be when it occurs.

3.4 Triangles and Pennants

Combinations of trend lines, resistance, support, and congestion give rise to special variants that have acquired names of their own. The most common include triangles and pennants. A triangle occurs when the peaks and troughs are converging. This may occur when the trend price is rising, falling, or fluctuating around some constant value. These triangles are said to be ascending, descending, and symmetrical, respectively. A pennant formation is a downtrend or uptrend with resistance and support lines paralleling the "trend" and each other.

3.5 Tops and Bottoms

Technical analysis is especially interested in finding turning points, when prices have reached a peak or top and are about to fall or when they have reached a trough or bottom and are about to rise. There are several types of top and bottom formations. Among the most common patterns are head and shoulders, inverse heads and shoulders, double tops or double bottoms, scallops, saucers, and round tops and bottoms. These and other patterns together with corresponding trading rules are illustrated in the following chapters.

3.6 Gaps

When the low (high) for the day lies above (below) the high (low) of the previous day, then a gap is said to exist. Gaps are preliminary indications of a possible "breakout" or a change in momentum.

3.7 Corrective Patterns

Corrective patterns include congestion patterns and triangles as well as some variations on these themes. These variations include the zig-zag, flat, irregular, and extension patterns. The *zig-zag* pattern consists of a trend with a significant but false reversal. The *flat* pattern consists of reversals concentrated with reversals without a clear trend emerging. An *irregular* pattern is similar to a flat pattern but contains a new high following an uptrend or a new low following a downtrend. Finally, an *extension* pattern is one that continues in the direction of a trend after a minor reversal but does so for a longer period than any previous movement in that direction for the history of the current trend.

4 TRADING CONSIDERATIONS

While the above terms and notions help specify the characteristic of recent price movements the following concepts help direct trading operations based in part on these observations.

4.1 Preliminary and Confirming Indicators

Technical analysts typically identify changes in market price direction in two steps. First, they specify occurrences that historically are thought to be preliminary indications of an impending move. Here, for example, a gap following a congestion phase may be such an indication. Second, they specify subsequent price patterns that, if encountered after the preliminary indications, are considered confirming patterns and sufficient reason for taking action. Confirming patterns may be another gap following the first one or some minor retracement or combination of these events over some period of observation after the preliminary indication.

4.2 Technically Weak and Technically Strong Price Movements

The notion of technically weak and technically strong price movements is defined in terms of the size of the price movement as well as the change in open interest. A technically strong price movement is said to exist when either a price increase of extraordinary dimension occurs in conjunction with an increase in open interest, or when a major price decrease occurs in conjunction with a decrease in open interest. A technically weak movement is said to exist when either a major price increase occurs in conjunction with a decrease in open interest or when a major price decrease occurs in conjunction with an increase in open interest. These definitions of market strength and weakness have a simple forecast interpretation: Technically strong markets indicate continued movement in the same direction while technically weak markets indicate a small likelihood of a continued price movement in the same direction. As with most forecasting rules they are rarely doubted but often wrong.

4.3 Technical Rally and Technical Reaction

When prices rise sharply without provocation by outside or fundamental factors they are often followed by a retracement. This pattern is called a technical reaction. It is most commonly attributed to profit taking owing to the market's assessment that prices moved without lasting cause, an assessment which may be self-fulfilling. When prices fall sharply without apparent outside cause and are followed by a retracement, the price increase is referred to as a technical rally. Here again, the cause of the rally is attributed to profit taking based on the belief that the price fall was an aberration and bound to reverse in the near future.

4.4 Price Objective and Stop Loss

The ultimate objective of technical analysis is to identify prices at which trades should be made and orders placed with a high chance of capturing a profit. When preliminary and confirming price patterns have been encountered, a long (buy) or short (sell) position may be taken. The price at which the position is to be liquidated is referred to as the price objective and ultimately requires some form of price forecast. In order to limit losses in case the preliminary and confirming indicators are erroneous, a second liquidation price is calculated. This loss-limiting liquidation price is placed a predetermined number of basis points from the position price and is called the stop-loss price. Its calculation can be determined by the trader's financial position and by estimates of how large an unanticipated price reversal must be before it is considered a significant and lasting reversal or by other methods such as the use of options valuation information as discussed in Chapter 5. To be sure, when prices are moving in a profitable direction one need not maintain the original stop-loss price. In this case the stop-loss should move with or "trail" the price "trend" and thereby help lock in profits as they emerge.

5 SUMMARY

The terms and perspectives discussed in this chapter permeate every aspect of commodity trading and, despite their often ambiguous definitions and inconsistencies, their importance cannot be ignored. There are, of course, many ways to quantify these notions and the following chapters provide the two basic alternatives: Charting or mathematical-statistical estimation and forecasting procedures. While different in style and technical rigor, their objectives and many of their procedures are remarkably similar.

6 BIBLIOGRAPHY

BROWN, R. G., *Smoothing, Forecasting and Prediction of Discrete Time Series.* Englewood Cliffs, N.J.: Prentice-Hall, Inc., 1963.

GOULD, BRUCE G., *Dow Jones Irwin Guide to Commodities Trading.* Homewood, Ill.: Dow Jones–Irwin, 1973.

GRANGER, C. W. J. and M. MATANAKA, *Spectral Analysis of Economic Time Series.* Princeton University Press, 1964.

HALLBERG, M. C., and V. I. WEST., *Patterns of Seasonal Price Variations for Illinois Farm Products.* Circular 861. Urbana: University of Illinois College of Agriculture, 1967.

HIERONYMUS, THOMAS A., *Economics of Futures Trading.* New York: Commodity Research Bureau, 1971.

KROLL, STANLEY, *The Professional Commodity Trader.* New York: Harper & Row, 1974.

———, and IRWIN SHISHKO, *The Commodity Futures Market Guide.* New York: Harper & Row, 1973.

LABYS, WALTER C., *Dynamic Commodity Models: Specification, Estimation, and Simulation.* Lexington, Mass.: Lexington Books, 1973.

LEFEVRE, EDWIN, *Reminiscences of a Stock Operator.* New York: Doran, 1923.

LOFTON, TODD, "Chartists Corner," *Commodities Magazine,* December 1974, pp. 14–23. (Two series of articles.)

TAYLOR, ROBERT JOEL, "The Major Price Trend Directional Indicator," *Commodities Magazine,* April 1972, pp. 16–22.

TEWELES, RICHARD J., CHARLES V. HARLOW, and HERBERT L. STONE, *The Commodity Futures Game, Who Wins? Who Uses? Why?* New York: McGraw-Hill, 1974.

TURNER, DENNIS, and STEPHEN H. BLINN, *Trading Silver—Profitably.* New Rochelle, N.Y.: Arlington House, 1975.

WATERS, JAMES J., and LARRY WILLIAMS, "Measuring Market Momentum," *Commodities Magazine,* October 1972, pp. 13–16.
WATLING, T. F., and J. MORLEY, *Successful Commodity Futures Trading.* London: Business Books, Ltd., 1974.

15

CHART ANALYSES
AND TECHNICAL TRADING RULES

|||||||||||||||||||||||||||||||||||||||||||||||||||||||||||||||||||||||||||||||||||||||||||||||||||||||||||||

1 INTRODUCTION

Charting is the summarization of information in a graphical display. Despite the plethora of perspectives on charting, it is one of the most commonly practiced forms of commodity analysis. While a number of chart species have evolved to accommodate the special needs of particular trading objectives, two general types of charts encompass them all: bar charts and point and figure charts. While other distinct types of charts exist they are not purely technical in nature but instead tend to be free associations of technical procedures and behavioral assumptions that transcend common charting techniques. These hybrids are not considered here. This chapter summarizes the essential elements of bar charts and point and figure charts and their corresponding analysis and trading rules. The presentation is heuristic as indeed it must be owing to the oral origins of the "discipline."

In the following sections the construction and interpretation of these charts are summarized together with illustrative examples of various price patterns. In addition the strengths and weaknesses of each approach are noted along with a summary and critique of trading rules based on them.

2 BAR CHARTS

The bar chart depicts price information as a discrete plot of points over time. In short it is graphic applied time series analysis. Bar chartists, therefore, are interested in each of the movements that typically characterize an economic time series: trends, cycles, seasonal movements, nonperiodic and nonrandom movements, and purely indeterministic irregular components. To be sure, the visual identification of these movements can vary dramatically with the perception of the beholder. However, some common ground does exist to catagorize these perspectives and this task is prerequisite to bar chart analysis.

2.1 Time Perspective

Time series are commonly viewed as composed of several distinct components: trends, cycles, seasonal movements, nonrandom irregular movements, and purely indeterministic irregular components. Following definitions employed by economic time series analysts a trend is an oscillation with a period in excess of the length of the observed series; a cyclical movement is an oscillation between two to six years in length; a seasonal movement completes its oscillation an integer (whole) number of times in a year; nonrandom irregular components are predictable but not oscillatory; and purely random components are not predictable. Figure 15.1 illustrates a time series of commodity prices over a several-year period and its various time series components.

As the time period and/or frequency of observation changes, the perspective of the analyst also changes and problems of time series decomposition emerge that cannot easily be overcome. These problems often lead to inconsistent use of common time series definitions for example, the "seasonal trend." As the frequency of observation is reduced, for example, from once a week to once every year, the higher-frequency components, such as the irregular and seasonal components, are absorbed and lost from view. Insofar as technical analysts rarely consider a frequency of observation of more than a week, and often no less than once a day, this issue is not paramount in importance. However, the length of the observation period is crucial. For example, consider the subperiod between t_0 and t_1 in Figure 15.1. Suppose this period of observation is the one from which the analyst must perceive the movements of the series. What was once a seasonal or irregular pattern within a longer period of observation now may be viewed as a "trend." Indeed technical analysts often speak in terms of the "recent trend" which has clear meaning to them but causes considerable uneasiness among time series analysts.

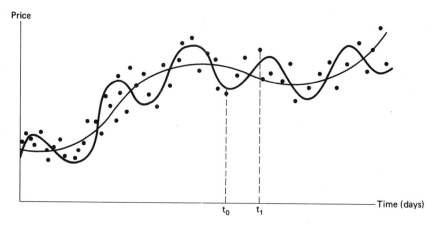

Price

Time (days)

t_0 t_1

Figure 15.1

ILLUSTRATIVE TIME SERIES

It would be unfair, of course, to imply that time series analysts also do not have problems of time series decomposition and identification. In fact they have much the same problem faced by chartists and, for all intents and purposes, their problems stem from the same origins. Be that as it may, the principal point to bear in mind with regard to bar charts is the importance of focussing on the message and not the terminology. Hopefully the plethora of possible perspectives indicated here will alert the reader to this problem and thereby help neutralize its potential for producing confusion. Finally it must be noted that bar charting is most common for interday price analysis and trading. However, it also may be used for intraday price analysis and trading, albeit with a less rich diversity of application and interpretation. Both inter- and intraday charting are presented below.

2.2 Interday Charting

2.2.1 Trend

As noted earlier the trend is typically identified as a succession of changing highs or lows. If the highs *and* lows are becoming higher with the passage of time, the market is characterized as being in a clear uptrend. Similarly if the highs and lows are becoming lower, the market is said to be in a clear downtrend. If the highs (lows) are constant and the lows (highs) are rising (falling) the market is said to be "thrashing" upward (downward), a situation which is thought to precede a new and "clear" trend direction. In all the above cases the distance between the trend line connecting the low points and the trend line connecting the high points is called the "trend channel." A "clear" and a "thrashing" uptrend are illustrated in Figure 15.2.

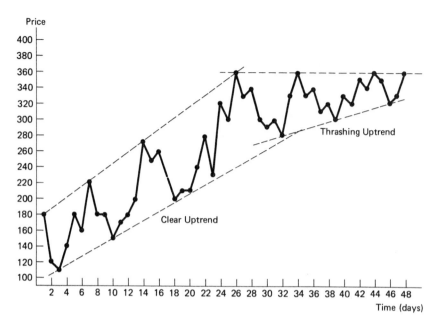

Figure 15.2

CLEAR AND THRASHING UPTRENDS

2.2.2 Turning Points: Top and Bottom Formations

The principle objectives of charting are to identify and "forecast" the direction of price movements. One of the most difficult tasks is to forecast, or identify on a timely basis, a reversal in direction. Once a trend has been identified, the timely recognition of a turning point requires constant vigilance for "top and bottom formations" that may signal a change in direction.

The reversal of an uptrend often is indicated when prices fall below the uptrend line and the subsequent high is not as high as the previous high achieved before the uptrend line was broken. Typically this pattern is referred to as a "head and shoulders pattern." The absolute high is called the "head" and the highs just preceding and following the head are called the "shoulders." The line connecting the troughs occurring between the shoulders and the head is referred to as the "neckline" or "turning point support line." This formation is illustrated in Figure 15.3. To be sure, there are several other types of "top" formations that may present themselves. They include the "multiple top" formation, the "head only" or "single peak" formation, and the "rounded top" or "mesokurdic" formation. These patterns are illustrated in Figure 15.4. Paralleling the "top" formations described above are "bottom" formations with patterns that mirror those already noted. Figure 15.5 illustrates the "inverted head and shoulders," "multiple bottom," "single

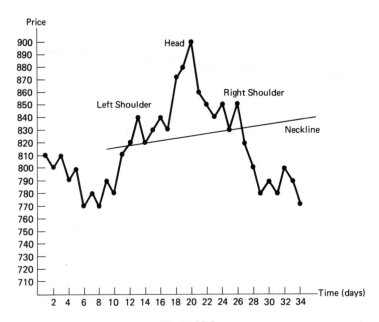

Figure 15.3

HEAD AND SHOULDERS TOP FORMATION

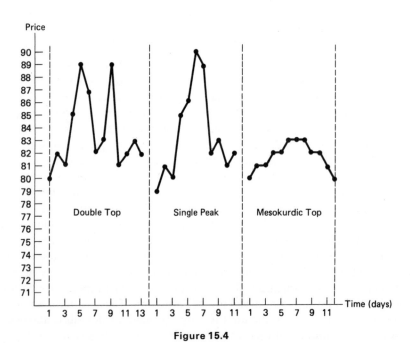

Figure 15.4

DOUBLE TOP, SINGLE PEAK, AND MESOKURDIC TOP FORMATIONS

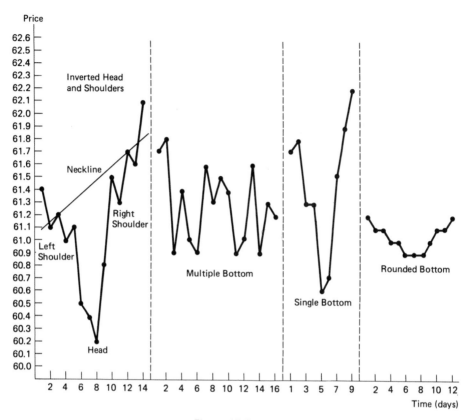

Figure 15.5

SELECT BOTTOM FORMATIONS

bottom," and "rounded bottom" formations, respectively. The distinction between these formations is the chartist's way of discerning between rates of change in prices—a not insignificant piece of information.

2.2.3 Intermediate or Mid-Formation Patterns

Between "tops" and "bottoms" are intermediate formations that are often distinguishable from top and bottom patterns. The most common intermediate patterns are "horizontal channels," also known as "congestion patterns" or "rectangles," "triangles," and "flags" or "pennants."

The horizontal channel or congestion area defines a range in which prices fluctuate for some period of time such that multiple tops occur at approximately the same high (the resistance level) and multiple bottoms occur at approximately the same low (the support level) as shown in Figure 15.6.

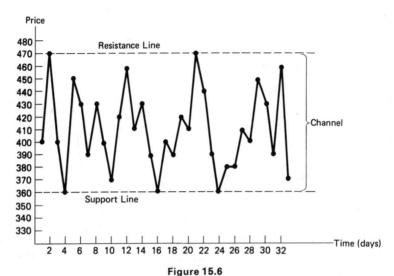

Figure 15.6

HORIZONTAL CHANNEL OR CONGESTION FORMATION

A "triangle" is said to exist when the resistance and support lines converge. This type of formation may have a more sharply rising support than falling resistance line level, or a more sharply falling resistance line than rising support level, or the support and resistance lines may be converging at near-equivalent rates. An illustrative case is shown in Figure 15.7.

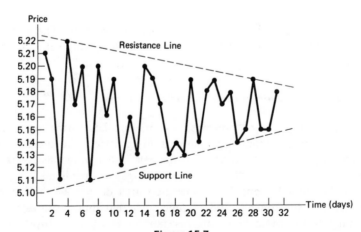

Figure 15.7

TRIANGLE FORMATION

A "flag" or "pennant" is depicted by a rising or falling channel and is distinguished from a trend channel in the same direction by its duration. Unfortunately the duration times are subjective and conditioned on the analyst's assumption of the continuation or reversal of the movement. Examples of a "flag" or "pennant" are given in Figure 15.8.

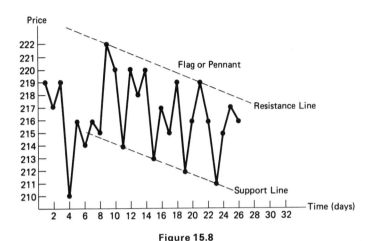

Figure 15.8

FLAG OR PENNANT FORMATION

2.3 Trading Rules Based on Interday Bar Charts

It is probably safe to conclude that at least as many trading rules have been developed from charting techniques as there are individuals who have seriously studied charts. While some of these rules, no doubt, have been profitable and others will never achieve that distinction, all of them can be fun to consider for the first time. Among the most common methods are the following: the thrust method, the congestion phase or N-day opposite method, the minor-trend method, the N-period rule, the wave or impulse-response rule and channel rules. Each is outlined below along with major variations on them.

2.3.1 The Thrust Method

The *thrust method* has two major variations: the thrust indication-confirmation rule and the double thrust rule. The thrust indication-confirmation rule has three distinct parts. First, prices are monitored for preliminary buy (sell) patterns. These preliminary signals include the following:

1. The current day's price falls (rises) to within a prescibed (by the analyst) number of basis points of the prior low (high).

2. A new low (high) is followed by a close higher (lower) than the previous day.

3. The range (distance between the high and low) for the current day is less than the previous day's range.

4. The current high (low) is above (below) the prior high (low).

5. Congestion develops near the prior low (high).

Second, if two or more of these preliminary indications are encountered, prices are monitored for a subsequent thrust confirmation. This confirmation is defined as a price the following day that is a prescribed number of basis points, z, away from the previous day's close in the same direction as the preliminary thrust. The basis point differential, z, of course, is commodity specific and typically determined by the volatility of the commodity. No hard and fast rules exist to calibrate this trigger differential but several have been proposed. One approach is to estimate the average absolute price change from day to day and set z equal to twice that value in order to reduce the frequency of false indications. A similar approach uses the standard deviation of daily price changes instead of the average absolute price change.

Third, if the confirmation is made, a long (short) position is taken and a price objective estimated on the basis of the trend anticipated to emerge.

The *double thrust rule* also has three parts. First, an indication of a trend (up or down) is said to occur if the current price is some prescribed distance (above or below) from the previous day's high or low respectively. Second, the trend is said to be confirmed if another thrust occurs immediately after the first one or after a congestion pattern subsequent to the preliminary thrust. Finally trading actions are taken if confirmation is made: Buy if the anticipated trend is up or sell if the anticipated trend is down.

2.3.2 The Congestion Phase N-Day Opposite Rule and the Theory of Runs

The *N-day opposite rule* is a trading rule for application during a congestion phase. For all intents and purposes it is an application of the theory of runs. The rule is straightforward: If the price of the commodity closes down, or down or unchanged, for $N - 1$ days in a row, then take an opposite position in the market early on day N. For example, if prices close down for three days in a row then take a long (buy) position early on the fourth day in anticipation of a rise, (i.e., reversal) in prices. The number of days, N, of course, must be determined and once again no hard and fast rule has been developed. Typically $N = 4$ days is chosen but different commodities may require different periods and the same commodity may require different periods during different stages of business activity. The underlying assumptions for this method are recognition of the congestion phase and the randomness of price movements during this phase. The latter point warrants further comment.

If prices are random the method has some statistical validity. For example, consider a wheat price of \$3.10 per bushel as of day t. For simplicity, assume the price of wheat can rise or fall by 10¢ from day to day. Over the next two days there are six possible arrangements of price changes. If these "runs" are random, that is, if any pair of changes is equally probable, then the probability of getting a price increase the second day given a price increase the first day is $\frac{1}{3}$:

$$\frac{\text{Prob (second change is upward}}{\text{given first change is upward)}} = \frac{\text{Prob (upward change both days)}}{\text{Prob (upward change first day)}}$$

$$= \frac{1/6}{1/2}$$

$$= \frac{1}{3}.$$

In this case, the appropriate action would be to sell at the end of the first day because the odds are two to one (odds $= \frac{2}{3}/\frac{1}{3}$) in favor of prices falling on the second day given they rose the first day.

2.3.3 Minor Trend Rule

The *minor trend rule* defines an uptrend and a downtrend as rising lows and falling highs, respectively. The trend is said to turn up when the most recent closing price (during a downtrend) is above its most recent high, and is said to turn down when the most recent closing price during an uptrend trades below its most recent low. The price is said to be congested or has not changed trend direction, otherwise. The trading rule is to buy (go long) when the minor trend turns up and sell (go short) when the minor trend turns down.

The price patterns that are most difficult for this rule to contend with are various types of congestion. Most notable among them is the case where highs and lows are trending in opposite directions, for example, highs that are falling and lows that are rising. These patterns typically are thought to precede a movement to a "clear" or major trend.

2.3.4 The N-day Rule

A variation on the minor trend rule is the *N-day rule*. Here, the current price is compared to previous highs and lows. Regardless of the trend direction (direction of highs and lows), if the current price exceeds the highest price in the past N days a further increase is indicated. Similarly if the current price falls below the lowest price during the past N days then a further price fall is indicated. Finally, if the current price lies between the highest high and lowest low of the past N days then a future price direction is not indicated. The trading rules for this approach also are straightforward: Buy when the most recent high is exceeded, sell when the low price is undercut, and do not take a position otherwise.

The most obvious technical question is how long is N? Ultimately the answer is an empirical one and is likely to vary from commodity to commodity and from period to period and typically relies on price volatility. One method for adapting the length of the observation period is to select a reference period, say N^*, and estimate the historical norm for the price variation over that period. The actual period of observation N_t then may be increased or decreased as the recent N^* period variation exceeds or falls below the historic norm in price variation. For example, if price variation is measured by the standard deviation in prices then the adaptive period of observation as of day t, N_t, may be determined by the equation

$$N_t = N^*\left(\frac{\text{``Normal'' } N^* \text{ period standard deviation}}{\text{Current } N^* \text{ period standard deviation}}\right)$$

or simple variations on this theme.

The procedure for determining N^* may benefit from historic simulations that use decision theory criteria that weigh the costs of too-frequent market entry against too-infrequent market entry. For the purist (the chartist without equations), normal price volatility and period of observation are determined through experience, a sharp eye, and an even sharper pencil. A common but highly arbitrary rule is to set N^* to four weeks.

2.3.5   The Wave or Impulse-Response Rule and a "Stabilizing" Market

The *wave or inpulse-response rule* is based on the notion of a "stabilizing" market. Here, the "steady state" price is defined as the average price during a period of congestion, and prices are viewed as moving from one steady state and period of congestion to another in an unending sequence of episodes. Each price change episode is characterized by a major price movement, usually defined as the establishment of a new high or low over some historical perspective, for example, four weeks. This price movement is referred to as the impulse and the subsequent price movements are referred to as the response to this "shock." A stabilizing market is one characterized by a narrowing band of highs and lows that approach some stable band around the new price equilibrium as shown in Figure 15.9.

The trading rules surrounding this view of the market are to sell (buy) near and usually shortly after the peak (low) of the "impulse," for example, the first lower (higher) closing price after the major price increase (decrease),

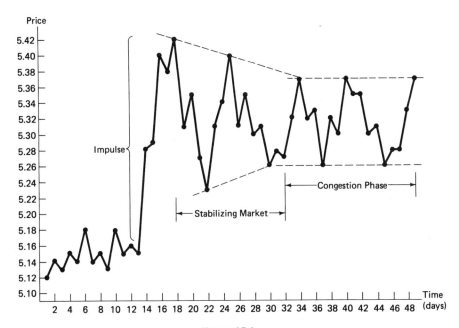

Figure 15.9

STABILIZING MARKET PATTERN

and place a liquidating order (i.e., price objective) some number of basis points away from the price at which a position was taken.

2.3.6 Channel Rules

The idea behind *channel rules* is to establish a band or channel of prices within which no trading activity takes place. If, however, the trading price of the commodity breaks out of the channel, then a buy or sell signal is triggered.

To construct a *simple channel rule* incorporating a profit target and stop-loss point, let

$$K_t = \frac{1}{3N} \sum_{j=0}^{N-1} (H_{t-j} + L_{t-j} + C_{t-j})$$

and

$$R_t = \frac{1}{N} \sum_{j=0}^{N-1} (H_{t-j} - L_{t-j}).$$

then, go long if $P_{t+1} > K_t + wR_t$ and hold until the profit target, π, is reached, $P_{t+k} \geq P_{t+1} + \pi$, or the stop loss is hit, $P_{t+k} \leq P_{t+1} - S$, where $k > 1$. Or, go short if $P_{t+1} < K_t - wR_t$ and hold until the profit target is reached, $P_{t+k} \leq P_{t+1} - \pi$, or the stop-loss is hit, $P_{t+k} \geq P_{t+1} + S$.

Here, w is a user-specified weight greater than zero, π is the profit or price differential, S is the stop-loss or price differential, H_t is the high price, L_t is the low price and C_t is the close or settlement price for day t.

When price changes are nonmonotonic, channel rules that accommodate reversals of positions can be implemented. A user-weighted *channel reversal rule* is: Go long if $P_{t+1} > K_t + wR_t$ and hold until $P_{t+k} < K_{t+k-1} - wR_{t-k-1}$; *then* go short and hold until $P_{t+k+\delta} > K_{t+k+\delta-1} + wR_{t+k+\delta-1}$, where $\delta > 0$. Or, go short if $P_{t+1} < K_t - wR_t$ and hold until $P_{t+k} > K_{t+k-1} + wR_{t+k-1}$; *then* go long and hold until $P_{t+k+\delta} < K_{t+k+\delta-1} - wR_{t+k+\delta-1}$, and so on.

2.4 Price Objectives and Price Forecasts

All of the trading methods outlined have two rules in common. First, once a new price direction has been revealed or is indicated, a position should be taken: Go long (i.e., buy) if the price direction is up, and go short, (i.e., sell) if the price direction is down. The goal, of course, is to capture a trading profit and the "price objective" is the price at which the position is to be liquidated at a profit (see Figure 15.10).

This price is as much a forecast as it is a desire and can be estimated in a variety of ways regardless of the bar chart method used. The various methods can be separated into four categories: extrapolation of previous support or resistance levels, basis point per time period extrapolations, "revelational" methods and mathematical estimation procedures. All but the latter are discussed here. The next two chapters summarize select mathematical estimation methods.

2.4.1 Support and Resistance Extrapolation

The extrapolation of the most recent previous support and resistance levels is one of the simplest price objectives to estimate. For example, if a price increase is indicated, a long position is taken and a sell order is placed at the resistance level most recently encountered. To be sure, the trader must also specify the length of time allowed for the price objective to be reached. This calculation, of course, depends not only on the length of time for the price move to complete its course but also on the costs the trader may incur waiting for the liquidation to materialize. These issues are discussed further in subsequent chapters dealing with trading examples.

2.4.2 Basis Point per Time Unit Extensions

Basis point per time period forecasts are simple time series extrapolations. Here, lengths of time in congestion periods are compared to the size of the price move to a new congestion phase and the length of time it takes to move from the end of one congestion phase to the beginning of another. For

Figure 15.10

TREND REVERSAL AND PRICE OBJECTIVE

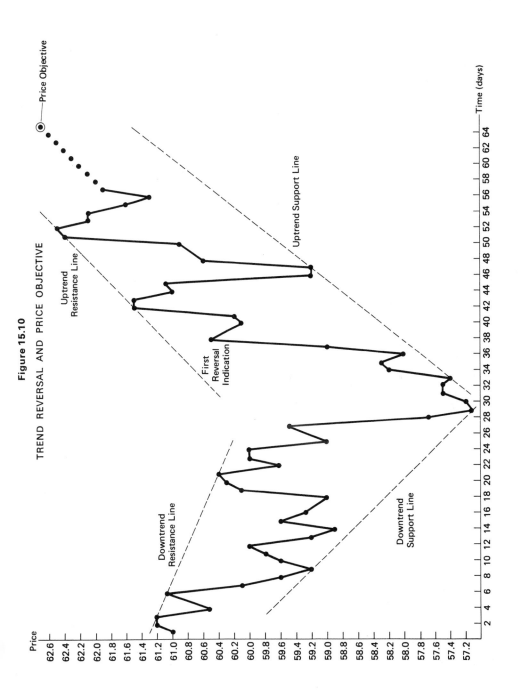

example, major price movements in silver may be 200 basis points per week for each week of the most recent congestion period, and this price movement may only take one-fourth the time in the congestion period to achieve the new congestion period; for example, a six-week congestion phase may imply a 1,200 basis point move in one-and-one-half weeks. Accordingly, the price objective would be placed at 1,200 basis points away from the mid-point of the congestion phase that was just broken out of and the trader would hold to this strategy for one-and-a-half weeks.

2.4.3 Revelational Methods

A number of interesting rules have sprouted up to "solve" for price objectives that are bastions of independence from any recognized science. They include

1. The *x* percent retrieval rule
2. The law of proportion
3. Fibonacci ratios and complements
4. The time-distance rule

The *x percent retrieval* rule postulates that an initial price movement of so many basis points will reverse itself by *x* percent within a given period after the initial price move. Accordingly, if the initial price move is up then a short position is taken just after the peak is reached and at the same time a buy order is placed at a price *x* percent below the price of the peak. The *x* percent differential typically is determined by casual empiricism and a "feel for the market" but historical estimates also are used.

The *law of proportion* follows the same rules as the retrieval rule except for the determination of the price differential. Instead of casual empiricism the percent retracements of price surges are estimated for a commodity during different stages of the business cycle and for different stages of futures contract maturity. The estimated proportions are grouped into one of the appropriate "theoretical" categories of $\frac{1}{2}, \frac{2}{3}, \frac{3}{4}, \frac{4}{5}, \frac{5}{6}, N/(N+1)$. These "reversal" proportions then are used to calculate the price objective for the particular stage of the business cycle, and stage of contract maturity.

The *Fibonacci ratio rule* bases the price differential on ratios of the Fibonacci series 1, 1, 2, 3, 5, 8, 13, 21, 34, . . . , F_n, $F_n + F_{n-1}$, ... The most commonly used ratios are $F_{n+1}/F_n = 1.618$, or $F_n/F_{n+1} = .618$, and its complement .382. A trend is defined as a price increase or fall of .618 from the historic and *persistent* congestion price. Upon reaching this mark one may then expect the price move to retreat .382 of the new price. The period over which these movements are to take place are not specified and the practitioner typically must determine these periods empirically for each commodity at various stages of the business cycle and each stage of futures contract maturity.

The *time-distance rule* is based on the assumption that each prolonged movement in a direction will be equal in length of time and distance in price as the preceeding prolonged movement in that direction. The prolonged movements are marked by minor retracements of the general trend and make the trend appear as coming in "waves." The uptrend trading rule is to take a long position just after a peak has been reached and a minor retracement has occurred and simultaneously to enter a sell order that is *y* percent of the wave above the price of the long position. Similar rules apply for a downtrend where a short position is taken just after the retracement and a buy order is placed *y* percent of the next wave below the short position price.

2.5 Intraday Bar Charts

Intraday bar charting focuses on two types of price movements within a day: typical or "normal" price movements and episodic movements in response to a major event. Because of the short time period of observation these charting methods are limited to day trading applications, that is, to taking a position and liquidating it all in the same day. Although trend, seasonal, and cyclical movements are not identifiable over a period of observation as short as a day, that is not to say that the influence of a trend, cycle, or seasonal movement may not be embedded in the intraday price behavior. Rather, it is to say that intraday price analysis must be conducted in the context of longer-term interday price movements in order to better anticipate intraday price movements. For example, if prices recently broke through a price support or resistance level, a new trend may be unfolding that can swamp the otherwise normal price movements that would have prevailed had this threshold not been crossed. With this caveat in mind the essentials of intraday bar charting and associated trading rules are summarized below.

2.5.1 Normal Intraday Price Patterns and Departures from the Norm

Intraday bar charts depict prices at fixed intervals within the day and plot the price history from the open to the close of trading. Trading rules for a "normal" day are based on estimates of the average price for the day, support and resistance levels, and bounds within which prices can be expected to fluctuate some given percent of the time, for example, 95 percent. The estimates of the average price and support and resistance levels as well as the 95 percent trading range may be estimated from some pet relationship and/or from surveys of floor brokers or some combination of methods.

In Figure 15.11 an illustrative intraday price pattern is combined with

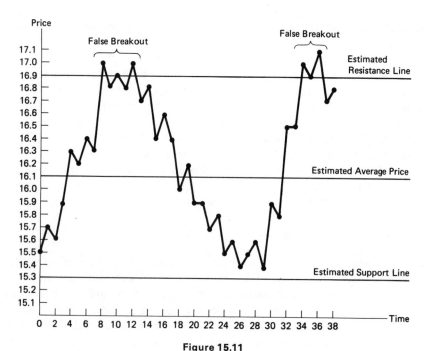

Figure 15.11

INTRADAY PRICE PATTERN AND ANTICIPATED AVERAGE PRICE,
SUPPORT, AND RESISTANCE LINES

an estimated average price and the intraday support and resistance lines (trading channel), when longer-term forces are not approaching interday support or resistance levels. Figure 15.12 illustrates a case where interday support and resistance lines threaten the intraday trading assessment.

In the "normal" case without interday pressures, illustrated in Figure 15.11, the trading rule is to sell when the price approaches a resistance line in anticipation of the price wandering downward and to buy when the price reaches a support level in anticipation of prices wandering upward.

If interday support or resistance levels overlap the daily trading range, the intraday trading rules typically are modified to shy away from the longer-term forces that may trigger a new trend. Here, for example, the trader may only work the downside if a long-term resistance threatens the short position of a day trade, or alternatively the trader may change to an "episodic day-trading rule" to be discussed shortly. If these strategies are not or cannot be followed in time, the trader is not without some tactical opportunities to save the day. Among the most common responses when a long-term support or resistance level has been breached and the market has moved against a position (e.g., gone higher after a short position was taken), is to "liquidate and

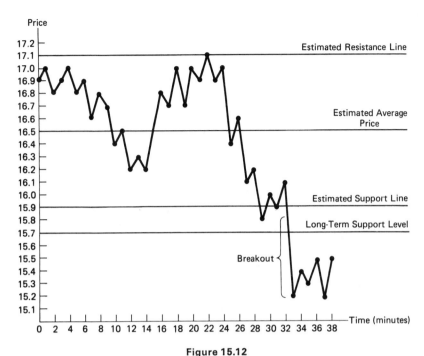

Figure 15.12

INTRADAY PRICE PATTERN AND ANTICIPATED AVERAGE, SUPPORT,
RESISTANCE, AND WITH LONG-TERM SUPPORT PRICES

double up"; that is, to liquidate the short position (at a loss) and double the
position but this time on the long side. This can be a costly tactic but can save
the day if the market breach of the resistance follows its anticipated move
upward.

2.5.2 Episodic Intraday Pattern and Trading Rules

Major news events or the breach of a long-term support or resistance
level may be viewed as episodic events and these are often followed by a
sharp change in prices as illustrated in Figure 15.13. After such an initial
shock the market price tends to "stabilize" around a new if temporary congestion phase. Often these congestion phases have diminishing volatility
around an average price and this pattern presents obvious day trading opportunities. The corresponding trading rule is to enter the market after an
episode, that is, after prices have changed sharply. If the change was positive
(negative) then a short (long) position is taken in anticipation of a possible
drop (rise) in prices as a new average level is sought. Alternatively, one can
wait until the prices begin to fluctuate around the new average level and

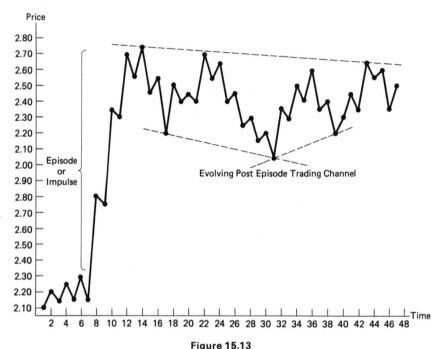

Figure 15.13

EVOLVING POST-EPISODE TRADING CHANNEL

orders may be placed at the extreme ranges of this variation. The principal problem with both of these alternatives is the recognition or estimation of the new price level. Here, there is no substitute for seasoned research and timely computational abilities including probability calculations and correspondences to past and surrounding events, for example, how did gold move in a similar situation and what was the reaction in London?

3 POINT AND FIGURE CHARTS

Point and figure charts record equal-size price movements regardless of the time interval between them. Typically the chart is depicted with price on the vertical axis and the price change "history" on the horizontal axis. The plot takes the form of vertically parallel columns of two different symbols, one denoting price increases, typically an *x*, and the other denoting price decreases, typically an *o*, as illustrated in Figure 15.14.

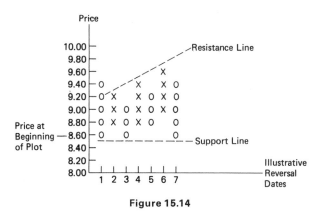

Figure 15.14

ILLUSTRATIVE POINT AND FIGURE CHART

Each *x* or *o* represents a price movement of a given size referred to as the box size and representing the smallest significant price move. These charts may be used for both interday and intraday commodity analysis. Typically the point and figure chart is developed from price movements that penetrate previous highs or lows. If the price sets a new high then a number of *x*'s are entered vertically from the old high to the new high. The number of *x*'s or positive boxes is determined by the box size. For example, if the price move is up 25¢ and the box size is 10¢ then two *x*'s would be recorded vertically; fractions of a box size are not counted. A similar treatment is given to a price decrease where a number of *o*'s would be entered, depending on how far prices fall. While this description captures the essence of point and figure charts it is, of course, far from complete and serves only as an introduction. Accordingly we defer for the moment the determination of box size and trading rules based on point and figure chart patterns in order to describe this chart construction more thoroughly.

3.1 Construction of a Point and Figure Chart

To begin let the symbol *t* denote the time of a high or low price; let *H* and *L* denote a high and low price, respectively; let *B* denote box size and let *R* indicate the number of boxes in a reversal. As prices unfold over time they reach new highs or set new lows or fluctuate somewhere in between. If prices fluctuate between the most recent highs and lows then they are in a period of congestion and no *x* or *o* entries are made on the point and figure chart. If prices do set new highs or lows (they can't set both at precisely the same time) the point and figure chart is adjusted as summarized in Table 15.1.

Table 15.1

SUMMARY OF POINT AND FIGURE CHART ALGORITHM

Step 1.	Begin at a specified price if starting a chart or, if a chart is in progress, begin at the current column (x's or o's).

Step 2.	If new high H_t is at least one box greater than the previous high H_{t-1} and a new low is not reached at the same time then calculate $(H_t - H_{t-1})/B$ and set number of new x's equal to the largest whole number of this ratio.	If new low L_t is at least one box lower than the previous low L_{t-1} and a new high is not reached at the same time then set the number of new o's equal to the largest whole number of the ratio $(L_{t-1} - L_t)/B$.
Step 3(a).	Plot number of x's vertically from beginning price or on top of column of x's.	Plot number of o's vertically below the beginning price or directly below the current column of o's.
3(b).	(Reversal) If the previous column is o's then move one column to the right and plot x's vertically (up) beginning one box above the previous low *provided* the new high is at least R boxes above the previous low; $R > 1$.	If the previous column is x's then move one column to the right and plot o's vertically (down) beginning one box below the previous high *provided* the new low is at least R boxes below the previous high; $R > 1$.
Step 4.	Do not make an entry otherwise.	Do not make an entry otherwise.
Step 5.	Continue sequentially from Step 1.	Continue sequentially from Step 1.

3.1.1 Box Size, B, and Reversal Rule, R.

The construction of a point and figure chart described above invoked two measures that the analyst must specify: the box size, B, and the number of boxes, R, that signals a significant price reversal. These parameters can be determined by the analyst's feel of the market or by financial considerations or they can be estimated in some other way from historical or survey data. Among the most common methods of establishing a box size, with the intent of separating meaningless chatter from meaningful market statements, is to set it equal to the smallest profitable price move or to the standard deviation of the commodity's price movements from trade to trade. The information for the latter may be obtained from historical intraday prices.

The number of boxes, R, signalling a reversal, typically is set equal to a fraction of the average number of reversal boxes preceding an uptrend or downtrend. This number also is an integer and will depend on the box size itself. If one sets the reversal number too high then a reversal may not be revealed until after it is over and there is no room left for possible trading profits. Obversely, if the reversal number is set too low the analyst may receive an excessive number of false reversal indications. This decision typically requires simulation based on the trading rule applied and the anticipated volatility of the market. The values of B and R selected are those providing the most profitable trading results.

In Figure 15.15 an historical price series of highs and lows are plotted alongside a corresponding point and figure chart where the box size is 20 basis points and the reversal number of boxes is two.

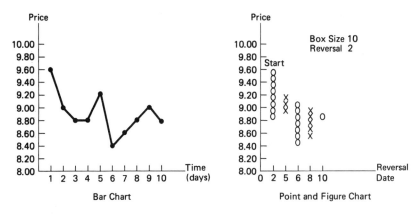

Figure 15.15

ILLUSTRATIVE COMPARISON OF A BAR CHART AND POINT
AND FIGURE CHART FOR THE SAME PRICE HISTORY

3.2 Point and Figure Chart Trading Rules

Point and figure charts can reveal the same patterns as bar charts, albeit from a different perspective. Similarly the trading methods described for bar charts also can be used here with virtually no modification. Illustrations of an uptrend, thrust, congestion phase, triangle, and impulse-response patterns are shown in Figure 15.16. The principle differences between the trading rules for point and figure charts and bar charts are (1) the translation of basis point price movements to equivalent numbers of boxes and vice versa, and (2) the way in which price objectives are calculated for liquidation. Conversion of basis point movements into numbers of boxes of a given size is straightforward arithmetic with only two procedural technicalities: The number of boxes must be an integer and the price at which an action is taken is either the extreme value in the last box or the mid-point in the last box. However, the calculation of the price objectives for point and figure chart trading rules is unique to this charting method.

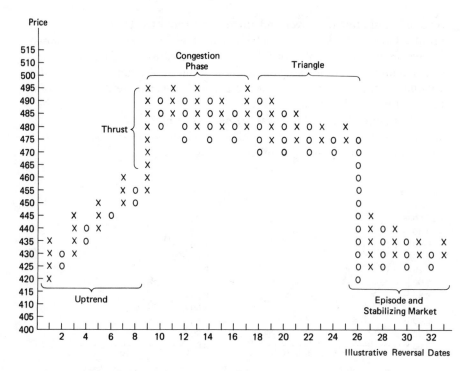

Figure 15.16

POINT AND FIGURE PATTERNS FOR AN UPTREND, THRUST,
CONGESTION PHASE, TRIANGLE, AND IMPULSE-RESPONSE
OR EPISODIC PRICE MOVEMENTS

3.3 Price Objectives from Point and Figure Charts

While some consider point and figure price objectives as being more
precise than bar chart methods, the added precision is little more than the
common acceptance of somewhat arbitrary rules of calculation. For the
most part point and figure price objectives and bar chart price objectives are
calculated in the same way: Once a movement has been discerned the past is
relied upon heavily to determine the price distance of that movement. Bar
chartists also must determine the length of time to reach the new price
whereas point and figure chartists do not consider time per se in keeping with
the nature of point and figure charts. The analyst may calculate point and
figure price objectives in either of two different methods or some weighted
combination of them: the vertical count method, the horizontal count
method, and the "weighted average" or "convex" count method.

3.3.1 Vertical Count Method

Vertical count price objectives are calculated as follows:

Upside Price Objective (long position taken)

$P_{ob}^s = P_L + \delta$ (number of boxes in the first reversal)

$\quad\quad\quad\quad\quad\quad\quad$ · (number of boxes signalling reversal) · (box size)

Downside Price Objective (short position taken)

$P_{ob}^b = P_H - \delta$ (number of boxes in the first reversal)

$\quad\quad\quad\quad\quad\quad\quad$ · (number of boxes signalling reversal) · (box size)

where $0 \leq \delta \leq 1$, and is assigned by the user; P_L and P_H are the previous low and high prices, respectively; the first reversal is the most recent price reversal and P_{ob}^s and P_{ob}^b are sell and buy price objectives, respectively. The speculative position is taken in the first reversal, typically near the end, and the liquidating order price or price objective is extrapolated in the anticipated price movement. A downside price objective is illustrated in Figure 15.17, where the number of boxes signalling a reversal is four.

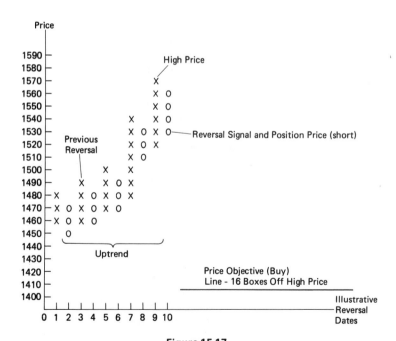

Figure 15.17

VERTICAL COUNT DOWNSIDE PRICE OBJECTIVE
(FOUR BOX REVERSAL, $\delta = 1$)

3.3.2 Horizontal Count

Horizontal price objectives are calculated as follows:

Upside Price Objective

$P_{ob}^{s} = P_L + \delta$ (number of columns between

the most recent major price reversals) $\cdot R \cdot B$

Downside Price Objective

$P_{ob}^{b} = P_H - \delta$(number of columns between

the most recent major price reversals) $\cdot R \cdot B$

where a major price reversal is defined as having occurred if the subsequent price reversal lies completely above or below its previous high or low, as the case may be. The number of columns are calculated between the most recent major reversal, but not including the reversal column, and the immediately preceding and opposite major price reversal including the reversal column. An upside price objective is illustrated in Figure 15.18.

3.3.3 Convex Count Method

In mathematics a region is said to be convex if it always contains the line segment joining any two points in the region. For a given price objective the vertical count price and the horizontal count price may be viewed as two distinct points. The convex count method is a weighted average of these two prices where the weights sum up to one and neither weight can be negative. In short, the convex count method calculates a price objective that is a "mid-point" between the vertical count and horizontal count prices. Whether the mid-point lies closer to the vertical count or the horizontal count depends on the weighting scheme used. Typically the criterion of equal ignorance is invoked and equal weights of $\frac{1}{2}$ are used. In general the convex count price objective is calculated as follows:

$$P_{ob}^{C} = w_1 P^H + (1 - w_1) P^V$$

where P_{ob}^{C} is the convex count price objective, $0 \leq w_i \leq 1$ is a weighting factor, and P^H and P^V are the horizontal and vertical price objectives, respectively. This formulation, of course, applies for the upside as well as the downside price objectives. A convex count price objective is illustrated in Figure 15.19 along with the component vertical and horizontal count price objectives.

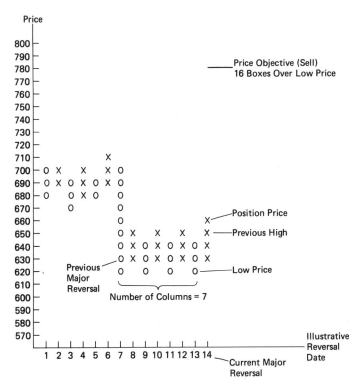

Figure 15.18

HORIZONTAL COUNT UPSIDE PRICE OBJECTIVE
(FOUR-BOX REVERSAL, $\delta = 1$)

3.4 Intraday Point and Figure Charts

The use of point and figure charts for day trading parallels, at least mechanically, the procedures described above. The principal differences are the box sizes and reversal signals must be recalibrated to intraday price variations and their daily limits, and as with bar charts, one must keep track of longer-term price movements represented by interday point and figure charts that have correspondingly larger box sizes and reversal signals. With regard to the problem of correspondence between interday and intraday point and figure charts and trading rules the procedures are much the same as those described in intraday bar chart analysis. When considering a day trade one must bear in mind the interday support and resistance levels. If these levels are outside the daily trading limits, then the penetration of one of them may not occur and the intraday trading rule may not be overridden for this reason. On the other hand, if the interday support and/or resistance levels lie

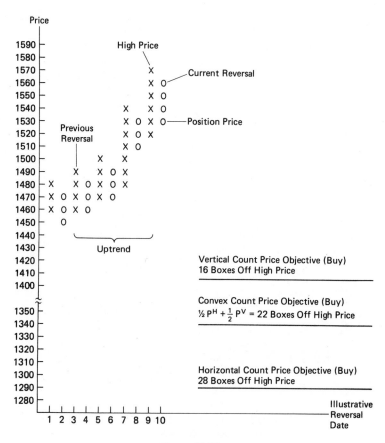

Figure 15.19

CONVEX COUNT DOWNSIDE PRICE OBJECTIVE
(4 BOX REVERSAL, $\delta = 1$ IN BOTH COUNT METHODS)

within the daily trading limits then an intraday pattern that has an intraday resistance level below the interday resistance may not be a good indicator of a buy if it is penetrated by a few boxes. The fact that prices have been trading below the interday resistance level may give rise to an unexpected intraday downward price spiral when a subsequent price increase (uptrend price objective) was anticipated.

4 SUMMARY

The charting methods and trading rules discussed in this chapter are among the most commonly used by analysts and traders. While many of these procedures are somewhat arbitrary and others seemingly transcend reason, their unsettling foundations are matched by their frequent profitability in the hands of seasoned practitioners. The approaches presented here are not the only ones and the next two chapters are dedicated to methods whose origins boast impressive scientific foundations but whose track record has yet to be established.

5 BIBLIOGRAPHY

ARMS, RICHARD W., JR., "Equivolume—A New Method of Charting," *Commodities Magazine,* April 1973, pp. 18–24.

DEVILLIERS, VICTOR, *The Point and Figure Method of Anticipating Stock Price Movements.* New York: Trader Press, 1966. (Reprint of 1933 edition)

DONCHIAN, RICHARD D., "Donchian 5- and 20-Day Moving Averages," *Commodities Magazine,* December 1974, pp. 10–16.

DUNNIGAN, WILLIAM, *One Way Formula.* Palo Alto, Calif.: Dunnigan, 1955.

——, *Select Studies in Speculation.* San Francisco: Dunnigan, 1954. (Includes "Gains in Grams," and "The Thrust Method in Stocks")

GOTTHELF, PHILIP, and CARL GROPPER, "Systems Do Work . . . But You Need a Plan," *Commodities Magazine,* April 1977, pp. 22, 23, 36, 37.

GANN, WILLIAM D., *The Basis of My Forecasting Method For Grain.* Pomeroy, Wash.: Lambert-Gann, 1976. (Originally 1935)

——, *Forecasting Grains by Time Cycles.* Pomeroy, Wash.: Lambert-Gann, 1976. (Originally 1946)

——, *Forecasting Rules for Cotton.* Pomeroy, Wash.: Lambert-Gann, 1976.

——, *Forecasting Rules for Grain-Geometric Angles.* Pomeroy, Wash.: Lambert-Gann, 1976.

——, *How to Make Profits In Commodities.* Pomeroy, Wash.: Lambert-Gann, 1976. (Originally 1942)

——, *Master Calculator for Weekly Time Periods to Determine the Trend of Stocks and Commodities.* Pomeroy, Wash.: Lambert-Gann, 1976.

HALBERG, M. C., and V. I. WEST, *Patterns of Seasonal Price Variations for Illinois Farm Products,* Circular 861. Urbana: University of Illinois College of Agriculture, 1967.

HAMBRIDGE, JAY, *Dynamic Symmetry, The Greek Vase.* New Haven, Conn.: Yale University Press, 1931.

——, *Practical Applications of Dynamic Symmetry.* New Haven, Conn.: Yale University Press, 1938.

HIERONYMUS, THOMAS A., *Economics of Futures Trading.* New York: Commodity Research Bureau, 1971.

————, *When to Sell Corn–Soy Beans–Oats–Wheat.* Urbana: University of Illinois College of Agriculture, 1967.

JILER, WILLIAM L., *Forecasting Commodity Prices with Vertical Line Charts.* New York: Commodity Research Bureau, 1966.

————, *Volume and Open Interest–a Key to Commodity Price Forecasting.* New York: Commodity Research Bureau, 1967.

KAUFMAN, PERRY J., and KERMIT C. ZIEG, JR., "Measuring Market Movement," *Commodities Magazine,* May 1974, pp. 20–25.

KROLL, STANLEY, *The Professional Commodity Trader.* New York: Harper & Row, 1974.

————, and IRWIN SHISHKO, *The Commodity Futures Market Guide.* New York: Harper & Row, 1973.

LABYS, WALTER C., *Dynamic Commodity Models: Specification, Estimation, and Simulation.* Lexington, Mass.: Lexington Books, 1973.

LOFTON, TODD, "Chartists Corner," *Commodities Magazine,* December 1974, pp. 14–23. (Two series of articles.)

————, "Moonlight Sonata," *Commodities Magazine,* July 1974, pp. 12–13.

MACKAY, CHARLES, *Extraordinary Popular Delusions and The Madness of Crowds.* New York: Noonday Press (Farrar, Straus & Giroux), 1932.

POLOUS, E. MICHAEL, "The Moving Average as a Trading Tool," *Commoditites Magazine,* September 1973. pp. 23–25.

TAYLOR, ROBERT JOEL, "The Major Price Trend Directional Indicator," *Commodities Magazine,* April 1972, pp. 16–22.

TEWELES, RICHARD J., CHARLES V. HARLOW, and HERBERT L. STONE, *The Commodity Futures Game, Who Wins? Who Uses? Why?* New York: McGraw-Hill, 1974.

THIEL, CHARLES, and R. E. DAVIS, *Point and Figure Commodity Trading: A Computer Evaluation.* West Lafayette, Ind.: Dunn & Hargitt, 1970.

TURNER, DENNIS, and STEPHEN H. BLINN. *Trading Silver Profitably.* New Rochelle, N.Y.: Arlington House, 1975.

WATERS, JAMES J., and LARRY WILLIAMS, "Measuring Market Momentum," *Commodities Magazine,* October 1972, pp. 13–16.

WATLING, T. F., and J. MORLEY, *Successful Commodity Futures Trading.* London: Business Books, Ltd., 1974.

WILLIAMS, LARRY, and MICHELLE NOSEWORTHY, "How Seasonal Influences Can Help You Trade Commodities," *Commodities Magazine,* October 1976, pp. 26–29, 43–46.

WINSKI, JOSEPH N., "A Sure Thing?" *The Dow Jones Commodities Handbook 1977,* Princeton, N.J.: Dow Jones Books, 1977.

16

UNIVARIATE FORECASTING METHODS AND TRADING SYSTEMS

||||||||||||||||||||||||||||||||||||||||||||||||||||||||||||||||||||||||||||||||||||||||||||||||||||||||

1 INTRODUCTION

Among the many problems facing the technical commodity analyst, that of forecasting future prices is one of the most important and difficult. This requirement is encountered in the estimation of price objectives and underlies the analyst's assessments of alternative trading algorithms. Forecasts of economic time series can be categorized into several groups: (1) naive methods that include mathematical fitting functions of time or combinations of auto-regressive and moving average methods; (2) leading indicators that attempt to identify economic activities that precede or lead the activity of the series under consideration; (3) sample survey results of predictions made by various forecasting procedures and/or oracles; (4) pressure methods that rely on important ratios of, or differences between, factors that are thought to influence the behavior of the activity in question; and (5) econometric techniques that attempt to describe the underlying economic structure of the commodity market and the forces that determine equilibrium prices and quantities and their evolution. This chapter focuses on the so-called naive methods of time series estimation and forecasting. In particular it summarizes moving averages and exponential smoothing, generalized adaptive exponential smoothing, mixed auto-regressive—moving average models, and the Kalman filtering approach sometimes referred to as "state space forecasting" owing to its sequential updating based on the addition of new information. These methods often are criticized as "measurement without theory." In their defense, more theoretically initiated procedures quickly outpace their measurability. Moreover, naive methods are often less costly to implement and no less inaccurate than their theory-based counterparts. For these reasons naive methods are popular and are therefore outlined in this chapter.

2 MOVING AVERAGES AND EXPONENTIAL SMOOTHING

Moving averages attempt to measure or estimate the true or underlying value of a time series corrupted by random noise by taking an average of recent values. Presumably the random elements are smoothed out and the true message revealed. A moving average estimate, M_t, of the underlying value of a time series, say P_t, may be denoted

$$M_t = \frac{P_t + P_{t-1} + \ldots + P_{t-n+1}}{n}$$

where n is the length of the moving average. This formulation may be recast into a computationally more efficient form

$$M_t = M_{t-1} + \frac{P_t - P_{t-n}}{n}.$$

When the underlying expected value of P_t is constant, the larger the length of the moving average the more accurate the moving average estimate: The standard error of the moving average estimate, S_M, is equal to the standard deviation of the noise component, S_e, divided by the square root of the length of the moving average, n; that is, $S_M = S_e/\sqrt{n}$. However, when the underlying value is evolving then long moving averages, that is, large values of n, will take longer to yield relevant estimates of the new underlying value when a change has taken place than when a shorter moving average is used. But shorter moving averages have larger standard errors than longer ones if the evolution permits. Since one may not know when or how frequently these evolutionary processes are moving one must balance these conflicting sources of error to obtain an optimal length n. One compromise suggested in findings by Meyer (1963) is

$$n_t = 2\left(\frac{1-a}{a}\right) + 1$$

where $a = S_{M,n_{t-1}}/S_e$ and $S_{M,n_{t-1}}$ is the standard error of the most recent moving average of length n_{t-1}. In this case if the moving average suddenly recorded an increase in its error variance relative to the variation in the noise, the length of the moving average would be shortened and one could more quickly estimate the new underlying value.

A moving average, like any average, gives some measure of central tendency. Here, the estimated value represents the mid-point of the moving average both numerically and in chronological correspondence. For odd values of n this does not pose a problem but even values of n require a decision as to the temporal positioning of the estimate. Frequently, the more recent position is used.

The simple moving average described here assumes also that the underlying process is a constant value buried in random noise; that is, $P_t = c_0 + e_t$ where c_0 is the constant value estimated by M_t and e_t is the random noise as of time t.

2.1 Higher-Order Models

When higher-order polynomials in time better represent the underlying "deterministic" component then higher-order averaging or exponential smoothing is required to estimate the underlying time series function. The transition from simple moving averages to more elaborate exponential smoothing requires two steps: first, to establish the relationship between a simple moving average and the exponential smoothing relationship for a constant c_0 corrupted by noise; second, to establish the relationships that enable one to estimate the higher-order model

$$P_t = c_0 + c_1 t + \frac{1}{2} c_2 t^2 + \ldots + \frac{1}{m} c_m t^m + e_t.$$

Simple exponential smoothing can be derived from a simple moving average by replacing c_{t-n} with the estimate of that value M_{t-1}. That is, the modified moving average

$$M_t^* = M_{t-1} + \frac{P_t - M_{t-1}}{n}$$

$$= \frac{1}{n} P_t + \left(1 - \frac{1}{n}\right) M_{t-1}$$

is the same as the exponential smoothing function

$$S_t = aP_t + (1 - a)S_{t-1}$$

where $a = 1/n$, and is called the smoothing constant.

This definition of simple or single smoothing can be extended to define multiple smoothing of order k as follows:

$$S_t^k = aS_t^{k-1} + bS_{t-1}^k$$

where k is the order of smoothing and $b = 1 - a$. For example, a second-order smoothing, $k = 2$, is a simple smoothing of a simple smoothing. Similarly, a third-order smoothing is a simple smoothing of a double smoothing, and so forth. For each successive smoothing the previously constructed smoothed series now is the series being smoothed.

Higher-order smoothing is used when the underlying process can be represented by a polynomial fitting function of time. That is, for a time series of the form $P_t = c_0 + e_t$, a single smoothing can provide enough information to estimate the underlying coefficient c_0. For a time series of the form $P_t = c_0 + c_1 t + e_t$, a second-order smoothing also would be necessary in order to estimate both c_0 and c_1. To be sure, the analyst may only be interested in smoothing the series until the residuals no longer have any serial correlation in order to determine how long a period is necessary to average out noise and reveal the true message.

2.2 Estimation and Forecasting Compendium

In order to forecast from exponential smoothing relationships one must invoke the notion of a Taylor series approximation and the Fundamental Theorem of Exponential Smoothing (Brown 1963). Taken together these theorems enable one to forecast τ time periods ahead using either of two equivalent procedures: one based on linear combinations of smoothed statistics $S_t^{(1)}, S_t^{(2)}, \ldots, S_t^{(k)}$ where k denotes the order of smoothing; and the other based on recursive estimates of the coefficients $c_0, c_1, \ldots$, as new information becomes available. The former approach is summarized below for constant, linear, and quadratic forms of the underlying time series. In what follows t is the most recent time period, τ is the lead time of the forecast, a is the smoothing constant, $b = 1 - a$, P_t is the value of the original observed series as of time t, $S_t^{(1)}$ is a single smoothing of P_t, and $S_{t-1}^{(1)}$ is the smoothed value of P_t up to and including but not beyond observation P_{t-1}.[1]

Constant Model:

$$P_t = c_0 + e_t$$

Forecast:

$$P_{t+\tau} = c_{0t}$$

Estimate of coefficient c_0 as of time t:

$$c_{0t} = P_t + b(S_{t-1}^{(1)} - P_t)$$

Linear Model:

$$P_t = c_0 + c_1 t + e_t$$

---

1. Robert Goodell Brown, *Smoothing Forecasting and Prediction*, (Englewood Cliffs, N.J.: Prentice-Hall Inc., 1963), pp. 122, 132–34, 143–44, 176–77, 192. Reprinted by permission of Prentice-Hall, Inc.

Forecast:

$$\hat{P}_{t+\tau} = c_{0t} + c_{1t}\tau$$

Estimate of coefficient c_0 as of time t:

$$c_{0t} = 2S_t^{(1)} - S_t^{(2)}$$

Estimate of coefficient c_1 as of time t:

$$c_{1t} = \frac{a}{b}[S_t^{(1)} - S_t^{(2)}]$$

Quadratic Model:

$$P_t = c_0 + c_1 t + \frac{1}{2}c_2 t^2 + e_t$$

Forecast:

$$\hat{P}_{t+\tau} = c_{0t} + c_{1t}\tau + \frac{1}{2}c_{2t}\tau^2$$

Estimate of coefficient c_0 as of time t:

$$c_{0t} = 3S_t^{(1)} - 3S_t^{(2)} + S_t^{(3)}$$

Estimate of coefficient c_1 as of time t:

$$c_{1t} = \frac{a}{2b^2}[(6 - 5a) S_t^{(1)} - 2(5 - 4a) S_t^{(2)} + (4 - 3a) S_t^{(3)}]$$

Estimate of coefficient c_2 as of time t:

$$c_{2t} = \frac{a^2}{b^2}[S_t^{(1)} - 2S_t^{(2)} + S_t^{(3)}]$$

It must be noted that initial estimates are needed for $S^{(1)}$, c_1, and c_2 in order to start the forecast algorithms presented above. These values may be obtained from historical calculations of $S^{(1)}$ and subjective estimates of c_1 and c_2. The latter typically are updated following the above algorithm over some historical period ending at time t (the most recent date, e.g., today) from which the τ period lead time forecast is "launched" (e.g., a forecast of tomorrow if $\tau = 1$ for a daily forecasting model).

3 GENERALIZED ADAPTIVE SMOOTHING

The moving average—exponential smoothing approach of estimating and forecasting a time series works well for underlying functions that may be represented by some linear expression of the form $P_t = c_0 + c_1 t + e_t$ where the noise element e_t is small. However, when the underlying process has an oscillatory component such as a seasonal movement represented by some sinusoidal function, or the noise element is relatively large, moving average methods to estimate the trend and seasonal components of such a series can introduce spurious correlation into the estimation and forecasting residuals. This effect is known as the Yule-Slutsky effect (Kendall and Stuart 1966). An approach developed by Brown (1963) can reduce this problem and offers computationally efficient methods for estimating and forecasting time series of this type. This approach is summarized below.

Let $f_i(t)$ denote the value of fitting function i as of time t. For example, for the fitting function $f_1 = 1$ the value of $f_1(t)$ is 1; for a fitting function of the form $f_1 = t$ then $f_1(t) = t$; for the fitting function $f_2 = t^2$ then $f_2(t) = t^2$; for a fitting function of the form $f_3 = \sin(wt)$ then $f_3(t) = \sin(wt)$, and so forth. The model under consideration may be described as follows:

$$P_t = c_0 f_0(t) + c_1 f_1(t) + \ldots + c_m f_m(t) + e_t$$

where the c_i are coefficients to be estimated, the $f_i(t)$ are fitting functions of time and e_t is random noise as of time t.

The τ period lead time forecasting model corresponding to this estimation model is of the form

$$P_{t+\tau} = c_0(t) f_0(t + \tau) + \ldots + c_m(t) f_m(t + \tau)$$
$$= C(t) F(t + \tau)$$

where $C(t)$ is a 1-by-$(m + 1)$ vector of coefficients estimated with data up to and including time t, and $F(t + \tau)$ is a $(m + 1)$-by-1 vector of values of the $m + 1$ fitting functions as of time $t + \tau$.

Because the coefficients c_i may evolve over time, one method of estimating them is to use discounted least squares so that more recent errors are given more weight and "avoided" more strongly. The estimated coefficients, in turn, more closely represent the latest true value. As shown by Brown (1963) these estimates, together with recursive relationships to shift the fitting functions of time period by period and the limiting values of the discounted products of the fitting functions, enable one to update, that is, to adapt the forecasting coefficients $C(t)$ as follows:[2]

$$C(t) = L'C(t - 1) + h[P_t - C(t - 1)F'(t)]$$

where L' is the transpose of the $(m + 1) \times (m + 1)$ matrix, L, of recursive shift operators for the $m + 1$ fitting functions of time and h is a vector of weights that revise the previous coefficient estimates on the basis of the most recent "forecast error," $P_t - C(t - 1)F'(t)$.

For example, consider a monthly model with a linear trend plus a seasonal component with trending amplitude.

$$P_t = c_0 + c_1 t + (c_2 + c_4 t)\sin\frac{2\pi}{12}t + (c_3 + c_5 t)\cos\frac{2\pi}{12}t + e_t$$
$$= c_0 f_0 + c_1 f_1 + c_2 f_2 + c_3 f_3 + c_4 f_4 + c_5 f_5 + e_t.$$

2. Ibid, p. 177.

The coefficients to be estimated are c_i, $i = 0, 2, \ldots, 5$. The fitting functions of time are $f_0 = 1$, $f_1 = t$, $f_2 = \sin \frac{2\pi}{12} t$, $f_3 = \cos \frac{2\pi}{12} t$, $f_4 = t \sin \frac{2\pi}{12} t$, and $f_5 = t \cos \frac{2\pi}{12} t$ where $\frac{2\pi}{12}$ is the frequency of the seasonal expressed in radians. The transition matrix L is

$$
L = \begin{bmatrix}
1 & 0 & 0 & 0 & 0 & 0 \\
1 & 1 & 0 & 0 & 0 & 0 \\
0 & 0 & \cos\frac{2\pi}{12} & \sin\frac{2\pi}{12} & 0 & 0 \\
0 & 0 & -\sin\frac{2\pi}{12} & \cos\frac{2\pi}{12} & 0 & 0 \\
0 & 0 & \cos\frac{2\pi}{12} & \sin\frac{2\pi}{12} & \cos\frac{2\pi}{12} & \sin\frac{2\pi}{12} \\
0 & 0 & -\sin\frac{2\pi}{12} & \cos\frac{2\pi}{12} & -\sin\frac{2\pi}{12} & \cos\frac{2\pi}{12}
\end{bmatrix}
\approx
\begin{bmatrix}
1 & 0 & 0 & 0 & 0 & 0 \\
1 & 1 & 0 & 0 & 0 & 0 \\
0 & 0 & .87 & .50 & 0 & 0 \\
0 & 0 & -.50 & .87 & 0 & 0 \\
0 & 0 & .87 & .50 & .87 & .50 \\
0 & 0 & -.50 & .87 & -.50 & .87
\end{bmatrix}
$$

and is derived from a Taylor series estimate of $F(t + 1)$ about $F(t)$.

The weighting function, h, is equal to $F^{-1}F(0)$, where $F(0)$ is the vector of fitting functions evaluated at time $t = 0$,

$$
F(0) = \begin{bmatrix}
f_0(0) \\
f_1(0) \\
f_2(0) \\
f_3(0) \\
f_4(0) \\
f_5(0)
\end{bmatrix} = \begin{bmatrix}
1 \\
0 \\
0 \\
1 \\
0 \\
0
\end{bmatrix}
$$

and F^{-1} is the inverse of the "steady state" matrix F defined as

$$
F = \sum_{t=0}^{\infty} \beta^t F(-t) F'(-t)
$$

where, following Brown (1963), $t = 0$ indicates the most recent time period and $-t$ indicates past time for discounting purposes. It can be shown that F, in the above case, is a symmetric six-by-six matrix of Z transforms that can be evaluated for any given value of β. For example, the element in the second row second column of F corresponds to

$$
\sum_{t=0}^{\infty} \beta^t t^2 = \frac{\beta(1 + \beta)}{(1 - \beta)^2}.
$$

A table of Z transforms can be found in Beightler et al. (1961).

For the example presented, and for $\beta = .983$ the weighting vector, h, is

$$h = \begin{bmatrix} h_0 \\ h_1 \\ h_2 \\ h_3 \\ h_4 \\ h_5 \end{bmatrix} \begin{bmatrix} .0335 \\ .0003 \\ .0060 \\ .0666 \\ .0001 \\ .0006 \end{bmatrix}.$$

While the calculations are not trivial, they do allow the construction of adaptive τ period ahead smoothed forecasts of prices with an oscillatory component.

4 ARIMA MODELS

Box and Jenkins (1970) popularized the building of mixed auto-regressive integrated moving average (ARIMA) models for discrete stochastic time series analysis and forecasting. The approach is popular for several reasons. First, it emphasizes model simplicity and a small number of parameters to be estimated in order to achieve adequate accuracy and representation. Second, it can be applied to nonstationary time series with or without seasonal or other oscillations. Third, it can accommodate more than one input as explanatory variables, that is, transfer function models. In this section we summarize the simple auto-regressive integrated moving average (ARIMA) model for univariate time series with and without seasonal or other oscillations. Multivariate-transfer function models are discussed in the next chapter.

4.1 Nonseasonal ARIMA Models

ARIMA models are predicated on a few rules and characteristics of time series. First, if the time series to be estimated and forecast, P_t, is nonstationary it must be transformed into a stationary process before any statistical estimation procedures can be applied with reasonable assurance of obtaining accurate coefficient estimates. This transformation may be accomplished by differencing the series, P_t, d times until the apparently stationary series, Z_t, is achieved. This operation can be denoted

$$Z_t = (1 - L)^d P_t$$

where L is the lag operator $L^d P_t = P_{t-d}$. An auto-regressive moving average model then is built to describe Z_t. The corresponding relationship for P_t is obtained by integrating back from Z_t to P_t, i.e., by undoing the differencing from P_t to Z_t.

Second, a finite moving average process can be written as the infinite length auto-regressive process and, conversely, a finite auto-regressive process can be written as an infinite length moving average process. In practice, a parsimonious representation of either infinite length auto-regressive process or infinite length moving average process will include both auto-regressive and moving average components of finite length. This practical representation can be denoted

$$Z_t - \phi_1 Z_{t-1} - \ldots - \phi_p Z_{t-p}$$
$$= e_t - \theta_1 e_{t-1} - \ldots - \theta_q e_{t-q}$$

or

$$\phi(L) Z_t = \theta(L) e_t$$

where

$$\phi(L) = (1 - \phi_1 L - \phi_2 L^2 - \ldots \phi_p L^p),$$
$$\theta(L) = (1 - \theta_1 L - \theta_2 L^2 - \ldots - \theta_q L^q)$$

and p and q are the finite length of the auto-regressive and moving average processes, respectively.

Third, for a stationary series the auto-correlation function of an auto-regressive process of order p tails off without end but its corresponding partial auto-correlation function ends at lag p. Conversely, the auto-correlation function of a moving average process of order q ends at lag q but its partial auto-correlation function tails off without end. A mixed auto-regressive–moving average process is indicated when both the auto-correlation and partial auto-correlation functions tail off. Because the auto-correlation and partial auto-correlation functions must be estimated, the length of the lags, p and q, may be identified using confidence intervals around the auto-correlation coefficients: Estimates that break through the confidence bounds are statistically significant at the prescribed level of assurance set by the user. For a pure auto-regressive model the maximum length lag, p, would correspond to the partial auto-correlation coefficient of the longest lag that is statistically significant. A similar rule would apply to the auto-correlation function for the pure moving average function to determine the maximum lag q. For mixed auto-regressive–moving average processes the determination of p and q are not so straightforward. Here one must estimate the character of the auto-correlations and partial auto-correlations as functions of the length of the lag. For example, auto-correlations that are significant and nearly constant from a lag of zero up to a lag of k and thereafter exhibit an oscillatory decay would imply a moving average process of order $q = k$ and an auto-regressive process of order p no less than 2. Box and Jenkins (1970, chs., 3, 4, 5) offer guidelines to help identify these structures. Finally, the coefficients in an ARIMA function are nonlinearly related to one another and therefore require nonlinear estimation techniques to obtain precise estimates of the parameters ϕ_1, $\phi_2, \ldots, \theta_1, \theta_2, \ldots$ in the model. Here, Box and Jenkins (1971) outline several alternative methods as do Goldfeld and Quandt (1972) and Himmelblau (1972).

Taken together these model-building guidelines offer the analyst both ease and flexibility in the construction of a time series model for forecasting purposes. The principal weaknesses of the approach are threefold. First, the model developed may not be unique. That is, an alternative combination of lags, p and q, may provide the same statistical accuracy and be no less parsimonious in terms of the number of coefficients to be estimated. While this is a potential problem to those who are interested in interpreting the model structure in detail, it is not a problem of great significance to those who are more concerned with ease of use and statistical accuracy. Second, and not unrelated to the first weakness, the specification of ARIMA processes is as much an art as it is a science. Here there is no substitute for experience. Third, sophisticated computational capabilities are essential.

4.2 ARIMA Models with Seasonal Oscillations

Economic time series often exhibit oscillations that complete themselves an integer number of times in a year. These oscillations are highly correlated with themselves one year earlier and special efforts must be taken to estimate them. These models may be thought of as having two components: a seasonal ARIMA model and a nonseasonal ARIMA model. The combined model must be able to distinguish between and capture both the "between-period" correlations (e.g., March to March between years), and the "within-period" correlations (e.g., February to March within the same year). The seasonal portion of the combined ARIMA model is of the form

$$(1 - \alpha_1 L^S - \alpha_2 L^{S2} - \ldots - \alpha_P L^{SP})(1 - L^S)^D P_t = (1 - \delta_1 L^S - \delta_2 L^{S2} - \ldots - \delta_Q L^{SQ})\epsilon_t$$

where L^S denotes a seasonal lag operator, for example, $L^S P_t = P_{t-s}$; $(1 - L^S)^D$ is a seasonal backward difference operator of order D, for example, for $D = 2$; $(1 - L^S)^2 P_t = P_t - 2P_{t-s} + P_{t-2S}$; and ϵ_t is the residual from this model estimation. Such a model links current behavior to that one or more years earlier. The order of the seasonal differencing, D, is dictated by the need to achieve stationarity in the "between-period" series. The determination of the orders of the seasonal auto-regressive and moving average operators P and Q follow the same procedures and guidelines as in the nonseasonal case but again for the "between-period" data.

The residuals from the seasonal ARIMA model, ϵ_t, are likely to be correlated within the seasonal period, that is, between time t and times $t - 1$, $t - 2, \ldots$. This possibility requires the analyst to consider a nonseasonal

ARIMA model for these residuals. Here, one follows the guidelines and rules noted earlier for nonseasonal ARIMA models. Such a model would be of the form

$$(1 - \phi_1 L - \phi_2 L^2 - \ldots - \phi_p L^p)(1 - L)^d \epsilon_t = (1 - \theta_1 L - \theta_2 L^2 - \ldots - \theta_q L^q) e_t,$$

and the complete combined model would be

$$(1 - \phi_1 L - \phi_2 L^2 - \ldots - \phi_p L^p)(1 - L)^d (1 - \alpha_1 L^S - \alpha_2 L^{S2} - \ldots - \alpha_p L^{SP})(1 - L^S)^{DP_t}$$
$$= (1 - \theta_1 L - \theta_2 L^2 - \ldots - \theta_q L^q)(1 - \delta_1 L^S - \delta_2 L^{S2} - \ldots - \delta_Q L^{SQ}) e_t.$$

4.3 Forecasting by ARIMA Models

There are several alternative forms in which an ARIMA forecasting equation can be expressed. One way is to solve the estimated difference equation for a forecasting equation that bears a strong family resemblance to general adaptive smoothing (see Box and Jenkins 1970, ch. 5). Another way is to use the estimated model directly and generate forecasts recursively. When seasonal components are present, forecasts are most easily generated direct from the "direct recursive forecast" approach. This method is illustrated below.

Let t denote the origin of the forecast, τ denote the lead time of the forecast and s the length of the seasonal period. A weekly ARIMA model with $p = 1, q = 1, d = 0, P = 1, Q = 1, D = 0, \tau = 2$ and $S = 52$ would be

$$(1 - \phi_1 L)(1 - \alpha_1 L^{52})P_t = (1 - \theta_1 L)(1 - \delta_1 L^{52})e_t$$

or

$$P_t = \phi_1 P_{t-1} + \alpha_1 P_{t-52} - \phi_1 \alpha_1 P_{t-53} + e_t - \theta_1 e_{t-1} - \delta_1 e_{t-52} + \theta_1 \delta_1 e_{t-53}.$$

For an τ-period-ahead forecast with perfect knowledge of the error terms (an impossibility) the forecasting equation would be

$$\hat{P}_{t+\tau} = \phi \hat{P}_{t+\tau-1} + \alpha_1 P_{t+\tau-52} - \phi_1 \alpha_1 P_{t+\tau-53} + e_{t+\tau} - \theta_1 e_{t+\tau-1}$$
$$- \delta_1 e_{t+\tau-52} + \theta_1 \delta_1 e_{t+\tau-53}.$$

Using conditional expectations for all variables beyond those that can be observed the $\tau = 2$ period forecasting equation would become

$$\hat{P}_{t+2} = \phi_1 \hat{P}_{t+1} + \alpha_1 P_{t-50} - \phi_1 \alpha_1 P_{t-51} - \delta_1 e_{t-50} + \theta_1 \delta_1 e_{t-51}$$

where $\hat{P}_{t-1}$ is calculated in a similar manner to $\hat{P}_{t+2}$ and the expected values of e_{t+2} and e_{t+1} are zero. The estimation residuals e_{t-50} and e_{t-51} may be expressed as $(P_{t-50} - \hat{P}_{t-50}^{(1)})$ and $(P_{t-51} - \hat{P}_{t-51}^{(1)})$, respectively, where $P_{t-\tau}^{(1)}$

denotes a forecast of $P_{t-\tau}$ made at time $t - \tau - 1$. With this final substitution the forecasting equation can be expressed completely in terms of previous actual and forecast values of P_t:

$$\hat{P}_{t+2} = \phi\hat{P}_{t+1} + (\alpha_1 - \delta_1)P_{t-50} + (\theta_1\delta_1 - \phi_1\alpha_1)P_{t-51} + \delta_1\hat{P}^{(1)}_{t-50} - \theta_1\delta_1\hat{P}^{(1)}_{t-51}.$$

4.4 Special Considerations of Daily Commodity Price Data for ARIMA Models

There are, of course, many problems one encounters in practice and all of them cannot be considered here. One problem encountered in the estimation and forecasting of a daily commodity price series is the treatment of seasonals when they are present. The principal problem here is the oscillatory character of the seasonal as opposed to a perfect periodicity. That is, in terms of daily observations a seasonal may be distributed between 360 and 370 days depending on holidays or other factors. Using a seasonal difference operator of $(1 - L^{365})^D$ may be precisely correct only a few times every few years and may result in a poor estimating and forecasting equation. One way to reduce this problem is to invoke the notion of a "band," b, around the average seasonal period. In the above case the band would be five days and would require a difference operator of the form

$$[1 - L(365,5)]^D = (1 - L^{360} - L^{361} - L^{362} - \ldots - L^{368} - L^{369} - L^{370})^D$$

where $L(365, 5)$ denotes a lag operator with a 5 day band around a 365 day lag. This leads to a proliferation of parameters to be estimated and the simplicity of the ARIMA approach is undercut.

5 KALMAN FILTERS

Kalman (1960) developed an approach to a class of estimation problems of special importance to commodity analysts. His efforts led to a linear minimum error variance sequential state estimation algorithm that distinguishes between a message model and an observation model in the context of a complete estimation and forecasting system. The recognition of a message model in conjunction with an observation model is of practical relevance for commodity market analysts. To appreciate its potential, suppose an analyst estimated a daily model of COMEX silver price movements (i.e., the message model) as a vehicle to make conditional forecasts of these prices one day ahead. Suppose further the analyst has other information on the one-period-ahead value of COMEX silver such as floor broker anticipations or opening prices in some other part of the world that often foreshadow

COMEX activity, for example, London silver prices. The Kalman approach enables one to systematically include this other information in the form of an observation model and in such a way that the revised values of the prior predictions may have greater forecasting accuracy than the prior predictions based solely on the message model. Another example of the Kalman approach is the estimation of a message model to predict prices and the inclusion of an observation model to reflect the effects of large-volume trades on the price actually captured in the market. Here the message model may predict a particular market price but entering the market at that price may force the market away from that price owing to the liquidity of the market in relation to the size of the trade. This "execution" effect may be reflected in the "observation" model. The Kalman approach can accommodate such distinctions systematically and in keeping with the tenets of estimation and prediction theory.

In general, the Kalman approach for univariate time series estimation and forecasting consists of a message model of the form

$$P_t = \phi P_{t-1} + {}^m e_t$$

and an observation model of the form,

$$J_t = HP_t + {}^o e_t,$$

where ϕ and H are known (estimated) coefficients and ${}^m e_t$ and ${}^o e_t$ are "state" and "observation" model random errors, respectively. It is assumed that ${}^m e_t$ and ${}^o e_t$ are serially uncorrelated.

In a forecasting context this system would produce a recursive one-period-ahead forecasting equation of the form,

$$\hat{P}_{t+1} = \phi \hat{P}_t + K_{t+1}(J_t - H\hat{P}_t)$$

where $\hat{P}_{t+1}$ is the one-period-ahead forecast of P_{t+1}, $\hat{P}_t$ is the one-period-ahead forecast of P_t, and K_{t+1} is the Kalman gain coefficient given by

$$K_{t+1} = \frac{\phi \, \text{var} \, (P_t - \hat{P}_t) H}{H \, \text{var} \, (P_t - \hat{P}_t) + \text{Var} \, {}^o e_t}$$

and where

$$\text{var} \, (P_t - \hat{P}) = \phi(\phi - K_t H) \, \text{var} \, (P_{t-1} - \hat{P}_{t-1}) + \text{var} \, {}^m e_t.$$

The Kalman gain coefficient is an adaptive correction factor that adjusts the most recent forecast for the most recent forecast error. It is adaptive owing to changes in the forecast error variance $\text{var} \, (P_t - \hat{P}_t)$ as well as changes in the observation model error variance var ^oe_t. The forecast error variance is estimated up to the time of the most recent forecast error available and can be calculated recursively as shown above.

The Kalman approach can accommodate nonstationarity in the model errors, a condition referred to as "colored" noise and explored by Sage and Melsa (1971). Furthermore, it may also accommodate independent variables as will be discussed in the next chapter.

The Kalman approach also can be used to accommodate seasonal as well as nonseasonal models. The latter is evident in the model outlined above. Seasonal oscillations can be accounted for in several ways. One of the easiest is to estimate the message model in seasonally adjusted terms and to construct an observation model on the unadjusted data of the form

$$J_t = h \cos wt\, P_t + {}^oe_t$$

where cos *wt* represents the seasonal oscillation. To be sure, more elaborate trigonometric functions may be used in the construction of the observation model. A variation of this approach can be used to capture residual seasonal oscillations in a supposedly seasonally adjusted series, or to capture changing seasonal patterns when both P_t and J_t are unadjusted for seasonal variation.

6   CHOOSING A METHOD

The several methods discussed here are especially designed to estimate and forecast a single time series. They vary in sophistication depending on the objectives of the analyst, the information available, and the sophistication of the research effort. To be sure, more elaborate models such as the Kalman approach are more costly to develop and maintain than simple exponential smoothing. Whether the additional effort of the Kalman approach over the exponential smoothing method is worthwhile depends of course on the character of the time series, the quality of the data, and the costs of imprecision. In short, which model is best is an empirical question. As a general but not infallible rule, time series that exhibit seasonal oscillations are better estimated and forecast using general adaptive smoothing, Box-Jenkins ARIMA models, or Kalman approaches. If the structure of the market and availability of the data afford the distinction between message and observation then the Kalman approach would be highly recommended. Otherwise the Box-Jenkins ARIMA model or general adaptive smoothing approach of Brown are most highly recommended. However, it must be noted that changes in market characteristics brought about by legislation or natural economic inertia often necessitate the obsolescence of one approach in favor of another. While "keeping it simple" is a practical virtue, the analyst must have a full range of these tools in order to meet the research needs of the market place.

7 UNIVARIATE FORECASTING METHODS AND TRADING SYSTEMS

The univariate forecasting methods summarized above can be used in conjunction with trading rules developed for technical chart analysis or may be combined with special trading systems of their own. When combined with chart analysis they are particularly useful in the calculation of price objectives and as checks against preliminary and confirming indicators of a price move. In their own right they give rise to trading systems that are based on confidence intervals. In the following paragraphs several illustrative trading systems are presented that apply univariate forecasting methods.

The particular combinations of forecasting methods and trading systems presented are not unique. To be sure, many of the forecasting methods and trading rules can be interchanged. Indeed, the variations are as numerous as the number of commodities and market conditions one may consider. In what follows all positions are liquidated upon the market price reaching the price objective or the first reversal or the stop-loss price, whichever comes first.

7.1 Trading Range Moving Average with Adaptive Volatility Adjustments

In the following equations $M(P_t)$ denotes a "simple" moving average of a particular commodity price P_t, B_t denotes some multiple of a variable that measures the volatility of the commodity price, P_{t+j} denotes a price forecast j periods into the future, and $\pi(i)$ denotes the minimum acceptable profit j periods in the future. The upper and lower bounds of the moving average are

$$M_t^{(+)} = M(P_t) + B_t$$

and

$$M_t^{(-)} = M(P_t) - B_t$$

respectively.

A common trading rule is if $(P_t - M_t^{(+)}) > 0$ and $P_t - P_{t-1} > 0$, then buy (go long). However, if $(P_t - M_t^{(-)}) < 0$ and $P_t - P_{t-1} < 0$, then sell (go short). The trading range defined by $M_t \pm B_t$ depends, of course, on the construction of B_t. Among the most popular calculations for B_t are

$$B_t = \eta \sigma_M$$

where σ_M is the standard deviation of $M(P_t)$, and η is a user-designated multiple;

$$B_t = \eta\sigma_P$$

where σ_P is the standard deviation of the commodity price over the same time period as the moving average and η is defined as above; and

$$B_t = \frac{1}{2}M(H_t - L_t)$$

where $H_t - L_t$ is the difference between the high and the low price as of time t, and $M(H_t - L_t)$ is a moving average of the difference $H_t - L_t$ and is of the same length as the moving average M_t.

The price objective in this system typically is based on a linear trend assumption, that is, $\hat{P}_{t+\tau} = c_0 + c_0\tau$; and forecast on the basis of smoothed estimates of the data. In this case the price objective calculated as of time t, from Section 2.3, would be

$$\hat{P}_{t+\tau} = c_0 + c_1\tau$$

where

$$c_0 = 2S_t^{(1)} - S_t^{(2)},$$

and

$$c_1 = \frac{a}{b}[S_t^{(1)} - S_t^{(2)}].$$

The length of the forecast τ is determined by the user's profit criterion and time horizon.

7.2. Velocity and Acceleration/Deceleration: a second-order smoothing system

Velocity indicates the direction of prices, and acceleration/deceleration indicates whether the prices are changing at an increasing, decreasing, or constant rate; for example prices are increasing (upward velocity) at a decreasing rate (decelerating). Because one must consider possible changes in rates of change, a second-order smoothing system (or the equivalent) is required. As noted above a second-order system is of the form

$$P_t = c + c_1t + \frac{1}{2}c_2t^2 + e_t.$$

For such a system velocity and acceleration/deceleration are given by

$$V_t = c_1 + c_2t$$

$$= \frac{a}{2b^2}[(6-5a)S_t^{(1)} - 2(5-4a)S_t^{(2)} + (4-3a)S_t^{(3)}] + \frac{a^2}{b^2}[S_t^{(1)} - 2S_t^{(2)} + S_t^{(3)}]t$$

and

$$A_t = c_2$$

$$= \frac{a^2}{b^2}[S_t^{(1)} - 2S_t^{(2)} + S_t^{(3)}]$$

respectively, where *a* and *b* are as defined in Section 2.1 of this chapter.

The trading rules for a velocity, acceleration/deceleration system are if $V_t > 0$, and $A_t > 0$, and $\hat{P}_{t+1} \geq \hat{P}_{t+2} \geq \cdots \geq \hat{P}_{t+\tau} \leq \hat{P}_{t+\tau+1}$, then buy, if $V_t < 0$, and $A_t < 0$, and $\hat{P}_{t+1} \leq \hat{P}_{t+2} \leq \cdots \leq \hat{P}_{t+\tau} \geq \hat{P}_{t+\tau+1}$, then sell; where the τ-period-ahead price objective is

$$\hat{P}_{t+\tau} = c_0 + c_1\tau + \frac{1}{2}c_2\tau^2.$$

Once again the precise holding period, τ, will be determined by user profit criteria, rates of time preference, and risk aversion.

7.3 General Adaptive Smoothing Systems

As noted earlier, general adaptive smoothing is well suited to estimate and forecast time series that include periodic or oscillatory components. For example,

$$P = c_0 + c_1 t + c_2 \sin wt + c_3 \cos wt + e_t$$

where *w* is the frequency of the oscillatory component. For such a system let $\sigma(\tau)$ denote the forecast error variance for a forecast τ time periods into the future. The trading rule is based on the notion of an uptrend or downtrend in the context of a projected confidence interval. Specifically, if $\hat{P}_{t+\tau} - \eta\sigma(\tau) \geq P_t + \pi(\tau)$, then buy; if $\hat{P}_{t+\tau} + \eta\sigma(\tau) \leq P_t - \pi(\tau)$, then sell; where $\pi(\tau)$ is a minimal acceptable profit for a waiting time of τ periods and η is a user-selected multiple based on desired levels of risk avoidance; for example, the larger η the more cautious the trading role. Figure 16.1 illustrates this system for an uptrend.

7.4 ARIMA Model Trading Systems

Auto-regressive moving average models lend themselves to trading systems that are not dissimilar from the general adaptive smoothing system described above. The principal differences are in the price forecasting mechanism and the corresponding calculation of forecast error variances needed to construct confidence about forecast prices. Here an illustrative estimation model would be

$$P_t = (1 + \phi)P_{t-1} - \phi P_{t-2} + e_t - \theta e_{t-1}.$$

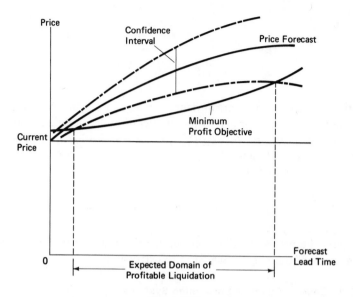

Figure 16.1

CONFIDENCE INTERVAL TRADING RULE

The corresponding forecasting equation would be

$$\hat{P}_{t+1} = (1 + \phi)P_t - \phi P_{t-1} - \theta e_t$$

or

$$\hat{P}_{t+\tau} = (1 + \phi)\hat{P}_{t+\tau-1} - \phi\hat{P}_{t+\tau-2}, \text{ for } \tau > 2,$$

where τ is the forecast lead time. The forecast error variance of lead time τ is given by

$$\sigma(\tau) = (1 + \sum_{j=1}^{\tau-1} \psi_j^2)^{1/2}\sigma_e$$

where the ψ's are calculated given the θ's and ϕ's using relationships analogous to those presented on page 309, and σ_e is the standard deviation of e_t.

To recapitulate, the trading rule would be if $\hat{P}_{t+\tau} - \eta\sigma(\tau) \geq P_t + \pi(\tau)$, then buy; if $\hat{P}_{t+\tau} + \eta\sigma(\tau) \leq P_t - \pi(\tau)$, then sell; where $\pi(\tau)$ is the minimally acceptable profit for a waiting time of τ time periods and η defines the width of the confidence interval. If one of the above conditions holds for several time periods then the waiting time may be set equal to that at which maximum profits are achieved.

7.5 Kalman Predictor Model

For the one-period-ahead forecasting equation $\hat{P}_{t+1} = \phi \hat{P}_t + K_{t+1}$ $(J_t - H\hat{P}_t)$, where K_{t+1} and var $(P_t - \hat{P}_t)$ are as defined earlier in Section 5, the trading rule is the same as those given for the ARIMA system: If $\hat{P}_{t+1} - \eta \text{var}(P_t - \hat{P}_t) \geq P_t + \pi(1)$, then buy; if $\hat{P}_{t+1} + \eta \text{var}(P_t - \hat{P}_t) \leq P_t - \pi(1)$, then sell.

An important distinction for the Kalman model in relation to the previous two approaches is the generation of forecasts more than one period ahead. In practice one may generate further forward forecasts using a sequence of successively longer one-period-ahead forecasts. These forecasts may be derived from parallel models based on different time units of measurement, for example, a daily model followed by a weekly model followed by a monthly model. Naturally, as the frequency of observation changes, the estimated models may reveal significant changes in character, for example, different coefficient estimates and/or different lag structures and error variances.

One other factor is unique to the Kalman system: the variance in the observation model. This may reflect the variability with which prices are captured in trading and may vary owing to the size of the trade in relation to liquidity of the market at the time of the trade. Accordingly some model of market liquidity may be required to project this error variance if necessary. Typically this involves some from of multivariate model building where, for example, market liquidity, measured by some combination of volume and open interest, may be an explanatory variable or may require a separate forecasting equation to be used in conjunction with the price forecasting model. These topics are discussed in the next chapter.

8 SUMMARY

The univariate estimating models and forecasting systems discussed here are among the most popular in commodity trading. To be sure, there are almost endless variations on these themes and combinations of these approaches. Their principal strength, simplicity, is also their major shortcoming. While conditions appear to arise with considerable frequency for these methods to be applied profitably, even the most ardent technical analyst would be hard pressed to consider them an adequate method for all occasions. The disposition of other factors often provides a "leading" indicator of near-term price movements, and technical analysis places considerable weight on other select factors. The incorporation of this additional data, of course, results in major changes in the character of the models used for trading purposes. These models and their trading systems bear a strong family resemblance to those already presented. However their correspondence is more apparent than it is real. As is often the case, a seemingly minor variation on a theme can involve more than first meets the eye. The extension of these simple technical systems to include the influence of other factors is covered in the next chapter.

9 BIBLIOGRAPHY

BEIGHTLER C. S., L. G. MITTEN, and G. L. NEMBAUSER, "A Short Table of *z*-Transforms and Generating Functions," *Operations Research,* 9, no. 4 (1961), 574–78.

BOX, G. E. P., and G. M. JENKINS, *Time Series Analysis Forecasting and control.* San Francisco: Holden-Day, 1970.

BROWN, R. G. D., *Smoothing, Forecasting and Prediction of Discrete Time Series.* Englewood Cliffs, N.J.: Prentice-Hall, Inc., 1963.

GOLDFELD, S. M., and R. E. QUANDT, *Nonlinear Methods in Econometrics.* Amsterdam: North Holland Publishing Co., 1972.

HIMMELBLAU, D. M., *Applied Nonlinear Programming.* New York: McGraw-Hill, 1972.

KALMAN, R. E., "A New Approach to Linear Filtering and Prediction Problems." *Journal of Basic Engineering;* 82D (March 1960), 655–60.

KENDALL, M. G., and A. STUART, *The Advanced Theory of Statistics,* Vol. 3. London: Charles Griffen & Company, Limited, 1966.

MEYER, R. F., "An Adaptive Method of Routine Short-Term Forecasting." Oslo, Norway: International Federation of Operational Research Societies, July 1963.

SAGE, A. P., and J. L. MELSA, *Estimation Theory with Applications to Communications and Control.* New York: McGraw-Hill, 1971.

17

MULTIVARIATE FORECASTING
MODELS AND TRADING SYSTEMS

IIIIIIIIIIIIIIIIIIIIIIIIIIIIIIIIIIIIIIIIIIIIIIIIIIIIIIIIIIIIIIIIIIIIIIIIIIIIIIIIIIIIIIIIIIIIIIIIIIIIIIII

1 INTRODUCTION

Technical commodity analysis often attempts to relate price movements
in a commodity to volume and/or open interest in that commodity or to
other commodity prices, volumes, and open interest that tend to foreshadow
price movements in the commodity under consideration. Time series models
that attempt to explain a single output, such as price, with multiple inputs,
such as volume and open interest, are referred to as multivariate models.
They are distinguished from univariate models such as those discussed in
Chapter 16 by the inclusion of independent variables such as volume and
open interest. There are, of course, many types of multivariate time series
models and all of them cannot be covered here. For the purposes of technical commodity analysis this chapter focuses on multivariate time series of
the form

$$P_t = G(L)X_{t-k} + N(L)e_t$$

where P_t is the value of the independent variable as of time t, $G(L)$ is a
"transfer" function of the lag operator L and is of the form $G(L) = g_k +$
$gL_{k+1}^2 + gL_{k+2}^2 + \ldots$ and relates the value of the independent variable X_t at
least k periods ago to P_t, and $N(L)e_t$ is a "noise" model that relates random
errors e_t to P_t. Here, both functions $G(L)$ and $N(L)$ take the form of some

auto-regressive moving average operator in order to capture the timing and intensity of the response in P_t to the impulse from the independent variable X and the noise e. To be sure it is not necessary that X_t lead P_t by k periods for estimation or forecasting purposes. However, for practical considerations of forecasting, the use of leading indicators avoids or reduces the need to condition forecasts on future values of the independent variables.

Even for the class of time series models considered here there are several ways to approach their estimation and forecasting. For practical and theoretical considerations three approaches are outlined below: the elementary first-difference model, the auto-regressive integrated moving average (ARIMA) approach, and the Kalman filter approach. The first-difference model is presented to serve primarily as an introduction and baseline. The ARIMA approach emphasizes parsimony in the size of the model, that is, the smallest number of coefficients needed to achieve a given level of accuracy. The Kalman approach includes the distinction between, and accommodation of, a message model in conjunction with an observation model.

2   ELEMENTARY FIRST-DIFFERENCE MODEL AND TRADING SYSTEM

As a point of departure consider the elementary first-difference model

$$\nabla P_t = \phi \nabla X_t + e_t$$

where ∇P_t is the change in P_t from time $t-1$ to time t, that is, $\nabla P_t = P_t - P_{t-1}$; ∇X_t is the change in the independent variable X from time $t-1$ to time t, that is, $\nabla X = X_t - X_{t-1}$; and e_t is a serially uncorrelated random error. For such a model simple least squares will suffice in the estimation of ϕ. In a forecasting context the τ period ahead change in P, $\nabla \hat{P}_{t+\tau}$, would be given by

$$\nabla \hat{P}_{t+\tau} = \phi \nabla X_{t+\tau}$$

assuming $\nabla X_{t+\tau}$ is known with certainty. In this case the τ-period-ahead forecast error variance would be

$$V(\tau) = \left(\frac{\nabla X_{t+\tau}^2}{\sum \nabla X_t^2} + 1 \right) \sigma_e^2$$

where $\sum \nabla X_t^2$ is the sum of the squared first differences in X over the estimation period up to time t, and σ_e^2 is the variance of the error term e_t. If $\nabla X_{t+\tau}$ is not known with certainty, and typically it is not, then the forecast error variance around $P_{t+\tau}$ will increase owing to the error variation around the prediction of $\nabla_{t+\tau} X$. One possible way of avoiding this cascade of forecast errors is to construct a model of ∇P_t that relies on an explanatory variable that precedes P_t by a sufficient number of time periods to eliminate, or reduce, the need to forecast the explanatory variable in order to forecast P_t; that is, to construct a model of the form

$$\nabla P_t = \nabla X_{t-k} + e_t$$

where k is the number of time periods X_t precedes P_t. This assumes, of course, that a leading indicator, X_t, can be found that offers sufficient accuracy and has a logical foundation for its use. To be sure, another model without a leading indicator may offer greater estimation accuracy than the leading indicator alternative. Insofar as the objective is to forecast ∇P_t, the criterion of choice will focus on forecast error variance and ease of implementation. In short, the selection of a leading indicator or some other model rests on performance. This model and those to follow give rise to trading systems in keeping with their statistical heritage. They are especially well suited for trading rules based on confidence intervals. These intervals are based in part on the error variance of the forecasts and the models enable one to calculate the variances with precision. To illustrate, trading rules for the elementary first-difference model consider a leading indicator model with an explanatory variable that precedes ∇P_t by k time periods. The τ-period-ahead forecast error variance is

$$V^2(\tau) = \left(\frac{\nabla X_{t+\tau}^2}{\sum \nabla X_t^2} + 1 \right) \sigma_e^2$$

Given the error variance of a τ-period-ahead forecast, $V^2(\tau)$, the 90 percent confidence interval corresponding to the point forecast $\hat{P}_{t+\tau} = P_t + \sum_{j=1}^{\tau} \nabla P_{t+j}$ would be

$$P_t + \sum_{j=1}^{\tau} \nabla P_{t+j} + U\left[\sum_{j=1}^{\tau} V^2(j) \right]^{1/2} \geq P_{t+j} \geq P_t + \sum_{j=1}^{\tau} \nabla P_{t+j} - U\left[\sum_{j=1}^{\tau} V^2(j) \right]^{1/2}$$

where U is some multiple (if e is normally distributed $U \approx 1.96$). Now if $\pi(\tau)$ denotes the minimum acceptable profit for a waiting period of τ time periods, a common trading rule is if $P_t + \pi(\tau) < \hat{P}_{t+\tau} - U(\sum_{j=1}^{\tau} V^2(j))^{1/2}$, then buy; if $P_t - \pi(\tau) > \hat{P}_{t+\tau} + U(\sum_{j=1}^{\tau} V^2(j))^{1/2}$, then sell. This rule is illustrated in Figure (16.1) for forecasts of P_t that suggest P_t first will increase and then will decrease. If the lower confidence bound lies above the minimum profit line as shown then a buy or long position is taken; a position is not taken otherwise.

The selection of the degree of confidence can be a user preference for some odds of success or can be based on comparative loss criteria that weigh the cost of too narrow a confidence band offering more frequent activity but higher odds of failure against a wider confidence band offering higher odds of success but a lower frequency of activity.

The elementary first-difference model is limited owing to its assumption that a change in the explanatory variable X leads to a single response in Y: Typically, an impulse in X has an effect on Y that is drawn out over considerably more than one time period. For these reasons the ARIMA transfer function–noise model can be an appropriate estimation and forecasting paradigm.

3   ARIMA TRANSFER FUNCTION–NOISE MODELS

The ARIMA approach to multivariate model building and forecasting parallels the univariate ARIMA procedure outlined in Chapter 16. The principal differences lie in the identification of the "transfer" function model linking one (or more) independent variable(s) to the dependent variable.

3.1   Estimation: single independent variable[1]

The basic procedure considers a single independent variable model

$$P_t = G(L)X_{t-k} + N_t$$
$$= g_{k-1}X_{t-k} + g_{k+1}X_{t-k-1} + \ldots + N_t$$
$$= U^{-1}(L)W(L)L^kX_t + N_t$$

where

$$U(L) = 1 - u_1L - u_2L^2 - \ldots - u_cL^c$$
$$W(L) = 1 - w_1L - w_2L^2 - \ldots - w_vL^v$$
$$L^kX_t = X_{t-k}.$$

and N_t is noise at time t.

The first step is to difference both series P_t and X_t sufficiently to achieve stationarity. The corresponding stationary model may be denoted

$$p_t = g_0x_{t-k} + g_1x_{t-k-1} + \ldots + n_t.$$

where

$$p_t = (1 - L)^dP_t$$
$$x_t = (1 - L)^dX_t$$

and

$$n_t = (1 - L)^dN_t$$

The second step is to "prewhiten" x_t by constructing a univariate ARIMA model for x_t. This is accomplished following the procedures out-

---

1. G.E.P. Box and G. M. Jenkins, *Time Series Analysis Forecasting and Control* (San Francisco: Holden-Day, 1970), pp. 415–16.

lined in Chapter 16 and yields a series α_t,

$$\alpha_t = \phi_x(L)\theta_x^{-1}(L)x_t,$$

that is a close approximation to random noise, save its relationship to p_t.

Third, the ARIMA process, $\phi_x(L)\theta_x^{-1}(L)$, estimated for x_t is used to transform p_t into the new series

$$\beta_t = \phi_x(L)\theta_x^{-1}(L)P_t$$
$$= G(L)\alpha_t + E_t$$

where

$$= \phi_x(L)\theta_x^{-1}(L)n_t.$$

Fourth, the coefficients g_i in $G(L) = g_0 + g_1L + g_2L^2 + \ldots$ then are estimated by

$$\hat{g}_i = \hat{r}_{\alpha\beta}(i)\frac{S_\beta}{S_\alpha}$$

where $\hat{r}_{\alpha\beta}(i)$ is the estimated correlation coefficient between α and β, i periods apart, S_β is the standard deviation of the series β_t and S_α is the standard derivation of the series α_t. Once again only those $\hat{r}_{\alpha\beta}(i)$ are "used" that are statistically significant at some prescribed level of significance, for example, 5 percent. If the $\hat{r}_{\alpha\beta}(i)$ are not statistically significant for the first $k-1$ lags then the delay between an impulse in x_t and the initial response in p_t is k periods.

Fifth, the preliminary estimates of the u's and w's are then calculated from the relationships

$$g_i = 0, \qquad\qquad i < k$$
$$g_k = w_0$$
$$g_{k-1} = u_1 g_k - w_1$$
$$g_{k-2} = u_1 g_{k+1} + u_2 g_k - w_2$$
$$g_{k+c+v} = u_1 g_{k+c+v-1} + \ldots - w_v$$

This calculation takes the form of a simultaneous solution of the above $c+v$ equations for the $c+v$ unknowns $u_1, u_2, \ldots, u_c, w_1, \ldots, w_v$.

Sixth, the residuals, E_t, are then modeled as an ARIMA model of the form

$$E_t = \phi_E^{-1}(L)\theta_E(L)e_t$$

where e_t is random noise. This estimation procedure follows the univariate estimation procedure outlined in Chapter 16 and is not repeated here.

Finally, the complete model is estimated using nonlinear estimation procedures like those referred to in Chapter 16. It is worth noting once again that the coefficients in this model, as in the simple univariate model, are nonlinearly related to each other and the nonlinear estimation is essential after the above "identification" process has been completed.

3.2　Multiple Independent Variables

More than one independent variable can be accommodated in these models through spectral methods outlined in Chapter 11 and in Box and Jenkins (1970). This process results in estimation residuals from the transfer function model of the form

$$E_t = P_t - \phi_{x_1}(L)\theta_{x_1}^{-1}(L)x_{1t} - \phi_{x_2}(L)\theta_{x_2}^{-1}(L)x_{2t} - \ldots - \phi_{x_m}(L)\theta_{x_m}^{-1}(L)x_{mt}$$

where $\phi_{x_j}(L)\theta_{x_j}^{-1}(L)$ is the auto-regressive moving average operator for independent variable x_j. There are m such operators in this example.

The residuals E_t are then estimated as a univariate ARIMA model of the form

$$E_t = \phi_E^{-1}(L)\theta_E(L)e_t.$$

The estimation of this model follows the univariate procedures outlined in Chapter 16.

Finally, the preliminary estimate of the complete transfer function-noise model must be refined or reestimated using nonlinear estimation techniques.

3.3　Seasonal Transfer Function–Noise Models

If P_t has seasonal components then either the independent variable X_{jt} will capture them perfectly or seasonal movements will be present in the residuals from the transfer function model. In the latter case the noise model will require the identification and estimation of a seasonal ARIMA process. These procedures are similar to those noted in Chapter 16.

3.4　Forecasts with Transfer Function–Noise Models

To reveal the procedure for forecasting from an "integrated" transfer function–noise model, consider the following illustrative weekly model:

$$P_t = \delta_1 P_{t-1} + \delta_2 P_{t-2} + w_1 X_{t-2} + w_2 X_{t-3} + e_t - \phi_1 e_{t-1} - \theta_1 e_{t-52} + \phi_1 \theta_1 e_{t-53}.$$

The recursive conditional forecasting equation for a two-period-ahead forecast will be

$$\hat{P}_{t+2} = \delta_1 \hat{P}_{t+1} + \delta_2 P_t + w_1 X_t + w_2 X_{t-1} - \theta_1 e_{t-50} + \phi_1 \theta_1 e_{t-51}$$

where $\hat{P}_{t+1}$ is a one-period-ahead forecast of P_{t+1}. Upon substitution of the expression $(P_t - \hat{P}_t)$ for e_t the forecasting equation becomes

$$\hat{P}_{t+2} = \delta_1 \hat{P}_{t+1} + \delta_2 P_t + w_1 X_t + w_2 X_{t-1} - \theta_1 P_{t-50} + \theta_1 \hat{P}_{t-50} + \phi_1 \theta_1 P_{t-51} - \phi_1 \theta_1 \hat{P}_{t-51}$$

where the one-period-ahead forecast $\hat{P}_{t+1}$ is calculated from a recursive equation similar to the one for $\hat{P}_{t+2}$ and past forecasts $\hat{P}_{t-50}$, $\hat{P}_{t-51}$ and actuals, P_{t-50} and P_{t-51}, of course, are known.

3.5 Trading Rules for Transfer Function–Noise Models

Trading rules for transfer function–noise models fall into two categories: (1) confidence interval systems when the forecast lead time does not exceed the lead time of the shortest leading indicator in the forecasting model, and (2) simulation–confidence interval systems when forecast lead times exceed the lead time of the shortest leading indicator. The former systems are similar to confidence interval trading systems already presented in Chapter 16 and for the elementary first-difference model. The simulation–confidence interval approach is an extension of the worst-case conditional projection systems outlined in the elementary first-difference model. The principal difference between those approaches and the ones presented here is the need to construct forecasts conditioned on outcomes for several explanatory variables.

Insofar as the independent variables may have different impacts and timing profiles with respect to the forecast dependent variable, simulation methods may simplify the calculation and comparison of alternative scenarios. The so-called simulation–confidence interval systems may be further separated into several categories. The two most popular are "worst-case"–confidence interval systems and Monte Carlo systems. In the worst-case–confidence interval system a worst-case assumption is made for each of the independent variables that must be forecast. Given the worst-case scenario, a confidence band then is constructed around it on the basis of the error variance for the estimation of the dependent variable, that is, on the basis of the error variance when the independent variables are known with certainty. Decisions then are made relative to the confidence interval.

The Monte Carlo simulation system takes a different approach. It generates forecasts that include random errors introduced into the forecast values of all the independent variables at each time period for which they are forecast. This results in a single forecast path for the dependent variable corrupted by random errors. This procedure is repeated a number of times until many such paths are constructed. This simulation results in a distribution of forecast outcomes for each forecast lead time. The user then may select a "trading bound" based on cumulative probabilities that reflect desired odds. An illustrative simulation is shown in Table 17.1. In Table 17.1 forecast

Table 17.1

LONG POSITION SIMULATION-ASSESSMENT SYSTEM

SILVER PRICE FORECAST INTERVAL	LEAD TIME	
	1	2
	Probability of Price >	Probability of Price >
17.01 to ∞	0	5
16.01 to 17.00	0	10
15.01 to 16.00	0	20
14.01 to 15.00	10	50
13.01 to 14.00	30	80
12.01 to 13.00	70	90
11.01 to 12.00	90	95
−∞ to 11.00	100	100

prices one period ahead have an estimated (simulated) probability of 90 percent of lying at or above the $11.01 to $12.00 range. Similarly, forecast prices two periods ahead have a probability of 90 percent of lying at or above the $13.01 to $14.00 range. If the trader had an opportunity to buy at $11.00 as of the time of the forecast and prefers no more than a 10 percent chance of not making a $1.00 profit for a waiting time of two periods, the simulation results in Table 17.1 would indicate a long position should be taken and held for two periods.

In general, simulation–confidence interval trading rules can be summarized as follows: If $\hat{P}_{t+\tau} - B_{t+\tau} > P_t + \pi(\tau)$, then buy at time t and hold for τ periods; if $\hat{P}_{t+\tau} + B_{t+\tau} < P_t - \pi(\tau)$, then sell at time t and hold for τ periods; where $B_{t+\tau}$ is the confidence bound calculated using either the worst-case—confidence interval approach or the Monte Carlo simulation approach.

4 KALMAN FILTERING: The Multivariate Case

The Kalman filtering approach to forecasting with a multivariate model is built around a structure consisting of a "message" model and an "observation" model. The message model with a single independent variable may be denoted

$$P_t = aP_{t-1} + bX_{t-k} + {}^m e_t$$

where a and b are known parameters (estimated coefficients), X_t is the independent variable with an impulse that precedes the corresponding response in P_t by k periods, $k \geq 0$, and ${}^m e_t$ is stationary random noise.

The observation model is of the form

$$Z_t = HP_t + {}^oe_t$$

where H is a known parameter (estimated coefficient) and ${}^oe_t$ is stationary random noise. Here, as in the univariate Kalman filtering approach, Z_t may be viewed as information about P_t from a source external to, or independent from, the information used in the message model.

In the context of a daily commodity forecasting model X_t may represent volume or open interest and Z_t may represent floor broker anticipations of P_t based on morning orders before the opening of business. From these two equations a recursive forecasting system can be derived for P_t that is a best linear sequential state predictor.

4.1 One-Period-Ahead Forecasts

Given the above model the one-period-ahead forecasting equation for P_t would be of the form

$$\hat{P}_{t+1} = a\hat{P}_t + bX_{t-k+1} + \hat{K}_{t+1}(Z_t - H\hat{P}_t)$$

where $\hat{P}_{t+1}$ is the one-period-ahead forecast of P_{t+1}, $\hat{P}_t$ is the one-period-ahead forecast of P_t, and K_{t+1} is the Kalman gain,

$$K_{t+1} = \frac{a \, \text{var} \, (P_t - \hat{P}_t)H}{H^2 \, \text{var} \, (P_t - \hat{P}_t) + \text{var} \, {}^oe_t},$$

and var $(P_t - \hat{P}_t)$ is the error variance in predicting P_t based on data up to and including, but not beyond, time t. It can be shown that

$$\text{var} \, (P_t - \hat{P}_t) = a \, (a - \hat{K}_t H) \, \text{var} \, (P_{t-1} - \hat{P}_{t-1}) + \text{var} \, {}^me_t$$

where var ${}^oe_t$ is the variance of the random error, ${}^oe_t$, in the message model.

As can be seen, the multivariate forecasting relationship is very similar to the univariate case presented in Chapter 16. The difference is the inclusion of bX_{t-k+1} in the multivariate forecasting equation. As in the multivariate ARIMA model it is recommended that leading indicators be used as explanatory variables (i.e., independent variables) in order to reduce or eliminate the need to condition forecasts on alternative future values of the independent variables. Several guidelines for the application of the univariate Kalman forecasting system also apply to the multivariate case. Among the most important is the accommodation of seasonal movements within the Kalman framework. If the seasonal movements in P_t are not captured perfectly by the independent variable or if spurious seasonal movements are introduced by the independent variable then the residual seasonal movement may be captured in the observation model as noted in Chapter 16.

4.2 Multiple Independent Variables

In the above example a single independent variable was contained in the message model. When more than one independent variable is used to explain the series P_t the mechanisms are almost the same. For two independent variables the message model would be of the form

$$P_t = aP_{t-1} + b_1 X_{1t-k_1} + b_2 X_{2t-k_2} + {}^m e_t$$

and the observation model would be

$$Z_t = HP_t + {}^o e_t$$

where X_{1t-k_1} and X_{2t-k_2} are independent variables that foreshadow P_t by k_1 and k_2 time periods, respectively. When a single variable is being explained (in this case P_t) the one-period-ahead forecasting equation may be written

$$\hat{P}_{t+1} = b_1 X_{t-k_1+1} + b_2 X_{t-k_2+1} + a\hat{P}_t + \hat{K}_{t+1}(Z_t - HP_t)$$

where the Kalman gain is the same as in the single independent variable case

$$\hat{K}_{t+1} = \frac{a \operatorname{var}(P_t - \hat{P}_t)H}{H^2 \operatorname{var}(P_t - \hat{P}_t) + \operatorname{var} {}^o e_t}$$

and $\operatorname{var}(P_t - \hat{P}_t)$ is defined as in Chapter 16.

4.3 Trading Rules for the Multivariate Kalman Filter Model

Trading rules for Kalman predictor models are not unlike those for the ARIMA model presented in Section 3.5. Specifically, the two most common systems are worst-case–confidence interval systems and Monte Carlo simulation confidence interval systems. The differences between these systems for ARIMA models and Kalman filter models lie in the qualitative construction of the simulations and in the construction of forecasts spanning several time periods. The qualitative distinction of the Kalman trading system reflects the segregation and simulation of message model and observation model errors. Here, for example, the observation error variance may reflect market liquidity and its effect on the ability to capture message model projected prices. The so-called qualitative distinction between the Kalman approach and the ARIMA model lies completely in the distinction between message and observation models and the practical knowledge this distinction offers. It does not lie in the quality of the estimates or assumptions per se. In short, the Kalman system may have all of the characteristics and required mechanics of an ARIMA system plus the added assumptions, simulation requirements, and information associated with the observation model.

A worst-case–confidence interval trading system for a Kalman model would use worst-case values for the independent variables in the message model and use a worst-case assumption for the recorded observation. With regard to the observation error assumption, suppose the observation error was 50 basis points below the expected observation but market assessment of future liquidity suggests that an observation error of 100 basis points may better adjust the forecast for the worst "liquidity" future. A confidence interval then would be constructed around this forecast and would be based on the error variance var $(P_t - \hat{P}_t)$. The Monte Carlo system would introduce a number of alternative outcomes for the observation error as well as introduce random errors into the value of the forecast independent variables. A forecast would be generated for each set of outcomes and errors and many sets of these outcomes would be simulated resulting in a distribution of forecast values for the dependent variable. The trading rule for a one-period-ahead forecast would be the same as that given for the ARIMA model.

When further forward forecasts are considered Kalman-based trading systems take on a recursive character that is similar to but different from the recursive structure of the ARIMA model. To illustrate, consider the Kalman one-period-ahead forecasting equation

$$\hat{P}_{t+1} = \phi \hat{P}_t + \theta X_{t-k+1} + K(Z_t - H\hat{P}_t)$$

where X_t is an indicator that leads P_t by k periods. For a two-period-ahead forecast where Z_{t+1} is not known the conditional expectation of P_{t+2} would be

$$\hat{P}_{t+2} = \phi \hat{P}_{t+1} + \theta X_{t-k+1}$$

or upon substitution

$$\hat{P}_{t+2} = \phi^2 \hat{P}_t + \phi\theta X_{t-k} + \theta X_{t-k+1} + \theta K(Z_t - H\hat{P}_t)$$

In general the τ-period-ahead forecasting equation for the above model can be written

$$\hat{P}_{t+\tau} = (1 - KH)\phi^\tau \hat{P}_t + \phi^{\tau-1} Z_t + \theta \sum_{j=1}^{\tau} \phi^{\tau-j} X_{t-k-1+j}.$$

This model could be used for worst-case–confidence interval trading systems, where the variance used to construct the confidence band would be var $(P_t - \hat{P}_t)$ as defined earlier.

For a Monte Carlo simulation the τ-period-ahead forecasting equation would include the simulated random errors between Z_{t+i} and HP_{t+i} for $i = 1, \ldots, \tau - 1$. This forecasting simulation equation can be written

$$\hat{P}_{t+\tau} = \phi^\tau \hat{P}_t + \theta \sum_{j=1}^{\tau} \phi^{\tau-j} X_{t-k-1+j} + \sum_{j=2}^{\tau} \phi^{\tau-j} K E_{t-j+1} + K\phi^{\tau-1}(Z_t - H\hat{P}_t)$$

where E_{t+i} is the simulated error between Z_{t+i} and HP_{t+i} for future values of both variables. Once again the simulation of a sequence of future values of P_t would be repeated many times for alternative values of X_t and the error terms that surround the model.

With these procedures in mind the trading rules would be similar to those presented for the ARIMA model. Specifically if $\hat{P}_{t+\tau} - B_{t+\tau} > P_t + \pi(\tau)$, then buy at time t and hold for τ periods; if $\hat{P}_{t+\tau} + B_{t+\tau} < P_t - \pi(\tau)$, then sell at time t and hold for τ periods; where $B_{t+\tau}$ is the confidence bound calculated using either the worst-case–confidence interval approach or the Monte Carlo simulation approach.

5 SUMMARY

As noted in the beginning of this part of the book, technically weak and strong markets are often assessed in terms of movements in volume and open interest. While not infallible the markets have at times have been profitable under relatively stable conditions when fundamental forces were not swamping the market. However, fundamental forces often do swamp the market and one must be able to switch methodologies quickly to keep in step with the market. This task has three parts: constant vigilance of the markets, the use of technical models designed for specific types of fundamental market conditions that can be switched on when appropriate, and some idea of the fundamental forces that influence the market, their timing and impact. The applications of fundamental analysis are as varied as the number of commodities and the number of trading objectives. A select tour of these applications is the subject of Part 4.

6 BIBLIOGRAPHY

Box, G. E. P., and G. M. Jenkins, *Time Series Analysis Forecasting and Control.* San Francisco: Holden-Day, 1970.

Chow, G., *Analysis and Control of Dynamic Economic Systems.* New York: John Wiley, 1975.

Sage, A. P., and J. L. Melsa, *Estimation Theory with Applications to Communication Control.* New York: McGraw-Hill, 1971.

Zellner, A., *An Introduction to Bayesian Inference in Econometrics.* New York: John Wiley, 1971.

IV

FUNDAMENTAL ANALYSIS AND TRADING APPLICATIONS OF ECONOMETRIC MODELS

Technical analysis tends to focus on short-term behavior of commodity prices, their levels, differentials, and movements. Analysts attempt to estimate these price patterns as functions of past prices, price movements, relationships to other prices, and the influence of volume and open interest. Their predictions are based on methods that range from highly subjective filters and rules to more disciplined techniques such as the ARIMA and state space models presented in Chapters 16 and 17. Fundamental analysis transcends technical analysis in both spirit and practice even though its principal objective is the prediction of commodity price behavior. It is concerned with the empirical content and application of economic theory. To this end it considers the structure and interaction of demand and supply together with the estimation and testing of these relationships and the practical implementation of the result. In short, it is the theoretical, empirical, and operational analysis of economic phenomena: It is econometrics.

The preliminary objective of fundamental analysis is a quantifiable representation of one or more markets to better forecast and understand commodity price behavior. To be sure, such a model of the real world cannot be perfect. Its modesty is derived from several sources: It is based on structural assumptions that often are close approximations at best; the data can be sparse and subject to error and revision; the truth may not be purely deterministic but hidden behind a veil of random elements; and the market place, like weather, is not well suited to controlled experimentation. Despite these obstacles, fundamental analysis can have redeeming value. While econometric theory and data collection methods have not resolved any of the above problems, they can reduce their distortion. Moreover, they can provide an efficient method to explore the interaction of large numbers of complex relationships. In so doing, fundamental analysis can not only reveal the effects of select conditions but also enable the user to redirect intellectual resources to more narrow and clearly defined areas of the unknown.

The final objective of fundamental analysis is better business decisions. These decisions tend to be long term in perspective and complementary to shorter-term technical operations. Because the response of economic activities to basic (i.e., fundamental) impulses are not always instantaneous but work themselves out over many weeks, months, or quarters, fundamental models tend to have a longer-term perspective than technical models. This longer-term perspective is reinforced by data considerations: The basic determinants of demand and supply are not readily available on a more frequent basis than once a month or once a quarter. For these reasons most fundamental models are quarterly in their time unit of measurement and their price and other estimates are representative of the entire period, for example, the quarterly average price. It is in this context that fundamental analysis has a long-term perspective and is a complement to daily and weekly technical analysis.

The purpose of the following chapters is to demonstrate the role of fundamental analysis and econometric models in commodity trading operations. The material presented in not intended to be an applied survey of econometrics. Indeed little is said about estimation methods and technical characteristics of the models, their solution, or simulation methodologies; the reader is referred to appropriate texts for these purposes. Rather, the intent is to summarize essential elements of fundamental analysis and to illustrate several different types of econometric models from various commodity trading perspectives. While some discussion, of course, is directed to the selection of a particular model structure, along with its estimation and simulation procedures, the primary emphasis is on the use of these models. Although some economic foundations are provided for each model, no attempt is made here to solicit the reader's belief in the models presented. The theoretical backdrop for such an effort is beyond the scope of this book. Moreover, seasoned maturity allows only one operational posture: Models are to be used, not believed. The following chapters are presented with this dictum in mind.

Chapter 18 presents select elements of demand, supply, and fundamental analysis. Included here are illustrative demand, production, and cost functions, and model building considerations such as identification and economic dynamics. In Chapter 19 an annual forecasting and simulation model of the world wheat market is outlined. An example of its use in speculative position taking also is presented. Chapter 20 summarizes a quarterly flow of funds–money market model for use in financial arbitrage positioning. A quarterly world gold market model is outlined in Chapter 21. The model is designed for speculative and intertemporal arbitrage operations and an example of its application is given. A quarterly exchange rate model is presented in Chapter 22. An application of the model is given for a multinational corporation seeking to hedge translation exposure.

18

ELEMENTS OF DEMAND, SUPPLY, AND FUNDAMENTAL ANALYSIS

||||||||||||||||||||||||||||||||||||||||||||||||||||||||||||||||||||||||||||||||||||||||||||||||||||||||||||||

1 INTRODUCTION

While technical analysis may offer practical short-term insights for commodity traders, economic fundamentals are all important when long-term price movements are considered. Here, the forces of demand and supply must be known and understood. To be sure, each commodity market has its own particular configuration and interaction of supply and demand forces. Nevertheless, several basic themes are common to all. The purpose of this chapter is to outline those elemental and in some cases elementary factors and relationships that all commodity markets share.

The elements of fundamental analysis presented here can help specify and interpret a model of a commodity market. In a model-building context the economic notions and perspectives presented must be applied with three criteria in mind:

1. The economic linkages must be rational,
2. The variables must be measurable either directly or by proxy,
3. The model should be amenable to prediction and simulation.

While the first two criteria are straightforward, the third warrants further comment. It would not be a gross overstatement to say that commodity traders are preoccupied with the future. It follows that any practical model of a commodity market must be able to assess alternative futures in order to help the trader take appropriate positions. This, of course, places a premium on a model's forecasting ability, its ease of use, and its accuracy. Unfortunately, ease of use and accuracy in a forecasting context often are not compatible with a model structure dictated by sound economic theory alone. Often, the more theoretical detail and informational intent the greater the cascade of estimation and data measurement errors and the more cumbersome the model. In short, forecasting ease and accuracy are not always compatible with rigorous economic theory and the availability of relevant data. This trade-off is one of the reasons why economic model building, is as much an art as a science. This comment of course, is not presented as license to disregard economic theory at every turn in the name of forecasting. Rather, it is to note that forecasting is a necessary condition of a practical econometric model and the detail, structure, and data comprising a model should be combined with this objective in mind.

No attempt is made here to consider any one commodity in detail. These analyses are done in subsequent chapters for select commodities and then only as econometric approximations to reality. Despite advances in economic theory, data reporting, and digital computers it is still not possible to describe a commodity market in absolute detail. Facts notwithstanding, reality forces one to consider a simplification of reality. These simplifications or *models* attempt to systematically and accurately capture some of the most important forces and relationships in a market. In so doing, models enable the user to study many economic questions efficiently and free otherwise committed time to issues not reflected in the model.

While there are many types of models of fundamental economic behavior, such as leading indicator models, single equation reduced-form models, and simultaneous equations models, they all must consider the character and interaction of demand, supply, and market structure.

2 DEMAND

Economic *demand* for a commodity is the amount of that commodity desired for possession at a given time and for a given price. That demand may be for final consumption, such as corn for human consumption, or it may be an intermediate or derived demand, such as corn for the production of corn oil or as animal feed. If a commodity has both uses, total demand for that commodity is the sum of both derived and final demands aggregated over all those demanding the commodity. Here, of course, one must be careful not to double count the same demands arising at different stages of the market allocation and distribution process. While different market segments may have different demands for a commodity, the structure of those demands and their basic elements are common to all.

2.1 Demand Functions: structure and elements

A *demand function* refers to the relationship between the quantity demanded of a commodity and all the factors or elements that influence that demand. Treating the quantity demanded as the dependent variable and the influencing factors or elements as independent variables an illustrative demand function for a particular market segment may be written

$$Q_t = Q(P_t, P_t^r, {}^eP_t, {}^eP_t^r, Y_t, {}^eY_t, A_t, A_t^r, T_t, T_t^r, N_t)$$

where

Q_t = Quantity demanded at time t

P_t = Price per unit of Q_t at time t

P_t^r = Prices per unit of complements and substitutes for Q_t at time t

${}^eP_t$ = Expected future price per unit of Q at time t

${}^eP_t^r$ = Expected future prices per unit of complements and substitutes for Q at time t

Y_t = Income at time t

${}^eY_t$ = Expected future income at time t

A_t = Advertising expenditurers for Q at time t

A_t^r = Advertising expenditures for complements and substitutes for Q, at time t

T_t = Technical attributes of Q at time t, e.g., reliability

T_t^r = Technical attributes of complements and substitutes for Q at time t

N_t = Size of market segment at time t.

Some of these factors may have an immediate and one-time influence on the quantity demanded. Others may have a delayed impact and/or an impact that "builds up" over time. These delays and buildups define the *dynamics of demand*.

2.2 Dynamic Demand Considerations

The response of demand to some impulse, or stimulus, rarely is instantaneous but instead builds up over time. For example, the effect of advertising on demand may take several weeks or months before its impact is felt and even longer before its full effect is realized. The length of the delay between the initial impulse and the first demand response together with the distribution of responses thereafter defines the dynamic structure between demand and the factor influencing it. This structure is sometimes referred to as the distributed lag function or just lag function.

Using discrete time notation, for example, weekly time units of measurement, the lag relationship between demand and a single factor, X, may be denoted

$$Q_t = a_0 X_{t-d} + a_1 X_{t-d-1} + \ldots + a_g X_{t-d-g}$$

where t denotes time, d is the *length of the delay*, $d + g$ is the maximum length of the lag and the a's describe the *lag structure*, that is, the numerical linkage of the lagged values of X to the current value of Q. This relationship says that a change in X does not impact on Q until d time periods have elapsed. At that time it brings about a change in Q equal to a_0 times the change in X. One period later the change in X has another impact on Q. This time the change in Q is equal to a_1 times the change in X. These *"lagged" impacts* continue until the last one is felt $d + g$ periods after the initial impulse.

Each of the variables in the illustrative demand function in Section 2.1 may have some form of lag structure linking it to demand. The specification and calibration of these relationships define the dynamic character of the demand function. Insofar as these dynamics are explicit within the demand function they are said to be *direct dynamics*. There are *indirect dynamics* as well. For example, the impact of a change in price expectations, ^eP, may be immediate and complete but the formation of these expectations may be the result of some distributed lag relationship. Taken together the direct and indirect dynamics can cascade into a demand function that is difficult to interpret without knowing the structure of the contributing functions. The purpose of a model is to provide this structural information.

2.3 Demand Curve

The *demand curve* is derived from the demand function by treating as constants all factors in the demand function other than the price of the commodity. From the demand function the corresponding demand curve (a constrained demand function) can be denoted

$$Q_t = Q(P_t).$$

Demand curves highlight the relationship between price and quantity whereas demand functions reveal the influence of all factors and can capture the net effect of several factors changing at the same time or changing over some time period.

2.4 Change and Elasticity

A *movement along a demand curve* occurs when there is a change in price while all other factors remain constant. A *shift in a demand curve* occurs when one or more of the variables other than price change. Regardless, if there is a movement along or a shift in a demand curve the response of demand to these impulses can be measured in two ways. First, it can be measured in "absolute" terms. For example, a one-dollar increase in the price of a substitute for wheat may lead to a 4 million metric ton increase in the demand for wheat. In the context of a simple linear demand function the numerical translation of such a price impulse to a demand response is captured by the price coefficient in the demand equation. For example, suppose the annual demand for wheat is

$$Q_t = 400 - 4P_t + 1.5P_t^s$$

where Q is the amount of wheat demanded in millions of metric tons, P is the price per bushel in dollars and P^s is the price per bushel of substitutes. Then the rate of change in demand for a small change in P^s would be

$$\frac{\partial Q_t}{\partial P_t^s} = \frac{\partial(400 - 4P_t + 1.5P_t^s)}{\partial P_t^s} = +1.5$$

That is to say, a one-dollar change in the price of substitutes per bushel leads to a 1.5 million metric ton change in the same direction in demand for wheat—for example, if the price went rise demand would fall.

Another measure of responsiveness is that of *elasticity*. This is a pure number and relates the percentage change in the quantity demanded to the percentage change in a variable that influences demand. Continuing with the above example, if $P^s = 8$ and $Q = 200$ the point demand elasticity of wheat with respect to the price of substitutes would be

$$E_{Q,P^s} = \frac{\partial Q_t}{\partial P_t^s} \cdot \frac{P_t^s}{Q_t}$$

$$= 1.5 \frac{8}{200}$$

$$= .06.$$

In general, the elasticity of demand with respect to the influencing variable x can be expressed either at a point or as an "arc" between two points. The *point elasticity* can be written

$$E_{Q,x} = \frac{\partial Q}{\partial x} \cdot \frac{x}{Q}.$$

The *arc elasticity* between two points can be denoted

$$\bar{E}_{Q,x} = \frac{Q_2 - Q_1}{x_2 - x_1} \cdot \frac{x_1 + x_2}{Q_1 + Q_2}$$

where the numerical subscripts denote the points defining the arc.

2.5 Demand Categories of Commodities

Commodities can be categorized according to their elasticities of demand. This categorization is summarized in Table 18.1. An inferior good might be spaghetti. If the price of spaghetti goes down its demand will go up but if household income falls, likewise the demand for spaghetti will go up.

Table 18.1

CATEGORIES OF COMMODITIES ACCORDING
TO ELASTICITY DEMAND INFLUENCING VARIABLE

	INCOME	OWN PRICE
Necessities	> 0	< 0
Luxuries	> 0	<> 0
Inferior	< 0	< 0

3 PRODUCTION, COST, AND SUPPLY

3.1 Production

Production can be defined as the process of transforming inputs into outputs. A *production function* is a technical statement of the relationship between inputs and outputs. In general, it may be denoted

$$Q = f(X_i, \ldots X_n)$$

where the X_i, $i = 1, \ldots, n$ are factor inputs and $f(\ \ )$ is the functional form linking the X_i's to output Q.

The specific form of a production function may be dictated by known engineering considerations or it may have to be estimated. If the function has to be estimated, several characteristics must be taken into consideration when selecting an appropriate representation. These include the marginal rate of technical substitution between inputs, the returns to scale of the production process, and the effect of technological progress.

3.1.1 Production Functions—Marginal Rate of Technical Substitution

For a given level of output the ratio at which one input may be reduced and another input increased such that the output level remains constant is known as the *marginal rate of technical substitution* (MRTS) between these two inputs. This ratio may be fixed, or it may vary in some way. Four types of production functions are commonly used for estimation purposes and each has different *MRTS* characteristics. They are the linear, Leontieff, Cobb-Douglas, and constant elasticity of substitution (CES) production functions.

3.1.1.1 Linear production function.

A *linear production function* implies that the inputs have constant marginal products. That is to say, for linear production functions, the rate of change in output in response to a one-unit change in an input is the same regardless of the amount of input from which the change takes place. Such a production function with two inputs can be denoted

$$Q = a_1 X_1 + a_2 X_2 + a_0.$$

In this production function the same amount of output can be produced by alternative combinations of inputs dictated by the ratio of MRTS's. For example, the MRTS between X_1 and X_2 in the above linear production function is a_1/a_2 and implies $X_1 = -(a_2/a_1)X_2$. That is, an increase in one unit of X_1 together with a decrease of a_2/a_1 units of X_2 will produce the same level of output as before the change in inputs:

$$Q^{(0)} = a_1 X_1^{(0)} + a_2 X_2^{(0)} + a_0$$

$$= a_1(X_1^{(0)} + 1) + a_2\left(X_2^{(0)} - \frac{a_1}{a_2}\right) + a_0$$

$$= a_1 X_1^{(0)} + a_1 + a_2 X_2^{(0)} - a_1 + a_0$$

$$= Q^{(0)}.$$

3.1.1.2 Leontieff production function.

The *Leontieff production function* is a fixed-proportions production function that does not allow any substitution among inputs. This production function may be denoted

$$Q = a_0\left[\min\left(\frac{X_1}{a_1}, \frac{X_2}{a_2}\right)\right]$$

where a_0 is a constant indicating the productivity of the process, and a_1 and a_2 are constants defining how X_1 and X_2 are to be combined. The level of output Q is equal to $Q(X_1/a_1)$ or $Q(X_2/a_2)$, whichever is smaller.

3.1.1.3 Cobb-Douglas production function.

The *Cobb-Douglas production function* is of the form

$$Q = a_0 X_1^{a_1} X_2^{a_2}$$

where a_0 is a constant representing the state of technology or productivity of the function, and a_1 and a_2 are the elasticities of production with respect to X_1 and X_2, respectively. In this production function the marginal products of X_1 and X_2, $\partial Q/\partial X_1$ and $\partial Q/\partial X_2$ respectively, decrease as long as $a_1 + a_2 < 1$. Moreover, the MRTS is $a_1 X_2/a_2 X_1$ and changes with the values of X_2 and X_1. However, the elasticity of substitution between X_1 and X_2 is 1.

3.1.1.4 Constant elasticity of substitution production function. The MRTS for a *constant elasticity of substitution production function* can vary with the level of inputs and, can have any constant elasticity of substitution between X_1 and X_2. This function can be denoted

$$Q = a_0 [a_1 X_1^{(e-1)/e} + (1 - a_1) X_2^{(e-1)/e}]^{[he/(e-1)]}$$

where a_0 is a productivity parameter $0 < a_0 < 1$, a_1 is a distribution parameter, e is the elasticity of substitution between inputs X_1 and X_2, and h is a parameter that determines returns to scale.

3.1.2 Returns to Scale

When all inputs in a production process are increased by the same proportion, that is, by the same scale, output will change by some corresponding proportion. Here, three outcomes may occur:

1. *Constant returns to scale:* Inputs and outputs change by exactly the same proportion
2. *Increasing returns to scale:* Outputs change by a greater proportion than input.
3. *Decreasing returns to scale:* Outputs change by a smaller proportion than inputs.

The four production functions noted above have the following returns to scale:

1. *Linear:* Constant returns to scale for $Q = a_1 X_1 + a_2 X_2$, decreasing but converging on constant returns to scale for $Q = a_0 + a_1 X_1 + a_2 X_2$.

2. *Leontieff:* Constant returns to scale.

3. *Cobb-Douglas:* Constant returns to scale if $a_1 + a_2 = 1$, decreasing if $a_1 + a_2 < 1$, and increasing if $a_1 + a_2 > 1$.

4. *CES:* May have constant, increasing, or decreasing returns to scale depending on whether $h = 1$, $h > 1$ or $h < 1$, respectively.

3.1.3 Technical Progress

With the same level of inputs, or even lesser amounts of input, the level of output may increase owing to technical progress. Here, several types of technical progress can be considered; *disembodied technical progress* for (1) all or (2) some subset of inputs and *embodied technical progress* for (3) all or (4) some subset of inputs of a particular vintage.

3.1.3.1   Disembodied technical progress.

Disembodied technical progress shifts the production function in such a way as to leave undisturbed over time the balance between inputs used in production. This form of technical progress can influence all inputs equally or all inputs of a certain generic type, such as labor or machines, regardless of their vintage. These forms of disembodied technical progress can be denoted

$$Q = f[X_1, X_2, T(Z)]$$

or

$$Q = f[T(Z)X_1, X_2]$$

for embodied technical progress that influences all inputs equally and influences only some (X_1), respectively. Here, $T(Z)$ is a function that describes the productive efficiency of technology to some factor(s) Z that determines it.

3.1.3.2   Embodied technical progress.

Embodied technical progress applies only to certain segments of inputs, typically to the latest addition or vintage of machines and their associated labor force. Here, any one type of input may no longer be considered homogeneous (the same) but may be treated as a stock of mixed vintages with different degrees of productivity owing to their level of technical progress. In these situations the production function and technical progress function varies from vintage to vintage. Those relationships can be denoted

$$_\tau Q = f[_\tau X_1, \, _\tau X_2, T(Z, \tau)]$$

for output, inputs, and technology of vintage τ where the technology applies to all inputs of vintage τ equally, and

$$_\tau Q = f[T(Z, \tau)_\tau X_1, \, _\tau X_2]$$

where the technology applies only to one input of vintage τ.

Examples of these types of production functions and technical progress are common in commodity analysis. For example, different countries may have different "vintages" of agricultural production, and gold may be mined by different "vintages" of mining machines.

3.1.3.3   The technical progress function.

With the importance of technological progress on production, an important consideration is the form of the *technical progress function*. In general, this function can be denoted

$$T = T(Z)$$

where T is the value of the function, that is, the multiple by which the "effective" level of input(s) increase, and Z is a factor or set of factors that determine T. Two types of technical progress functions are common. One is a simple *growth function* of the form

$$T = e^{mt}$$

where e is the base of the natural logarithm, m is a rate of growth, and t represents time. The other is a *logistics function* of the form

$$T = \frac{k}{1 + e^{a+bz}}$$

where k is an upper asymptote, e is the base of the natural logarithm, and a and b are parameters. The term Z in this case may be time or the amount of funds spent on research and development or some other factor that may be related to technological progress.

3.2 Costs and Supply

Given the production function and the costs of the various inputs one can determine the relationship of total variable costs to the level of output. Here the distinction between a "short-run" and the "long-run" perspective comes into sharp relief. Neither term has any unit of time involved in its definition: In the *short-run* some factor input(s) are constant and in the *long-run* all factor inputs are variable. To be sure, the length of the analyst's time horizon may make one perspective more appropriate than another. In both cases, the optimal amounts of the inputs can be determined by the minimization of costs subject to an output constraint.

3.2.1 Short-Run Production Efficiency and Costs

The *short-run cost efficient amount of inputs* to utilize and the corresponding total and marginal cost curves are obtained (conceptually) as follows. First, the objective of the producer is to minimize costs subject to an output constraint and the fixed amount of one or more inputs. This objective can be denoted

$$\min_{w.r.t. X_1 X_2} TC = P_1 X_1 + P_2 X_2 + P_3 X_3^0 + C$$

subject to

$$Q^0 = Q(X_1, X_2, X_3^0)$$

where $P_3 X_3^0 + c$ is fixed cost, $P_1 X_1 + P_2 X_2$ is total variable cost, P_j is the price per unit of input j, X_j is the amount of input j used, Q^0 is the given (constraint) level of output, $Q(X_1, X_2, X_3^0)$ is the production function, and X_3^0 is a given level of a fixed input.

The achievement of this objective requires the following first-order conditions be satisfied simultaneously

$$\frac{TVC + \lambda[Q^0 - Q(X_1, X_2, X_3^0)]}{\partial X_j} = 0 \text{ for } j = 1, 2$$

$$\frac{TVC + \lambda[Q^0 - Q(X_1, X_2, X_3^0)]}{\partial \lambda} = 0.$$

The solution of these equations for X_1, X_2, and λ that satisfies the above conditions yield input order quantity rules of the following form

$$X_j^* = X_j(P_1, P_2, X_3^0, Q^0) \text{ for } j = 1, 2.$$

That is, the cost efficient input utilization rules (i.e., *derived demand curves*) equate the amount of an input to some function of the prices of the inputs, the level of the fixed input(s), X_3^0, and the target level of output Q^0.

If these rules are followed, the least total variable cost, TVC^*, and therefore least total cost TV^* will be achieved. Moreover, given these rules, TC^* can be reduced to a function, V, of output where input prices, P_1, P_2, and P_3, and X_3^0, but not all of the inputs are treated as constants. That is,

$$TC^* = P_1 X_1^* + P_2 X_2^* + P_3 X_3^0 + C$$
$$= P_1 \cdot X_1(P_1, P_2, X_3^0 Q^0) + P_2 \cdot X_2(P_1, P_2, X_3^0, Q^0) + P_3 X^0 + C$$
$$= V(Q^0).$$

This *least total cost function* consists of least variable costs plus fixed costs. The derivative or rate of change of this function with respect to the level of output dTC/dQ, evaluated at all levels of output yields the *marginal cost function* of the production process. The *supply function* of the commodity is the marginal cost function. In fact, it is the rising portion of the marginal cost function that typically defines the supply curve:

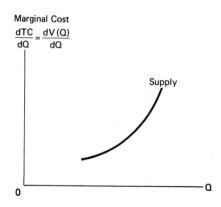

Marginal Cost
$$\frac{dTC}{dQ} = \frac{dV(Q)}{dQ}$$

Supply

0

Q

As with a demand function one can explore movements along the supply curve and shifts in the supply curve. In the short run, shifts in the supply curve can occur for several reasons. They include a change in input price, a change in technology, and a change in the level of some "fixed" inputs. Here again, one may explore the absolute response of supply to these forces or may use elasticity as a pure measure of responsiveness. For example, the point *input price elasticity* of supply would be

$$E_{Q^s, P_j} = \frac{\partial Q^s}{\partial P_j} \cdot \frac{P_j}{Q^s}$$

where Q^s is the quantity supplied and P_j is the price of the jth input.

3.2.2 Long-Run Efficiency and Costs

In the long run the analytical construction of the least variable cost function follows similar lines to the short run. The principal difference is all inputs are allowed to vary. Because there are no inputs held constant there are more decision rules or equations describing how inputs should be utilized in order to meet given production goals. In the context of the above production function where all variables, X_1, X_2, and X_3, are allowed to vary, these rules can be denoted

$$X_j = X_j(P_1, P_2, P_3, Q^0) \text{ for } j = 1, 2, 3.$$

The functions, $X_j(\ )$, are different from their short-run counterparts owing to the variability of all inputs and the corresponding change in the interconnectendness of the inputs. As in the short run, the decision rules are functions of the prices of the inputs and the level of output to be achieved. As before, one may explore the response of supply, now long run, to changes in any of these factors. Here one may use both absolute measures of responsiveness or elasticities. In the long run the relationship between the level of output and the amount of inputs defines the expansion path.

The utilization of inputs is said to be efficient when (1) the highest level of output is achieved for the given amounts of inputs, or (2) the costs of production are at a minimum for a given level of output. An *expansion path* shows the least cost combination of inputs as the level of output is expanded. As will be discussed later, the expansion path gives rise to the *long-run cost function* and is determined as much by MRTSs as the prices of the inputs and the budget.

4 INVESTMENT IN CAPITAL STOCK AND INVENTORIES

Long-run supply, of course, is determined in part by the productive capacity of the industry and this in turn is determined in part by investment in capital stock. Short-run supplies are determined in part by the available stocks, that is, inventories. Inventories also may be viewed as an investment. Any fundamental analysis would be incomplete without some comment on each of these types of investment.

4.1 Investment in Capital Stock

The literature on investment in capital stock is long, varied, and complex. In the authors' opinion the outstanding work in this area is that of Jorgenson (1965) and it is this theme that is presented here. In general, the amount of investment at any time is a function of the quantity of output, prices for output, the rate of depreciation, capital stock, tax rate, capital consumption allowances, and the rate of interest. In particular the typical form of an industry investment function can be written

$$I_t = \frac{\gamma(L)}{W(L)}\left(\alpha \frac{P_t X_t}{C_t} - \alpha \frac{P_{t-1} X_{t-1}}{C_{t-1}}\right) + \delta K_{t-1}$$

where I_t is the amount of investment in period t, $\gamma(L)$ and $W(L)$ are distributed lag functions, P_t is the price of output at time t, X_t is the amount of output of time t, δ is the rate of depreciation, K_t is the capital stock at time t, α is the elasticity of output with respect to capital, and C_t is the user cost of capital defined as

$$C_t = q_t\left[\left(\frac{1 - uv}{1 - u}\right)\delta + \left(\frac{1 - uw}{1 - u}\right)r - \left(\frac{1 - ux}{1 - u}\right)\frac{\dot{q}}{q}\right]$$

where q is the price of capital, $\dot{q}$ is the time rate of change in q, r is the cost of capital (rate of interest), v is the proportion of depreciation charged against revenue less outlay, w and x are similar proportions for cost of capital and capital loss, respectively, and u is the tax rate.

Estimates of these functions for various industries can be found in Jorgenson (1965).

4.2 Investment in Inventories

While current harvests may be poor, current prices may not go up if there are plentiful inventories to meet demands through to the next harvest. By the same token, an expected good harvest may not reduce current prices if current inventories are scarce relative to demand. Similar observations can be made in the manufacturing industries that produce and utilize nonagricultural commodities. In short, inventories can play an important role in determining prices. Inventories, of course, are not free and represent an alternative investment to placing an equivalent amount of money in treasury bills or some other asset.

As with investment in capital stock the literature on inventory investment is voluminous and only an illustrative discussion is presented here. In particular the model structure has two parts which, with some variation, are common to most forms of inventory investment model. First, the actual change in inventories from time $t - 1$ to time t, ΔI_t, is postulated to be some proportion, $0 < d < 1$, of the difference between the level of inventory at time $t - 1$, I_{t-1} and the "desired" level of inventory at time t, I_t^*, that is,

$$\Delta I_t = d(I_t^* - I_{t-1})$$

Second, the "desired" level of inventory typically is postulated to be a function of several factors including unfilled orders (i.e., excess demand), D^x, current sales, S, and capacity utilization, CU. One form of the function describing the desired level of inventories is

$$\frac{I_t}{S_t} = a + b\frac{D_t^x}{S_t} + g\,(CU)$$

where $g(CU)$ is some function of capacity utilization CU, and a and b are parameters to be estimated.

A variation on this theme by Holt et al. (1960) is

$$I_t^x = a + b\bar{S}_t + c\lambda$$

where $\bar{S}_t$ is anticipated sales, λ is some function of the inventory constraint (e.g., only so much warehouse space), and a, b, and c are parameters to be estimated.

5 MARKET CLASSIFICATION AND DISEQUILIBRIUM

Fundamental analyses are greatly influenced by the competitive nature of the market and the character of the price-forming process. They help specify demand and supply relationships and the way in which they interact to determine prices.

5.1 Market Classification

The analysis and modeling of the price-forming process can be facilitated by recognizing the type of market that exists. This recognition can enable the analyst to better identify the market participants, to determine what aggregations can or must be made, to specify more accurately the response mechanisms of the various market forces to economic and other stimuli, and, in turn, to better design a useful model of the market process. There are eight major market categories. These categories and their identifying characteristics are as follows:

Pure and Perfect Competition

1. *Pure competition:* (a) The number of buyers and sellers in the market is so large that no one buyer or seller can influence price by virtue of their actions; and (b) the technical or pathological character of the commodity is homogeneous among sellers.

2. *Perfect competition:* (a) and (b) as above, plus (c) all producers, factors of production and consumers have perfect knowledge of prices and other relevant economic data; (d) all factors of production have perfect mobility; and (e) there are no impediments to arbitrage.

Imperfect Competition on the Supply Side

3. *Monopolistic competition:* There are a large number of sellers but with product differentiation.

4. *Oligopoly:* A market consists of a few sellers with homogeneous or differentiated products.

5. *Monopoly:* There is a single seller.

Imperfect Competition on the Demand Side

6. *Monopsonistic competition:* There are many buyers of the commodity but each buyer has a unique attribute to offer the sellers (e.g., delivery flexibility).

7. *Oligopsony:* There are a few buyers of a homogeneous or differentiated but generically common product.

8. *Monopsony:* There is a single buyer of a homogeneous or differentiated but generically common product.

5.2 Disequilibrium

The interaction of supply and demand together determine the price and quantity that will prevail in the marketplace. While buyers and sellers may reach an agreement on how much to transact at a certain price this equilibrium may not be self-perpetuating. That is, the price and quantity achieved between buyers and sellers in any period may not remain unchanged and, if it does change, it may not return to its original position or settle on a new one. When this occurs the market is said to be in *disequilibrium*.

It is the rule, not the exception, that commodity markets are constantly searching for a new equilibrium. Accordingly, fundamental models must be designed to describe the disequilibrium dynamics of the market. That is not to say that equilibrium in the historical accounting (i.e., ex-post) sense does not exist. To be sure, the amount bought equals the amount sold at that price. Rather, it is to say that decisions are often based on desires and expectations and that this ex-ante equilibrium is very elusive.

Disequilibrium can occur for many reasons. In the commodities markets the sluggishness of supply responses to changes in price brought about by changes in demand is one of the most common. With low inventories a surge in the demand for wheat, owing to bad harvests in the Soviet Union, typically cannot be met by immediate responses in the supply of these commodities. The production processes are too long. An immediate increase in output is not a likely response to higher prices. If those higher prices persist, then production will expand and prices will drop, but only after enough time has passed for the added production efforts to mature. The technical rigidity of supply in the short run, of course, is not limited to wheat. The same argument can be made for coffee, cocoa, soybeans, and almost every other commodity with the possible exception of currencies and financial instruments. With regard to currencies and financial instruments, one may encounter rigidities on the demand side (for dollars or treasury bills) in relation to their supply. These rigidities can result in equally dramatic price changes as in gold or agricultural commodities. Whether or not prices will constantly fluctuate and never settle down to a "steady state" is an issue of stability and depends on the precise character of demand and supply.

6 MODEL DESIGN

There are several types of fundamental models one may develop. Among the three most common are:

1. *Leading indicator models:* An activity or price is preceded regularly by one or more other activities.
2. *Single equation behavioral models:* A model typically estimated using regression methods where price or quantity are explained by some collection of factors.
3. *Simultaneous system models:* A collection of structural equations that collectively describe the mechanics and interdependencies of the various market forces.

While each of the above models are different they all may be classified as dynamic, causal, stochastic, historical models. They are dynamic because economic responses to economic or other impulses often are delayed and/or distributed over time. The models are causal insofar as the linkage between variables is dictated by economic reason and a priori knowledge. They are stochastic to the extent that random or chance happenings cloud the structural relationships. Finally, the models are historical owing to the need to calibrate and corroborate the models using historical data.

6.1 Features of Dynamic Models

The design features of all dynamic models include the following:

1. Constructions or specifications of ex-ante (i.e., desired) economic behavior
2. Accounting identities

3. Linkages between ex-ante desires and ex-post realizations
4. Estimation of the impulse response characteristics between variables
5. Solution and operation procedures
6. Identification of demand and supply for interpretive purposes

6.2   A Comment on Identification

While the purpose of this chapter is not to examine problems of econometrics, the *problem of identification* is central to the problems of specification, estimation, and interpretation, and warrants further comment. Simply stated, the problem of identification can be posed as the following question: Given quantity and price as time series, can the demand and supply curves be deduced? To illustrate the problem consider the following model:

$$Q_t^D = a + bP_t + u_t \quad \text{(demand)}$$
$$Q_t^S = g + hP_t + v_t \quad \text{(supply)}$$
$$Q_t^D = Q_t^S \quad \text{(equilibrium)}$$

where a b, g, and h are parameters to be estimated and u and v are stochastic variates with zero means. In order to identify demand and supply in this system one must be able to deduce the values of a, b, g, and h. In terms of deviations from their means, the above model could be written:

$$q^D = bP_t + u_t$$
$$q^S = hP_t + v_t$$
$$q^D = q^S.$$

This produces the result

$$q_t^* = \frac{bv_t - hu_t}{b - h}$$

$$P_t^* = \frac{v_t - u_t}{b - h}$$

In order to obtain b and h, u_t and v_t would have to be known. Unfortunately, they are not known. Regression of q_t on p_t will not succeed unless $u_t = 0$, which is a special case bordering on the trivial.

Now if a lag is introduced, say on the supply side, the model could be written:

$$q_t^D = bP_t + u_t$$
$$q_t^S = hP_{t-1} + v_t$$
$$q_t^D = q_t^S.$$

Now a regression of q_t on p_t would give b and a. Similarly, a regression of q_t on p_{t-1} would give h. In this case, the demand and supply parameters would be identified.

The critical point to note is that the design of the model will determine its dynamics, interpretability, and practical usefulness. Here, identifiability can play an important role.

7 FUNDAMENTAL MARKET FACTORS AND STRUCTURES

While each commodity market has its own unique collection of demand and supply forces, there are nevertheless several general interactions and factors that provide a checklist when performing fundamental analyses. These interactions and factors are summarized in Table 18.2. To be sure, the degree of detail depends on the commodity in question and the objectives of the fundamental analysis. An illustrative flow chart for an international commodity market model is shown in Figure 18.1.

Table 18.2

FUNDAMENTAL FACTORS AND STRUCTURES

1. Market Stratification	Identification and distinction of market participants by (a) economic role, e.g., final consumers, hedgers, speculators, arbitragers; (b) political affiliation, e.g., Soviet bloc economies; (c) level of technology, e.g., primitive agriculture.
2. Demand	Total demand consists of domestic consumption plus exports plus domestic stocks (may be treated as a supply). Domestic consumption broken down by use, e.g., gold demand for manufacturing and gold demand for investment where gold demand for jewelry may or may not be separated out from investment demand depending on the research objectives; demand for an agricultural product broken down into human, feed, and seed demands and demands for derivative products such as meal and oil from soybeans.
3. Production and Supply	Total supply consists of production plus imports and stocks (unless treated as a demand). Production may be segregated by type of commodity (different grade), production technology, political origin, and production cycle (crop year or mining period or pattern of new issues of financial instruments).
4. Market Structure and Price	Type of market, e.g., price leadership oligopoly as in the case of coffee and the dominance Brazil has as a producer.
5. Expectations	A consideration that may influence producers as well as consumers, e.g., expected harvest, expected carry-over, expected price. Here the expectations mechanisms must be spelled out as they can influence the dynamics of the market: Past activity is especially important.

Table 18.2 (Continued)

6. External Influences Excluding Government Influences

These factors may include weather patterns and effects, quality of ore, transport costs, per capita income, rates of inflation, fiscal and monetary policies.

7. Government Influences

Domestic price supports, import restrictions, export constraints, subsidies for production, technology incentives, strategic stocks.

8. Integration

Tie together demands and supplies into a consistent integrated market structure. Here accounting identities and rules for identification of specific market behavior are especially important.

9. Short-Run and Long-Run Distinctions

Fixed and variable factors of production, evolving tastes.

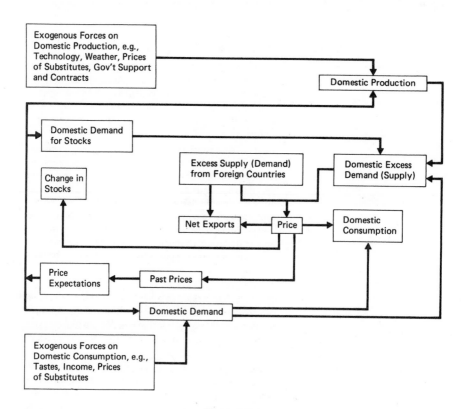

Figure 18.1

ILLUSTRATION FLOW CHART OF INTERNATIONAL
COMMODITY MARKET

Fundamental models can vary in degree of analytical detail, type of estimation, and commodity of reference. Nevertheless they all have a common developmental heritage. The common considerations and assumptions guiding these efforts include the following:

1. The world is not entirely random in its behavior.
2. More accurate, more timely, and more relevant information used in a proper framework can improve investment decisions.
3. Specific economic activity and prices are determined in part by market, regional, and world events including social, economic, and natural phenomena.
4. The many-faceted, interrelated character of a commodity market demands a "mathematical" approach to efficiently assimilate the diverse and changing information that influences the market.
5. Many economic phenomena are dynamic and not instantaneous in response to some impulse.
6. A common conceptual structure including:
   • demand for consumption
   • demand for stocks
   • production
   • price expectations
   • producer and retail price adjustment mechanisms
   • accounting and logical identities
   • constraints.
7. Economic theory dictates general design; data and ease of use help determine operational configuration.

The operation of a model also follows a common three-tier process:

1. Monitoring the marketplace and relevant factors.
2. Projecting prices, trade flows, and other economic activity through model simulation.
3. Evaluating and comparing alternative investment decisions based on the price projections generated by the conditional simulations and their associated probabilities.

The following chapters are presented in this context.

9 SUMMARY

Fundamental analysis captures the elements of supply and demand in a formal mathematical structure. This structure requires the use of economic theory and econometric modeling techniques. The quality of the fundamental approach then becomes a function of the ability of the analyst to follow the guidelines set out above. The greater popularity of technical analysis, in comparison to fundamental analysis, comes not so much from a recognized theoretical superiority but from the recognition that fundamental analysis rarely embodies daily decision-making and is often more difficult to construct.

10 BIBLIOGRAPHY

ALLEN, R. G. D., *Macro-Economic Theory: A Mathematical Treatment.* New York: St. Martins Press, 1967.

HOLT, C. C., F. MODIGLIAN, J. F. MUTH, and H. A. SIMON, *Planning Production, Inventories and Work Force.* Englewood Cliffs, N.J.: Prentice-Hall, Inc., 1960.

JORGENSON, D. W., "Anticipations and Investment Behavior," in *The Brookings Quarterly Econometric Model of the United States,* ed. Duesenberry et al. Chicago: Rand McNally, 1965.

LANCASTER, K., *Consumer Demand: A New Approach.* New York: Columbia University Press, 1971.

BRIGHAM, E. F. and J. L. PAPPAS, *Managerial Economics,* 3rd ed. Hinsdale, Ill.: Dryden Press, 1979.

THEIL, H., *Economic Forecasts and Policy,* 2nd ed. Amsterdam: North Holland Publishing Co., 1961.

19

WORLD WHEAT ANALYSIS

||||||||||||||||||||||||||||||||||||||||||||||||||||||||||||||||||||||||||||||||||||||||||||||||||||||||||||||||

1 INTRODUCTION

There are several considerations in the construction of an operational econometric model of a world agricultural crop. First, from a business perspective, the myriad of information that is generated must be translated into digestible form relevant to decisions such as whether to hedge, to reverse a position, or to go long. This requires the estimation of the cash price at one or more forward dates and in relation to their corresponding future market prices. The cash and futures markets are alternative pricing arenas albeit closely interconnected. Second, a commodity such as wheat that is produced by many countries or regions and demanded by many others requires a comprehensive and detailed model for each country and region. There is a common source of inadequacy in more aggregative models, which consist of a handful of equations to explain world demand supply. It is their inherent inability to measure the effects of specific country influences, such as changes in import and export duties, tariffs, regional weather conditions, and exchange rates. Alternatively a world agricultural commodity model must explain the demand and supply of the commodity in each country or region as well as the linkage of the excess supplies to all other regional excess demands. Without this level of detail a model may be forced by design to produce estimates that are untenable or that limit the exploration of distributional impacts that may have dramatic effects on prices. The world wheat model presented here is an illustrative attempt to satisfy these requirements. Moreover the linkage of the model's predicted cash to corresponding futures prices is highlighted to show the practical application of this or any other model.

2 MODEL STRUCTURE[1]

The model divides the world wheat market into 43 major countries or regions. The 43 countries or regions considered are summarized in Table 19.1. This "decomposition" was selected on the basis of importance in the market-

Table 19.1

COUNTRIES AND REGIONS

United States	Yugoslavia
Canada	East Germany
Central America	Poland
Argentina	Czechoslovakia
East South America	Hungary
West South America	Rumania
Norway	Bulgaria
Sweden	Russia
Morocco	West Asia
Algeria	India
Tunisia	Pakistan
Egypt	Other South Asia
West Africa	Southeast Asia
East Africa	Japan
South Africa	Other East Asia
Turkey	China
	Oceania

Denmark
Britain
Belgium
Netherlands
West Germany
France
Spain
Portugal
Italy
Other Europe

1. This model is an adaptation of one developed by LLOREX Corporation and D. Warner. See Dennis Warner, "An Econometric Analysis of the World Wheat Economy," PHD. dissertation, Princeton University, 1979.

place, and geographic location and political persuasion. To be sure, several other alternatives could be considered.

For each country or region the model provides estimates of human, feed, and seed consumption; domestic and export prices; quantities produced, yields, hectares planted and harvested; stocks; weather effects indices; and world trade patterns. The estimation of demand and supply for each of these countries or regions, of course, requires appropriate price and quantity data. While quantities of similar items in different countries can be aggregated with relative ease to create a regional value for that factor, the same ease of construction is not the case for prices. Here, exchange rates, government subsidies, and other factors must be taken into consideration in order to construct a representative regional price. In this model, the regional prices are weighted averages of the individual country prices in the region, where the weights assigned to each country in a region parallel their value of wheat consumption relative to the region's value of wheat consumption.

Each country contains a block of 12 equations. Five equations for demand: human consumption, feed demand, seed demand, demand for stocks, and total demand. The first four of these are estimated and the last is an accounting identity. On the supply side there are five equations: one equation each for area harvested and yield, one equation defining production as the product of area harvested times yield, one equation for area planted, and one equation for weather effects. An illustrative representation of these equations is presented in Table 19.2. To be sure not all of the equations referred to in Table 19.2 apply to each country or region. Some regions such as Other South Asia are not significant producers of wheat while the United States and the Soviet Union plant and harvest two wheat crops—winter wheat harvested in the spring and spring wheat harvested in late summer. Moreover, the Northern and Southern Hemispheres plant and harvest wheat at different times and these phase differences are accounted for in the model crop year and weather effects factors. In addition, some countries with "planned" economies can dramatically change area planted and/or cattle, and poultry production which, in turn, can introduce, remove, or change these equations from year to year. Historically these shifts are a matter of record and easily accounted for. In a forecasting-simulation context alternative model structures must be used to accommodate these anticipated events.

A detailed summary of most of the models estimation results can be found in Warner (1979). In general, the estimated prices and quantities for the major producers and consumers are within a few percent of the actual values. In model simulation these errors cascade somewhat but remain within 5 to 10 percent of the actual values.

The excess demands and supplies are aggregated and together solve for prices and trade flows that minimize total transport costs subject to trade

Table 19.2

REPRESENTATIVE STRUCTURE FOR A COUNTRY OR REGION

Demand

Human	$HD = H(PW, IN, BD, PR, PP, T)$
Feed	$FD = F(PW, PC, NOC, NOP, PS)$
Seed	$SD = S(APE, T)$
Stock	$ST = T(QH, PWX, ST_{-1})$
Total	$TD = HD + FD + SD + (ST - ST_{-1})$

Production

Quantity Harvested	$QH = YL \cdot AH$
Yield	$YL = Y(SWW, FI, WH)$
Area Harvested	$AH = A(AP, PG, PP, PW, WH)$
Area Planted	$AP = P(PG, PP, PW, WH, PS, PC, PR)$
Weather Effects	$WH = W(TE, MO, VTE, VMO)$

Trade

Excess Demand (+) or Supply (−)	$EX = TD - QH$
Import Constraints on Country j	$IL_j \leq IM_j \leq IU_j$
Export Constraints on Country j	$XL_j \leq XP_j \leq XY_j$
Trade Identity	$EX - \sum_j IM_j = 0$, if $EX > 0$
	$EX + \sum_j XP_j = 0$, if $EX < 0$

Price Constraints

Domestic Price	$PG \leq PW$
Export Price	$PXL \leq PWX \leq PXU$

Mnemonics

PW	= Price of wheat—domestic	PG	= Government support price of wheat
IN	= Gross National Income	PWX	= Export price of wheat
BD	= Population	PXL	= Lower bound export price of wheat
PR	= Price of rye	PXU	= Upper bound export price of wheat
PP	= Consumer Price Index	HD	= Human consumption demand
T	= Time	FD	= Feed demand
PWX	= Export price of wheat	SD	= Seed demand
PC	= Price of corn	ST	= Stock demand
NOC	= Number of cattle	TD	= Total demand
NOP	= Number of poultry	QH	= Quantity harvested
PS	= Price of soybeans	YL	= Yield
APE	= Area planted—expected	AH	= Area harvested
FI	= Soil fertility index	AP	= Area planted
WH	= Weather effects index	SWW	= Type of wheat—spring or winter
AP	= Area planted		
EX	= Excess demand (+) or supply (−)		
TE	= Temperature—average of select stations at select times		
MO	= Moisture—average of select stations at select times		
VTE	= Variance of TE		
VMO	= Variance of MO		

IL_j = Lower bound imports from country j ⎫
IM_j = Imports from country j ⎬ of Wheat
IU_j = Upper bound imports from country j ⎭

XB_j = Lower bound exports to country j ⎫
XP_j = Exports to country j ⎬ of Wheat
XU_j = Upper bound exports to country j ⎭

constraints for each country as well as the constraint that total exports equal total imports. The solution requires a fixed point algorithm owing to the nonlinear and discontinuous character of the regional excess demand schedules.

3 MODEL OPERATION

The model is solved for conditional values of the exogenous variables. Each such simulation produces demands, production, prices, and trade flows for each of the 43 countries or regions. The model is annual and estimates July export (import) prices of wheat. Select portions of one such simulation are illustrated in Tables 19.3 through 19.5.

For investment analysis purposes, simulations are conducted for combinations of outcomes for select exogenous variables. The simulations are conducted for alternative weather, stockpiling, and exchange rate scenarios. Subjective probabilities are included for each outcome for each variable, and the simulation results are summarized as probability distributions for select variables; the U.S. July cash price is given special attention. The simulated price distribution then is compared to futures prices as of the simulation date and investments comparisons are made. Here the expected price differentials are compared as well as the odds of achieving a given differential. Because weather conditions, political events, exchange rates, and other factors change over time, the model is restimulated each month to take advantage of new information on a timely basis. This in turn leads to investment reassessments as the harvest year unfolds. An example of the model's application is presented below.

4 MODEL APPLICATION: February 1979 Assessment of July 1979 World Wheat Market[2]

As of February 1979, three areas appear especially important for world wheat prices and trade in the commodity markets. One is on the supply side and two are on the demand side of the market:

Weather

Anticipated war stockpiling

Exchange rates

2. Excerpts of LLOREX Corporation presentation at the Eighth International Commodities Conference, Chicago, Illinois, March 1979.

Table 19.3

EX-POST 1973 CROP YEAR SIMULATION WHEAT EXPORTER SUMMARY STATISTICS

EXPORTING REGIONS

	U.S.A.	Canada	Argentina	Sweden	France	Spain	Russia	Oceania
Demand[a]								
Human Consumption	15,084.55	1,785.42	3,877.11	457.30	4,705.74	3,413.79	53,259.20	1,306.39
Feed Demand	15,009.32	2,124.52	50.00	216.00	4,299.91	1,332.32	41,071.01	934.01
Seed Demand	1,486.03	1,009.68	513.51	79.39	736.10	499.84	8,346.87	475.87
Total Region Demand	31,579.89	4,919.62	4,440.61	752.69	9,741.75	5,245.95	102,677.17	2,716.27
Production								
Quantity Harvested[a]	43,778.72	16,484.71	8,306.25	1,074.85	17,134.76	4,916.50	102,694.44	10,771.27
Area Harvested[b]	18,781.87	9,918.72	4,962.66	249.61	3,874.96	3,692.99	66,814.69	8,235.72
Yield	2.33	1.66	1.67	4.31	4.42	1.33	1.54	1.31
Stocks[a]								
Change	−7,322.57	78.70	−325.66	12.96	−168.94	−102.28	600.70	−365.21
Level	6,009.93	19,809.58	1,280.0	716.17	1,590.40	935.60	2,770.01	512.07
Trade[a]								
Net Exports	20,916.17	13,091.66	3,786.28	304.21	7,282.36	−400.95	−583.37	8,175.87
Prices[c]								
Domestic Price, Local	78.81	77.73	81.37	409.83	533.67	568.12	101.26	69.56
Domestic Price, US$	78.81	78.06	81.37	89.29	113.35	99.76	101.26	103.51

[a]All quantities in thousands of metric tons.
[b]All areas in thousands of hectares.
[c]All prices in U.S. dollars per metric ton.
SOURCE: LLOREX Corporation 1977. All rights reserved.

Table 19.4

EX-POST 1973 CROP YEAR SIMULATION WHEAT IMPORTER SUMMARY STATISTICS

IMPORTING REGIONS

	Egypt	West Africa	East Africa	South Africa	Turkey	West Asia	India	Pakistan	Other South Asia
Demand[a]									
Human Consumption	2,507.14	508.08	668.17	1,462.87	6,938.68	2,650.28	23,404.08	4,070.42	1,808.95
Feed Demand	1,961.66	397.54	522.79	0.0	5,429.04	2,073.66	101.00	3,184.82	1,415.38
Seed Demand	392.92	79.63	104.72	0.0	1,087.44	415.36	2,043.92	637.92	283.50
Total Region Demand	4,861.73	985.24	1,295.68	1,698.31	13,455.15	5,139.29	25,549.00	7,893.16	3,507.84
Production									
Quantity Harvested[a]	2,933.60	41.76	633.76	1,658.56	10,162.57	2,500.01	22,391.96	6,912.26	2,904.08
Area Harvested[b]	745.81	41.76	657.00	1,400.04	8,663.97	2,705.35	-18,552.78	6,141.06	3,000.00
Yield	3.93	1.02	0.96	1.18	1.17	0.93	1.21	1.13	0.97
Stocks[a]									
Change	0.0	0.0	0.0	69.01	-136.88	-9.0	-216.22	-78.64	-30.50
Level	211.00	0.0	18.0	576.42	2,000.00	100.0	4,683.78	653.29	348.98
Trade									
Principle Importing Region	U.S.A.	Argentina	Oceania	Oceania	U.S.A.	U.S.A.	Oceania	Oceania	Oceania
Total Imports[a]	1,928.20	943.47	661.92	108.76	3,155.70	2,630.27	2,940.76	902.26	573.26
Prices[c]									
Domestic Price, Local	40.18	107.26	107.26	59.09	143.86	111.62	925.31	1,120.23	112.80
Domestic Price, US$	102.76	107.26	107.26	87.80	102.76	111.62	112.80	112.80	112.80

[a]All quantities in thousands of metric tons.
[b]All areas in thousands of hectares.
[c]All prices in U.S. dollars per metric ton.

SOURCE: LLOREX Corporation, 1977. All rights reserved.

Table 19.5

EX-POST 1973 CROP YEAR SIMULATION WORLD WHEAT TRADE FLOW PATTERNS

IMPORTING REGIONS	U.S.A.	Canada	Argentina	Sweden	France	Spain	Russia	Oceania	Total Imports
U.S.A.	22,862.46	0.0	0.0	0.0	0.0	0.0	0.0	0.0	-0.00
Canada	0.0	3,393.02	0.0	0.0	0.0	0.0	0.0	0.0	-0.00
Central America	1,520.96	0.0	0.0	0.0	0.0	0.0	0.0	0.0	1,520.96
Argentina	0.0	0.0	4,519.96	0.0	0.0	0.0	0.0	0.0	-0.00
East South America	0.0	0.0	3,042.98	0.0	0.0	0.0	0.0	0.0	3,042.98
West South America	0.0	523.11	255.76	0.0	0.0	0.0	0.0	0.0	778.86
Norway	354.41	0.0	0.0	0.0	0.0	0.0	0.0	0.0	354.41
Sweden	0.0	0.0	0.0	770.64	0.0	0.0	0.0	0.0	-0.00
Denmark	0.0	0.0	0.0	0.0	0.0	0.0	0.0	0.0	0.0
Britain	0.0	124.33	0.0	0.0	2,953.25	0.0	0.0	0.0	3,077.59
Belgium	0.0	0.0	0.0	0.0	801.76	0.0	0.0	0.0	801.76
Netherlands	0.0	0.0	0.0	0.0	1,236.47	0.0	0.0	0.0	1,236.47
West Germany	0.0	0.0	0.0	0.0	1,286.59	0.0	0.0	0.0	1,286.59
France	0.0	0.0	0.0	0.0	9,852.39	0.0	0.0	0.0	-0.00
Spain	0.0	400.95	0.0	0.0	0.0	4,916.50	0.0	0.0	400.95
Portugal	0.0	472.71	0.0	0.0	0.0	0.0	0.0	0.0	472.71
Italy	0.0	0.0	0.0	0.0	1,004.29	0.0	0.0	0.0	1,004.29
Other Europe	218.17	0.0	0.0	0.0	0.0	0.0	0.0	0.0	218.17
Yugoslavia	640.51	0.0	0.0	0.0	0.0	0.0	0.0	0.0	640.51
East Germany	742.74	1,097.96	0.0	0.0	0.0	0.0	0.0	0.0	1,840.70
Poland	633.02	935.77	0.0	0.0	0.0	0.0	0.0	0.0	1,568.78
Czechoslovakia	456.34	674.59	0.0	0.0	0.0	0.0	0.0	0.0	1,130.94
Hungary	0.0	0.0	0.0	0.0	0.0	0.0	0.0	0.0	0.0

EXPORTING REGIONS

Region									Total World Trade
Rumania	0.0	0.0	0.0	0.0	0.0	0.0	0.0	0.0	0.0
Bulgaria	0.0	0.0	0.0	0.0	0.0	0.0	0.0	0.0	0.0
Russia	0.0	279.23	0.0	304.21	0.0	0.0	102,694.44	0.0	583.37
Morocco	1,004.07	0.0	0.0	0.0	0.0	0.0	0.0	0.0	1,004.07
Algeria	911.73	0.0	0.0	0.0	0.0	0.0	0.0	0.0	911.73
Tunisia	389.18	0.0	0.0	0.0	0.0	0.0	0.0	0.0	389.18
Egypt	1,928.20	0.0	0.0	0.0	0.0	0.0	0.0	0.0	1,928.20
West Africa	0.0	0.0	487.56	0.0	0.0	0.0	0.0	455.92	943.47
East Africa	0.0	0.0	0.0	0.0	0.0	0.0	0.0	661.92	661.92
South Africa	0.0	0.0	0.0	0.0	0.0	0.0	0.0	108.76	108.76
Turkey	3,155.70	0.0	0.0	0.0	0.0	0.0	0.0	0.0	3,155.70
West Asia	2,630.27	0.0	0.0	0.0	0.0	0.0	0.0	0.0	2,630.27
India	0.0	0.0	0.0	0.0	0.0	0.0	0.0	2,940.76	2,940.76
Pakistan	0.0	0.0	0.0	0.0	0.0	0.0	0.0	902.26	902.26
Other South Asia	0.0	0.0	0.0	0.0	0.0	0.0	0.0	573.26	573.26
Southeast Asia	0.0	0.0	0.0	0.0	0.0	0.0	0.0	190.52	190.52
Japan	6,330.38	0.0	0.0	0.0	0.0	0.0	0.0	0.0	6,330.88
Other East Asia	0.0	0.0	0.0	0.0	0.0	0.0	0.0	4,937.87	4,937.87
China	0.0	2,595.65	0.0	0.0	0.0	0.0	0.0	0.0	5,987.65
Oceania	0.0	2,595.39	0.0	0.0	0.0	0.0	0.0	0.0	2,595.39
Total Exports	20,916.17	13,091.66	3,786.28	304.21	7,282.36	-0.00	0.0	10,771.26	53,556.56

Note: All quantities in thousands of metric tons

SOURCE: LLOREX Corporation, 1977. All rights reserved.

Four weather alternatives are examined. In conjunction with each of the four weather alternatives two stockpiling alternatives are examined. And, for each of the eight combined weather and stockpiling alternatives, three exchange rate alternatives are examined. In all, 24 different alternatives are simulated. The alternative simulations are shown in Table 19.6. The simula-

Table 19.6

1979 LLOREX SIMULATION ALTERNATIVES

	A	*B*	*C*	*D*
Weather[a]	Normal	23% drought in the Soviet Union	23% drought in China	23% drought in the Soviet Union and China

	1		*2*	
Stockpiling	Normal		10% war precautionary stockpiling by the Soviet Union and China	

	X	*Y*	*Z*
Exchange Rates	No change (as of 2/79)	Japan and Europe rise by 10% and U.S. falls by 10%	Japan and Europe fall by 10% and U.S. rises by 10%

Note: Simulation A1X denotes the "norm."
[a]Percentage drought is measured relative to LLOREX's regional weather effects index.

tion **A1X** denotes the state of "normal conditions" with respect to the three variables under consideration. Every other simulation is recorded as a deviation from this norm. For example, our system predicts that for simulation **A2Z**, world price will change by +22 percent from what we would expect if weather conditions are normal, international tensions abate in Asia, and exchange rates do not deteriorate or improve. The alternative price forecasts are summarized in Table 19.7 along with probability estimates of their occurrence.

Under "normal conditions" the expected outcome for July 1979 is a price of $3.47 per bushel. However, normal conditions are not anticipated to prevail. A Soviet drought and Asian stockpiling are considered most likely. This scenario produces a July 1979 price of $4.08. Table 19.7 summarizes the simulation results along with MaxMin and Expected Value decisions for the 1979 crop year. In addition, speculative positions at four to one odds also are given. In retrospect the model has performed well: the July 1979 wheat price rose to within 5% of that anticipated.

Table 19.7

INVESTMENT ANALYSIS—
JULY 1979 FUTURES PRICES IN COMPARISON TO FEBRUARY 1979
ESTIMATES OF JULY 1979 PRICES

	PRICE INTERVALS $ per bushel				
	$0–3.495	$3.500–3.745	$3.750–3.995	$4.000–4.245	$4.250–∞
Probability	.0833	.125	.1667	.250	.3750
Payoff—Long[a]	$−0.05	$0.154	$0.404	$0.654	$1.030
Payoff—Short[a]	$0.05	$−0.154	$−0.404	$−0.654	$−1.030

DECISION CRITERION STRATEGY DECISIONS

MaxMin: Long July 1979 futures
MaxMax: Long July 1979 futures
Max Expected Value: Long July 1979 futures

FOUR TO ONE ODDS POSITIONS

Long July futures at any price up to $3.74
Short July futures at any price over $4.50

[a]Payoff basis calculated from July 1979 futures price of $3.47, as of February 1979.

5 SUMMARY

The world wheat markets are influenced by events and factors in individual countries and regions. The model referred to here provides a framework from which to measure some of the most important of these forces. The information supplied by monitoring efforts is combined with alternative market assumptions to generate alternative market outcomes. The various market scenarios can focus on alternative exchange rate profiles, war precaution stockpiling, transportation costs, weather conditions, and select other considerations for each of the 43 different countries and regions. The price information from these simulations is assembled to reveal the distribution of prices that may emerge. Prospective profit-risk profiles of cash or physicals positions in relation to the futures markets may be calculated and evaluated using common decision criteria. This process results in alternative investment positions depending on the decision criterion used. The model is demonstrated with an example that assesses long-term speculative or hedging positions. These results, of course, may be complemented by short-term technical analyses.

6 BIBLIOGRAPHY

ALIBER, ROBERT Z., "Speculation and Price Stability Once Again," *Journal of Political Economy,* 72 (1964), 607–9.

BAER, JULIUS B., and OLIN G. SAXON, *Commodity Exchanges and Futures Trading.* New York: Harper & Brothers, 1949.

BAUMOL, W. J., "Speculation, Profitability and Stability," *Review of Economics and Statistics,* 39 (August 1957), 263–71.

BOARD OF GOVERNORS OF THE FEDERAL RESERVE, *The Monthly Report of the Federal Reserve System.* Washington, D.C.: 1961–62.

BOX, G. E. P., and G. M. JENKINS, *Time Series Analysis: Forecasting and Control.* San Francisco: Holden-Day, 1970.

BRENNAN, M. J., "The Supply of Storage," *American Economic Review,* 40 (March 1958), 50–72.

CHICAGO BOARD OF TRADE, *The Statistical Annual of the Chicago Board of Trade.* Chicago: Chicago Board of Trade, 1965, 1968.

COMMODITY EXCHANGE AUTHORITY, *Commitments of Trades in Commodity Futures.* Chicago: Commodity Exchange Authority, 1961–72.

COMMODITY RESEARCH BUREAU, *The Commodity Yearbook.* New York: Commodity Research Bureau, Inc., 1968–74.

COOTNER, PAUL H., "Returns to Speculators: Telser versus Keynes," *Journal of Political Economy,* 68 (August 1960), 397–403; reply by Telser, pp. 404–15; rejoinder by Cootner, pp. 901–11.

——, "Common Elements in Futures Markets for Commodities and Bonds," *Proceedings of the American Economic Association,* 51 (May 1961), 173–83.

——, "Speculation and Hedging," *Food Research Institute Studies,* 7, Supp. (1967), 65–106.

DOW, J. C. R., "The Inaccuracy of Expectations," *Economica,* 8 (May 1941), 57–68.

DULAY, H., "On the Variance Effects of a Buffer-Stock Scheme: A Simulation Study of a Floor Price Plan for Wood," *Australian Economic Papers,* 4 (June-December 1965), 79–92.

EHRICH, ROLLO L., "The Impact of Government Programs on Wheat-Futures Markets, 1953–63," *Food Research Institute Studies,* 6 (1966), 313–38.

——, "Cash-Futures Price Relationships for Live Beef Cattle," *American Journal of Agricultural Economics,* 51 (February 1969), 26–39.

FAMA, E. F., L. FISHER, M. C., JENSEN, and R. ROLL, "The Adjustment of Stock Prices to New Information," *International Economic Review,* 10 (February 1969), 1–21.

FISHMAN, G. S., "Price Behavior under Alternative Forms of Price Expectations," *Quarterly Journal Of Economics,* 78 (May 1964), 281–98.

FOOTE, RICHARD J., J. W., KLEIN, and M. CLOUGH, *The Demand and Price Structure for Corn and Total Feed Concentrates.* U.S. Department of Agriculture, Technical Bulletin No. 1061. Washington, D.C.: U.S. Government Printing Office, October 1965.

GOLD, G., *Modern Commodity Futures Trading.* New York: Commodity Research Bureau, Inc., 1959.

GRANGER, C. W. J., and M. HATANAKA, *Spectral Analysis of Economic Times Series.* Princeton, N.J.: Princeton University Press, 1964.

GRAY, ROGER W., "The Seasonal Pattern in Wheat Futures Prices under the Loan Program," *Food Research Institute Studies,* 3 (February 1962), 23–24.

———, "Fundamental Price Behavior Characteristics in Commodity Futures." *Futures Trading Seminar, II.* Madison: Mimir Publishers, 1963.

HATHAWAY, D. E., "Food Prices and Inflation," *Brookings Papers on Economic Activity,* 1 (1974).

HAWTREY, R. G., "A Symposium on the Theory of the Forward Market: III. Mr. Kaldor on the Forward Market," *Review of Economic Studies,* 7 (June 1940), 196–205.

HICKS, J. R., *Value and Capital,* 2nd ed. Oxford: Clarendon Press, 1965.

HIERONYMUS, T. A., *Uses of Grain Futures Markets in the Farm Business.* Agricultural Experiment Station Bulletin No. 696. Urbana: University of Illinois, 1963.

———, *Economics of Futures Trading.* New York: Commodity Research Bureau, Inc., 1971.

HIMMELBLAU, D. M., *Applied Nonlinear Programming.* New York: Mc-Graw-Hill, 1972.

HOFFMAN, G. W., and J. W. T. DUVEL, *Grain Prices and the Futures Market: A 15-Year Survey, 1923–38.* U.S. Department of Agriculture Technical Bulletin No. 747. Washington, D.C.: U.S. Government Printing Office, January 1941.

HOUCK, JAMES P., *Demand and Price Analysis of the U.S. Soybean Market.* Agricultural Experiment Station Technical Bulletin No. 244. Minneapolis: University of Minnesota, 1963.

———, and J. S. MANN, *Domestic and Foreign Demand for U.S. Soybeans and Soybean Products.* Agricultural Experiment Station Technical Bulletin No. 256. Minneapolis: University of Minnesota, 1968.

———, "The Relationship of Direct Price Flexibilities to Direct Price Elasticities," *Journal of Farm Economics,* 46 (August 1964), 789–92.

HOUTHAKKER, H S., "Commodity Futures IV: An Empirical Test of the Theory of Normal Backwardation." Cowles Foundation Discussion Paper, Economics No. 2124, June 22, 1955.

———, "Can Speculators Forecast Prices?" *Review of Economics and Statistics,* 39 (1957), 143–51.

————, "Restatement of the Theory of Normal Backwardation." Cowles Foundation Discussion Paper No. 44, December 18, 1957.

————, "The Scope and Limits of Futures Trading," in *Allocation of Economic Resources: Essays in Honor of B.F. Haley*, ed. M. Abromovitz. Stanford, Calif.: Stanford University Press, 1959.

————, "Systematic and Random Elements in Short Term Price Movements," *Proceedings of the American Economic Association*, 51 (May 1961), 164–72.

————, "Free and Stable Commodity Markets." Statements to the National Advisory Committee on Food and Fibre, September 1966.

IRWIN, H. S., "Seasonal Cycles in Aggregates of Wheat Futures Contracts," *Journal of Political Economy*, 43 (1935), 278–88.

JENKINS, G. M. and D. G. WATTS, *Spectral Analysis and its Applications*. San Francisco: Holden-Day, 1969.

JOHNSON, LELAND L., "The Theory of Hedging and Speculation in Commodity Futures," *Review of Economic Studies*, 27 (June 1960), 139–51.

KEMP, MURRAY C., "Speculation, Profitability and Price Stability," *Review of Economics and Statistics*, 45 (May 1963), 185–89.

KENDALL, M. G., and A., STUART, *The Advanced Theory of Statistics*, Vol. 3, New York: Hafner Publishing Company, 1966.

KING, G. A., *The Demand and Price Structure for By-Product Feeds*. U.S. Department of Agriculture Technical Bulletin No. 1183. Washington, D.C.: U.S. Government Printing Office, August 1958.

LABYS, W. C., and C. W. J. GRANGER, *Speculation Hedging and Commodity Price Forecasts*. Lexington, Mass.: Heath Lering Books, 1970.

LARSON, ARNOLD, "Evidence on the Temporal Dispersion of Price Effects of New Market Information." Ph. D. dissertation, Stanford University, 1960.

————, "Estimation of Hedging and Speculative Positions in Futures Markets." *Food Research Institute Studies*, 2 (November 1961), 203–12.

LLOREX CORP., "Wheat—A Mathematical Approach." Paper presented at the 8th International Commodities Conference, Chicago, 1979.

————, "Wheat Model Sees Higher Prices Ahead" *Commodities Magazine*, July 1979, pp. 47–49.

MCKINNON, RONALD I., "Futures Markets, Buffer Stocks, and Income Stability for Primary Producers," *Journal of Political Economy*, 75 (December 1967), 844–61.

MANDELBROT, B., "Forecasts of Future Prices, Unbiased Markets and 'Martingale' Models," *Journal of Business Security Prices*, 39, Supp. (January 1966), 242–55.

MEINKEN, K. W., *The Demand and Price Structure for Wheat*. U.S. Department of Agriculture Technical Bulletin No. 1136. Washington, D.C.: U.S. Government Printing Office, November 1955.

——, et al., "Measurement of Substitution in Demand for Time Series Data: Synthesis of Three Approaches." *Journal of Farm Economics*, 38 (August 1956), 711–35.

MILLS, E. S., "The Use Reply by M. Nerlove, of Adaptive Expectations in Stability Analysis," *Quarterly Journal of Economics*, 75 (May 1961), 330–38.

——, *Price Output and Inventory Policy.* New York: John Wiley, 1962.

MOSBEAK, E. J., and H. O., WOLD, *Interdependent Systems: Structure and Estimation.* New York: American Elsevier, 1970.

MUTH, J. F., "Rational Expectations and the Theory of Price Movements," *Econometrica*, 29 (July 1961), 315–35.

NERLOVE, MARC, "Adaptive Expectations and Cobweb Phenomena," *Quarterly Journal of Economics*, 73 (May 1958), 227–40.

——, *Distributed Lags and Demand Analysis for Agricultural and Other Commodities.* U.S. Department of Agriculture Agricultural Handbook No. 141. Washington, D.C.: U.S. Government Printing Office, 1958.

——, "On the Nerlove Estimate of Supply Elasticity," *Journal of Farm Economics*, 40 (August 1958), 723–28.

——, "Spectral Analysis of Seasonal Adjustment Procedures." Report No. 6227, Rotterdam, The Netherlands: Econometric Institute, 1964.

——, *The Dynamics of Supply: Estimation of Farmers' Response to Price.* Baltimore: Johns Hopkins Press, 1958.

——, and WILLIAM ADDISON, "Statistical Estimation of Long-Run Elasticities of Supply and Demand," *Journal of Farm Economics*, 40 (November 1958), 861–80.

OECD, *Agriculture Policy in the United States.:* Organization for Economic Cooperation and Development, 1974.

PAARLBERG, DONALD, *Princes of Soybeans and Soybean Products.* Agricultural Experimental Station Bulletin No. 538. Lafayette, Ind.: Purdue University, September 1949.

PULINO, LEONARDO A., "A Recursive Model of the U.S. Domestic Soybean Market." Ph.D. dissertation, Michigan State University, 1966.

ROCKWELL, CHARLES S., "Profits, Normal Backwardation, and Forecasting in Commodity Futures." Ph.D. dissertation, University of California at Berkeley, 1964.

SAMUELSON, PAUL., "Intertemporal Price Equilibrium; A Prologue to the Theory of Speculation," *Weltwirtschaftliches Archiv,* December 1957, pp. 181–219.

——, "Proof that Properly Anticipated Prices Fluctuate Randomly," *Industrial Management Review,* 6 (Spring 1965), 41–49.

SARGENT, THOMAS J., "Commodity Price Expectations and the Interest Rate," *Quarterly Journal of Economics,* 83 (February 1969), 126–40.

SHEPHERD, GEOFFREY S., *Agricultural Price Analysis.* Ames: Iowa State University Press, 1966.

TELSER, LESTER G., "A Theory of Speculation Relating Profitability and Stability," *Review of Economic Studies,* 41 (August 1959), 295–301.

———, "The Supply of Speculative Services in Wheat, Corn and Soybeans," *Food Research Institute Studies,* 7, Supp. (1967), 131–76.

TEWELES, J., C. V. HARLOW, and H. L., STONE, *The Commodity Futures Trading Guide.* New York: McGraw-Hill, 1969.

TOBIN, J., "Liquidity Preference as Behavior Toward Risk," *Review of Economic Studies,* 25 (February 1948), 240–262.

UNITED NATIONS, *Food and Agricultural Organization: Production Yearbook,* New York: 1962–72.

———, *Food and Agricultural Organization: Trade Yearbook,* New York: United Nations, 1962–72.

U.S. DEPARTMENT OF AGRICULTURE, *Crop Production Reports, Prospective Plantings Report, and Annual Summary,* Washington, D.C.: U.S. Gov't. Printing Office, 1961–72.

———, *Fats and Oils Situation Reports.* Washington, D.C.: U.S. Gov't. Printing Office, 1961–72.

———, *Food Grain Statistics.* Washington, D.C.: U.S. Gov't. Printing Office, 1961–72.

———, *Grain Market News.* Washington, D.C.: U.S. Gov't. Printing Office, 1961–72.

———, *The Feed Situation Report.* Washington, D.C.: U.S. Gov't. Printing Office 1961–72.

———, *Wheat Situation Report.* Washington, D.C.: U.S. Gov't. Printing Office 1961–72.

———, *Margins, Speculation and Prices in Grains Futures Markets.* Washington, D.C.: Economic Research Service, December 1967.

U. S. DEPARTMENT OF COMMERCE, *The Survey of Current Business.* Washington, D.C.: U.S. Gov't. Printing Office, 1967–72.

———, *The Quarterly Stock of Grain in All Positions Report.* 1967–72.

WARNER, D., "An Econometric Study of the World Wheat Economy." Ph.D. dissertation, Princeton University, 1979.

WOLD, H. O., "Nonlinear Estimation by Iterative Least Squares Procedures," in *Festschrift for J. Neyman,* ed. New York: John Wiley, 1966.

WOOD, D. B., ed., "The Use of The Earth Resources Technology Satellite (ERTS) for Crop Production Forecasts." Draft of final report of the Task Force on Agricultural Forecasting, Goddard Space Flight Center, July 24, 1974.

WORKING, HOLBROOK, "The Investigation of Economic Expectations," *American Economic Review,* 39, No. 3, May 1949, pp. 150–166.

———, "Theory of the Inverse Carrying Charge in Futures Markets," *Journal of Farm Economics,* 30 (February 1948), 1–28.

———, "The Theory of Price of Storage," *American Economic Review,* 39 (December 1949), 1, 43–62.

———, "A Theory of Anticipatory Prices," *American Economic Review,* 48 (May 1958), 188–99.

20

FINANCIAL SECTOR ANALYSIS

||||||||||||||||||||||||||||||||||||||||||||||||||||||||||||||||||||||||||||||||||||||||||||||||||||||||||||||||||

1 INTRODUCTION

The determination of interest rates from either microeconomic or macroeconomic theoretical foundations has not found a consensus among economists or market practitioners. Economic theory notwithstanding, the importance of finding good predictors for the spectrum of interest rates has spawned competition among model builders.

The model of the financial sector presented in this chapter combines a bank reserves approach to short-term interest rate determination with a structural model of the corporate bond market based upon the flow of funds accounts.[1] It is designed for quarterly forecasting with special emphasis on Federal Reserve policy. The long-term interest rate is determined by the clearing of the bond market rather than by the use of reduced-form, term-structure equations, models.

Many financial sector models employ reduced-form approaches to determine various financial yields by aggregating different financial assets by risk and maturity class. This approach may be analytically unacceptable. It ignores the possibility of market segmentation and the important role of market structure. Recent work in efficient markets and rational expectations

1. This model is an adaptation of one developed by N. Sheflin (1979).

358

cast doubt on the appropriateness of the term structure equations used in such models. While flow of funds models that determine asset yields through the clearing of specific markets have been developed, few have been designed or found suitable for forecasting and investment analysis purposes. The model presented here incorporates this flow of funds approach in a standard framework and does so with the intent of providing an efficient forecasting mechanism.

The model makes special efforts to accommodate alternative Federal Reserve policies. It is structured to reflect and switch between either a federal funds rate target or a monetary aggregate target. In the former case the federal funds rate target is treated as an exogenous variable. The federal funds rate is linked to the level of free reserves and the corresponding value of unborrowed reserves. Unborrowed reserves in turn also enters the banking sector through demand deposits which in turn helps determine the money supply. The three-month T-bill rate is solved for through the equilibration of the banking sector relationships. In the latter case, the money supply target is treated as an exogenous variable. This in turn helps determine deposits and unborrowed reserves. The three-month T-bill rate is then solved as before and the federal funds rate is obtained from the level of free reserves. These two different policy structures were estimated and can be simulated depending on which policy version is "switched on."

While the model is small, it produces reasonable and stable asset demand and supply equations over a volatile sample period covering 1960 through 1975. The model also produces reasonable in-sample solutions for the corporate bond rate and T-bill rate.

2 HIGHLIGHTS OF MODEL STRUCTURE

The model provides estimates for up to 26 variables in the financial sector, depending on the operational objective of Federal Reserve policy. These variables are summarized in Table 20.1.

The complete model consists of 22 stochastic equations, 8 identities, and a set of structural switching rules to reflect Federal Reserve policy. The basic structure of the system is as follows: The sectoral supply and demand for corporate bonds (CB), dependent on various financial yields and flows, and real sector variables, serves to determine the bond rate. The demand for reserves, dependent on the volume of deposits and the desire for free reserves by banks, together with nonborrowed reserves, determines the market yield on 90-day treasury bills. Commercial loans depend on the treasury bill yield and the bond rate and in turn are an important determinant of free reserves. Among the major endogenous variables are the sectoral CB flows; the bond, treasury bill, and commercial loan rates; deposits; free reserves; and commer-

Table 20.1

ENDOGENOUS VARIABLES

CBAMSA	= Net purchases of corporate bonds—mutual savings banks
CBALIA	= Net purchases of corporate bonds—life insurance companies
CBPAPPA	= Net purchases of corporate bonds—private pension funds
CBASRA	= Net purchases of corporate bonds—state and local government retirement funds
CBAOIA	= Net purchases of corporate bonds—other insurance companies
CBAHHA	= Net purchases of corporate bonds—households
CBABCL	= Net issues of corporate bonds—nonfinancial corporate business
CBAFCL	= Net issues of corporate bonds—finance companies
TMAMSL	= Deposit flows at mutual savings banks
RMALIL	= Flow of life insurance reserves less policy loans
FMSDA	= Demand deposit component of the money stock
FMSTD	= Time deposit component of the money stock
FCMFR	= Free reserves
FCLICX	= Commercial loans
FYRCL	= Rates on commercial loans
FMSCU	= Currency
FYGL	= Rate on long-term government bonds
FYCP	= Rate on six-month commercial paper
FSPHGM	= Rate on state and local government bonds
FYMR	= Rate on FHA-insured residential mortgages
FYSM3	= Market yield on three-month treasury bills
FGMA	= Market yield on Government National Mortgage Association certificates
FCB	= AAA corporate bond rate
FFR	= Federal funds rate: alternative exogenous target
MS	= Money supply: alternative exogenous target
FCMRUB	= Unborrowed reserves

cial loans. Exogenous are all real sector variables including the household and business sector deficits, various Federal Reserve policy instruments, and several financial assets and yields.

The money supply measures are linked back to the federal funds rate through the required reserve identity and the free reserves relationship. This linkage brings the federal funds rate and money supply—the two alternative Federal Reserve "targets"—together. Insofar as unborrowed reserves is a reasonable measure of Federal Reserve open market operations (see De-Leeuw 1969), the possibility arises that Federal Reserve money market stability and money supply objectives may be at odds under certain conditions. This problem and its handling in this model warrant some comment.

For some time, perhaps as early as 1969, the Federal Reserve has pursued two operation targets: short-run money market stability and long-run growth in monetary aggregates. As Meek and Cox (1966) point out, the former is a long-standing responsibility of the Federal Reserve and has been affected through short-term open market operations designed to avoid or reduce sharp jumps in the federal funds rate. Frequently, since 1969–70 the Federal Reserve also has aimed its open market operations toward adequate rates of growth in money supply in order to help the economy achieve employment and output goals or to help curb inflation. Typically, the money market operations have a short-term seasonal character owing to seasonal changes in currency float and other technical factors (see Meek and Cox 1966). However, open market operations aimed at influencing the rate of growth in monetary aggregates tend to focus on long-term trends in net new or unborrowed reserves. At any point in time, open market operations may have to face the needs of both policy objectives and the necessary open market operations may be at odds with one another.

In practice, it appears that open market operations tend to follow a switching policy that focuses on money market conditions (or monetary aggregates) until such time that departures from money supply goals (or money market conditions) require more open market attention. In an operational modeling context, these switches in policy can be reflected in the alternate exogeneity of the federal funds rate and money supply. On the one hand, when the federal funds rate is the primary target, its "desired" value (and some range around it) may be treated as an exogenous variable that helps determine nonborrowed reserves and, in turn, influences money supply and credit. On the other hand, when conditions are such that money supply and credit are dominant considerations, then money supply may be treated as an exogenous "target" variable. In this case the deposit equation and reserve identities are used to solve for unborrowed reserves, free reserves, and the implicit federal funds rate. In a forecasting-simulation mode the actual switching between Federal Reserve "target" variables must be determined judgmentally outside the model by seasonal considerations, rates of inflation, and the size, length, and the severity of the departure of the federal funds rate and/or money supply from their targets.

The "target" values of the federal funds rate and money supply also are determined outside the model. These values and their "acceptance intervals" are designed to reflect the most recent Federal Reserve policy announcements, market anticipations, or possibilities.

A total of 30 equations define the model. The general character of each is summarized in Table 20.2. The equations, of course, vary widely in their estimated form: Some are estimated in first differences and others in logs; some exogenous variables have elaborate distributed lags and some have none. The specific set of equations used and their precise form depend on the Federal Reserve policy target selected.

In general the estimation results produce interest rate estimates with standard errors ranging from 11 basis points on the long-term government bond rate to 38 basis points on the commercial paper rate. The integrated simulation of the model over the estimation period produced root mean

Table 20.2

MODEL SUMMARY

Net Purchases of Corporate Bonds
   Mutual Savings Banks
      $CBAMSA = M(CBSMSA_{-1}, FUYTAA, FYGM3, TMAMSL, SD1, SD2, SD3)$
      $TMASL \quad = B(TMSMSL, KNAFA, FYGM3, KNAFA, NAFA1, T)$
   Life Insurance Companies
      $CBALIA \quad = L(RMSLIL, FYGM3, FYUTAA, SD1, SD2, SD3)$
      $RMALIL \quad = R(RMSLIL, KNAFA, FYGM3, NAFA1)$
   Private Pension Funds
      $CBPAPPA = P(RPAPDL, FYUTAA, P8CPI, CBSPPA_{-1})$
   State and Local Government Retirement Funds
      $CBASRA \quad = S(RPSSRL_{-1}, FYUTAA, FSPMGM, CBSSRA, RPASRL, RMSLIL, SD1,$
                  $SD2, SD3, t)$
   Other Insurance Companies
      $CBAOIA \quad = I(CBAOIA_{-1}. PPSOIL, GSPHGM, FYUTAA)$
   Households
      $CBAHHA \quad = H(CBSHHA_{-1}, KNAFA, FYUTAA, FYGL, FYGM3, NAFA1)$
Net Issues of Corporate Bonds
   Nonfinancial Corporate Business
      $CBABCL \quad = N(CBSBCL, KDEFB1, FYUTAA, FYGM3, M12CBS, GIN, GUP, CLICX)$
   Finance Companies
      $CBAFCL \quad = F(CTAHHL, FYUTAA, FYGM3, M12CBS, FCLICS, W2)$
      where $W2 = CTSHHL_{-1} + FCLICX_{-1}$
Bond Market Clearing Constraint (to solve for equilibrium quantity and rate)
      $CBABCL + CBAFCL + SRESID = CBAMSA + CBALIA + CBAPPA + CBASRA$
                          $+ CBAOIA + CBAHIA + DRESID$

Money and Credit
   Demand Deposits Component of the Money Stock
      $FMSDA \quad = D(GNP, FMSDA_{-1}, GNP72, FYGM3, FYRTD, RFYGM3)$
   Time Deposits at Commercial Banks
      $FMSTD \quad = T(FMSTD_{-1}, GNP, FYRTD, FYGM3, GNP72, KNAFA, GD)$
   Commercial Loans
      $FCLICX \quad = C(FCLICX_{-1}, GV, FIVA, DEFB1, GNP, GV, FIVA, FYGM3, FYRCE,$
                  $KDEFB1, M12RAT)$
   Currency
      $FMSCU \quad = K(FMSCU_{-1}, GC, FYUTAA)$
   Money Supply
      $MS \quad = FMSDA + FMSTED = FMSCU$
Bank Reserves
   Nonborrowed Reserves Identity (to solve for T-bill rate)
      $FCMRNB = FCMFR + RRDD \cdot RATDD*(FMSGD + FMSDA) + RRTD + RATTD$
                          $*FMSTD$
   Free Reserves (for money supply target)
      $FCMRF \quad = FR(FCMFR_{-1}, S, FYGM3, FYGD, FYGM3, DRES, DCL, DRR)$
      $DRES \quad = (1 - RR)(FCMRNB - FCMRNB_{-1})$
      $DCL \quad = RRDD(FCLICX - FCLICX_{-1})$
      $DRR \quad = FMSDA_{-1}(RRDD - RRDD_{-1}) + FMSTD_{-1}(RRTD - RRTD_{-1})$
      $S \quad = .25*(FMSDA_{-1} + FMSDA_{-2} + FMSDA_{-3} + FMSDA_{-4})$

Table 20.2—Continued

Free Reserves (for federal funds rate target)

$\qquad$ $FFR \qquad = FR(FCMFR)$

Interest Rates

Rate on Commercial Loans

$\qquad$ $FYRCL \qquad = CL(FYRCL_{-1}, GYGM3, M12RCS, FMSTED, FMSDA, FCLICX, FYUTAA)$

Rate on Long-Term Government Bonds

$\qquad$ $FYGL \qquad = G(FYGL_{-1}, FYUTAA)$

Rate on Six-Month Commercial Paper

$\qquad$ $FYCP \qquad = CPC(FYGM3)$

Rate on State and Local Government bonds

$\qquad$ $FSPHGM \qquad = MU(FYUTAA, FSPHGM)$

Rate on FHA-Insured Residential Mortgages

$\qquad$ $FYMR \qquad = RM(FYGM3, FYUTAA)$

Rate on Eight Percent GNMA Certificates

$\qquad$ $FGMA \qquad = GM(FYMR)$

Mnemonics for Equation Summary

$CBAMSA$	= Net purchases of corporate bonds—mutual savings banks
$CBSMSA$	= Stock of corporate bonds—mutual savings banks
$FYUTAA$	= Yield on new issues of AAA corporate utility bonds
$FYSM3$	= Market yield on three-month treasury bills
$TMAMSL$	= Flow of deposits at mutual savings banks
$TMSMSL$	= Stock of deposits at mutual savings banks
$SD1$	= Seasonal dummy variable = 1 in quarter 1
$SD2$	= Seasonal dummy variable = 1 in quarter 2
$SD3$	= Seasonal dummy variable = 1 in quarter 3
$CBALIA$	= Net purchases of corporate bonds—life insurance companies
$RMSLIL$	= Stock of reserves minus policy loans—life insurance companies
$RMALIL$	= Flow of reserves minus policy loans—life insurance companies
$CBAPPA$	= Net purchases of corporate bonds—private pension funds
$RPAPPL$	= Flow of reserves—private pension funds
$P8CPI$	= Eight-quarter moving average of percent change in CPI
$CBSPPA$	= Net purchase of corporate bonds—private pension funds
$CBASRA$	= Net purchases of corporate bonds—state and local government retirement funds
$RPSSRL$	= Stock of reserves—state and local government retirement funds
$FSPHSM$	= Yields on high-grade municipal bonds
$CBSSRA$	= Stock of corporate bonds—state and local government retirement funds
$RPASRL$	= Flow of reserves—state and local government retirement funds
$TIME$	= Time trend 1 = 1960/1
$CBAOIA$	= Net purchases of corporate bonds—other insurance companies
$PPSOIL$	= Stock of policies payable—other insurance companies
$CBAHHA$	= Net purchases of corporate bonds—households
$KNAFA$	= Cumulative net accumulation of financial assets—households
$CBSHHA$	= Stock of corporate bonds—households
$FYGL$	= Market yields on long-term government bonds (FRB)
$NAFA1$	= Net accumulation of financial assets—households
$CBABCL$	= Net issues of corporate bonds—nonfinancial corporate business
$CBSBCL$	= Stock of corporate bonds—nonfinancial corporate business
$M12CBS$	= Twelve-month moving average spread between $FYUTAA$ and $FYGM3$

Table 20.2—Continued

GIN	= Nonresidential fixed investment (NIA)
*KDEFB*1	= Cumulative financing deficit
SUP	= Undistributed profits (NIA)
FCLICX	= Stock of commercial and industrial loans of commercial banks
CBAFCL	= Net issues of corporate bonds—finance companies
CTSHHL	= Stock of household consumer credit liabilities
SRESID	= Exogenous supply component
DRESID	= Exogenous demand component
FCMRNB	= Nonborrowed reserves
FCMRB	= Borrowed reserves
FCMFR	= Free reserves
RRDD	= Implicit weighted reserve requirement against demand deposits
RATDD	= Ratio of member bank to total demand deposits
FMSGD	= Demand deposit component of the money stock
RRTD	= Reserve requirement against time deposits
RATTD	= Ratio of member bank to total time deposits
FMSTD	= Time deposits (including large negotiable CDs)
GNP	= Gross National Product
*GNP*72	= Gross National Product (1972 dollars)
FYRTD	= Average yield on passbook savings deposits at commercial banks
*RFYGM*3	= Ratio of T-bill yield to past peak
GD	= Implicit GNP deflator
*DCD*1	= Dummy variable for CD ceiling = 1 in 66/3, 66/4, 68/2, 69/1, 70/2
FYGD	= Discount rate at N.Y. Federal Reserve Bank
GV	= Change in inventories
GIVA	= Inventory valuation adjustment
*FYRC*1	= Rate on commercial loans
*M*12*RAT*	= Twelve-month moving average of *FCLICX/KDEFB*1
*M*12*RCS*	= Twelve-month moving average of *FYRC*1*-FYGM*3
FMSCU	= Currency component of the money stock
GC	= Consumption
FYMR	= Rate on FHA-insured residential mortgages
FFR	= Federal funds rate

square errors on the interest rate variables ranging from 37 basis points for the corporate bond sector to 56 basis points for the commercial loan rate.

3   MODEL APPLICATION: Hedging and Speculative Decisions as of October 1, 1979

As of October 1, 1979, the rate of inflation had been growing at or near double digit rates for several months. The president of the United States had announced intentions of stabilizing prices and a new chairman had been appointed to the Board of Governors of the Federal Reserve. Although many analysts in the financial markets anticipated credit tightening by the Federal Reserve in order to help dampen rising prices, their expectations as to the timing and intensity of such a move varied widely. Although similar economic conditions existed in late 1972 and the Federal Reserve subsequently embarked on a policy that raised short-term interest rates 300 basis points in a short period, the political and economic conditions through the third quarter of 1979 mitigated against an imminent repeat of those actions. A gradual but firm tightening was believed to be more likely in the first or second quarter of 1980: After all, the Federal Reserve chairman was new to his post and economic indicators were mixed as to the future direction of the economy.

Regardless of the political and economic climate, the time to hedge or speculate against a possible rise in interest rates is before the rise takes place. This could be accomplished by taking appropriate positions and actions in the futures markets. If the markets remained stable these positions could be switched forward as the futures contracts neared maturity. Moreover, stop-loss orders could be entered to liquidate the futures contracts in order to reduce mounting opportunity losses owing to an unanticipated lowering of interest rates. While the timing and intensity of future Federal Reserve actions were not clear, a consensus emerged among market analysts that if the Federal Reserve embarked on a money- and credit-tightening policy, near-term rates ultimately would rise by a few hundred basis points. A survey of analysts and reports in leading financial publications produced the profile of changes in the federal funds rate shown in Figure 20.1. The anticipated changes in the

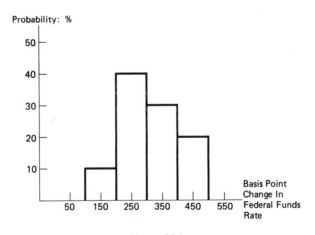

Figure 20.1

PROBABILITY PROFILE OF ANTICIPATED CHANGE
IN THE FEDERAL FUNDS RATE

federal funds rate together with no change or simple growth rate extrapolations for the other exogenous variables in the model produced the distributions of rates for commercial paper, three-month treasury bills, long-term government bonds, GNMAs, and AAA corporate bonds given in Table 20.3.

Table 20.3

ESTIMATED PROBABILITY DISTRIBUTIONS OF
SELECT RATES OF INTEREST

INTEREST RATE INTERVAL

INSTRUMENT	8–9 %	9–10 %	10–11 %	11–12 %	12–13 %	13–14 %	14–15 %	15–16 %	EXPECTED VALUE
Commercial Paper					.20	.40	.20	.20	13.90
Three-Month Treasury Bills			.10	.40	.30	.20			12.55
Long-Term Government Bonds		.90	.10						10.05
GNMAs	.30	.60	.10						9.75
AAA Corporate Bonds	.30	.60	.10						9.75

As of October 1, 1979, the implicit rates of interest on March 1980 futures contracts were 12.40, 10.00, 9.20, and 9.85 percent per annum for commercial paper, treasury bills, long-term government bonds, and GNMAs, respectively. While a perfect correspondence for AAA corporate bonds does not exist in the futures markets, a combination of existing futures contracts does offer an approximation. One such approximation is the following:

AAA corporate bond rate = .71 Long-term Gov't rate + .29 GNMA rate

This implies an effective March 1980 futures rate of 9.36 for AAA corporate bonds.

For a $10 million long position in each of these instruments the investor could take the following hedge positions in the futures markets:

Commercial Paper
    Long 10 March 80 contracts at 12.40 or better
    Stop-loss order at 12.00

Three-Month Treasury Bills
    Short 10 March 80 contracts at 90.00 or better
    Stop-loss order at 90.40

Long-Term Government Bonds
    Short 100 March 80 contracts at 86.50 or better
    Stop-loss order at 87.00

GNMA Certificates
    Short 100 March 80 contracts at 81.50 or better
    Stop-loss order at 82.00

AAA Corporate Bonds
    Short 70 March 80 long-term government bonds at 86.50 or better
    Short 30 March 80 GNMAs at 81.50 or better
    Stop-loss order at any combination producing a yield of less than 9.16

For speculative purposes one must also consider the odds of capturing profitable differentials. The current interest rates on futures contracts together with the projected interest rate profiles from the model give rise to the probability distributions of speculative profits summarized in Table 20.4.

Table 20.4

DISTRIBUTION OF BASIS POINT DIFFERENTIALS BETWEEN
PROJECTED CASH MARKET RATES AND CURRENT MARCH 80
FUTURES MARKET RATES

	BASIS POINT DIFFERENTIAL							
	(March 80 Futures Rate–Projected Cash Market Rate)							
INSTRUMENT	0–50	50–100	100–150	150–200	200–250	250–300	300–350	350–400
Commercial Paper			.20	.30	.30	.10	.10	
Three-Month Treasury Bills			.20	.30	.30	.10	.10	
Long-Term Government Bonds	.90	.10						
GNMAs	.90	.10						
AAA Corporate Bonds	.90	.10						

With minimally acceptable odds of 4 to 1 and a minimally acceptable profit of 150 basis points for commercial paper and three-month treasury bills and 50 basis points for long-term government bonds, GNMAs, and AAA corporate bonds, the following speculative positions would be taken in the interest rate futures market:

Commercial Paper
        Long March 80 at any rate up to 13.45
        Short March 80 at any rate over 14.70
Three-Month Treasury Bills
        Short March 80 at any price down to 88.50
        Long March 80 at any price below 87.50
Long-Term Government Bonds
        Short March 80 at any price down to 86.50
        Long March 80 at any price below 86.05
GNMAs
        Short March 80 at any price down to 80.60
        Long March 80 at any price below 80.15
AAA Corporate Bonds
        Short 7 March 80 long-term governments at any price down to 86.50
        Short 3 March 80 GNMAs at any price down to 80.60
        Long 7 March 80 long-term governments at any price below 86.05
        Long 3 March 80 GNMAs at any price below 80.15

New simulations are made and revised in response to new information. In retrospect the application of the model offered profit opportunities. While the forecasts were not perfect, the direction and relative positioning of rates were captured. The suggested futures positions, for a rise in rates, would have faired well.

4 SUMMARY

A primary objective of this model is to predict a handful of major interest rates. They include the rate on commercial loans, the rate on long-term government bonds, the rate on six-month commercial paper, the rate on state and local government bonds, FHA insured residential mortgages, the rate on eight percent GNMA mortgages, the three-month Treasury bill rate and, depending on the version employed, Federal Reserve policy. Moreover, the model gives high relief to the flow of funds among the major economic sectors of the economy as well as special detail for the banking sector.

Through its design the model exemplifies a practical econometric model: it offers simulation of future interest rates and other select variables from a rich selection of sources that the user may vary. In this way it provides not only predictions but sensitivity analyses and insight into the workings of the financial sector. As with most econometric models, its decision frequency is longer term and is a complement to shorter-term technical analyses. The application of the model focuses on its use for hedging and speculation in the cash and futures markets. In this context the statistical accuracy of the model is used to help determine stop-loss positions. The exact positions taken in the markets, of course, are dictated in part by liquidating considerations as well as by the trading horizon and cash position of the user.

5 BIBLIOGRAPHY

BAIN, A. D., "Surveys in Applied Economics: Flow of Funds Analysis," *Economic Journal,* December 1973, pp. 1055–93.

BOARD OF GOVERNORS OF THE FEDERAL RESERVE SYSTEM, *Introduction to Flow of Funds.* Washington, D.C.: Board of Governors of the Federal Reserve System, February 1975.

——, *Flow of Funds Accounts 1946–1975.* Washington, D.C.: Board of Governors of the Federal Reserve System, 1976.

——, *Quarterly Econometric Model.* Washington, D.C.: Board of Governors of the Federal Reserve System, March 1977*a*.

——, *Flow of Funds Accounts, Assets and Liabilities Outstanding 1965–1976.* Washington, D.C.: Board of Governors of the Federal Reserve System, December 1977*b*.

————, *Federal Reserve Bulletin.* Washington, D.C.: Board of Governors of the Federal Reserve System, March 1978*a*.

————, *Flow of Funds Accounts, Second Quarter 1978, Revisions for 1972–1977*. Washington, D.C.: Board of Governors of the Federal Reserve System, 1978*b*.

BOSWORTH, BARRY, and JAMES S. DUESENBERRY, *A Flow of Funds Model and Its Implications.* Washington, D.C.: The Brookings Institution, Technical Reprint T005, 1974.

BRAINARD, WILLIAM C., and TOBIN, JAMES, "Pitfalls in Financial Model Building," *American Economic Review*, 57 (May 1968), 99–122.

CAGAN, PHILLIP, and ROBERT E. LIPSEY, *The Financial Effects of Inflation.* Cambridge, Mass.: Ballinger Publishing Co., 1978.

CHOW, G. C., "Tests of Equality between Subsets of Coefficients in Two Linear Regressions," *Econometrica*, 28 (1960), 591–605.

CHRIST, CARL F., "Econometric Models of the Financial Sector," *Journal of Money, Credit and Banking*, 3, pt. 2 (May 1971), 252–69.

COPELAND, MORRIS A., *A Study of the Money Flows in the United States.* New York: National Bureau of Economic Research, 1952.

CRAINE, ROGER, ARTHUR HAVENNER, and JAMES BERRY. "Fixed Rules vs. Activism in the Conduct of Monetary Policy," *American Economic Review*, 68 (December 1978), 769–83.

DELEEUW, FRANK, "A Model of Financial Behavior," in *The Brookings Quarterly Econometric Model of the United States*, ed. J. S. Duesenberry et al. Chicago: Rand McNally, 1965.

————, "A Condensed Model of Financial Behavior," *The Brookings Model: Some Further Results*, Chicago: Rand McNally, 1969.

DOUGALL, HERBERT E., and JACK E. GAUMNITZ, *Capital Markets and Institutions*, 3rd ed., Englewood Cliffs, N. J.: Prentice-Hall, Inc., 1975.

DUESENBERRY, J. S., "A Process Approach to Flow of Funds Analysis," in *The Flow-of-Funds Approach to Social Accounting, a Report of the National Bureau of Economic Research*, pp. 173–94. Princeton N.J.: Princeton University Press, 1962.

————, and B. BOSWORTH, "Policy Implications of a Flow-of-Funds Model," *Journal of Finance, Papers and Proceedings*, May 1974, pp. 331–63.

DURBIN, J. "Testing for Serial Correlation in Least Squares Regression When Some of the Regressors are Lagged Dependent Variables," *Econometrica*, 1970, pp. 410–21.

DUTTA, M., N. SHEFLIN, and H. NEUMANN, "Iterative Instrumental Variables Estimation of the Wharton Quarterly Econometric Model of the United States." New Brunswick, N. J.: Rutgers University, 1975. Mimeographed.

ENZLER, JARED, LEWIS JOHNSON, and JOHN PAULUS, "Some Problems of Money Demand," *Brookings Papers on Economic Activity*, 1 (1976).

FRIEDMAN, BENJAMIN M., "A Structural Model of the Long-Term Corporate

Debt Market." Discussion Paper No. 348, Harvard Institute of Economic Research, February 1974.

———, "Substitution and Expectation Effects on Long-Term Borrowing Behavior and Long-Term Interest Rates." Harvard University, July 1976, rev. Mimeographed.

———, "Financial Flow Variables and the Short-Run Determination of Long-Term Interest Rates," *Journal of Political Economy*, 85 (August 1977), 513–41.

GOLDFELD, STEPHEN M., *Commercial Bank Behavior and Economic Activity*. Amsterdam: North Holland Publishing Co., 1966.

———, "The Demand for Money Revisited," *Brookings Papers on Economic Activity*, 3 (1973), 577–646.

———, "The Case of the Missing Money," *Brookings Papers on Economic Activity*, 3 (1976), 683–730.

GRAMLICH, E. M., and J. H. KALCHBRENNER, "A Constrained Estimation Approach to the Demand for Liquid Assets." Federal Reserve Board Special Studies Paper No. 3, December 1969.

HALL, BRONWYN, "Time Series Processor Users Manual Version 3.2." 1975. Mimeographed.

HENDERSHOTT, P. H., "Recent Development of the Financial Sector of Econometric Models," *Journal of Finance*, March 1968, pp. 75–92.

———, *Understanding Capital Markets, Vol. 1: A Flow-of-Funds Financial Model*. Lexington, Mass.: Heath, 1977.

HENDERSON, JAMES M., and RICHARD E. QUANDT, *Microeconomic Theory: A Mathematical Approach*, 2nd ed. New York: McGraw-Hill, 1971.

JOHNSTON, J., *Econometric Methods*, 2nd ed. New York: McGraw-Hill, 1972.

KUH, EDWIN, and RICHARD L. SCHMALENSEE, *An Introduction to Applied Macroeconomics*. Amsterdam: North Holland Publishing Co., 1973.

MADDALA, G. S., *Econometrics*. New York: McGraw-Hill, 1977.

MARKOWITZ, HARRY, "Portfolio Selection," *Journal of Finance*, 7 (March 1952), 77–91.

McCARTHY, MICHAEL D., *The Wharton Quarterly Econometric Forecasting Model—Mark III*. Philadelphia: Economics Research Unit, Wharton School of Finance and Commerce, 1972.

MEEK, P. and J. W. COX, "The Banking System-Its Behavior in the Short-Run," *Monthly Review*, Federal Reserve Bank of New York, April 1966.

MODIGLIANI, FRANCO, ROBERT RASCHE, and PHILLIP J. COOPER, "Central Bank Policy, the Money Supply and the Short-Term Rate of Interest," *Journal of Money Credit and Banking*, May 1970, 200–27.

MODIGLIANI, FRANCO, and ROBERT J. SHILLER, "Inflation, Rational Expectations, and the Term-Structure of Interest Rates." *Economica,* 40 (February 1973), 12–43.

MODIGLIANI, FRANCO, and RICHARD SUTCH, "Innovations in Interest Rate Policy." *American Economic Review,* 56 (May 1966), 178–97.

NATIONAL BUREAU of ECONOMIC RESEARCH, *Machine Readable Databank Directory.* New York: National Bureau of Economic Research, 1977.

NEWBOLD, P., and C. W. J. GRANGER, "Spurious Regressions in Econometrics." *Journal of Econometrics,* 2 (July 1974), 111–20.

PORTER, RICHARD D., and EILEEN MAUSKOPF, "Some Notes on the Apparent Shift in the Demand for Demand Deposits Function." May 1978. Mimeographed.

SAMUELSON, PAUL ANTHONY, *Foundations of Economic Analysis.* New York: Atheneum, 1974.

SHEFLIN, N., "Forecasting Macro Financial Behavior: A Bank Reserves-Flow of Funds Approach." Ph.D. Dissertation, Rutgers University, 1979.

SILBER, WILLIAM L., *Portfolio Behavior of Financial Institutions.* New York: Holt, Rinehart & Winston, 1970.

TAYLOR, STEPHEN P., "Uses of Flow of Funds Accounts in the Federal Reserve System." *Journal of Finance,* 18 (May 1963), 249–58.

WHITE, WILLIAM L., "Debt Management and the Form of Business Financing." *Journal of Finance,* 29 (May 1974), 565–77.

ZWICK, BURTON, "The Market for Corporate Bonds," *Quarterly Review Federal Reserve Bank of New York,* 2 (Autumn 1977), 27–36.

21

GOLD: A Distributional Model

||||||||||||||||||||||||||||||||||||||||||||||||||||||||||||||||||||||||||||||||||||||||||||||||||||||||||||||||||

1 INTRODUCTION

The market for gold has grown dramatically in recent years and in the eyes of many has become the de facto monetary numeraire for the world. Yet despite the increasing amount of interest in the gold market, precious little has been done to develop forecasting models that reflect the structure of the market. The model presented here is a preliminary effort to meet this need. To be sure, its structure is not sacrosanct and other objectives may well require an alternative design. Be that as it may, the taxonomy and character of this model of this enigmatic commodity were guided by several considerations. Among the most important were the types of demand, the regional character of demands and supplies, the dominance of stocks in relation to production, the activities of governments, the role of price expectations and political instability, and, of course, data considerations.

Gold is a commodity traded for several reasons: It is traded as a financial asset with the hope of speculative gains, arbitrage profits, or the maintenance of asset value; it is also traded for manufacturing uses. These reasons can be reflected in two general demand categories: hoarding demand and manufacturing demand. While some analysts consider jewelry demand as a separate category, the majority consider jewelry as a not-so-disguised form of hoarding. Moreover, trading for arbitrage profits requires stocks and these stocks are also combined with other private stocks that define hoarding demand.

These demands are influenced by many factors including the level of economic activity, the rate of inflation, interest rates, and sociopolitical risk. These factors, of course, vary widely in their intensity and influence from country to country. The repositioning of other assets into gold stocks and their redistribution from one location to another can strongly influence the price of gold. This is one reason why the gold model presented here is regional in nature: The net price effects of changes in regional socioeconomic factors can be revealed and studied. The production of gold also is regional in character. It is dominated by the Soviet Union and South Africa and their actions in the market are often precipated by widely divergent considerations. Here again a regional- or country-specific analysis is required to capture and distinguish between the actions and impacts of these players.

The stock of gold is very large in comparison to net flows. Some analysts estimate the gold stock is sufficient to satisfy almost 200 years of manufacturing demand at current rates. This places special emphasis on the analysis accorded the demand for and adjustments to these stocks. Here the market for gold is divided into two "sectors": a "financial" sector that focuses on the demand for and supply of stocks by financial transactors and a "real" sector that focuses on demand flows for manufacturing and supply flows, that is, production.

In addition, private and government holdings of gold exist side by side on a world scale and, for the most part, on a country and regional scale. Yet their actions most often are dictated by different considerations or objectives. Accordingly, the model distinguishes between them. Here, government accumulation or decumulation of gold is treated as an exogenous variable.

Investor demand for gold is influenced by several factors such as wealth, rates of inflation, and interest rates. These factors notwithstanding, two considerations are generally placed above all others: price expectations and country risk, that is, political instability. While various relationships can be used to estimate price expectations a measure of country risk is either a major task or a relatively simple one. Opting for the latter, insurance rates on business offered by international insurance companies are used as a proxy. Presumably, as this risk increases the amount of gold held in that country would diminish ceteris paribus.

Owing to data constraints the model developed here divides the world gold market into the following countries and regions: North America, West Europe, Latin America, South Africa, Japan, Asia (excluding Japan), Mid East, the Soviet Union and the rest of the world. The Soviet Union is treated exogenously and the model only considers their excess demand or supply, that is, whether they are a net demander or supplier to the rest of the world. Each of the other countries is treated in a common fashion. The excess demands or supplies are solved together for a price at which they balance.

Finally, it must be noted that the individual hoarding demand equations are for private stocks located in that country—no attempt is made here to trace ownership by region or country.

In summary, the model structure is rich in its ability to estimate the effects of country-specific phenomena and trace their impacts on price and physical location. However, it offers little information on ownership save the net redistributions that can take place. From a practical perspective this limitation is not severe. The model can still reveal the effects of a change in political uncertainty in a specific region or country as well as the effects of several factors for different regions or countries. With an annual frequency of observation the model offers long-range market assessments of price directions and distributional profiles of trading activity. It is intended for use in long-term price analyses for investment purposes. In the following sections its structure is presented in more detail along with an example of its application.

2   MODEL STRUCTURE: A Summary

The model divides the world market for gold into nine countries or regions and provides estimates for 39 variables. The countries or regions and the endogenous variables are listed in Table 21.1.

Each country or region has several blocks of equations to describe their demands, supplies, and trade. On the demand side the model has a private

Table 21.1

WORLD GOLD MARKET: REGIONAL TAXONOMY AND ENDOGENOUS VARIABLES

Countries or Regions	*Endogenous Variables for Each Country or Region*
Japan	Hoarding Demand
Latin America	Industrial Demand
United States & Canada	Production
West Europe	Support Price (South Africa only)
South Africa	Excess Demand or Supply
Asia (excluding Japan)	*Endogenous Variables: World*
Soviet Union[a]	*Aggregates*
Mid East	Price Expectations
Rest of World	Equilibrium Price

[a] Exogenous

stock or hoarding demand equation and an equation for industrial demand for gold. On the supply side there is a production equation and a relationship to explain price support activity by the producer. This takes the form of a price support stock equation that could be considered another form of demand and applies only to South Africa where private hoarding is not allowed.

The trade block consists of an excess demand (+) or supply (−) identity that includes as an exogenous input the accumulation or decumulation of gold stocks by the government except for South Africa, which is treated endogenously. Also included here are balancing constraints that ensure gold inflows equal excess demand or gold outflows equal excess supply. These relationships are summarized in Table 21.2.

In addition to the country-specific relationships the model also has a world price expectations equation and exchange rate index. They are

$$PE = E(P, PS, CPI, XR)$$

$$XR = X(USBT, USY)$$

where XR is defined by a trade-weighted average of dollar/yen ($/¥) and dollar/deutschemark ($/DM) exchange rates. The model solves for the price of gold and the distribution of quantities through the world market clearing constraint

$$\sum_i EX_i = 0.$$

While a detailed summary of the model's analytical and statistical foundation is beyond the scope of this chapter, a few general comments are in order. First, the government of South Africa often enters the gold market to support the price of gold in order to maintain a favorable exchange rate. Moreover, producers often enter the market in order to maintain prices and stem inventory losses. These price support activities are the object of the price support stock equation. The price support level is estimated by a moving average of the world price.

Second, the degree of industrialization is measured by the ratio of industrial output to total output. For regions this ratio is a weighted average of the countries in the region or the ratio for the dominant country in the region depending on the availability of data. Where weights are required they are equal to a specific country's proportion of total GNP for the region.

Third, the model is annual in its frequency of observation. The price of gold is the U.S. price given by average daily spot prices on the Commodity Exchange Incorporated. Missing data were interpolated using simple averages of surrounding data.

Fourth, as noted earlier the exchange rate variable is a weighted average of $/¥ and $/DM exchange rates. The weights are normalized trade shares

Table 21.2

MODEL SUMMARY FOR A REPRESENTATIVE COUNTRY

Demand
  Hoarding

$$HD = H(WR, i, PE, R, CR, HD_{-1})$$

  Industrial

$$ID = I(GNP, P, PS, DI)$$

Production and Other Stocks
  Production

$$Q = Q(P, K)$$

  Price Support Stocks

$$SS = S(P, SP, SS_{-1})$$

Trade
  Excess Demand (+) or Supply (−)

$$EX = HD + ID - Q - (SS - SS_{-1}) - B$$

  Balancing Constraints

$$EX - \sum_j IN_j = 0, EX > 0$$

$$EX + \sum_j OUT_j = 0, EX < 0$$

Mnemonics

HD	= Hoarding demand
WR	= Wealth
i	= Rate of interest
PE	= Expected price of gold one period ahead
R	= Rate of inflation
CR	= Country risk index
ID	= Industrial demand
GNP	= Gross National Product
P	= Spot price of gold
PS	= Price index for gold substitutes in manufacturing
DI	= Degree of industrialization [(Manufacturing + Services)/Total Output]
Q	= Production of gold
K	= Production cost per unit
SS	= Price support stocks
SP	= Producer support price of gold
B	= Decumulation of central bank gold stock (+); accumulation (−)
EX	= Excess demand (+) or supply (−)
IN_j	= Gold inflow to country or region j
OUT_j	= Gold outflow to country or region j
CPIE	= Expected consumer price index one period ahead
XR	= U.S. exchange rate index
USBT	= U.S. balance of payments
USY	= U.S. Gross National Income

for Japan and Germany. No attempt is made to explain the individual exchange rates or the trade shares: In estimation and ex-post simulation actual values are used. In a forecasting mode the exchange rate variable is projected on the basis of anticipated $/¥ and $/DM exchange rates together with the most recent trade share weights.

Finally, the model was estimated and then simulated over the period from 1967 through 1979. The estimation and simulation results are mixed. On the negative side the demand and production equations for the rest of the world and production equations in general leave a lot of room for improvement: The squared coefficients of correlation range from about .70 to .90. These results are the product of several factors, including the heterogeneity of some groups and the difficulty of linking ore quality to extraction costs. Moreover, degrees of freedom were a problem and for some equations two-stage least squares could not be used. Here iterative least squares methods were used instead. These results proved to be extremely sensitive to lag structures, and a unique model remained an elusive objective. On the positive side model simulations yielded price estimates within 8 percent of actuals and provided estimates of the gold stocks for major countries and regions within 2 percent for North America and West Europe. Furthermore the empirical results supported the significance of key simulation variables including country risk and price expectations.

3 MODEL OPERATION: An Illustrative Simulation

The long-term investment application of the model begins with a set of assumptions intended to capture the possible combinations of events that are anticipated in the coming period. In the following example a set of one-period-ahead (1980) simulations were generated to reveal the effects of alternative changes in country risk for the Rest of the World, a worsening exchange rate for the United States, and large imports of grain by the Soviet Union requiring substantial sales of gold to finance these purchases. For each of these variables several alternative outcomes were considered. These alternatives are summarized in Table 21.3. The values of the other exogenous variables are either lagged and use known historical values or are forecast using no- change or constant growth rate extrapolations from their 1978–79 values.

The simulations produced the expected demands, production, and trade flows summarized in Table 21.4 and the distribution of prices given in Table 21.5. The results suggest that hoarding demand in the Rest of the World will go up by about 8.5 million ounces.

Table 21.3

ALTERNATIVE OUTCOMES FOR SELECT
DETERMINANTS OF GOLD PRICES

FACTOR	*ALTERNATIVE OUTCOME*	*PROBABILITY OF OCCURRENCE*
Rest of World Country Risk	Unchanged	.20
	Up 25%	.40
	Up 50%	.20
	Up 75%	.10
	Up 100%	.10
Soviet Net Exports of Gold	Unchanged	.05
	Up 50tons	.15
	Up 100tons	.25
	Up 150tons	.35
	Up 200tons	.10
	Up 250tons	.10
U.S. Exchange Rate	Unchanged	.10
	$ drops 5%	.60
	$ drops 10%	.20
	$ drops 15%	.10

Table 21.4

1980 EXPECTED DEMANDS, SUPPLIES, AND TRADE

REGION	*DEMAND*		*PRODUCTION*	*NET EXPORTS* (+) *OR IMPORTS* (−)
	Hoarding	Industrial		
North America	110	0.66	2.8	−3.9
Latin America	50	0.27	1.1	−1.0
West Europe	240	1.27	0.5	−6.8
Japan	12	0.25	0.2	−1.5
Asia	155	0.55	0.7	−4.3
South Africa	—	0.08	23.7	+16.0
Mid East	20	0.00	—	−4.0
Soviet Union	—	—	—	+8.5
Rest of World	51	0.25	3.4	−3.0

Millions of ounces

The investment strategies based on these results are relatively straight-forward. To be sure, the assumptions and probabilities made here are likely to change as the forecast year unfolds in actuality. This new information, of course, gives rise to new simulations and reassessments of investment strategies.

Table 21.5

DISTRIBUTION OF ESTIMATED 1980 GOLD PRICE

PRICE INTERVAL	ESTIMATED PROBABILITY	CUMULATIVE PROBABILITY GREATER THAN OR EQUAL TO	CUMULATIVE PROBABILITY LESS THAN OR EQUAL TO
∞ to 530	3.0	3.0	100.0
529 to 520	8.9	11.9	97.0
519 to 510	12.6	24.5	88.1
509 to 500	30.9	55.4	75.5
499 to 490	28.5	83.9	44.6
489 to 480	10.9	94.8	16.1
479 to 470	4.8	99.6	5.2
469 to ***	0.4	100.0	0.4

On the basis of these results, the odds are better than four to one that average gold prices in 1980 will be at least $490 an ounce. With an average 1979 spot price of about $410 an ounce (as of October 1979) there would be odds of about four to one in favor of a long position capturing an $80 profit per ounce in 1980 and an infinitesimal chance of losing money on a long position at $410 an ounce or lower. In terms of the futures markets a long position in December 1980 COMEX gold futures at $450 or better would have odds of about four to one in favor of making a $40 per ounce profit. To the extent the outcomes presented above foreshadow coming events, prudent investors should consider adding gold to their portfolio as of October 1979. Of course as these inputs change, prudent investors must reassess and adjust their positions accordingly. The model presented here offers a vehicle to help perform these calculations. In retrospect, country risks were understated and gold rose to over $800 an ounce in 1980.

4 SUMMARY

The market for gold is international in scope and byzantine in character. Despite the arguments of many scholars, it is widely regarded as an excellent financial asset. That is not to say that its price is stable. Indeed, its price is among the most volatile of commodities. While some of its price fluctuation stems from technical trading considerations, there are long-term movements in the price of gold that can be captured in an econometric structure. The model presented here gives special emphasis to the types of demand, the regional character of demand and supply, the role of stocks in relation to production, the character of production and socio-economic factors such as political instability. Although the model offers little information on ownership it does offer a logical structure that can trade the effects of country or region specific phenomena on the world price of gold and its geographic physical redistribution. Because of the paucity of data the model is annual in its frequency of observation. The application of the model, of course, is intended for long-term price analysis.

The example given demonstrates the simulation of the model. Here, three conditions were explained: (1) alternative changes in country risk for the rest of the world relative to the United States; (2) a worsening exchange rate for the United States; and (3) large sales of gold by the Soviet Union owing to poor grain harvests. Several alternative values were considered for each of these variables. These alternatives were combined with each other to generate simulations from which price profiles and their odds were constructed. These profiles, in turn, were used to assess long-term investment positions in gold. The model of course could have been used to assess the need for hedging a position in gold just as easily. Because of the annual frequency of the model, the positioning of a hedge in the futures market would have to be determined outside the model, that is, by liquidating considerations of the gold futures contracts and the precise time horizon of the hedger.

5 BIBLIOGRAPHY

BARATTIERI, V., and R. N. BROWN, "The Gold Price and Gold Output," *The Banker*, November 1973, pp. 1257–58.

BAUMOL, W. J., "Speculation, Profitability and Stability," *Review of Economics and Statistics*, August 1957, pp. 163–178.

BROWN, R. N., "Gold: Prospects for the Two-Tier System," *Journal of World Trade Law*, January-February 1971, pp. 101–10.

CAGAN, P., "The Monetary Dynamics of Hyperinflation," in *Studies in the Quantity Theory of Money*, ed. Milton Friedman, pp. 25–117. Chicago: University of Chicago Press, 1956.

CONWAY, V., "Understanding Gold and the World Gold Markets," in *Commodity Yearbook 1976*. New York: Commodity Research Bureau, 1976.

DEPARTMENT OF MINES, "Explanatory Memorandum on 'Relief to Needy Gold Mines.'" South Africa, 1968.

EDGERTON, DAVID L., "Some Properties of Two-Stage Least-Squares as Applied to Nonlinear Models," *International Economic Review*, February 1972, pp. 26–32.

FELLS, P. D., *Gold 1974*. Johannesburg: Consolidated Gold Fields, Ltd., 1974.

———, *Gold 1975*. Johannesburg: Consolidated Gold Fields, Ltd., 1975.

FRENKEL, J. A., "Inflation and the Formation of Expectations," *Journal of Monetary Economics,* 1 (1975), 403–21.

FRIEDMAN, M., "The Case for Flexible Exchange Rates," in *Essays in Positive Economics,* pp. 157–203. Chicago: University of Chicago Press, 1953.

GOLDSMITH, O. S., "Market Allocation of Exhaustive Resources," *Journal of Political Economy,* October 1974, pp. 1035–40.

Government Gazette, "Relief to Needy Gold Mines." South Africa, 1968.

HIRSCH, F., "Influences on Gold Production," IMF Staff Papers, November 1968, pp. 405–90.

HOTELLING, H., "The Economics of Exhaustible Resources," *Journal of Political Economy,* April 1931, pp. 137–75.

HOUGHTON, D. H., *The South African Economy.* London: Oxford University Press, 1964.

JOHNSON, H. G., "Destabilizing Speculation: A General Equilibrium Approach," *Journal of Political Economy,* February 1976, pp. 101–8.

KALDOR, N., "Speculation and Economic Stability," *Review of Economic Studies,* 1939–40, pp. 1–25.

KELEJIAN, HARRY H., "Two-Stage Least Squares and Econometric Systems Linear in Parameters but Nonlinear in the Endogenous Variables," *Journal of the American Statistical Association,* June 1971, pp. 373–74.

KEYNES, J. M., *The General Theory of Employment, Interest, and Money.* New York: Macmillan, 1936.

LEAMER, E. G., and R. M. STERN, *Quantitative International Economics.* Boston: Allyn and Bacon, 1970.

LERNER, ABBA P., *The Economics of Control.* New York: Macmillan, 1944.

MICHALOPOULOS, C., and R. C. VAN TASSEL, "Gold as a Commodity: Forecasts of Use in 1975," *Western Economic Journal,* June 1971, pp. 157–71.

SALANT, S., "Exhaustible Resource Cartels: A Nash-Cournet Approach." Paper presented at Econometric Society Meetings at Dallas, Texas, December 1975.

SHIRATORI, M., and R. N. BROWN, "Private Demand for Gold." Unpublished paper, IMF, 1974.

SOUTH AFRICAN GOVERNMENT, *The Official Yearbook of the Union of South Africa,* 1960.

TOBIN, JAMES, "The Theory of Portfolio Selection," in *The Theory of Interest Rates,* ed. F. Hahn and F. Brechling, ch. 1. London: Macmillan, 1965.

TOBIN, JAMES, "A General Equilibrium Approach to Monetary Theory," *Journal of Money, Credit and Banking,* 1 (1969), 15–29.

TRANSVAAL and ORANGE FREE STATE CHAMBER OF MINES, *The Outlook for Gold Mining.* Johannesburg: Gold Producers' Committee, 1974.

WARNER, D, "Econometric Study of the World Wheat Economy." Ph.D. dissertation, Princeton University, 1979.

WEINSTEIN, M. C., and R. J. ZECKHAUSER, "The Optimal Consumption of Depletable Natural Resources," *Quarterly Journal of Economics*, August 1975, pp. 371–92.

WILSON, F., *Labor in South Africa Gold Mines.* London Univ. : Cambridge: 1972.

WOLD, H., *Demand Analysis.* New York: John Wiley, 1953.

22

FOREIGN EXCHANGE

||||||||||||||||||||||||||||||||||||||||||||||||||||||||||||||||||||||||||||||||||||||||||||||||||||||||||||||||||||||||||||||||||||||||||||||

1 INTRODUCTION

Foreign currencies have become some of the most actively traded "commodities" in the world and their markets promise to grow in the foreseeable future. The impetus behind this activity, of course, is the growth of international trade. The foreign exchange markets have evolved to meet the varied needs of the market participants. Government-to-government foreign exchange transactions withstanding, arbitrage, hedging, and speculation are the primary motives for trading foreign exchange.

To meet these needs two types of currency markets have evolved: (1) the direct placement and brokered market where firms, individuals, and sometimes governments buy and sell currency among themselves at agreed-upon rates and delivery dates; and (2) the organized futures markets where contracts to buy and sell specific amounts of currency at specified dates in the future are contracted in an open outcry market. Governments, banks and private firms engage in direct placement activities and private firms and individuals dominate trade in foreign exchange futures contracts. For private traders as well as governments such as Brazil or the People's Republic of China, the futures markets offer both a substitute for, and a complement to, the direct placement markets. Arbitragers and speculators operating in both markets have helped to narrow price differentials between markets, to real-

383

locate resources over time to better meet the market's time preferences, and to redistribute risk from those seeking to avoid it to those willing to take it.

While these activities play an important efficiency role, the backbone of the direct placement and futures markets is hedging and lending activities related to international trade. Exporters, importers, and multinational corporations all contract forward foreign exchange in order to lock in profits and reduce the risks of adverse exchange rate fluctuations. Typically, the sellers or lenders of foreign exchange are financial intermediaries whose international operations form a natural basis for foreign currency balances. To be sure, international manufacturing and trading companies also perform this role. Be that as it may, the lesson of history is clear: As foreign trade expands and exchange rates are allowed to fluctuate, trading in foreign exchange will increase in volume and the markets will widen their domain of currency coverage.

Regardless of the growth in these markets, foreign exchange rate projections are important information for all market participants. The arbitrager and speculator place their positions in the different markets based on these anticipations and their relation to the average thought prevailing in the marketplace. Hedgers also consider alternative exchange rate profiles that may come to pass. For example, the investment decisions of multinationals can depend heavily on translation exposure. This exposure is a reflection of anticipated foreign exchange rate fluctuations. The direction and intensity of these fluctuations may precipitate a reconsideration of foreign investments as well as the positions the firm may take in the futures or direct placement markets. In short, long-term projections of foreign exchange rates are a necessary consideration for all foreign investors.

This chapter sets forth and illustrates the application of a model to simulate and forecast select foreign exchange rates. The model focuses on a handfull of major currencies. They include, British pounds (£), Japanese yen (¥), German marks (DM), Canadian dollars (C$), and Swiss franks (SF). While the model has a single-minded objective to forecast exchange rates between these currencies, its design characteristics are drawn among three often antagonistic goals: theoretically sound structures, data availability, and operating efficiency. To the technical analyst the model no doubt pays too much in lost operating efficiency to meet the needs of economic theory. At the same time, international trade economists are likely to cringe at some sacrifices in structure to appease data limitations and cost constraints. But econometrics is an art as well as a science for these very reasons. The model presented here is no exception to this rule.

While many applications of the model are possible, the one presented here illustrates its use in assessing the effects of alternative financial practices by a multinational enterprise faced with possible devaluation exposure. Here the costs and risks of intersubsidiary lending, futures hedging, and options are considered. The model, of course, is used to generate alternative exchange rate scenarios that give rise to the expected outcome and the odds of incurring a loss.

2 MODEL STRUCTURE

The model concentrates on trade flows and prices, in its causal structure to explain spot foreign exchange rates. Special emphasis is given to the type of imports and exports and their prices. Here three categories are studied: goods, services, and petroleum. Their prices and quantities are determined in part by domestic price indices, levels of economic activity, potential levels of economic activity, and exchange rates, among other factors. Together these considerations lead to estimates of the current account. Following an asset balance approach (Branson 1977) spot exchange rates are then estimated from the current account balances. Forward foreign exchange rates are obtained from interest rate parity relationships where the term structure of interest rates is exogenous input and combined with the spot exchange rates derived from the model.

In part, the model follows the work of Halttunen and Warner (1979) and draws on the work of others to calibrate the model. However, the model presented here differs from others on several important points owing primarily to its emphasis on forecasting. Some theoretical economic detail is passed over in favor of more practical forecasting structures. Furthermore, the estimation is Bayesian and follows procedures developed by Kalman (1960) and Sage and Melsa (1971).[1] This was done for a variety of reasons. Among the most important are the evolving nature of the data and trade shares between countries and regions.

The model contains five blocks of equations for each foreign exchange pair. The first block contains the spot exchange rate equations that relate changes in an exchange rate to the current account of each country represented in the specific exchange rate pair. The next block of equations describes the current accounts of each country as the difference in value between imports and exports of goods, services, and petroleum and the net contribution of government transfers, investment income, and other items. The import and export values of goods, services, and petroleum make up the third and fourth blocks. The import and export values are products of price indices and quantities. The price indices are estimated as adaptive-integrated autoregressive moving average models that include domestic prices and select foreign prices as explanatory variables. The quantities imported are based in part on actual and "full employment" levels of GNP. The quantities exported

1. See Chapter 14 of this text.

are based on the GNP of select other countries and an index of GNP for the rest of the world. These relationships also are estimated as adaptive-integrated auto-regressive moving average models. The last block of equations describes the GNP levels and follows the lead of Halttunen and Warner (1979) in this regard. In addition, there are accounting identities and definitions that construct estimated exchange rates from their past levels and estimated changes and construct indices from select exogenous variables. The estimated spot exchange rates together with exogenous interest rates and the interest rate parity relationships produce forward foreign exchange rates.

The model has 18 equations per country including estimated relationships, constructs and accounting identities plus 1 equation for each exchange rate. The equations defining the model are presented in Table 22.1.

Table 22.1

EXCHANGE RATE FORECASTS

Equation Summary

1. Exchange Rate Block

   $\nabla E_{ij} = \epsilon_{ij} C_i + \phi_{ij} C_j$ where i, j denote exchange rate pair, e.g., $i = \$, j = DM$

2. Current Account Block

   $C_i = (PXG_i \cdot XG_i - PMG_i \cdot MG_i) + (PXS_i \cdot XS_i - PMS_i \cdot MS_i)$
   $\quad\quad + (PXP_i \cdot XP_i - PMP_i \cdot MP_i) + G_i + Z_i + R_i$

3. Import and Export Price Block

   $PXG_i = h_i (PDG, r)$
   $PXS_i = g_i (PDS, r)$
   $PXP_i = $ Exogenous
   $PMG_i = \sum_j m_{ij} PXG_j$
   $PMS_i = \sum_j s_{ij} PXS_j$
   $PMP_i = $ Exogenous

4. Import and Export Block

   $XG_i = \sum_j m_{ij} MG_j$
   $XS_i = S_i (MS)$
   $MG_i = W_i MGS_i$
   $MS_i = (1 - W_i) MGS_i$
   $MGS_i = M_i (Y_i, \bar{Y}_i, PD_i, PMGS_i, E_{ij})$
   $PMGS_i = \lambda (PMS_i, PMG_i)$
   $MP_i = f_i (GNP_i, t, PMP)$
   $XP_i = \sum_j \theta_{ij} MP_j$

5. GNP Block

   $Y = \pi \prod_k L_k^{\alpha_k} K_k^{P_k}$, $k = $ Agriculture, Industry, Private Services, Public Services
   $\bar{K}_k = Q_k^* \cdot V_k \bar{Y}$
   $G_k = \bar{K}_k - K_k$
   $K_k = \bar{K}_k - \dfrac{G_k^*(11 - t)}{11}$ where $G^* = G$ as of 1979
   $I_k = \nabla K_k + \delta_k K_k$

Table 22.1—Continued

Mnemonics
1. Exchange Rate Block
   - ∇E_{ij} = Change in i/j exchange rate
   - ϵ_{ij} = Coefficient on current account balance for country i
   - ϕ_{ij} = Coefficient on current account balance for country j
2. Current Account Block: For Country i
   - C = Current account balance
   - G = Government transfers (exogenous)
   - Z = Other items (exogenous)
   - R = Investment income
3. Import and Export Price Block: For Country i
   - PXG = Price deflator for exports of goods
   - XG = Exports of goods in billions of 1975 dollars
   - PMG = Price deflator for imports of goods
   - MG = Imports of goods in billions of 1975 dollars
   - PXS = Price deflator for exports of nonfactor services
   - XS = Exports of nonfactor services
   - PMS = Price deflator for imports of nonfactor services
   - MS = Imports of nonfactor services
   - PXP = Price deflator of petroleum exports (exogenous)
   - XP = Exports of petroleum (exogenous)
   - PMP = Price deflator of petroleum imports (exogenous)
   - MP = Imports of petroleum in billions of 1975 dollars
   - r = Rate of interest on one-year government notes (exogenous)
4. Import and Export Block: For Country i
   - XG = Exports of goods in billions of 1975 dollars
   - XS = Exports of services in billions of 1975 dollars
   - MG = Imports of goods in billions of 1975 dollars
   - MS = Imports of services in billions of 1975 dollars
   - MGS = Imports of goods and nonfactor services
   - $PMGS$ = Price deflator for imports of goods and nonfactor services (exogenous)
   - PDG = Domestic price deflators for goods in select countries (exogenous)
   - PDP = Domestic price deflators for petroleum in select countries (exogenous)
   - PDS = Domestic price deflators for services in select countries (exogenous)
5. GNP Block: For Country i
   - Y = GNP in billions of 1975 dollars
   - $\bar{Y}$ = GNP at full employment in billions of 1975 dollars
   - $\bar{K}_k$ = Full-employment capital stock in sector k
   - L_k = Labor force in sector k (exogenous)
   - K_k = Capital stock in sector k
   - I_k = Investment in sector k
   - Q_k^* = Full-employment capital output ratio for sector k (exogenous)
   - V_k = Value added share for sector k (exogenous)
   - t = Time (exogenous)
   - δ_k = Depreciation rate for sector k (exogenous)

A large portion of the model did not have to be estimated owing to the availability of parameter estimates made by others. Here, for example, full-employment capital output ratios, depreciation rates, and full-employment–unemployment rates reflect estimates summarized by Halttunen and Warner (1979). Value added shares were calculated as moving averages of recent values and extrapolated using exponential smoothing for forecasting purposes. Estimation and extrapolation of the integrated auto-regressive moving average processes follow the procedures outlined in Chapter 16.

While it opts for parsimony in exchange for precise theoretical structures, the model in general lies within a reasonable economic framework. If the current account shows a deficit, the capital account shows a surplus and the private sector liquidates net foreign assets. This decumulation, in turn, has a short-term impact on exchange rates. Changes in exchange rates, in turn, influence trade flows and the current account which ultimately influence exchange rates. Hence, a current account deficit of country *j* will cause its currency to depreciate in the short run and a long-run dynamic adjustment of the exchange rate will be affected through the interaction of the exchange rate, trade, and GNP blocks of the model.

Although the model is rich in its dynamics and simulation capability, for changes in petroleum prices, exports, economic growth and development decisions for individual countries and regions, many of the precise structural linkages are not unique. Consequently, a number of alternative structures could be postulated that would correspond to this reduced form model: that is to say many economic interpretations are possible. This is, no doubt, a source of concern for those seeking to accept or refute a particular economic view of the world. While these issues are of interest, they are secondary to the forecasting applications of the model.

3   MODEL APPLICATION: Hedging Strategies to Reduce Potential Multinational Conversion Losses

To illustrate the use of the exchange rate model, consider the following problem faced by a multinational U.S. corporation. The parent company has made loans in early 1979 to subsidiary 1 in country 1 and loans to subsidiary 2 in country 2. The parent company is to be repaid these loans in late 1980 and must decide how to manage these repayments so as to minimize possible conversion losses. That is, it wants to minimize losses stemming from the repayment of the debts at exchange rates different from those at the time the loans were made. Because the currencies do not have a liquid foreign exchange market, currency swaps with a financial intermediary are untenable. However, the value of the currencies in country 1 and country 2 vary inversely with the $/¥ and $/DM exchange rates, respectively. To be sure, such perfect correlation is rarely encountered. But this problem may be addressed through portfolios of traded currencies (see Chapter 24).

In order to achieve its goals the parent can follow any combination of several strategies. They include taking DM and ¥ positions in the forward and/or futures markets, increasing "local" loans owed in a country with a weak currency and shifting the funds to a stronger currency, or purchasing standby commitments, that is, options to sell (or buy) currency at an agreed-upon rate.

The costs of these alternatives are not equal and depend on the size and variability of the expected currency devaluations. The purchase of yen and deutschemarks through sales of the dollar in the direct placement forward market carries a premium over spot that typically equals interest rate differentials and the expected change in the foreign exchange rates at the time of forward commitment. Here the firm runs the risk that the currency 1 and currency 2 devaluations will be larger than the DM or ¥ revaluations.

Buying yen and deutschemark futures contracts is another alternative for the firm. The difference between this alternative and similar operations in the direct placement forward market is the brokerage differential and the volatility costs of futures trading. With regard to the latter cost, stop-loss orders typically are placed in futures trading to unlock the hedge if exchange rates move against the hedge. If the rates fluctuate, the hedger may encounter "whipsaw" costs from repeatedly putting on and taking off the hedge, incurring a slight loss each time. Here the expected volatility of the exchange rates has a direct effect on the expected cost of hedging in the futures markets.

The redistribution of loans from one subsidiary to another has insignificant transaction costs but runs the risk of unanticipated exchange rate losses if the market should reverse itself or if the relative weakness of the two currencies change unexpectedly.

Finally, the parent could buy standby commitments, that is, options for given amounts of DM and yen at agreed-upon rates. Here the parent must weigh the costs of the options against the costs of the other alternatives. The cost of the option, of course, is based in part on the expected value of the currency and its variance over the period in question.

Before a decision can be made, the exchange rate profiles of the foreign currencies must be estimated. Each of the strategies mentioned above has costs and, depending on the size and variability of the exchange rate changes, one strategy may offer a superior risk-return profile.

The exchange rate profiles for yen and deutsche marks were estimated using the alternatives for the exogenous variables summarized in Table 22.2. The outcomes are considered equally likely and independent (within the one-year time horizon of the problem). These alternatives in combination and

Table 22.2

1980 SIMULATION OF
ALTERNATIVE VALUES OF SELECT EXOGENOUS VARIABLES

VARIABLE	ALTERNATIVE OUTCOMES (percent change from 1979 average levels)
Petroleum Prices	+10, +20, +30
Labor Productivity	
United States	+ 2, 0, − 2
West Germany	+ 1, + 2, + 3
Japan	+ 1, + 2, + 3
Rest of World	Unchanged
Domestic Prices	
United States	+ 7, +10, +13
West Germany	+ 3, + 5, + 7
Japan	+ 2, + 4, + 6
Domestic Rate of Interest	
United States	+15, +25, +35
West Germany	+ 5, +10, +15
Japan	+ 5, +10, +15

conjunction with no-change and simple growth rate extrapolations produce the distribution of exchange rates given in Table 22.3. The expected change in the $/¥ exchange rate is a drop of −3.25 percent. An increase of 16.5 percent is expected for the $/DM exchange rate. Thus, the foreign exchange rate of country 1 is expected to appreciate by 3.25 percent and that of country 2 is expected to drop by 16.5 percent.

Table 22.3

1980 SIMULATION OF THE PROBABILITY
DISTRIBUTION OF $/¥ AND $/DM EXCHANGE RATES

EXCHANGE RATE	ESTIMATED PROBABILITY OF PERCENT CHANGE									
	−20	−15	−10	−05	0	5	10	15	20	25
$/¥		.20	.40	.25	.15					
$/DM						.10	.15	.25	.35	.15

For a $1 million loan to both subsidiaries the cost of an option for subsidiary 2, as of September 1979, would be $100,000—based on the standard deviation of the $/DM distribution of changes in exchange rates. Because the currency of country 1 is expected to appreciate, the parent need not hedge against expected losses. Indeed, the distribution of exchange rates in this case has odds of less than one in five of resulting in a conversion loss.

The loan to subsidiary 2 also could be hedged in the futures markets. Here, 14 deutschemark futures contracts could be purchased with stop-loss orders placed 4¢ from the position price based on the hedge ratio from the option valuation (see Chapter 5). With a standard deviation of 5 percent, past experience indicates that the number of whipsaws will lie between one and three a year. Taking the worst outcome, that is, the most frequent number of whipsaws, the cost of the futures hedging strategem is $210,000: (.12 $/DM) × 1,750,000 DM.

A loan redistribution from country 2 to country 1 is virtually cost free and offers a net conversion gain. This result comes about because any amount lent by subsidiary 2 to subsidiary 1 becomes a current asset for subsidiary 2 against which subsidiary 2 can borrow local currency. By virtue of the 16.5 percent devaluation of currency 2, subsidiary 2 has a 16.5 percent gain in local currency or a 13.44 percent gain in dollars. Subsidiary 1 can use the funds from subsidiary 2 to buy short-term paper denominated in local currency. Interest on the short-term paper aside, the exchange gain by subsidiary 1 is 3 percent in local currency and 3.9 percent when converted to dollars. The exchange gain together with the intersubsidiary loan provide a gross exposure offset of 17.34 percent or a net gain of 0.84 percent, that is, $8,400. However, this is an expected outcome and there is substantial variation around it. The convolution of the exchange rate distributions given in Table 22.3 indicates an almost 10 percent chance of exchange rates moving against the loan alternative, with a loss of up to 5 percent. Hence the expected net cost of this alternative is $21,000 − $8,400 = $12,600, assuming 10 percent of the loan is hedged in the futures markets and subject to proportional whipsaw costs in alternative 2. If an option contract were taken on 10 percent of the face value, the net cost would be $1,600 for "complete" coverage.

While the outcome seems to favor a loan redistribution between subsidiaries together with an option on a portion of the face value of the exposure, the use of futures contracts together with the loan redistribution cannot be counted out. The costs associated with the option are guaranteed: The costs of the futures contract hedging are expected and a worst case at that. Thus the multinational may be faced with a choice between alternative hedging strategies that trade off increased possibilities of cost reduction against higher "fixed" costs. Because the number of observations is rather small to base much faith in probability estimates of exchange rate variability and its corresponding frequency of whipsaws, decision theory methods are not especially appealing to solve the problem. One factor that may be worth considering is the ease and cost of adding options or futures as market conditions may require. Here the liquidity of the markets for options and foreign exchange futures may outweigh a $11,000 difference for 10 percent coverage. But this issue transcends the illustration at hand and the ultimate choice is left to the hedger's preferences and the characteristics of the markets.

4 SUMMARY

A model consisting of an exchange rate block, current account block, import and export block, and a GNP block was used to simulate and forecast select exchange rates. The design features of the model considered trade-offs among theory, data availability and operating efficiency.

The focus of the model presented here is spot exchange rates and their connected trade flows. Given the interest rate parity theorem and the term structure of interest rates a complete set of conditional forward exchange rates can also be determined.

After estimation and simulation various strategies were profiled to assess cost trade-offs between options and futures hedging. While the model's forecasts and simulations suggest decisions, final hedging choices must take account of the preferences of the hedger with respect to the trade-off between the benefits of higher exposure coverage and the cost of higher exposure.

5 BIBLIOGRAPHY

ARTUS, J. R., and R. R. RHOMBERG, "A Multilateral Exchange Rate Model," *IMF Staff Papers.* 10, no. 3 (November 1973), 987–1011.

BASEVI, GEORGIO, "Commodity Trade Equations in Project Link," in *The Internation Linkage of National Economic Models,* ed. R. J. Ball. Amsterdam: North Holland Publishing Co., 1973.

BRANSON, W. H., *Asset Markets and Relative Prices in Exchange Rate Determination.* Sozialcuissiuschaftliche Annalsu, Band 1, 1977.

———, and H. HALTTUNEN, "Asset-Market Determination of Exchange Rates: Initial Empirical and Policy Results," in *Trade and Payments Adjustment Under Flexible Exchange Rates,* ed. J. P. Martin and A. Smith. London: Macmillan, 1978.

———, and P. MASSON, "Exchange Rates in the Short Run: The Dollar-Deutschemark Rate," *European Economic Review,* 2 (1978), 82–107.

BRANSON, W. H., and L. PAPAEFSTRATIOU, "Income Instability, Terms of Trade and the Change of Exchange Rate Regimes." Unpublished paper, 1978.

DAPPLER, M. C., and D. C. RIPLEY, *"The World Trade Model: Merchandise Trade,"* IMF Staff Papers, (March 1978), 240–272.

DORNBUSCH, R., and P. KRUGMAN, "Flexible Exchange Rates in the Short Run," *Brookings Papers on Economic Activity,* No. 3, 1976.

HALTTUNEN, H., and D. WARNER, *A Model of Trade and Exchange Rate Projections.* Working Paper 389. Cambridge, Mass.: National Bureau of Economic Research, Inc., 1979.

HOUTHAKKER, H. S., and S. P. MAGEE, "Income and Price Elasticities in World Trade," *Review of Economics and Statistics,* 2 (May 1969), 217–39.

JONSON, P. D., and M. W. BUTLIN, "Price and Quantity Responses to Monetary Impulses in a Model of a Small Open Economy," Research Discussion Paper 7703, Reserve Bank of Australia, July 1977.

KALMAN, R. E. "A New Approach to Linear Filtering and Prediction Problems," *Trans. ASME, Series D, J. Basic Engr.,* Vol. 82, 34–45, 1960.

SAGE, A. P., and J. L. MELSA, *Estimation Theory with Applications to Communications and Control,* New York: McGraw-Hill, 1971.

SAMUELSON, L., "A New Model of World Trade," *OECD Economic Outlook,* Occasional Studies, December 1973.

STERN, R. M., J. FRANCIS, and B. SCHUMACHER, eds., *Price Elasticities in International Trade.* London: Macmillan, 1976.

TAPLIN, G. B., "A Model of World Trade," in *The International Linkage of National Economic Models,* ed. R. J. Ball. Amsterdam: North Holland Publishing Co., 1973.

V

TRADING OPERATIONS:
Theory, Guidelines, and Examples

All commodity trading must weigh return against risk. In an operational context this involves the recurrent determination of trading prices and quantities for different commodities and different time horizons for given degrees of risk and risk preference. These considerations in turn involve three tasks: the specification of trading strategies and tactics, the selection and management of a commodity portfolio, and the integration of multicommodity trading operations.

All commodity trading involves the specification of trading guidelines regardless of whether one is buying or selling outright positions or spreads or is hedging. These guidelines can be used to help determine the price at which a speculative position should be taken, at what price to stop losses, and at what price to take profits. The specification of trading strategies and tactics also facilitates ex-post assessments of trading performance which in turn is vital information for improving future trading performance.

Portfolio selection and management is always an important consideration to commodity traders. Many commodities have technical linkages to some commodities but are independent of others and inversely correlated with still others. These varying degrees of interconnectedness open opportunities for trading and taking positions that in combination may be more profitable for any given level of risk than an equivalent monetary investment in a single asset. These potential benefits from diversification apply to hedgers as well as speculators. Often an asset to be hedged does not have a corresponding futures or option contract. This lack of correspondence may be in the commodity or in the time horizon or both. Here, combinations of available commodity contracts may provide the hedging assurance required despite apparent differences in commodity type and timing between the asset of reference and the hedging vehicle.

A multicommodity operation requires the integration of these activities into a coordinated effort if the firm's resources are to be used most efficiently. To be sure, the various trading desks of a multicommodity trading operation may be profitable when they trade independent of one another. Nevertheless, they may be even more profitable when their operations are integrated: Working together they may uncover combinations of trading opportunities that otherwise would go unnoticed or with no hope of capture. Here, coordination means the resource constraints of the firm together with the inventory and forward contracting constraints of the individual trading desks must be satisfied simultaneously. This includes the determination of the profit maximizing borrowing and lending profile for the firm as a whole and for each of the individual trading desks.

The following chapters focus on these issues. Chapter 23 considers the essential elements of trading strategies and tactics. Included here are the planning horizon, objective, capital limitation, and the probability of ruin as well as procedural guidelines to help avoid the pitfalls of commodity trading. Portfolio selection and analysis are presented in Chapter 24. Among the topics covered are selection methodology and the distinction between and implications of operational and estimation errors on portfolio selection and maintenance. Integrated commodity trading is the subject of Chapter 25. Here, the role of inventory management is tied to the simultaneous determination of intercommodity, intertemporal trading positions. As in the other chapters, illustrative examples also are presented.

To be sure, many topics are not covered in these chapters: risk preference and the estimation methods used to forecast future prices are among the most obvious. But these topics are the subject of earlier chapters and need not be repeated here. Indeed, the subjects presented thus far are prerequisites for the chapters to follow and are assumed knowledge.

23

TRADING STRATEGIES AND TACTICS:
The Essential Elements

||||||||||||||||||||||||||||||||||||||||||||||||||||||||||||||||||||||||||||||||||||||||||||||||||||||||||||

1 INTRODUCTION

A commodity trader has little hope of making a perfect trade every time; there is no such thing as a risk-free trade. For the speculator taking an outright position the possible risks of an adverse price movement are obvious to all. But similar risks surround hedgers and arbitragers. While futures markets offer a hedging vehicle against direct placement spot and forward commitments, futures prices do not always move in lock step with their cash counterparts. This fluctuation in the "basis" is a risk for the hedger. Similarly, the use of options to hedge a "physical" position is not risk free. Here the risk is that the hedger may execute the option before maturity only to have the market reverse itself and offer an opportunity the trader no longer can take advantage of. The use of futures markets to hedge options also is not without risk. Here, too, market volatility and uncertainty can trigger actions such as hedging too large a percent of the option that rob potential profits by increasing hedging costs.

The arbitrager also is not free of market risk. Even though a price differential may arise between two markets for the same commodity, for example, New York and Chicago silver prices, the purchase of one and the sale of the other does not necessarily ensure a profit. If the markets are *liquid,* that is, have many traders and much trading, the price differentials between the two markets may be narrow, and taking and making of delivery between the markets may not be worthwhile. In this case the arbitrager often "puts on" the intermarket spread with the intention of liquidating the spread before maturity at a profitable price differential. For example, buying COMEX silver at $11.00 an ounce and selling CBT silver at $11.10 an ounce and then, at some subsequent time before either silver contract matures, selling the COMEX contract at $10.90 an ounce and buying back the CBT contract at $10.90 an ounce. Here the "arbitrager's" initial position locks in a gross trading profit of 10¢ an ounce which may not be profitable if deliveries have to be made and taken. However, the "arbitrager" now has time to liquidate the trades before maturity if a profitable opportunity arises. In this case the liquidation would capture a 10¢ an ounce profit and no delivery costs. To be sure, if the trader had taken a net short position on the CBT the profit would have been 20¢ an ounce. However, the risk exposure would have been much greater: Prices could have gone the other way and the trader could have lost money. In the case presented, the "arbitrager" could have liquidated at any equal price between COMEX and the CBT and still capture a profit.

Regardless of the risk, successful traders do not trust all to luck: Their efforts are systematic and disciplined. The purpose of this chapter is to set forth the essential elements of a trader's strategy and tactics. The specific game plan, of course, will vary from trader to trader and from time to time. There are no set formulas to guarantee profits. However, there are guidelines. The very recognition of these considerations offers a checklist against surprises that, unprepared for, can catch a trader off balance and turn a profit into a loss or a loss into a catastrophe. The essential elements of a trading strategy are (1) trading objective, (2) planning horizon, (3) capital position and probability of ruin, (4) trading limits and stop-loss orders, (5) diversification and market coverage, and (6) expectations, risk preference, and research. Together these elements give shape and meaning to a trading strategy. The development of trading rules to execute that strategy is a tactical issue. Here again there are no formulas for guaranteed success, only guidelines to help ensure discipline and logical integrity. The following paragraphs summarize these strategic and tactical guidelines as a precursor for the material to be covered in the remainder of the text. The intent here is not to offer answers but to help identify major questions and aims; subsequent chapters are designed to help answer or approach them.

2 ELEMENTS OF A TRADING STRATEGY

The six essential elements of a trading strategy noted above are not independent of one another. Changes in one will influence the character of another and a large number of combinations can be generated. Accordingly, only the primary role and linkages of each element are set forth below.

2.1 Objective

All trading objectives can be viewed as the desire to achieve profits or avoid losses. While the business details of these obvious goals will vary owing to the commodity, market, and type of commodity trading one is engaged in (speculation, hedging, or arbitrage), the steps in setting an objective are common to all but not as trivial as one might expect.

First, one must determine the commodity or commodities to trade in, along with the maturity structure of the position and whether to go long or short.

Second, a profit objective or profile must be established, that is, when to liquidate "in the money." Here one may have a single number or a profile giving profit levels or rates of return at which a trade will be liquidated at a profit. For example, the trader may have a 20 percent per annum profit objective with a time horizon of six weeks. That is, any time over the next six weeks if a 20 percent per annum profit can be realized it will be taken. Figure 23.1 illustrates this objective together with an isolated probability line

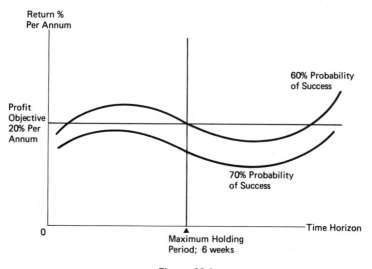

Figure 23.1

ILLUSTRATIVE PROFIT OBJECTIVE AND MARKET PROFILE

showing the return and holding period for a given probability of capturing at least that return. Whether a single number or a profile, the trader's risk preference and time horizon play an important role in setting this objective.

Third, one must have a "stop-loss" objective, that is, when to liquidate when the market has moved against the position. Here, again, one may have a single number or a profile indicating when a position would be liquidated at a loss before the maximum holding period is up. As with the profit objective the stop-loss objective will be determined by the trader's risk preference and time horizon. In addition, it will be determined in part by the trader's capital position.

2.2 Planning Horizon

The planning horizon defines the time period the trader is going to follow a strategy. For speculators basing their trades on fundamental developments, this time horizon may extend out for six to eighteen months and typically from six to twelve months. When technical considerations dictate the trader's time perspective, the planning horizon tends to be from one day to six months, although longer periods are not uncommon. For the hedger the planning horizon is set by external factors. Here, for example, sales or production commitments for some time in the future determine the length of the hedge trading horizon: sales made six months forward need to be hedged for the next six months. Arbitrage trading horizons can vary from one day to many months depending on the nature of the arbitrage: between markets, between maturities, between commodities, or between some combination of markets, maturities, and commodities. Typically the planning horizon is dictated by the forward position of the most active contracts. Generally, these most active contracts are spot, three months forward and six months forward or the nearest futures contract to these time periods. If a position is taken and nothing is done by the time the planning horizon reaches maturity, the trader must reassess trades in these commodities and either (1) liquidate, (2) switch the position forward to a new time horizon, or (3) change to a new commodity and time horizon.

2.3 Capital and the Probability of Ruin

For the speculator, trading capital is often viewed as the amount of money that can be lost and still remain on the sunny side of catastrophe. This, of course, depends on the speculator's "aversion to loss" and financial resources. As a rule of thumb, the smallest amount of capital should be at least equal to three times the margin requirement on a contract. One-third of that amount will be used for initial margin. The remaining two-thirds are set aside to cover a large percent of margin calls before prices may reverse and make the position profitable. The rule is based on the observation that more than two consecutive limit moves are not common and this much reserve reduces the probability of ruin (i.e., the probability of losing all of one's capital), to acceptable odds for many traders.

The probability of ruin in relation to the trader's capital and the size of each "bet" has been spelled out in Chapter 10. The probability of ruin can be expressed as follows:

$$q_k = \left(\frac{1-A}{1+A}\right)^k, \ k = \frac{c}{b}$$

where q_k is the probability of eventual ruin, C is the dollar amount of capital, b is the *size of a trade* in dollars, that is, the initial margin, and A is a percent measure of the advantage the trader has over the market in general.[1]

For example, suppose the trader has \$15,000 in capital, the trade size is \$1,500 and the advantage is 10 percent or .10 in decimal fractions. Here the probability of ruin would be

$$q_k = \left(\frac{1-.1}{1+.1}\right)^{15,000/1,500}$$

$$= .134.$$

Alternatively, the trader can specify the acceptable probability of ruin and work back to determine the amount of capital needed to at least meet this requirement given the dollar size of a trade, b, and the trader's advantage, A. This formulation is

$$C = \frac{b \ln q_k}{[\ln (1-A) - \ln (1+A)]}$$

The above relationship also can be modified to determine the probability of ruin before reaching a profit objective starting from any accumulated position. This relationship for a long position can be written

$$q_{k,a} = \frac{[(1+A)/(1-A)]^{(P^*-P^0)/b} - 1}{[(1+A)/(1-A)]^{C+(P^*-P^0)/b} - 1}$$

where P^* is the price objective, P^0 is the long position price, $(P^* - P^0)$ is the profit objective and $(P^* - P^0)/b$ is the profit objective expressed as the number of trading units. This formula can be used to help construct and assess profit objective profiles for a given probability of ruin, q_k, capital, C, trading unit size, b, advantage, A, and initial position price, P^0. Alternatively, one can use this to determine required amounts of capital to achieve a desired profit objective given the acceptable probability of ruin, q_k, advantage, A, and trading unit size, b.

Variations in interpretation apply to this theme for hedgers. For the hedger the amount of capital for hedging is determined in part by the value of the physical commodity to be hedged and the initial margin requirements. However, fluctuations in the basis may make net demands for *"hedge main-*

1. See Chapter 10.

tenance" capital. For hedge maintenance capital the probability of ruin, that is, the probability of exceeding the hedge maintenance capital, is given as

$$q_H = \left(\frac{q}{p}\right)^{(C-K-M)/b}$$

where C is the total amount of capital available, K is the capital invested in the cash position, M is the original margin, q is the probability of a margin call, p is the probability of a margin receipt, and b is the average amount of margin payed or received when payment is made or received.

For example, suppose one has initial capital of \$1,000,000, a cash commitment of \$990,000 in some commodity, \$5,000 in original margin for the hedge against the cash commitment in the futures market, and average margin payment or receipt is \$1,000, and $q = .40$. In this case the probability of ruin, that is the probability of margin calls taking all of the residual capital and forcing a reduction in the amount hedged, is

$$q_H = \left(\frac{2}{3}\right)^5 = .1317.$$

2.4 Trading Limits, Stop-Loss Orders, and Reinvestment

While the amount of capital available to the trader is the extreme limiting amount to lose there are other rules to establish when to liquidate at a loss. These rules culminate in a *stop-loss order:* an order to execute trades at prices that limit one's losses to prescribed levels. In some cases, the liquidation is indicated when the market offers technical or fundamental signals that are just the opposite of what had been signaled when the position was put on. Select technical and fundamental trading rules have been described in detail in previous chapters. However, they do not specify a liquidation price when technical and fundamental signals are not clear but prices nevertheless have moved against the position. Here many rules have come into popularity and none can be professed above another. One rule discussed in Chapter 5 is to use option valuation methods to establish prices at which a stop-loss order should be placed. This rule is based on the stochastic character of the price series, the profit objective, and the expected volatility of the market, and may accommodate anticipated price trends based on fundamental considerations.

Regardless of the rule it is imperative to have a stop-loss or liquidation trigger when the market is not going in favor of the position. Moreover, this liquidation trigger should be as automatic as possible, for example, specific liquidation orders left with the broker. When the market turns decidedly against a position it is important to be able to "bail out" as quickly as possible in order to limit one's losses.

The size of the "bet" or investment can be modified on *successive reinvestment* in order to offset previous losses and leave the trader with a net profit. The most typical schemes are linear (i.e., additive) and geometric (i.e., multiplicative). Linear trade extrapolations increase the size of the old position by one or more contracts each time a position is liquidated at a loss. Geometric growth in position size, sometimes referred to as a *Martingale system*, increases the size of the trade by some percent after each liquidation. For example, if the trader loses on a one-contract position, a new position of two contracts will be taken. If that position also ends in a loss, a subsequent position of four contracts will be taken and so on. As soon as the position "wins" the trader will recapture all previous losses, plus a profit. There are, of course, two practical limitations to extrapolative trading size schemes. First, the trader may run out of capital before a "win" is encountered. Second, there are either de jure or de facto trading size limits on all exchanges. *De jure size limits* are legal restrictions on cornering a market. For many commodities too large a position in the futures markets constitutes evidence of potential market manipulation. De facto limitations exist on all exchanges and in direct placement. One defacto limitation is market liquidity: There may not be enough buyers or sellers to satisfy the size of the desired position. Another is few brokerage houses are willing to accept a position so large that the trader's ability to meet margin is in doubt.

2.5 Diversification and Market Coverage

It has long been recognized that *diversification* can reduce risk for a given rate of return by taking advantage of the covariability between investments. To illustrate the potential advantage from diversification consider the following example. Two investments with identical rates of return and the same amount of variability in their returns may exhibit price divergences around their respective returns that are opposite to one another. By investing equally in both, the resulting portfolio or combination of investments would have an expected rate of return equal to either of its individual investments but would have zero variation around that expected return. Investing all of the available funds in just one of the investments would capture the same expected rate of return but would have a higher degree of risk as measured by the variation around the return. To be sure, the real world rarely offers opportunities with benefits from diversification as clear as this example: The deviations rarely are perfectly offsetting. However, they may be offsetting enough for diversification to pay.

While diversification is well established in the securities markets, the same opportunities for improving the risk-return profile exist in commodities investments, although they are not yet as widely recognized. Here, as in securities diversification, considerable effort must be made to identify the best combination of commodities to invest in. In practical terms, this diversification can be over time, across markets, across commodities, or some combination of these dimensions.

For the *speculator*, the principal area of diversification is across commodities where market and timing (contract maturity) are determined in part by liquidity. For the *hedger* there is less freedom across commodities than for the speculator as might be expected: The hedger, after all, is hedging a specific item. Consequently, matters of timing and market are of special importance. However, not all items to be hedged have corresponding futures contracts of reference and those that do often exhibit variations between the futures price and the "physical" price being hedged. In both cases the hedger may have to select a combination of maturities and/or a combination of markets and similar commodities in order to reduce the variation between the "physical" price being hedged and the price of the constructed hedging vehicle. For example, AAA corporate bonds may be hedged to a significant extent using a combination of GNMA, and long-term government bond futures contracts, as discussed in Chapter 20.

Diversification for arbitragers can also pay, but the operational problems can be formidable. On the one hand, it offers more opportunities for liquidation at a profit since the arbitrager now has many more combinations of possibilities to take advantage of. In the same context, diversification offers more opportunities to put on a profitable spread. On the other hand, the disadvantage for the arbitrager is the difficulty with which a trader can assess the convolution of investments and differentials that must be considered and acted upon on a moment's notice.

Market coverage is related to diversification but distinct enough to warrant special comment. In short, *market coverage* means being able to do business in all four commodity markets: spot, forward, futures, and options. Arbitragers, of course, spend a great deal of their resources capturing differentials between these markets and in so doing help establish consistent prices in various markets for a commodity. Hedgers also must be active in all of these instruments since each offers an alternative and sometimes complementary way of hedging their asset of reference. Speculators are somewhat less in need of being able to establish themselves in all of these markets. Nevertheless, the complete speculator would be well advised to be able to play in any of these markets: the liquidity of these markets is not always uniform: one market may offer a trading opportunity that otherwise would not be available. For example, an investor may make a larger profit by exchanging a futures contract for physicals with one party and then selling (buying) the physical commodity to (from) a third party than if the speculator simply liquidated the futures contract in the futures market. Here the act of arbitrage may enhance the speculator's return and reduce risk insofar as the number of opportunities for business have been increased.

2.6 Expectations, Risk Preference, and Research

A trader's actions, in part, are based on expectations about future prices. These *expectations*, either implicitly or explicitly include not only the anticipated changes in prices and their *payoffs* but the *probabilities* of those changes and the risks associated with each alternative action open to the trader. These expectations together with the trader's risk-taking disposition ultimately determine the trader's actions.

To be sure, the character of these efforts can vary widely from trader to trader. Price expectations can be little more than a hunch or determined through the use of elaborate market analyses, technical, and/or econometric models. Similarly, the probability estimates can range from an arbitrary whim to estimates based on empirical evidence such as past relative frequencies or survey information from select market participants. In addition, the trader's risk-taking disposition may or may not be precisely defined or consistent. Moreover, the coordination between and systematic application of these efforts can vary from haphazard to careful and deliberate.

Successful traders rarely rely on whim or are haphazard in their operations. The *role of research* is to help bring order and consistency to trading operations together with more and better information. That is not to say that research alone is sufficient to guarantee profits. It is to say that research can offer a systematic method of estimating payoffs and probabilities and specifying consistent decision criteria. Research can help develop a trade plan, establish rules to follow it, and, if done correctly, show the trader how to adapt to evolving market conditions and to modify the trading plan accordingly. To be sure, the markets may move in a way they have never moved before or in a way that is contrary to reason. But without a systematic trading plan and detailed records the likelihood of recognizing a new pattern in the market and subsequently capturing profits is reduced to the level of pure chance. While research will not find all the answers to all the questions or even identify all the questions, it can find some and offers a means of finding new ones.

The operational objectives of research are severalfold. Briefly, they are as follows:

1. To identify factors influencing the short-term and long-term movements in prices
2. To estimate the impulse response characteristics between prices and the factors influencing those prices
3. To estimate the probability distribution of prices around their expected values
4. To distinguish between major price movements and minor ones and between long-term and short-term movements
5. To provide a means of determining price objectives and stop-loss orders

6. To establish rules to achieve the correct timing and diversification of trades

7. To provide a means of evaluating trading opportunities with different risk-return profiles

8. To determine how to allocate capital

9. To determine the size of trades and reinvestment rules, for example, as a linear extrapolation of previous investments or as a geometric extrapolation such as a Martingale scheme where the size of the investment is increased as some multiple of the previous trade

10. To identify the trading tasks and their sequence of operation

3 TRADING TACTICS

Trading tactics set forth the techniques of securing the objectives designated by the trading strategy: They define the art and science of deploying resources to achieve the targeted commodity trading goals. Among the most important tactical rules to follow are the following:

1. Complete all market assessments and trading objectives before the opening of business each day. This includes knowing the exact value and maturity structure of the current positions, the available lines of credit, the prices and character of markets opened in other parts of the world, as well as technical and fundamental market analyses.

2. Determine the value and maturity structure of each trade together with remaining available capital and net position immediately after conducting each trade. In short, the trader must always know the current position.

3. To the extent other business commitments permit, orders should be placed in quantities the market can assimilate readily and not in quantities so large that the weight of the trade forces the market against the position as the order is being filled.

4. Stop-loss orders should be entered in advance with instructions to execute "at the market if touched."

5. When a position is liquidated, all associated orders such as stop-loss orders should be canceled at that time.

6. Monitor the location of stop-loss orders in the various markets. If one market penetrates a stop-loss level another market may have a sympathetic reaction.

7. Always attempt to liquidate at the predetermined objective. If the objective should change during the life of the position make sure that the former and subsequent objectives are recorded together with a detailed market price history during the life of the position. This is critical for postoptimality trading analysis, that is, to explore how trading may be improved.

8. Monitor information services continuously during the day in order to be aware of information that may influence the market and require a trading response. This vigilance must be maintained throughout the life of the position.

9. Play the odds. Estimate the probabilities of price differentials and price levels and the positions that offer high odds in favor of a profit. While high odds do not guarantee a profit they do suggest how to bet. The key element here is the accuracy of the probability estimates. This is a research issue and emphasizes the need for research to be geared toward operational trading issues.

In addition to the above list of positive actions there are several "don'ts" that, if followed, can help avoid some common and serious pitfalls:

1. Don't trade without a plan or in violation of the plan. To do so invites chaos and makes adaptation more difficult.

2. Don't trade without keeping a detailed trading record. This record may help reveal profitable changes in trading operations that otherwise would go unnoticed.

3. Don't disguise losses by changing to a spread position from an outright position or by switching to another spread position from a spread position unless the spread positions have been assessed on their own merits and in conjunction with the original position and the repositioning promises to be profitable.

4. Don't trade without experienced brokers or with a brokerage house that does not have a timely and accurate back office to manage margin payments.

5. Don't ignore other markets in other commodities or in other forms of contracting. To do so limits the possibilities of arbitrage and profitable liquidation opportunities.

4 SUMMARY

There are several aspects to a successful trading strategy. They include the objective, time horizon, capital and probability of ruin, trade limits, stop-loss positions, reinvestment rules, diversification, expectations and risk preference, and the use of research. Each of these elements must be spelled out, monitored and adherded to or an otherwise sound system will become haphazard at best. The tactical aspects of trading commodities are no less important than the strategic ones. They consist of simple do's and don'ts that make up an important check list for the neophite and experienced trader alike. Indeed, it is often the case that an experienced trader makes a costly error because these rules were not followed during an emotional flurry of activity.

To be sure, following the strategic and tactical guidelines presented here does not guarantee successful trading performance. However, they do provide a system from which assessments and improvements can be made in an objective and consistent way. A system is the only way to ensure that one's trading performance will be deliberate and repeatable, and not purely the elusive product of chance.

5 BIBLIOGRAPHY

FELLER, W., *An Introduction To Probability Theory and Its Applications,* Vol. 2. New York: John Wiley, 1971.

KAUFMAN, P. J., *Commodity Trading Systems and Methods.* New York: John Wiley, 1978.

MAO, J. T. C., *Quantitative Analysis of Financial Decisions.* London: Macmillan, 1969.

KROLL, S., and I. SHISHKO, *The Commodity Futures Market Guide.* New York: Harper & Row, 1973.

TEWELES, R. J., C. V. HARLOW, and H. L. STONE. *The Commodity Futures Game. Who Wins? Who Loses? Why?* New York: McGraw-Hill, 1974.

CHICAGO BOARD OF TRADE, *Commodity Training Manual.* Chicago: Chicago Board of Trade, 1980.

24

COMMODITY PORTFOLIOS:
Selection and Management

▬▬▬

1 INTRODUCTION

A great deal has been written about the selection and management of investment portfolios and a wealth of general conclusions and guidelines have emerged. Yet, to date, the literature has focused on portfolios of securities, even though commodity portfolios are common if not widely publicized. In part, this seeming neglect stems from legal impediments on commodities as investment media: Apparently the "prudent man" does not invest in gold or other commodities and for this reason pension funds and other institutional "investors" have been barred from investing in commodities such as gold and interest rate futures. Moreover, commodities have unique characteristics that demand knowledge and understanding distinct from the securities markets: Commodity investment portfolios are drawn from the futures markets where everyday settlements and spotty daily liquidity pose operational problems that securities managers are not accustomed to. Furthermore, their exchanges have evolved for different market segments. Nevertheless, the basic principles of modern portfolio analysis apply to commodities and commodities are becoming more popular investment media.

The objective of this chapter is to summarize the essential elements of portfolio analysis in the context of commodities investments and to highlight topics that are of special importance. While portfolio analysis includes technical and fundamental analyses of individual investments this chapter focuses on portfolio selection and management. No attempt is made here to recapitulate the fundamental and technical analyses of individual investment alternatives. These are prerequisites to portfolio selection and earlier chapters provide guidelines for these purposes. Rather, the chapter focuses on the selection and management of efficient portfolios with special emphasis on applications and the impacts of operational errors.

The chapter is organized as follows: Section 2 summarizes essential concepts of commodity portfolio analysis. Included here are notions of return, risk, diversification, and efficiency as well as select peculiarities of the futures markets. Section 3 outlines standard portfolio selection methods. The topics covered include representative objective functions and constraints together with practical solution procedures. The problem of errors in operation also is considered in this section. Finally special applications of commodity futures portfolios are presented in Section 4.

2 COMMODITY PORTFOLIO ANALYSIS: An Overview

Commodity portfolios are collections of investments in various commodity positions. The selection of the positions is based on considerations of risk and return. The actual methods involved, while bearing a strong resemblance to security portfolio selection, have several unique twists. These include the measurement of return and risk, and special procedures owing to the possibility of short positions. Each of these issues is discussed as a prelude to the application of portfolio theory to commodities.

2.1 Expected Returns and Risk: Outright and Spread Positions

Historical returns on commodity futures can be calculated in relation to the stream of margin payments and receipts incurred over the holding period, as discussed in Chapter 6. This is expost analysis, i.e., after the fact. Portfolio selection is ex-ante in intent, i.e. anticipatory. However, future margin flows are not known. Moreover, the holding periods are not long enough to assume the maintanence margin flows sum to zero if they are random. Consequently, the expected returns are calculated on the basis of initial position prices in relation to their anticipated future prices. This is applied to long and short positions as well as to outright and spread positions.

The anticipated gross return on an outright position is equal to the anticipated price less the position price divided by the position price. This return may be converted to an annualized rate by taking account of the number of days that it takes for this gross return to be realized relative to a year. For example,

$$r = \left(\frac{\hat{P}_{t+N} - P_t}{P_t}\right)\left(\frac{N}{365}\right)$$

where P_t is the position price and $\hat{P}_{t+N}$ is the anticipated price N days into the future. The anticipated price $\hat{P}_{t+N}$, of course, must be forecast in some way (see Parts 3 and 4). Insofar as the forecast is not perfect, there may be some random error surrounding the forecast value. That is $P_{t+N} = \hat{P}_{t+N} + e_{t+N}$. If these errors are unbiased, that is, if $E(e_{t+N}) = 0$, then the "expected value" of the return will be equal to the true return. But expected values are not the same thing as results. The error term indicates that the actual return N days from the date the position is taken may be higher or lower than its expected value. This variation in the expected return, of course, may be viewed as the risk surrounding the expected outcome.

Outright positions in different commodities or different commodity contract maturities may have different expected returns and different variances around them. An outright position in one-year forward gold may have an expected rate of return of 13 percent per annum but a standard deviation of 5 percent per annum, while an outright position in three-month forward silver may have an expected rate of return of 11 percent per annum but a standard deviation of only 2 percent per annum. Here gold has the highest expected rate of return but also the highest amount of risk as measured by the standard deviation of the expected return.

A spread position in a commodity also may be viewed in terms of return and risk. Here the difference in price and the length of time between the near and far positions determine the rate of return. Unlike an outright position, a spread assures the investor of the return dictated by the price differential and time interval. For example, one could invest in a silver spread by purchasing spot silver at $15.00 an ounce and selling one-year forward silver on the COMEX at $16.50 and capture a capital gain of 10 percent per annum before insurance, storage, delivery, and brokerage costs (which are small for moderate quantities of 25,000 ounces or more). However, spread positions can have both "certain" and "stochastic" elements in their estimated or predicted returns if one does not intend to hold to maturity. However, spreads may widen or narrow unpredictably as they mature. Consequently an opportunity may arise to liquidate the spread position before the nearest contract matures and capture a profit greater than that built into the spread. Moreover, if the "near side" of the spread matures, the portfolio manager need not wait for the "far side" of the spread to mature but may, if the opportunity arises, liquidate the far side of the spread for a speculative profit.

Regardless of the type of position, technical and fundamental analyses are essential to estimate the returns, their variabilities, and the odds associated with various investment outcomes. Moreover portfolio selection must weigh expected returns against risks for and between each investment alternative. For technical and fundamental reasons the expected rate of return on an investment may vary systematically with returns on other investments. This covariability may be strong or weak, and positive or negative. Be that as it may, portfolio selection theory takes these factors into consideration.

2.2 Portfolio Objectives and Strategies

The portfolio manager ultimately is concerned with the achievement of financial objectives defined in terms of the performance of the collection of investments as whole. Typically these objectives are defined in terms of capturing a desired rate of return with the lowest possible variability in that return, or in terms of its "dual," the maximization of return subject to a constraint on the acceptable variability in that return. Here the variability of the portfolio return is a measure of risk and depends on the variabilities of, and covariabilities between, the individual investments in the portfolio. The role of the portfolio manager is to adjust the amounts of each investment in the portfolio so as to maintain or improve upon the return and risk characteristics of them as a whole.

As noted in Chapter 6 portfolio selection strategies for investments with uncertain returns are bounded by two extreme states of the world. On the one hand, there may be complete and perfect positive correlation between the investment alternatives. In this case the allocation of investment funds to only one alternative cannot be improved upon if one cannot go short. If the outcomes of several tossed coins were equal to the outcome of one of them, then one could be no more certain of the group outcome than the outcome for any one of the tossed coins. Perfect negative correlation between investments, offers zero risk but is never found. On the other hand, if the investment alternatives are completely independent of one another, then diversification of investable funds between the various investments can reduce the risk of a given "general" outcome: One may not be able to predict the outcome of a single toss of a coin with confidence but may with confidence predict the general or average outcome of several coins tossed independently. As Samuelson (1967) has shown, diversification pays. Indeed, if the returns were independent and identically distributed, then a uniform distribution of investments (equal allocation of funds to investment alternatives) would minimize the variability (risk) of portfolio return.

2.3 Common Foundations and Special Character of Commodity Portfolios

Investment returns in practice are rarely perfectly correlated and the problem confronting the portfolio manager cannot be treated by the simple bromides or a single investment. For this reason most of the work in portfolio theory and its applications are designed to deal with partially interdependent investments. A variety of portfolio selection criteria and computational schemes have arisen to meet this challenge. For the most part these results can be applied to commodity portfolios. Among the most important are the path-breaking works of Markowitz (1959), Wolf (1957), and Sharpe (1970). These efforts are milestones in basic theory, solution methodology, and practical operating design, respectively. That is not to say that commodities portfolios can be viewed in all respects as securities portfolios. Indeed, there are important differences that must be recognized.

2.3.1   *Marking to Market and Liquidity*

Investments in commodity futures contracts, unlike their securities counterparts, must be "marked to market," that is, settled every day. To be sure, securities portfolios can be "marked to market" daily in an accounting context without true liquidation. This is often done to assess performance from the point of view of opportunity gains or losses. But in many cases security portfolios can opt to ride out a momentary storm by holding their position until more favorable market conditions reappear. Commodity portfolios have no alternative but to take or make settlements every day for a portfolio of commodity futures.

Because of daily settlements, portfolio managers must contend with the problem of spotty daily liquidity to a much greater extent than a securities portfolio manager with more time to "manage the account." Consequently, commodity portfolio managers are especially responsive to profit opportunities that emerge during the day. These fleeting opportunities offer certain safety to an otherwise uncertain settlement and the possibility of a serious cash drain. Unfortunately, the markets often are "shallow" and trades cannot be expected "at the market" price: The size of the trade in relation to market volume may force the price against the trade. In short, market prices are not always good indicators of "execution" prices and this introduces the problem of errors in variables into the expected returns and variabilities on which a portfolio selection is made. The practical importance of this problem is straightforward: Insofar as the allocation of investable funds is determined in part by returns and variabilities based on recorded data, unrecognized errors in these data can lead to improper decisions. Improper decisions in turn can lead to overall investment performance far from desired or attainable with correct information. While solutions to this problem may not be perfect, the approaches discussed below at least recognize the problem and indicate operating procedures that show promise.

2.3.2   *Short Positions*

One may invest in a long or short position with equal ease in commodity futures unlike in securities. This distinction gives rise to an important methodological issue in portfolio selection. For securities portfolios the relative proportions of the alternative investments are non-negative and sum to 1 or 100% of virture of a budget constraint. In commodities futures portfolios, each investment alternative can be either long or short. Consequently there are twice as many possible positions and the longs have the opposite sign of the shorts. Because of the different signs of the long and short positions, the budget constraint takes the form of absolute values of the relative proportions that sum to 1 or 100%. Because of the sign differences and the nature of the budget constraint the simple application of security portfolio selection methodologies to commodities will not suffice. A formal solution requires non-linear programming algorithms.

Formal requirements not withstanding, a common approach to this problem, that has the virtue of using the more well known solution methodology, is a two-stage conditional selection algorithm. In the first stage the investor decides which commodities will be long or short but not their relative proportions. Given this information the rows and columns for the short position commodities in the portfolio covariance matrix are changed in sign: this allows the portfolio solution algorithm to treat a short position as a long position. The adjusted covariance matrix together with the expected returns and the budget constraint (standard linear constraint) then are used to solve for the relative proportions of the commodity investments. This method is not as weak as some think: hedgers and speculators often are constrained by other business considerations to knowing in which commodities they must be either long or short. The following discussion focuses on the second stage. From a mechanical vantage the first stage is exogenous to the selection of the relative proportions. Moreover, the possible reasons for determining long or short position apriori are two many to consider. It is the second stage that offers the analytical richness of portfolio selection and is outlined below.

3 PORTFOLIO THEORY

Portfolio theory is concerned with investment decisions involving interrelated and uncertain outcomes. It contains two principal stages: the evaluation of each investment opportunity and the selection of investments to be made based in part on these evaluations. This section focuses on the second stage. In particular it sets forth the basic commodity portfolio selection problem in terms of an elementary mathematical programming problem and extends this discussion to include index models and errors in variables.

3.1 Commodity Portfolios: the mathematical programming approach

As Markowtitz (1959) has shown, the portfolio selection problem can be cast as a nonlinear programming problem. To set the stage consider an investor who must select a portfolio of commodities $x_1, x_2, \ldots, x_n$ where $0 \leq x_i, i = 1, 2, \ldots, n$ are the proportions of available funds invested in the ith asset, and $\sum_i^n x_i = 1$. In addition to these constraints there may be one or more constraints on the values of select weights. One such constraint for commodity investors is the proportion of funds invested in treasury bills as a safeguard to meet possible variation margin calls. This may be denoted $x_k = b$ where b is the prescribed proportion of treasury bills. The objectives of the portfolio manager are defined in terms of the return and risk on the portfolio as a whole.

The expected return on the portfolio, R, is measured by the weighted average of the expected returns from the commodity investments. That is,

$$\hat{R} = \sum_{i=1}^{n} x_i \hat{r}_i$$

where the $\hat{r}_i$ are the expected returns on the $i = 1, 2, \ldots, n$ investment alternatives and the x_i are the investment allocation weights. The risk of the portfolio, V, is measured by the variance in the expected portfolio return and is given by

$$V = E[\hat{R} - E(\hat{R})]^2 = \sum_{i=1}^{n} \sum_{j=1}^{n} \sigma_{ij} x_i x_j$$

where σ_{ij} is the covariance between the ith and jth investment returns when $i \neq j$ and is the variance of the ith investment return when $i = j$.

Of all the feasible portfolios (i.e., sets of weights $x_1, \ldots, x_n$) that satisfy the constraints, the portfolio manager will select only an efficient portfolio. A portfolio is said to be efficient if there is no other collection of investments (i.e., set of weights $x_i, i = 1, \ldots, n$), with a higher return and lower risk, or higher return at the same level of risk or lower risk at the same level of return.

3.1.1 The Basic Problem

Taking all of these considerations into account, one way (among many) the portfolio selection problem may be summarized is as follows:

$$\max_{\substack{w.r.t. x_i \\ i=1,\ldots,n}} Z = \sum_{i=1}^{n} x_i \hat{r}_i - A \sum_{i=1}^{n} \sum_{j=1}^{n} \sigma_{ij} x_i x_j$$

subject to

$$\sum_{i=1}^{n} x_i \leq 1$$

$$x_k = b$$

$$x_i \geq 0 \text{ for } i - 1, \ldots, n$$

where A is a parameter set by the portfolio manager and reflects the desired degree of risk aversion (see Chapter 13). The solution to this problem requires the derivation of the analytical conditions that must be satisfied in order to achieve the constrained objective and an efficient method of solving for the numerical values of the x_i once those conditions are known. The first aspect has been resolved by Kuhn and Tucker (1951) and the second by Wolf (1957).

3.1.2 *Kuhn-Tucker Conditions*

The Kuhn-Tucker conditions for the above problem may be expressed as follows:

$$\sum_{h=1}^{n} 2A\sigma_{ih}x_h + S_{n+1} - S_j = \hat{r}_j \text{ for } j = 1, 2, \ldots, n$$

$$\sum_{\substack{i=1 \\ i \neq k}}^{n} x_i + x_{n+1} = 1 - b$$

$$x_i \geq 0 \text{ for } i = 1, 2, \ldots, n + 1$$
$$S_i \geq 0 \text{ for } i = 1, 2, \ldots, n + 1$$
$$x_i S_i = 0 \text{ for } i = 1, 2, \ldots, n + 1$$

where S_{n+1} is a constant of proportionality and the S_i's and x_{n+1} are slack variables.

Because the objective function is concave and the constraints are linear (and therefore convex) the Kuhn-Tucker theorem implies that a collection of investment weights $x_1, \ldots, x_n$ is optimal (satisfies the objective and all of the constraints) provided there exist values of $x_{n+1}, S_1, \ldots, S_{n+1}$ such that the values of $x_1, \ldots, x_{n+1}, S_1, \ldots, S_{n+1}$ satisfy the above conditions.

A linear programming–simplex approach to finding such a feasible solution was developed by Wolf (1957). With the exception of the last condition, $x_i \cdot S_i = 0$, the Kuhn-Tucker conditions may be viewed as linear programming constraints for $2(n + 1)$ variables. The last restriction, $x_i \cdot S_i = 0$, states that both variables cannot be solved for at the same time—this would involve using the same equation to solve for two different unknowns.

3.1.3 *Linear Programming Formulation of Kuhn-Tucker Conditions*

Because the $\hat{r}_i$ in the first n conditions are positive an obvious starting point does not present itself. For this reason an artificial variable, V_i, is introduced to each of the first n conditions. This enables one to start with the $x_i = 0$, $i = 1, \ldots, o$ and the V_i, $i = 1, \ldots, n$ equal to their respective $\hat{r}_i$. The objective now is to decrease the V_i to zero in order to obtain the optimal values for the x_i. Taking all of these considerations into account the problem now may be stated as follows:[1]

$$\min C = V_1 + \ldots + V_n$$

subject to

$$\sum_{h=1}^{n} 2A\sigma_{ih}x_h + S_{n+1} - S_i + V_i = \hat{r}_i \text{ for } i = 1, \ldots, n$$

$$\sum_{\substack{i=1 \\ i \neq k}}^{n} x_i + x_{n+1} = 1 - b$$

$$x_i \geq 0 \text{ for } i = 1, \ldots, n+1$$

$$S_i \geq 0 \text{ for } i = 1, \ldots, n+1$$

$$V_i \geq 0 \text{ for } i = 1, \ldots, n+1.$$

This problem now may be solved as a linear programming problem.

3.2 An Illustrative Portfolio Selection Problem

To illustrate the entire process consider the following example:

$$\max Z = .09x_1 + .15x_2 + .12x_3 - A (.08x_2^2 + .04x_3^2 - .20x_2x_3)$$

subject to

$$x_1 + x_2 + x_3 \leq 1$$

$$x_1 = .20$$

In this example there are three commodity investments with expected returns per annum of $\hat{r}_1 = .09$, $\hat{r}_2 = .15$ and $\hat{r}_3 = .12$. Here the percent of funds invested in asset 1, x_1, is fixed at 20 percent (.20 as a decimal fraction). Moreover, x_1 does not have any variance in its rate of return, for example, a spread position or a "riskless" asset such as a treasury bill. The variance of the return on the second and third investments is .08 and .04, respectively, and their covariance is $-.20$ indicating an inverse relationship between departures from their expected returns. The unspecified coefficient, A, may be viewed as the coefficient of risk aversion and the effect of it on the composition of the portfolio will be simulated.

1. The "first-order" conditions were multiplied by -1, thus changing the objective from maximization to minimization. This change together with the addition of artificial slack variables V_i to establish a starting point and appropriate transformation of variables completes the transition to the minimization problem.

Because x_1 is fixed and its return has no variation the maximization need only focus on x_2 and x_3 subject to the constraint $x_2 + x_3 \leq .80$. The Kuhn-Tucker conditions are

$$A .16x_2 - A .20x_3 + S_4 - S_2 = .15$$
$$-A .20x_2 + A .08x_3 + S_4 - S_3 = .12$$
$$x_2 + x_3 + x_4 = .80$$
$$x_i \geq 0 \text{ for } i = 2, \ldots, 4$$
$$S_i \geq 0 \text{ for } i = 2, \ldots, 4$$
$$x_i S_i = 0 \text{ for } i = 2, \ldots, 4.$$

With the addition of artificial slack variables to the first-order conditions on x_2 and x_3, the linear programming problem corresponding to the above Kuhn-Tucker conditions can be written

$$\min C = V_2 + V_3$$

subject to

$$A .16x_2 - A .20x_3 + S_4 - S_2 + V_2 = .15$$
$$-A .20x_2 + A .08x_3 + S_4 - S_3 + V_3 = .12$$
$$x_2 + x_3 + x_4 = .80$$

and

$$\text{all } x_i \geq 0, S_i \geq 0, V_i \geq 0.$$

The solution to this problem is

$$x_1 = .20$$
$$x_2 = .35 + \frac{.0469}{A}$$
$$x_3 = .45 - \frac{.0469}{A}$$
$$x_4 = 0$$
$$S_2 = 0$$
$$S_3 = 0$$
$$S_4 = .3325$$
$$V_2 = 0$$
$$V_3 = 0$$

and

$$A \geq .1042.$$

The effect of different degrees of risk aversion on the composition of the portfolio is shown in Figure 24.1. As the degree of risk aversion increases, that is, as A increases, the portfolio becomes more heavily weighted toward the third investment which has the highest expected return in relation to the variation in its expected return.

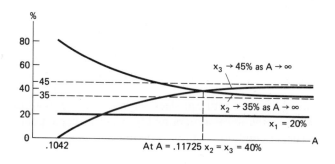

Figure 24.1

ILLUSTRATIVE PORTFOLIO DISTRIBUTION
FOR DIFFERENT DEGREES OF RISK AVERSION

3.3   The Commodity Portfolio Index Model

Sharpe (1970) has shown that if one or more indices can be found that describe the systematic variation in the various investment media then this linkage can be used to reduce the number of covariance terms in the model and reduce its computational difficulty. Theoretically, the portfolio selection outlined above is independent of the method used to generate the expected investment returns. When these returns are obtained from a linear regression model the portfolio selection procedure takes on two important operational attributes. The first, popularized by Sharpe (1970) and most often cited, is improved computational efficiency. In brief, the "Index Model" approach enables one to reduce the number of covariances needed in the calculations and thereby reduces the numerical problems associated with large portfolio selection problems. The second is informational and shows the effect of improved estimates on the selection of a portfolio: While one investment may have higher historical rates of return and lower variances, its operational problems may more than outweigh these virtues. This discussion emphasizes the latter attribute as a prelude to the problem of spotty daily liquidity.

3.3.1   The Portfolio Perspective of Improved "Indices"

The regression model approach uses one or more "indices" as explanatory variables in the prediction of rates of return. These indices may be based on fundamental or technical considerations. The variances of the residuals from estimating equations represent the unexplained variances of the rates of return. These residuals are independent of one another. Their variances together with the variance(s) of the indices and weighting factors make up the total variance of the expected return on the portfolio return. The absence of covariability between the estimation residuals leads to sparse matrices (large blocks of zero entries) that are less difficult to invert than full matrices without large numbers of zero entries.

The informational contribution of this approach can be shown easily by example. To illustrate this attribute reconsider the portfolio selection problem of the last section where the true returns are given by the following models:

$$r_2 = a_2 + b_2 I + e_2$$
$$r_3 = a_3 + b_3 I + e_3$$

where I is the explanatory variable (index), the a's and b's are estimated regression coefficients and the e's are random error terms. If the estimates of these returns are unbiased the expected values of the returns, conditioned on a prescribed value of the index, I^*, would be

$$\hat{r}_2 = a_2 + b_2 I^*$$
$$\hat{r}_3 = a_3 + b_3 I^*$$

and the return on the portfolio could still be written

$$\hat{R} = \hat{r}_2 X_2 + \hat{r}_3 X_3.$$

The variance of the expected portfolio rate of return would now be

$$V = \sum_{i=2}^{3} X_j^2 \sigma_j^2 + B^2 \sigma_I^2$$

where

$$B = \sum_{i=2}^{3} X_j b_j,$$

σ_i^2 is the variance of e_i, and σ_I^2 is the variance of the explanatory variable I. The maximization problem now can be written

$$\max Z = X_2 \hat{r}_2 + X_3 \hat{r}_3 - A(\sigma_2^2 X_2^2 + \sigma_3^2 X_3^3 + X_2^2 b_2^2 \sigma_I^2 + X_3^2 b_3^2 \sigma_I^2 + 2X_2 X_3 b_2 b_3 \sigma_I^2)$$

subject to

$$\sum_{i=2}^{3} X_i \le .8$$
$$X_i \ge 0 \text{ for } i = 2,3.$$

The corresponding Kuhn-Tucker conditions are

$$A(2\sigma_2{}^2 + 2b_2{}^2\sigma_I{}^2)X_2{}^2 + A(2b_2b_3\sigma_I{}^2)X_3 + S_4 - S_2 = \hat{r}_2$$
$$A(2b_2b_3\sigma_I{}^2)X_2 + A(2\sigma_3{}^2 + 2b_3{}^2\sigma_I{}^2)X_3 + S_4 - S_3 = \hat{r}_3$$
$$X_2 + X_3 + X_4 = .8$$
$$X_i \geq 0 \text{ for } i = 2,3,4$$
$$S_i \geq 0 \text{ for } i = 2,3,4$$
$$X_iS_i = 0 \text{ for } i = 2,3,4.$$

Adding artificial slack variables, V_i, the linear programming form of the Kuhn-Tucker conditions can be written

$$\min C = V_2 + V_3$$

subject to

$$A\sigma_2^* X_2 + A\sigma_{2,3}^* X_3 + S_4 - S_2 + V_2 = \hat{r}_2$$
$$A\sigma_{2,3}^* X_2 + A\sigma_3^* X_3 + S_4 - S_5 + V_3 = \hat{r}_3$$
$$X_2 + X_3 + X_4 = .8$$

and

$$\text{all } X_i \geq 0, S_i \geq 0, V_i \geq 0$$

where

$$\sigma_2^* = (2\sigma_2{}^2 + 2b_2{}^2\sigma_I{}^2),$$
$$\sigma_{2,3}^* = (2b_2b_3\sigma_I{}^2),$$
$$\sigma_3^* = (2\sigma_3{}^2 + 2b_3{}^2\sigma_I{}^2).$$

The solution to this problem is

$$X_1 = .2$$
$$X_2 = \frac{(\hat{r}_3 - \hat{r}_2) + A(.8)(\sigma_{2,3}^* - \sigma_3^*)}{2A\sigma_{2,3}^* - A\sigma_3^* - A\sigma_2^*}$$
$$X_3 = \frac{(\hat{r}_2 - \hat{r}_3) + A(.8)(\sigma_{2,3}^* - \sigma_2^*)}{2A\sigma_{2,3}^* - A\sigma_3^* - A\sigma_2^*}$$
$$X_4 = 0$$
$$S_1 = 0$$
$$S_2 = 0$$
$$S_3 = 0$$
$$S_4 = \frac{A[\sigma_2^*\sigma_3^* - (\sigma_{2,3}^*)^2]0.8 + \sigma_{2,3}^*(\hat{r}_2 + \hat{r}_3) - \sigma_3^*\hat{r}_2 - \sigma_2^*\hat{r}_3}{2\sigma_{2,3}^* - \sigma_3^* - \sigma_2^*}$$
$$V_2 = 0$$
$$V_3 = 0.$$

This solution, of course, is dependent on specific values of $\sigma_2{}^2, \sigma_3{}^2, b_2, b_3$, and $\sigma_I{}^2$. To be sure another explanatory variable or "index" may produce the same expected returns but may have different variances and b coefficients. These differences in turn could change the investment allocation solution. Indeed they could lead to a more efficient portfolio.

3.3.2 An Example

For example, suppose the parameters in the above problem were $\sigma_2{}^2 = .02$, $\sigma_3{}^2 = .02$, $b_2 = .9$, $b_3 = .7$, $\sigma_I{}^2 = .10$, $\hat{r}_2 = .15$, $\hat{r}_3 = .12$, $\hat{r}_1 = .10$, and $A = .50$. The corresponding solution for X_1, X_2, X_3, E, V, and Z would be

$$X_1 = .200$$
$$X_2 = .458$$
$$X_3 = .342$$
$$E = .1297$$
$$V = .0039$$
$$Z = .1278.$$

Now suppose another explanatory variable produced the following parameters: $\sigma_2{}^2 = .01$, $\sigma_3{}^2 = .01$, $b_2 = .9$, $b_3 = -.9$, $\sigma_I{}^2 = .08$, $\hat{r}_2 = .15$, $\hat{r}_3 = .12$, $r_1 = .10$, and $A = .50$. The solution for X_1, X_2, X_3, E, V, and Z would be

$$X_1 = .20$$
$$X_2 = .507$$
$$X_3 = .293$$
$$E = .1313$$
$$V = .0062$$
$$Z = .1282.$$

In this case the alternative estimating procedure produces both a different distribution of funds to investment alternatives as well as a higher portfolio rate of return and a higher (i.e., more efficient), value of Z. While this may not always be the case it is clear that alternative estimating equations can lead to different investment allocations and portfolio efficiencies. In short, accuracy of estimation is as much a practical determinant of portfolio allocation as historical variability and return.

3.4 Errors in Estimation and Errors in Operation

While trades in the futures markets are rarely if ever nonexistent the volume often can be very low. This poses several problems that have operational implications for portfolio managers. In particular, the periodic absence of high trading volume, or liquidity, can lead to difficult order execution. A model based on historical data may correctly estimate the rate of return for an investment. If volume is low, however, the size of the individual sale or purchase may impinge on the price or rate of return captured in the market. That is, an otherwise modest sale may be disproportionately large on an unexpected low-volume day. Under these conditions an offer (to sell) may force the market price down, that is, against the sale; similarly, a bid (to buy) could force the price up against the desired purchase. This state of affairs can increase the variation in the price at which the order is executed in relation to the variance of the estimation error. This problem has parallels to the *generalized errors in equation model*.

3.4.1 Portfolio Implications of Errors in Operation

In the context of the portfolio example given above, consider an "index" or message model described in the previous section,

$$r_{it} = a_i + b_i I_t + e_{it}.$$

Moreover, let the actual return captured, r_{it}^*, be related to the message model return by the addition of a random "operational" error, ε_{it}, stemming from random changes in liquidity. That is,

$$r_{it}^* = r_{it} + \varepsilon_{it}$$

where e_{it} and ε_{it} are uncorrelated for any time difference between them. Taken together these relationships lead to an operational model of the form

$$r_{it}^* = a_i + b_i I_t + e_{it} + \varepsilon_{it}$$
$$= a_i + b_i I_t + n_{it}$$

where the variance of n_{it} is

$$\sigma_n^2 = \sigma_e^2 + \sigma_\varepsilon^2.$$

On the surface this system is similar to the index model discussed in the previous section. However, several important differences and implications are worth noting. First, the operational error variance σ_ε^2 is likely to vary from commodity to commodity, for different maturity positions and different periods of general economic activity. Second, for practical purposes the rates of return considered in portfolio selection must be based on capturable rates of return, that is, based on r_{it}^*'s and not $\hat{r}_{it}$'s. Third, and following directly from the previous two conditions, changes in one or more of the operational error variances, all other characteristics remaining the same, can lead to sizable shifts in portfolio composition.

To demonstrate the latter point reconsider the portfolio example given above and make the following substitutions:

$$\sigma_2{}^2 = \sigma_{e2}{}^2 + \sigma_{82}{}^2$$

$$\sigma_3{}^2 = \sigma_{e3}{}^2 + \sigma_{83}{}^2.$$

This leads to the following portfolio weights x_2 and x_3:

$$x_2 = \frac{(r_3{}^* - r_2{}^*) + A(.8)\{2b_2b_3\sigma_I{}^2 - [2(\sigma_{e3}{}^2 + \sigma_{83}{}^2) + 2b_3{}^2\sigma_I{}^2]\}}{2A(2b_2b_3\sigma_I{}^2) - A[2(\sigma_{e3}{}^2 + \sigma_{82}{}^2) + 2b_3{}^2\sigma_I{}^2] - A[2(\sigma_{e2}{}^2 + \sigma_{82}{}^2) + 2b_2{}^2\sigma_I{}^2]}$$

$$x_3 = \frac{(r_2{}^* - r_3{}^*) + A(.8)\{2b_2b_3\sigma_I{}^2 - [2(\sigma_{e2}{}^2 + \sigma_{e2}{}^2) + 2b_2{}^2\sigma_I{}^2]\}}{2A(2b_2b_3\sigma_I{}^2) - A[2(\sigma_{e3}{}^2 + \sigma_{82}{}^2) + 2b_3{}^2\sigma_I{}^2] - A[2(\sigma_{e2}{}^2 + \sigma_{82}{}^2) + 2b_2{}^2\sigma_I{}^2]}$$

When $\sigma_{e2}{}^2 = .01$, $\sigma_{82}{}^2 = .01$, $\sigma_{e3}{}^2 = .01$, $\sigma_{83}{}^2 = .01$, $b_2 = .9$, $b_3 = -.7$, $\sigma_I{}^2 = .10$, $r_2^* = .15$, $r_3^* = .12$, and $A = .50$, the value of the weights are $x_2 = .458$ and $x_3 = .342$. Holding these factors constant except for a change in $\sigma_{82}{}^2$ from .01 to zero the weights become $X_2 = .668$ and $X_3 = .132$. While these differences may not be dramatic they are significant. In this case the interpretation is straightforward: An increase in liquidity for commodity 2 leads to a decrease in the operational error variance for that commodity which, in turn, leads to a larger proportion of the portfolio allocated to the second investment. To be sure, if many investments are considered, the results may not be as straightforward as those illustrated. Combinations of changes in operational error variances may lead to unintuitive shifts in portfolio composition. Be that as it may, changes in operational error variances, just as changes in estimation error variances, can have pronounced effects on portfolio management decisions.

3.4.2 *Practical Considerations in Estimation*

The above results and operational implications depend, of course, on measurements of the estimation error variance and the operational error variance. For commodities that have not been traded by the firm the index or message model error variance can be estimated directly from the regression results. The operational error variance must be obtained through other means. Here a common approach is to extrapolate from other commodity trading experience or from floor broker experience in that commodity and update the prior estimates as trading results become available. For commodities that have been traded by the firm the total variance, that is, the index model estimation error variance plus the operational error variance, is a matter of record as is the operational error variance. The former can be estimated from company trading data and the latter subjectively estimated from floor broker or trader experience or from historical data kept on operational error variance per se.

4 HEDGING NONFUTURES ASSETS WITH PORTFOLIOS OF FUTURES CONTRACTS

Investors, manufacturers, and others often have positions in a commodity for which a corresponding futures contract does not exist. For example, AAA corporate bonds and Brazilian cruzeiros do not have corresponding futures contracts of reference. In these cases one may be able to hedge them by selecting a portfolio of futures contracts for other investment media or foreign exchange, respectively. Indeed, a hedge portfolio in such a case may require the inclusion of futures contracts on commodities that are seemingly quite dissimilar from the object of the hedge.

While a perfect hedge in the futures markets may not be possible in these circumstances, a close hedge may be within reach. One method to select the hedge portfolio is least squares, a variation of quadratic programming. In general, the problem may be viewed as one to minimize the variation of the value of the portfolio around the value of the commodity being hedged. That is,

$$\min_{w.r.t. Z_i} V = \sum_{j=1}^{n} \left(r_j - \sum_{i=1}^{m} f_{ij} Z_i \right)^2$$

where r_j is the jth observed value of the commodity being hedged, f_{ij} is the jth observed value of the ith hedge asset with a corresponding futures contract, and Z_i is the hedge weight assigned to the ith hedge asset. The Z_i need not be constrained to nonnegative values if long and short positions are allowed. If sign conventions are followed to adjust the f_{ij} for long and short positions so that the Z_i will all be positive then one can add the sum of the $Z_i = 1$ to reflect the exhaustive allocation of hedging funds. In this case the hedge portfolio selection problem becomes a constrained least squares problem, another variation on quadratic programming.

4.1 A Possible Hedge for Cruzeiros

To illustrate the selection of a hedge portfolio consider an exporter of Brazilian goods to the United States. Because the cruzeiro may devalue relative to the dollar the exporter seeks an appropriate hedge. Setting aside alternatives such as currency swaps and financing arrangements in currencies that may provide a hedge for cruzeiros (see Chapter 3), the futures markets in foreign exchange offer an indirect hedging alternative. Here, some combination of British pounds, deutschemarks, and Japanese yen may provide a sufficient cover for the exporter. A simple least squares estimate of the dollar/cruzeiro exchange rate from the dollar/pound, dollar/deutschemark, and dollar/yen exchange rates produces the following results

$$\$/C = .01 \ \$/£ - .00004 \ \$/DM + .09 \ \$/Y$$

with an $R^2 = .98$ and a standard error of the estimating equation of .00006. The corresponding positions in the futures markets would parallel these results in those futures contracts that are closest in maturity to the exporter's time horizon.

For example, if the exporter had a six-month exposure horizon based on forward commitments, positions would be taken in the foreign exchange futures contracts maturing in that month. If futures contracts do not exist for the month corresponding to the importer's exposure horizon then combinations of the futures contracts surrounding the maturity horizon would be selected. Here linear prorating schemes typically are used to make the contract maturity allocations. Typically, these are based on the number of days from the futures contract maturity to the exposure horizon month: As the near side of the hedge comes to maturity the far side takes on a greater percent of the hedge allocation. Alternatively, the hedger can allocate all of the hedge funds to the nearest maturing futures contract and just before it matures switch the hedge forward to the next futures contract.

For a $10 million hedge and six-mosth time horizon the exporter would take the following positions in the futures markets as of December 1979:

Short $1,000,000 June British pounds

Short $9,000,000 June Japanese yen

In this example the deutschemark does not have a large enough impact to warrant its inclusion in a hedge of only $10 million.

Foreign exchange, of course, is not the only candidate for these hedging activities requiring portfolios of futures contracts. Other examples include securities manufactured items and construction among others. To be sure, portfolios of futures contracts may not always offer an adequate hedge: The correlations between the commodity being hedged and the commodities for which futures contracts exist may not be strong enough. Then again they may be highly correlated and their futures contracts can offer an excellent hedging alternative. Ultimately, this is an empirical question and least squares, constrained or otherwise, is one method of selecting a hedge portfolio.

5 SUMMARY

Portfolios of commodities while not well publicized are nevertheless popular and promise to grow in popularity in the foreseeable future. The foundations of portfolio selection apply to commodities as they do to securities but commodities have some unique aspects that warrant special consideration. Among the most important are the requirement for daily marking to market, spotty daily liquidity and accommodating short positions.

While no effort is made here to combine commodities with securities to explore the efficiency of the combined portfolio, even a cursory view of the two markets strongly suggests that such an amalgamation may be surprisingly efficient and rewarding, especially when viewed from a future that holds tightening commodity supplies and greater reliance on foreign trade. Be that as it may, commodity portfolios of outright and/or spread positions can be selected and managed with the same rigor and procedures found in the securities markets, an affinity that no doubt must appeal to the "prudent man."

6 BIBLIOGRAPHY

BAUMOL, W. J., "An Expected Gain-Confidence Limit Criterion for Portfolio Selection," *Management Science,* Vol. 10, No. 1, October 1963, pp. 174–182.

HILLIER, F. S., and G. J. LIEBERMAN, *Operations Research.* San Francisco: Holden-Day, 1967.

KUHN, H. W. and A. W. TUCKER, "Nonlinear Programming" in Jerzy Neyman (ed.), *Proceedings of the Second Berkeley Symposium on Mathematical Statistics and Probability,* Berkeley: University of California Press, 1957, pp. 481–492.

MAO, J. C. T., *Quantitative Analysis of Financial Decisions.* New York: Macmillan, 1969.

MARKOWITZ, H. M., *Portfolio Selection: Efficient Diversification of Investments.* New York: John Wiley, 1959.

SAMUELSON, P. A., "General Proof that Diversification Pays," *Journal of Finance and Quantitative Analysis,* March 1967, pp. 1–13.

SCHOLES, M., and J. WILLIAMS, "Estimating Betas from Non-Synchronous Data." University of Chicago, 1977.

SHARPE, W. F., *Portfolio Theory and Capital Markets.* New York: McGraw-Hill, 1970.

THEIL, H., *Econometrics.* New York: John Wiley, 1971.

WOLF, P., "A Simplex Method for Quadratic Programming." RAND P-1205, 1957.

25

INTEGRATED MULTIPLE COMMODITY TRADING: The Money Desk

IIIIIIIIIIIIIIIIIIIIIIIIIIIIIIIIIIIIIIIIIIIIIIIIIIIIIIIIIIIIIIIIIIIIIIIIIIIIIIIIIIIIIIIIIIIIIIIIIIr

1 INTRODUCTION

This chapter summarizes in a unified framework the objectives and activities of a Money Desk operation. A Money Desk is an investment banking operation within a company. Its objectives are twofold: to improve investment efficiency between profit centers, that is, commodity trading centers within a company, and to act as a distinct profit center for a company. To a large extent, the ideas and procedures presented here are drawn from material presented in previous chapters. However, some important new ground is broken. Most important, the notions presented here integrate the activity of traders, finance, accounting, and research in the establishment of an efficient multicommodity trading operation. That is not to say that all of the problems and issues for each of these areas have been identified let alone resolved. Rather, it is to say that the activities outlined here can be used as a guideline to develop a coordinated multicommodity trading operation.

The chapter is organized as follows: In Section 2 the objectives, activities, and constraints of a Money Desk are set forth. Here special attention is given to inventory and risk management. In Section 3, select Money Desk trading examples are presented to illustrate the operation of the system and highlight its information requirements.

Illustrative "trading assessment profiles" (TAPs) and transaction reporting forms (TRFs) are presented in Section 4. The TAPs provide spread information along with inventory availability and Money Desk borrowing and lending rates. The TRFs are for record keeping. One TRF is intended for use by specific commodity traders and the other by the Money Desk. Together, these two TRFs provide the double-entry accounting information necessary to monitor and assess the Money Desk operation. Mathematical programming applications to Money Desk operations are given in Section 5 and the chapter is summarized in Section 6.

2 OBJECTIVES, ACTIVITIES, AND CONSTRAINTS OF THE MONEY DESK

In part, a "Money Desk" borrows money from and/or lends money to different commodity trading centers within the company in order to capture potential arbitrage opportunities between them. In addition, the Money Desk can perform these activities between internal profit centers and opportunities outside the company in the money markets per se. In short, a Money Desk performs financial alchemy: It can transform excess wheat inventory into silver or gold or treasury bills and back again when it is profitable to do so.

2.1 Objectives and Activities

The principal objective of the Money Desk is to better utilize financial resources by opening commodity trading to a wider range and possible compounding of arbitrage opportunities.

For the most part the Money Desk performs two basic operations: (1) borrowing and lending between a commodity "department" or profit center within the company and an outside market, and (2) borrowing and lending between two or more profit centers within the company. For example, if a profit center within the company can borrow money in a commodity market by buying a switch at 4 percent per annum and the money markets offer an investment opportunity with a yield of 6 percent per annum with a corresponding (to the switch) maturity, the Money Desk would borrow from the commodity desk and "loan" those funds in the money market and capture the 2 percent per annum "profit." Here the Money Desk operates as a profit center.

Another Money Desk operation is borrowing and lending completely within the company. For example, a spread in one commodity may offer 7 percent per annum, and a spread in some other commodity may cost 4 percent per annum. Here, the Money Desk could borrow at 4 percent per annum from the latter profit center and loan that money to the former profit center and capture a 3 percent per annum profit. In this case, the Money Desk would act as a catalyst to enable profit centers to borrow and lend between one another.

In both of the above cases it is essential that net inventories, that is, inventories in excess of hedging or other business requirements, be available to the borrowing profit center in order to conduct the spread. This requirement, in turn, raises some important inventory management issues that weigh heavily on the operation of a Money Desk.

2.2 Inventory Management and Money Desk Constraints

Commodity inventories are necessary for the operation of the Money Desk. Without inventories, funds cannot be raised in a commodity market by buying a switch, that is, selling near and buying forward. Although inventories are necessary, they are not by themselves sufficient to do profitable Money Desk business. At least two other conditions are required. It also is essential to know the inventory position of each commodity by vintage every day, for example, 10,000 ounces of platinum from March 18 to April 16 as of February 28, 1979. The amount of excess inventory that may be invested through the Money Desk must be determined. This requirement, of course, places special demands on commodity inventory record keeping and information processing. Each of these issues are discussed below.

Despite attractive Money Desk arbitrage opportunities, it may not be profitable to dedicate all inventories to these investments. Expected other business activity may promise even greater rewards and some reserve or buffer inventories should be kept on hand. The conflict here arises from the "dual" or competing roles of commodities inventories. On the one hand, inventories incur holding costs that include the cost of foregone investment opportunities available through the Money Desk. Accordingly, the lower the level of inventories owing to Money Desk investments of those inventories, the lower the inventory "opportunity" holding costs. If D denotes the investment profit differential then the cost of not allocating inventories, C_h, is D times the amount of inventories I, that is, $C_h = DI$. On the other hand, inventories are necessary to take advantage of special investment opportunities that may arise, for example, a break in the market offering exceptional arbitrage opportunities. In this case, the lower the level of inventories the greater the potential loss (i.e., opportunity cost), from not being able to take advantage of fleeting market opportunities. In short, too few inventories also can result in inventory opportunity costs. These costs, referred to as inventory depletion costs, are inversely related to the amount of inventory on hand for any given level of market volatility. As the volatility of the market increases the greater the likelihood of special arbitrage opportunities. Thus, inventory depletion costs are conditioned on expected market volatility and are inversely related to the level of inventory on hand to take advantage of opportunities as they arise. Together these factors give rise to an inventory depletion cost function of the form $C_d = VA/I$ where V is the expected volume of arbitrages that can be captured for a given degree of market volatility, C_d denotes depletion cost, and A is the estimated arbitrage profit the traders can capture under a given degree of volatility.

Together these two inventory costs make up total inventory opportunity cost (*TIOC*) to the company, $TIOC = C_h + C_d$. If I^* is the amount of inventory that minimizes *TIOC* then the differential $I - I^*$ is investable. The question to answer now is how does one determine I^*? The answer to this question can be found by weighing incremental opportunity holding costs against incremental opportunity depletion costs.

2.3   Optimal Inventory Levels I^*

Because holding costs go up with higher levels of inventories and depletion costs go up with lower level of inventories, there may exist some positive level of inventories, I^*, such that any inventory level above or below that amount will incur higher combined inventory cost; for example, a further reduction in inventory holding cost is more than offset by an increase in inventory depletion costs. These costs are illustrated in Figure 25.1.

In Figure 25.1, I^* represents the "most efficient" (cost minimizing) level of inventory to be kept on hand by a specific commodity profit center. With respect to Money Desk operations, only those inventories in excess of the "optimal" level, I^*, would be available for Money Desk opportunities.

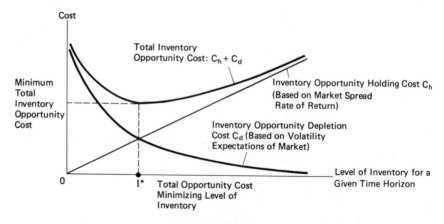

Figure 25.1

ILLUSTRATIVE INVENTORY OPPORTUNITY COST SCHEDULES

The solution for I^* can be illustrated with the help of some differential calculus. Before this is done the arbitrage profit factor and the volume estimate must be spelled out. In practice the arbitrage profit factor A is based on historical performance of the commodity traders under varying degrees of market volatility. This relationship may be estimated by a function of the form

$$A = A_0 + A_1\sigma$$

where A_0 is some minimum basis point profit per trade, A_1 indicates the rate at which their "baseline" profit changes as volatility changes, and σ is the standard deviation of commodity prices (one of several alternative measures of volatility). Similarly, the volume of trades V also may be represented by some function of volatility σ. Here a common approach is a relationship of the form

$$V = Q\sigma\gamma$$

where Q is the average size of a trade and γ is a parameter to be estimated. This function states that the volume of profit opportunities increases by $Q\gamma$ for every one unit increase in market volatility.

Combining the estimates of A and V the inventory depletion cost can be written

$$C_d = \frac{VA}{I}$$

$$= \frac{Q\sigma\gamma(A_0 + A_1\sigma)}{I}$$

$$= \frac{\gamma A_0 Q\sigma + \gamma Q A_1 \sigma^2}{I}.$$

Combining this cost with the inventory holding cost, C_h, the total inventory cost function, TIC, becomes

$$TIC = DI + \frac{\gamma A_0 Q\sigma + \gamma A_1 Q\sigma^2}{I}.$$

The minimization of this cost function with respect to the inventory level, I, is achieved at an inventory level of

$$I^* = \sqrt{\frac{\gamma Q(A_0\sigma + A_1\sigma^2)}{D}}.$$

This optimal value of inventory when subtracted from the actual value of inventory reveals the amount of "excess" inventory, I_x, that can be allocated to Money Desk opportunities. That is, excess inventory, also referred to as investable inventory, is equal to

$$I_x = I - I^*$$

To be sure I_x may be negative at times. This condition would indicate over-commitment of inventories relative to expected market volatility and current profit opportunities. Here the profit center would benefit from letting its inventories build up to optimal amounts or borrowing money to temporarily increase inventories to "safe" levels.

Before turning to examples of Money Desk operations one additional topic of inventory management must be considered: the accuracy of the volatility, volume, and arbitrage profit estimates. These parameters are not known with certainty but are estimated from past performance, as is typically the case for V and A, or estimated in some other way, such as a survey, as may be the case for σ. Because they must be estimated, the true values of these parameters will lie in some interval around their estimated values a certain percentage of the time. This suggests that a "worst-case" value for I^* may be more appropriate than one based on expected values of σ, V, and A. The worst-case alternative is easy to calculate and accommodates the additional objective of establishing a given level of risk in the inventory investment decision. This calculation would assign worst-case values for A_0, A_1, σ, and γ. Denoting these values with a w the optimal level of inventory under the worst-case scenario would be

$$I^w = \sqrt{\frac{\gamma^w Q[A_0{}^w \sigma^w + A_1{}^w (\sigma^w)^2]}{D}}$$

and the corresponding amount of investable inventories would be

$$I_x^w = I = I^w.$$

2.4   Maturity Profiles

Finally, it must be noted that the available amount of inventory for Money Desk operations typically will vary by maturity and commodity. That is to say, for each commodity there could be several possible "excess" inventory levels, one for each different maturity category, for example, from two months forward to four months forward. This inventory maturity profile is dictated by normal trading activity. These profiles must be available every morning for each commodity and segregated by vintage and time interval of availability. Once invested through the Money Desk, the "excess" inventories would not become available again until the maturity of these investments.

3   MONEY DESK TRADING OPERATIONS

In this section several examples are presented to illustrate the operation of the Money Desk. Each example is presented in a separate table. At the top of each table the basic market conditions are stated. The trading activity is summarized along with the net financial results of the Money Desk operation. The illustrative transactions do not include transactions (brokerage) cost and therefore the financial results are gross trading profits before taxes.

Three arbitrage examples are given: one between the "outside" money markets and an "inside" profit center; another between two "inside" profit centers; and the third between two "inside" profit centers and the "outside" money markets. Where futures contracts are traded, such as COMEX gold futures, common industry notation is used for the maturity months. Specifically, F for January, G for February, H for March, J for April, K for May, M for June, N for July, Q for August, U for September, V for October, X for November, and Z for December.

3.2 Wheat Market, Gold Market Arbitrage Example

The Wheat Desk has excess inventory from December to July. Wheat prices on the CBT over this period are flat. Gold prices on the COMEX are rising by 11 percent per annum over the same period. Moreover, Gold dealers are willing to borrow Gold at 13 percent per annum during this period.

Transactions as of September 21, 1979	*Trading Operations*
Wheat Desk borrows money on CBT; buys December-July switch at 0% p.a.	Sell 5 Z at 449½ per bu. ($112,375). Buy 5 N at 449½ per bu. ($112,375).
Wheat Desk loans money to Money Desk at 10% p.a. for period from December to July.	Loan $112,000 cash in December to Money Desk for July repayment of $117,600, i.e., at N $117,600.
Money Desk loans money to Gold Desk at 12% p.a. for period from December to June.	Lend $112,000 cash in December to Gold Desk for June repayment of $117,600, i.e., at M, $117,600.
Gold Desk sells COMEX December-June switch at 11% p.a. and loans gold to dealer from December to June at 13% p.a.	Buy 3 Z COMEX gold @ 373.34; sell 3 M COMEX gold @ 390.45; loan $112,000 gold to dealer at M, $118,066.65.

PROFIT POSITION AS OF JULY 1980

GOLD DESK	WHEAT DESK	MONEY DESK	COMPANY
$ 118,066.65	$ 117,600	$ 117,600.00	$ 118,066.65
−117,600.00	−112,000	−117,600.00	−112,000.00
$ 466.65	$ 5,600	$ 0.00	$ 6,066.65

3.1 Money Market, Silver Market Arbitrage Example

The Silver Desk currently has an excess inventory for the next six months. COMEX silver prices are "moving forward" at 7 percent per annum over the next six months. Bankers acceptances are offering 12 percent per annum over the same period.

Transactions as of September 21, 1979	*Trading Operations*
Silver trader borrows money on COMEX; buys a switch at 7% p.a.	Sell 1 (U) at $15.75 per oz. Buy 1 H at $16.30 per oz.
Silver trader loans money to Money Desk at 10% p.a.	Loan $78,750.00 cash to Money Desk at March repayment of $82,687.50.
Money Desk invests borrowings in Money Market at 12% p.a.	Borrow $78,750.00 cash from Silver Desk for March repayment of $82,687.50.
	Invest $78,750.00 cash in bankers acceptance with March maturity at $83,475.

PROFIT POSITION AS OF END MARCH 1980

SILVER DESK	MONEY DESK	COMPANY
$ 82,687.50	$ 83,475.00	$ 83,475.00
−78,750.00	−82,687.50	−78,750.00
$ 3,937.50	$ 787.50	$ 4,725.00

3.3 Multiple Market Reallocation Example

In this example, the Wheat Desk has excess funds but the Silver Desk does not and has an opportunity to capture a London-New York arbitrage through an exchange of physicals with another firm. The Money Desk invests surplus funds in bankers acceptance at 12 percent per annum.

Transactions as of September 21, 1979	*Trading Operations*
Wheat Desk sells 35,000 bu. in cash Market at $4.32 per bu.; buys 7 Z CBT Wheat at $4.45 per bu.	Sell 35,000 bu. at $4.32 per bu. ($151,-200); buy 7 Z at $4.45 per bu. ($155,750).
Wheat Desk loans 150,000 to Money Desk at 16% p.a. for 3 months.	Loan $150,000 to Money Desk for 90 days at Z = $156,000.
Money Desk loans $150,000 for 3 days to Silver Desk at 20% p.a.	Loan $150,000 to Silver Desk for 3 days for September 24 repayment of $150,250.
Silver Desk buys London spot silver at $14.925 per oz.; exchanges London physicals for COMEX deposits; and sells 2 U on COMEX at $15.75 per oz.	Buy 10,000 oz. London spot silver at $14.925 per oz. ($149,250); exchange of physicals −10,000 oz. London silver, +10,000 oz. New York silver; Sell 2 U COMEX at $15.750 per oz. ($157,750).
Silver Desk repays Money Desk loan.	Repay 3-day loan to Money Desk $150,250.
Money Desk buys bankers acceptance at 12% with December maturity.	Purchase 3-month bankers acceptance at $150,000 for December maturity of $154,500.

WHEAT DESK	SILVER DESK	MONEY DESK	COMPANY
$ 151,200	$ 150,000	$ 150,000	$ 151,200
−155,750	−150,250	−156,000	−155,750
−150,000	−149,250	−150,000	−149,250
156,000	157,750	150,250	157,750
$ 1,450	$ 8,250	−150,000	−150,000
		154,500	154,500
		$ −1,250	$ 8,450

4 TRADING ASSESSMENT PROFILES AND TRADING BOOKS

In order to facilitate and monitor the execution of Money Desk operations, commodity trading assessment profiles and trading books must be
kept. The purpose of the trading assessment profiles is to help identity profitable trading opportunities and their maturity structure. The trading books
are for double-entry bookkeeping purposes, for example, one book would be
used to record the wheat traders' side of a Money Desk transaction and a
parallel book would be used by the Money Desk to record transactions with
the wheat traders and some other commodity trader or the "outside" money
markets.

With regard to the trading assessment profiles, several additional comments are in order. First they require information on available (investable)
inventories. The determination of these quantities has been described above.
Second, the firm must have information on spreads and their associated
percent per annum switch "rates of return." Third, the sheets require Money
Desk borrowing and lending rates and borrowing and lending rates on money
market, that is, "outside" sources and uses of funds. These data are illustrated
in Tables 25.1, 25.2, 25.3 and 25.4.

In the examples, Table 25.1 shows the excess inventories of wheat to
be valued as of September 21, 1979. Here, the Wheat Desk has $150,000 in

Table 25.1

MATURITY PROFILE OF AVAILABLE INVENTORIES BY
WHEAT DESK AS OF SEPTEMBER 21, 1979
(IN 000's OF BUSHELS)

	SEPTEMBER	OCTOBER	NOVEMBER	DECEMBER
September	20	18	10	15
October		18	10	15
November			16	15
December				15

437

Table 25.2

ILLUSTRATIVE SPREAD TRIANGLE FOR
CASH AND CBT WHEAT PRICE AS OF SEPTEMBER 21, 1979
(PERCENT PER ANNUM)

	DECEMBER '79	MARCH '80	MAY '80	JULY '80	SEPTEMBER '80
Cash	7.32	5.02	7.19	7.94	9.59
December '79		2.68	7.01	8.07	10.16
March '80			13.38	12.03	13.80
May '80				10.44	13.74
July '80					16.68

Table 25.3

MONEY DESK BORROWING (UPPER TRIANGLE) OR LENDING
(LOWER TRIANGLE) RATES AS OF SEPTEMBER 21, 1979
(PERCENT PER ANNUM)

FROM: NUMBER OF MONTHS FORWARD	TO: NUMBER OF MONTHS FORWARD						
	0	1	2	3	4	5	6
0		10	11	12	12	11	11
1	11		11	12	12	11.5	11
2	12	12		12	12	12	11.5
3	13	13	13		12	12	11.5
4	13	13	13	13		12	11.5
5	12	12.5	13	13	13		11.5
6	12	12	12.5	12.5	12.5	12.5	

funds from September to December. Table 25.2 reveals the minimum rate of interest the Wheat Desk would require to replace a near sale with a forward purchase of the same quantity, for example selling one bushel in the cash market requires a price 7.32 percent per annum higher to replace that bushel in December as of September 21, 1979. Table 25.3 reveals the interest rates the Money Desk is willing to pay for forward funds (the upper triangle position) or is asking for loanable funds (the lower triangle positions).

There are, of course, many sources and uses of funds that determine Money Desk borrowing and lending rates. Within the company the "switch" rates of return must be considered for each commodity traded. Outside the company (e.g., in the money markets) several investments are highly liquid and especially attractive. An illustrative compendium of outside sources and uses of funds is summarized in Table 25.4.

The data shown in the tables can be obtained daily (every morning) and percent annum cost-return schedules can be generated for the Money Desk. Here automation is essential. Among the most important computer programs

Table 25.4

ILLUSTRATIVE COMPENDIUM OF
MONEY DESK "OUTSIDE" SOURCES
AND USES OF FUNDS

OUTSIDE SOURCE AND USE	TIME HORIZON
Borrowing	
Prime Loan Rate	Demand
Eurodollar Rate	Call–90 days
Bankers Acceptance	7–90 days
Eurodollar Rate Bankers Acceptance	90–180 days
Treasury Bills Treasury Notes	180–360 days
Investing	
Call Eurodollars	48 hours
Repurchase Agreements	2–30 days
Bankers Acceptances	2–90 days
Treasury Bills	91–180 days
Treasury Notes (2ndry mkt)	180–260 days

are ones to identify the lowest-cost–highest-return money market instruments or combinations of instruments that correspond in maturity to a potential commodity switch, the preparation of the trading assessment sheets and the recording of trades ("money books") that automatically update the maturity profile of available funds.

5 MATHEMATICAL PROGRAMMING AND MONEY DESK OPERATIONS

The Money Desk operations described above are amenable to mathematical programming algorithms that can perform difficult allocations in a fraction of the time it would take by hand. Moreover, it can do so with assurance of achieving maximum profit. The intent here is not to summarize the theory of mathematical programming but instead to show how Money Desk problems can be recast in terms of a mathematical programming problem and to illustrate its solution. While several types of mathematical programming are acceptable to Money Desk operations, multiperiod linear programming is especially well suited to meet these needs. It reflects the return on, the cost of, and the availability of funds by each profit center for each time period, achieves the maximum profit for the entire set of alternatives taken as a whole, and ensures the optimal allocation will satisfy the constraints of the problem.

5.1 Money Desk Operations: a multiperiod linear programming format

To illustrate a multiperiod linear programming formulation of Money Desk operations consider a two-commodity trading operation with a Money Desk (a third trading operation with respect to outside borrowing and lending) and a two-period investment horizon. Let I_{ijk} denote the amount invested from the beginning of period i to the end of period j at use (investment medium) k. Let B_{ijk} denote the amount borrowed from the beginning of period i to the end of period j by source (borrowing medium) k. Let K_{ijk} denote the amount of funds available for borrowing from period i to period j from source k. For a commodity desk per se this constraint would correspond to the value of the excess inventory available from period i to period j from commodity desk k. This information is contained in Table 20.1 together with current commodity prices. For the Money Desk this constraint would be the total amount of funds the firm can borrow from banks, commercial paper issues, and so forth, over some time interval. Finally, let r_{ijk} and c_{ijk} denote the returns and costs, respectively from the beginning of period i to the end of period j for medium k. (This information would be contained in Tables 25.2, 25.3, and 25.4.)

The objective of this Money Desk problem is to maximum profits over the two-period time horizon by selecting the appropriate amounts of borrowing and investing, B_{ijk} and I_{ijk}, respectively, for $i = 1, 2, j = 1, 2$ where $i \leq j$ (no short sales) subject to the constraint each period that one invests what is borrowed plus net returns and cannot borrow more than is available. The relationships are summarized below:

Objective Function

$$\max_{w.r.t. I_{ijk}, B_{ijk}} \pi = \sum_{k=1}^{3} \sum_{i=1}^{2} \sum_{\substack{j=1 \\ i \leq j}}^{2} ((1+r_{ijk})I_{ijk} - (1+c_{ijk})B_{ijk})$$

Profit over two periods where short sales, $i > j$, are not allowed.

Constraints

$$\sum_{j=1}^{2} \sum_{k=1}^{3} I_{ijk} = \sum_{j=1}^{2} \sum_{k=1}^{3} B_{ijk}$$

Period 1: Amount invested equals amount borrowed.

$$I_{ijk} B_{ijk} = 0$$

Medium k cannot be an investment source *and* a borrowing source over the same interval.

$$\sum_{k=1}^{3} I_{22k} = \sum_{k=1}^{3} (1 + r_{11k})I_{11k} + \sum_{k=1}^{3} B_{22k}$$
$$- \sum_{k=1}^{3} (1 + c_{11k})B_{11k}$$

Period 2: Amount invested equals amount borrowed plus net returns from period 1 one-period investments.

$$B_{111} \leq K_{111}$$

Period 1 loanable funds from medium 1.

$$B_{112} \leq K_{112}$$

Period 1 loanable funds from medium 2.

440

$B_{121} \leq K_{121}$	Period 1 to 2 loanable funds from medium 1.
$B_{122} \leq K_{122}$	Period 1 to 2 loanable funds from medium 2.
$\left. \begin{array}{l} B_{113} + B_{123} \leq K_3 \\ B_{123} + B_{223} \leq K_3 \end{array} \right\}$	Line of credit to Money Desk for two-period time horizon.
$B_{221} \leq K_{221}$	Period 2 loanable funds from medium 1.
$B_{222} \leq K_{222}$	Period 2 loanable funds from medium 2.

Most of the above relationships are straightforward, for example, profits and available loanable funds based on "excess inventory" or "outside" lines of credit. However, two of the above relationships warrant some elaboration. The constraint

$$\sum_{k=1}^{3} I_{22h} - \sum_{k=1}^{3} (1 + r_{11k})I_{11k} - \sum_{k=1}^{3} B_{22k} + \sum_{k=1}^{3} (1 + c_{11k})B_{11k} = 0$$

reflects the maturity of one-period investments made in the first period as additional funds available for a subsequent one-period investment together with a similar cash withdrawal for repayment of funds borrowed plus interest for one period in the first period. Second, the condition

$$I_{ijk}B_{ijk} = 0$$

notes that a medium (k), from the beginning of i to the end of j, cannot be both a lender and an investor for itself at the same time: Medium k for period i, j must be a net investor (borrower) or lender (investor). Thus, if a trading desk (k) has "excess" inventories for a given period, then it is a source of borrowed funds and $B_{ijk} > 0$ and $I_{ijk} = 0$. Excess inventories, of course, are known before the Money Desk allocation is made and the zero value variable I_{ijk} or B_{ijk} is pruned from the linear programming formulation.

Taken together these relationships give rise to a set of equations that may be partitioned into three clusters of relationships: linking constraints, linking variables, and intraperiod decision variables. The linking constraints coordinate the trading desks by making them share the firm's resources that are available during one or more time periods. The linking variables coordinate the time periods by representing the activities that affect the operation of any desk for two or more time periods. The intraperiod decision variables represent the subproblems concerned with the optimization of the trading desks during one of the time periods considered in isolation. This system can be structured in psuedorecursive form as shown in Chapter 13.

5.2 Multiperiod Multicommodity Linear Programming: an illustrative example

To illustrate the application of the multiperiod multicommodity linear program outlined above, consider the following simple case of a firm with a Wheat Desk, a Gold Desk, a Money Desk and a two-month time horizon. Let I_{ijk} denote an investment opportunity by desk k from the period i to the end of period j and let B_{ijk} denote loanable funds by desk k from the beginning of period i to the end of period j. The rates of return, costs of funds, and constraints on the investment and borrowing opportunities are given as follows:

MEDIUM 1 WHEAT DESK		MEDIUM 2 GOLD DESK		MEDIUM 3 MONEY DESK	
Variable in Dollars	Interest p.a. in Dec. Frac.	Variable in Dollars	Interest p.a. in Dec. Frac.	Variable in Dollars	Interest p.a. in Dec. Frac.
I_{111} —	.12	$I_{112} = 0$	—	$I_{113} = 0$	—
I_{121} —	.16	I_{122} —	.15	$I_{123} = 0$	—
I_{221} —	—	I_{222} —	.17	$I_{223} = 0$	—
$B_{111} = 0$	—	$B_{112} \leq 2,000$	.11	$B_{113} + B_{123} \leq 3,000$	.10
$B_{121} = 0$	—	$B_{122} = 0$	—	$B_{123} + B_{223} \leq 3,000$	.10
$B_{221} = 1,000$	.12	$B_{222} = 0$	—		

Converting to monthly equivalents and adjusting for the length of time borrowed or invested, the problem faced by the firm can be summarized as follows:

$$\max_{w.r.t.\, I_{ijk}, B_{ijk}} \pi = 1.010 I_{111} + 1.027 I_{121} + 1.014 I_{222} + 1.025 I_{122} - 1.009 B_{112}$$
$$- 1.010 B_{221} - 1.008 B_{113} - 1.008 B_{123} - 1.008 B_{223}$$

subject to the constraints

$$I_{111} - B_{112} - B_{113} - B_{123} + I_{121} + I_{122} = 0$$
$$.010 I_{111} - I_{222} + B_{221} + B_{223} + .009 B_{112} + .008 B_{113} = 0$$
$$B_{112} \leq 2,000$$
$$B_{221} \leq 1,000$$
$$B_{113} + B_{123} \leq 3,000$$
$$B_{123} + B_{223} \leq 3,000.$$

The solution to this problem is

$$I_{111} = 5{,}000$$
$$I_{121} = 0$$
$$I_{122} = 0$$
$$I_{222} = 4{,}008$$
$$B_{112} = 2{,}000$$
$$B_{221} = 1{,}000$$
$$B_{113} = 3{,}000$$
$$B_{123} = 0$$
$$B_{223} = 3{,}000$$
$$\pi = 74.20.$$

In brief, the results state that the largest investment will be made in wheat in period 1: $5,000.00 yielding "interest" of $50.00 at the end of the first period. This period 1 investment is financed by a $2,000.00 loan for one period from the Gold Desk and a $3,000.00 loan for one period from the Money Desk. These loans carry "interest" charges of $18.00 and $24.00, respectively. At the end of period 1 the $5,000.00 in loans and $42.00 in "interest" charges are paid off through the maturity of the one-period wheat investment. After repayment of the loans and interest charges due at the end of period 1, a net balance of $8.00 profit remains to be invested in period 2 for one period. These profits together with a $1,000.00 loan from the Wheat Desk and $3,000.00 loan from the Money Desk, are invested in the gold market for period 2. At the end of period 2 the one-period gold investment matures together with its "interest" of $100.20. At the same time, the loans from the Money Desk and the Wheat Desk mature along with their one-period interest of $10.00 and $24.00, respectively. Taken together, these transactions produce a cumulative profit of $74.20 over the two-period time horizon.

To be sure, the above example is a simple one and other kinds of mathematical programming procedures may be better suited to meet special needs. Nevertheless, the model presented here does accommodate a wide variety of problems in investment management common to multiple commodity investment operations and illustrates the combined use of the information, objectives, and constraints facing an integrated multiple commodity trading operation.

6 SUMMARY

The Money Desk performs investment banking operations within a multicommodity trading operation: It transfers surplus funds from one or more commodity trading desks, that is, profit centers, to one or more trading desks that have investment opportunities, or it may borrow or invest funds in the money markets and operate as a distinct profit center. The information requirements for such an operation include the availability of excess funds by each trading desk, borrowing and investment opportunity profiles for each trading desk, and borrowing and investment opportunities in the money markets. This information, of course, must be made available on a timely basis. Inventory control considerations can help determine the availability of funds at each trading desk and mathematical programming procedures can help make large numbers of profit-maximizing borrowing and lending allocations efficiently. Depending on the size of the problem and its characteristics, multiperiod linear programming is one method especially well suited to meet the demands of a Money Desk.

7 BIBLIOGRAPHY

BYRNE, R. F., et al., eds., *Studies in Budgeting*. New York: American Elsevier, 1971.

HILLIER, F. S., and G. J. LIEBERMAN, *Operations Research*. San Francisco: Holden-Day, 1967.

MAO, J. C. T., *Quantitative Analysis of Financial Decisions*. New York: Macmillan, 1969.

SENGUPTA, J. K., and K. A. FOX, *Optimization Techniques in Quantitative Economic Models*. New York: American Elsevier, 1971.

TEICHROW, O., *An Introduction to Management Science*. New York: John Wiley, 1964.

TABLE OF WEIGHTS AND MEASURES

METRIC EQUIVALENTS

1 meter	(m)	=	39.37	inches
1 hectare	(ha)	=	2.471	acres
1 liter	(l)	=	.9081	dry quarts, or
			1.0567	liquid quarts
1 kilogram	(kg)	=	2.204622	pounds
1 quintal	(100 kgs)	=	220.462	pounds
1 ton	(1,000 kgs)	=	2,204,622	pounds
1 ton	(1,000 kgs)	=	1,102.311	short tons

BUSHEL WEIGHTS

POUNDS PER BUSHEL		BUSHELS PER TON		
		Metric ton (bushels)	Short ton (bushels)	Long ton (bushels)
Soybeans	60	36.7437	33.3333	37.3333
Wheat	60	36.7437	33.3333	37.3333
Corn (shelled)	56	39.36825	35.7143	40.0
Oats	32	68.89444	62.500	70.0
Barley	48	45.929625	41.6667	46.6667
Rye	56	39.36825	35.7143	40.0
Sorghum grain	56	39.36825	35.7143	40.0
Rice, rough	45	48.991	44.4444	49.7778
Flaxseed	56	39.36825	35.7143	40.0

OUNCE WEIGHTS

Troy ounce—a weight used chiefly to measure gold and silver. Each troy ounce has 20 penny-weights, each of 24 grains. There are 12 troy ounces to the troy pound.

Avoirdupois ounce—a traditional weighting scheme with 16 ounces to the avoirdupois pound. The avoirdupois pound has 7000 grains and the troy pound has 5760 grains.

APPENDIX: Immunization and Hedging Strategies

|||||||||||||||||||||||||||||||||||||||||||||||||||||||||||||||||||||||||||||||||||||||||||||||||||||||||||||||

1 IMMUNIZATION

A major objective of hedging is to safeguard against unanticipated changes in the value of cash market positions over some prescribed time period. This objective is sometimes referred to as *immunization*. The formal character of immunization can be shown using the sum, J, of the cash and hedge positions. This sum can be denoted

$$J = X_C P^C + X_H P^H,$$

where X_c and X_H are the number of units in the cash commodity and hedge position respectively, and P^C and P^H are the cash and hedge market prices per unit, respectively. In the context of differential calculus the immunization condition can be written

$$\frac{dJ}{dt} = 0,$$

which implies

$$X_C \frac{dP^C}{dt} = -\left(\frac{dX_H}{dt} P^H + X_H \frac{dP^H}{dt}\right),$$

assuming the cash position X_C is fixed. This condition simply states that the change in the value of the cash position is the opposite of the change in the value of the hedge position over the time interval.

The goal of a hedging strategy is to satisfy the above immunization condition. In general there are two classes of hedging strategies—static and dynamic.

2 STATIC HEDGING STRATEGIES

A static hedge is said to exist when the size of the hedge position, X_H, is constant over the hedge period. In this case the immunization condition becomes

$$X_C \frac{dP^C}{dt} = -X_H \frac{dP^H}{dt}.$$

This relationship, in turn, implies the optimal size of the cash position in relation to the hedge position, that is, the optimal *hedge ratio*

$$HR \equiv \frac{X_C}{X_H} = -\frac{dP^H}{dP^C}.$$

In practice dP^H/dP^C is not known with certainty and some estimation method must be used to determine the hedge ratio. Four commonly used methods are the naive, expected value, minimum variance, and elasticity estimates.

2.1 Naive Hedge Ratio

The naive hedge ratio method equates X_H with X_C. If the cash market and hedge position assets of reference are identical this rule is sufficient for immunization. Often the cash market and hedge position assets of reference are not identical and the naive ratio of 1 is not a good approximation.

2.2 Expected Value Hedge Ratio

The expected value hedge ratio method determines the hedge ratio as the expected value of dP^H/dP^C. Here, the estimate of the expected ratio is an average of a sample of past ratios. That is

$$\frac{X_C}{X_H} = -\bar{R}$$

where $\bar{R}$ is the average of n finite ratios $\Delta P^H/\Delta P^C$, $\Delta P^C \neq 0$. A principal shortcoming of this approach is that the sample history may not be an accurate base from which to predict the future.

2.3   Minimum Variance Hedge Ratio

The value of J can vary over the hedge period. The minimum variance method derives a hedge ratio that minimizes the variation in J. The variance of J can be written

$$\text{Var}\,(J) = X_H^2[\sigma_H^2 + (HR)^2\sigma_C^2 + 2(HR)\sigma_{CH}],$$

where σ_C^2 and σ_H^2 are the variance of P^C and P^H over the hedging period respectively, σ_{CH} is the covariance between P^C and P^H, and HR is the hedge ratio X_C/X_H.

The hedge ratio that minimizes $\text{Var}\,(J)$ is

$$HR^* = -\frac{\sigma_{CH}}{\sigma_C^2}$$

or

$$HR^* = -\rho\frac{\sigma_H}{\sigma_C}$$

where ρ is the coefficient of correlation between P^C and P^H. In practice ρ, σ_{CH}, σ_C and σ_H are historical estimates and may not be accurate predictors.

2.4   Elasticity Hedge Ratio

Another method of estimating the hedge ratio is to recast the ratio of price changes into the product of the ratio of their average price levels and their average elasticity. This method is most often used when the cash market and hedge position assets of reference are measured in different units. This ratio can be denoted

$$HR = -\frac{\overline{P^H}}{\overline{P^C}}E_{CH}$$

where the elasticity E_{CH} is an average of sample ratios of the percent change in the cash market price divided by the percent change in the hedge asset price, and $\overline{P^H}$ and $\overline{P^C}$ are average values of P^H and P^C, respectively, over the estimation period. Here, as in the other methods, a potential shortcoming is the predictive inaccuracy of the statistical estimates.

2.5   Hedge Ratios for Financial Assets

Hedging cash market positions in financial assets, such as treasury bills or corporate debt issues, has become extremely popular owing to the volatility of interest rates. Popularity notwithstanding, there are many potential pitfalls in hedging financial assets. At the core of the problem lies the potential imperfect correspondence between the cash market asset to be hedged and the asset underlying the hedge position. Among the most important of these differences are the risk category and the term to maturity. For example, a corporate issue to be hedged against an unanticipated rise in rates would not correspond perfectly in risk category to any asset underlying an interest rate futures contract. Moreover, the term to maturity may not correspond. While no sure bromides exist to cure these problems some guidelines have evolved. Two are especially noteworthy. They are (1) the hedge ratio for T-bills with nonmatching terms to maturity, and (2) duration hedge ratios where both the risk category and maturity may differ between the cash and hedge assets of reference.

2.5.1   T-Bill Hedge Ratio For Nonmatching Terms to Maturity

The minimum variance hedge ratio as given above may be written

$$HR_k = -\frac{k\sigma_{CH}}{k\sigma_C^2}$$

where the added subscript k denotes the term to maturity of the T-bill. Here, the term to maturity is assumed to be the same for the cash and hedge positions.

When the yield curve is flat, the relationship between a change in the price per dollar face value of a $k < 90$-day T-bill, ΔP_k, and a change in the price per dollar face value of a 90-day T-bill, ΔP_{90}, is

$$\Delta P_k = \frac{k}{90} \Delta P_{90}.$$

The introduction of this relationship into the derivation of the minimum variance hedge ratio results in the following correspondence

$$HR_k = \frac{k}{90} HR_{90}.$$

That is, the minimum variance hedge ratio for a k-day to maturity T-bill is equal to $k/90$ times the minimum variance hedge ratio for a 90-day T-bill.

When the yield curve is unknown over the hedging period the hedge ratio may be derived from the minimum variance condition. This hedge ratio can be denoted

$$HR_k = -\frac{\sigma_{k,90}}{\sigma_k^2}$$

or

$$HR_k = -\rho \frac{\sigma_{90}}{\sigma_k}$$

where the subscript k denotes the term to maturity of the cash position ($k < 90$) and the subscript 90 denotes the term to maturity of the hedge position.

2.5.2 Duration Hedge Ratio

Duration, D, is a measure of the maturity horizon of a financial asset. It may be written

$$D = \frac{\sum_{t=1}^{n} t \frac{C_t}{R_t}}{\sum_{t=1}^{n} \frac{C_t}{R^t}},$$

where C_t is the payment received at t, $R^t = (1 + r)^t$, r is the yield to maturity, and n is the time to maturity. The expression $\sum_{t=1}^{n} C_t/R^t$ is the price, P, of the security. D may be recast as an elasticity:

$$D = -\frac{dP/P}{dR/R}.$$

Using superscripts C and H to denote the cash market and hedge positions respectively, the hedge ratio $-dP^H/dP^C$ can be rewritten in terms of duration as

$$HR = -\frac{R^C}{R^H} \cdot \frac{dR^H}{dR^C} \cdot \frac{D^H}{D^C} \cdot \frac{P^H}{P^C}.$$

This rendition of the hedge ratio distinguishes between relative price effects, changes in the elasticity of the cash market rate of discount with respect to the hedge market rate of discount, and the ratio of the cash and hedge market durations. The effects of each, or some combination, of these influences on the hedge ratio can be studied. In this way various anticipated financial market conditions can be simulated and the corresponding hedge ratios derived. In practice the components must be estimated. Typically these estimates are based on some combination of past values and forecasts and may be perfectly accurate.

3. Adaptive Hedge Strategies

An adaptive hedge is one in which X_H is allowed to vary over the hedging period. In general there are two schemes that can determine the variation in X_H. In either case the intent is to change X_H so as to better achieve immunization. On the one hand, the scheme can be purely heuristic. Typically this approach is based on the hedger's belief about future ratios of price changes and is applied without resort to a formal criterion and methodology. On the other hand, the scheme can be derived from some formal dynamic optimization method. Here the immunization condition is recast as some form of control problem and decision rules are derived that guide the adaptive hedge. One common method in this regard is dynamic programming. Applications of this method, together with a discussion of select optimal control problems, are presented in Chapter 13.

4. Bibliography

FRANKLE, C. T., "The Hedging Performance of the New Futures Market: Comment," *Journal of Finance,* 35, No. 5, 1273–79.

KOLB, R. W. and R. CHIANG, "Duration, Immunization, and Hedging with Interest Rate Futures," in *Interest Rate Futures: Concepts and Issues,* ed. G. D. Gay and R. W. Kolb, pp. 353–64. Richmond: R. F. Dame, Inc, 1982.

INDEX